Unsnarling the World-Knot

Unsnarling the World-Knot

*Consciousness, Freedom,
and the Mind-Body Problem*

David Ray Griffin

UNIVERSITY OF CALIFORNIA PRESS
Berkeley   Los Angeles   London

University of California Press
Berkeley and Los Angeles, California
University of California Press
London, England

Copyright © 1998 by The Regents of the University of California

Library of Congress Cataloging-in-Publication Data

Griffin, David Ray, 1939–
    Unsnarling the world-knot : consciousness, freedom, and the mind-
body problem / David Ray Griffin.
        p.   cm.
    Includes bibliographical references and index.
    ISBN 0–520–20944–3 (alk. paper)
    1. Philosophy of mind.   2. Consciousness.   3. Mind and body.
4. Free will and determinism.   I. Title.
BD418.3.G75   1998
128'.2—dc21
                                                              97–8390
                                                              CIP

Printed in the United States of America

1 2 3 4 5 6 7 8 9

The paper used in this publication meets the minimum requirements of American
National Standard for Information Sciences—Permanence of Paper for Printed Library
Materials, ANSI Z39.48-1984 ⊗

For Charles Birch, who inspired it

Science seems to have driven us to accept that we are all merely small parts of a world governed in full detail (even if perhaps ultimately just probabilistically) by very precise mathematical laws. Our brains themselves, which seem to control all our actions, are also ruled by these same precise laws. The picture has emerged that all this precise physical activity is, in effect, nothing more than the acting out of some vast (perhaps probabilistic) computation—and, hence, our brains and our minds are to be understood solely in terms of such computations. . . . Yet it is hard to avoid an uncomfortable feeling that there must always be something missing from such a picture.

ROGER PENROSE, *THE EMPEROR'S NEW MIND*

I am confident that in our entire philosophical tradition we are making some fundamental mistake, or set of fundamental mistakes in the whole discussion of the free will problem.

JOHN SEARLE, "THE MIND-BODY PROBLEM"

The idea that the mind-body problem is particularly perplexing flows from our unjustified and relatively modern faith that we have an adequate grasp of the fundamental nature of matter at some crucial general *level of understanding.*

GALEN STRAWSON, *MENTAL REALITY*

Almost all really new ideas have a certain aspect of foolishness when they are first produced.

ALFRED NORTH WHITEHEAD, *SCIENCE AND THE MODERN WORLD*

CONTENTS

ACKNOWLEDGMENTS

My primary intellectual debts for this book are to those authors I have cited extensively. Besides Alfred North Whitehead and Charles Hartshorne, these are especially Daniel Dennett, Nicholas Humphrey, William James, Jaegwon Kim, William Lycan, Geoffrey Madell, Colin McGinn, Thomas Nagel, William Seager, John Searle, Galen Strawson, and Peter Strawson.

The immediate stimulus for writing this book was the conference "Consciousness in Humans, Animals, and Machines" held in October 1994 under the auspices of the Center for Process Studies in Claremont, California. I am especially indebted to Charles Birch, who proposed the conference, and Robert Valenza of Claremont McKenna College, who primarily made it possible. This book began as a "background paper" for that conference. I am also grateful to Peter Farleigh and Granville Henry who, along with Birch and Valenza, helped plan the conference and to those participants who gave helpful criticisms of the manuscript, especially (besides the aforementioned) John Cobb and Donald Griffin. The hope that the conference would enable me to improve the manuscript was also fulfilled because of presentations of some of the participants, especially William Seager on intentionality and Colin McGinn on supervenience; the latter led to the addition of chapter 10, on Jaegwon Kim's position.

I am grateful to Jaegwon Kim for reading chapter 10 and for assuring me that I had not misrepresented his position, and also to Donald Sherburne and two anonymous readers for the press, all of whom made many valuable suggestions that led to improvements.

Special thanks are due to my secretary, Sharon Thompson, who went far beyond the call of duty in getting this manuscript ready.

My primary ongoing debt is to my wife, Ann Jaqua, who, among many other things, provides a context in which I can focus on matters such as the mind-body problem.

KEY TO ABBREVIATIONS

AI	Alfred North Whitehead, *Adventures of Ideas.*
AO	Walter F. Elsasser, *Atom and Organism: A New Approach to Theoretical Biology.*
BABF	Gerald M. Edelman, *Bright Air, Brilliant Fire: On the Matter of the Mind.*
BH	Charles Hartshorne, *Beyond Humanism: Essays in the Philosophy of Nature.*
BM	Keith Campbell, *Body and Mind,* 2d ed.
BP	William S. Robinson, *Brains and People: An Essay on Mentality and Its Causal Conditions.*
C	William G. Lycan, *Consciousness.*
CE	Daniel E. Dennett, *Consciousness Explained.*
CI	Charles Hartshorne, "The Compound Individual."
CIP	William Seager, "Consciousness, Information, and Panpsychism."
CM	Colin McGinn, *The Character of Mind.*
CN	Jacques Monod, *Chance and Necessity: An Essay on the Natural Philosophy of Modern Biology.*
CR	Owen Flanagan, *Consciousness Reconsidered.*
CS	Colin McGinn, "Consciousness and Space."
CSPM	Charles Hartshorne, *Creative Synthesis and Philosophic Method.*
DL	Charles Hartshorne, *The Darkness and the Light: A Philosopher Reflects upon His Fortunate Career and Those Who Made It Possible.*
EM	H. D. Lewis, *The Elusive Mind.*
EOS	W. D. Hart, *The Engines of the Soul.*
ES	H. D. Lewis, *The Elusive Self.*
FAR	Peter F. Strawson, *Freedom and Resentment and Other Essays.*
FOR	Alfred North Whitehead, *The Function of Reason.*
FR	John C. Eccles, *Facing Reality.*
FU	David Chalmers, "Facing Up to the Problem of Consciousness."

GET	J. T. Fraser, *The Genesis and Evolution of Time.*
HBP	John L. Pollock, *How to Build a Person: A Prolegomenon.*
HM	Nicholas Humphrey, *A History of the Mind.*
HS	John C. Eccles, *How the Self Controls Its Brain.*
IHM	Thomas Reid, *An Inquiry into the Human Mind,* ed. Timothy Duggan.
JS	Ernest Lepore and Robert van Gulick, eds., *John Searle and His Critics.*
M	J. J. C. Smart, "Materialism."
MAC	Paul M. Churchland, *Matter and Consciousness: A Contemporary Introduction to the Philosophy of Mind,* rev. ed.
MBP	John R. Searle, "The Mind-Body Problem."
MBS	John R. Searle, *Minds, Brains and Science: The 1984 Reith Lectures.*
MBSC	Ted Honderich, "Mind, Brain, and Self-Conscious Mind."
MBWP	John R. Searle, "Minds and Brains without Programs."
MC	William Seager, *Metaphysics of Consciousness.*
MM	Geoffrey Madell, *Mind and Materialism.*
MMB	Curt J. Ducasse, "Minds, Matter and Bodies."
MMBP	Michael E. Levin, *Metaphysics and the Mind-Body Problem.*
MN	John B. Cobb, Jr., and David Ray Griffin, eds., *Mind in Nature: Essays on the Interface of Science and Philosophy.*
MQ	Thomas Nagel, *Mortal Questions.*
MR	Galen Strawson, *Mental Reality.*
MT	Alfred North Whitehead, *Modes of Thought.*
MW	Colin Blakemore and Susan Greenfield, eds., *Mindwaves: Thoughts on Intelligence, Identity, and Consciousness.*
NYR	Thomas Nagel, "The Mind Wins!"
OCC	Karl R. Popper, *Of Clocks and Clouds.*
PC	Colin McGinn, *The Problem of Consciousness: Essays Towards a Resolution.*
PCH	Lewis Edwin Hahn, ed., *The Philosophy of Charles Hartshorne: Library of Living Philosophers XX.*
POP	William James, *Principles of Psychology,* vol. 1.
PP	Charles Hartshorne, "Physics and Psychics: The Place of Mind in Nature."
PR	Alfred North Whitehead, *Process and Reality: An Essay in Cosmology*
PRE	John Passmore, *Philosophical Reasoning.*
PS	Sewall Wright, "Panpsychism and Science."
PU	William James, *A Pluralistic Universe* (published with *Essays in Radical Empiricism*), ed. Ralph Barton Perry.
RM	John R. Searle, *The Rediscovery of the Mind.*
RIM	Alfred North Whitehead, *Religion in the Making.*
SAB	Karl R. Popper and John C. Eccles, *The Self and Its Brain: An Argument for Interactionism.*
SB	Lynne Rudder Baker, *Saving Belief: A Critique of Physicalism.*

SM	Jaegwon Kim, *Supervenience and Mind: Selected Philosophical Essays.*
SMP	Roger Sperry, *Science and Moral Priority: Merging Mind, Brain, and Human Values.*
SMW	Alfred North Whitehead, *Science and the Modern World.*
UU	David Bohm and B. J. Hiley, *The Undivided Universe: An Ontological Interpretation of Quantum Theory.*
VN	Thomas Nagel, *The View from Nowhere.*
VRE	William James, *Varieties of Religious Experience.*
WJP	Marcus P. Ford, *William James's Philosophy: A New Perspective.*

Introduction

This book suggests both a formal procedure for making progress on the mind-body problem and a substantive solution to it, with special attention to consciousness and freedom. The mind-body problem, which Arthur Schopenhauer called the "world-knot," has arguably been the central problem in modern philosophy since its inception in the seventeenth century. With regard to the twentieth century in particular, John Searle in *The Rediscovery of the Mind* (1992) has expressed his considered judgment that, "contrary to surface appearances, there really has been only one major topic of discussion in the philosophy of mind for the past fifty years or so, and that is the mind-body problem" (*RM*, 29).

As indicated by the titles of a number of recent books—for example, Nicholas Humphrey's *Consciousness Regained* (1983), William Lycan's *Consciousness* (1987), Paul Churchland's *Matter and Consciousness* (1988), Alastair Hannay's *Human Consciousness* (1990), Colin McGinn's *The Problem of Consciousness* (1991), William Seager's *Metaphysics of Consciousness* (1991), Daniel Dennett's modestly titled *Consciousness Explained* (1991), and Owen Flanagan's *Consciousness Reconsidered* (1992)—consciousness has widely come to be seen as lying at the heart of the mind-body problem. Consciousness, says McGinn, is "the hard nut of the mind-body problem" (*PC*, 1). Dennett says (somewhat optimistically), "Human consciousness is just about the last surviving mystery" (*CE*, 21). Seager, speaking of the difficulty of fitting psychology into the hierarchy of the sciences, says that "the source of the difficulty is consciousness" (*MC*, 185–86). Humphrey, in *A History of the Mind* (1992), says, "The mind-body problem is the problem of explaining how states of consciousness arise in human brains" (*HM*, 2–3). John L. Pollock, in *How To Build a Person* (1989), has said, "The most perplexing problem for any materialist theory of the person is that of making sense of consciousness" (*HBP,* 28). Thomas Nagel, whose work, especially "What Is It Like to Be a Bat?" has provoked much of the current ferment, says, "Consciousness is what makes the mind-body problem really intractable" (*MQ,* 165). In *Mental Reality* (1994), Galen Strawson, using "experience" synonymously with "consciousness," says that "the existence of experience is the only hard part of the mind-body problem for materialists" (*MR,* 93).

The problem of consciousness, as the central feature of the mind-body problem, is also widely seen as a problem for science (not simply for philosophy). Colin Blakemore and Susan Greenfield, editors of *Mindwaves: Thoughts on Intelligence, Identity, and Consciousness* (1987), say that "the nature of consciousness may come to be seen as the central problem of research on the brain" (*MW,* vii). A few recent books (besides some of those already mentioned) illustrating this point are Roger Penrose's *The Emperor's New Mind: Concerning Computers, Minds, and the Laws of Physics* (1989), Gerald M. Edelman's *Bright Air, Brilliant Fire: On the Matter of the Mind* (1992), and Israel Rosenfield's *The Strange, Familiar, and Forgotten: An Anatomy of Consciousness* (1992).

Whereas it is now widely recognized by dualists and materialists alike that human consciousness creates a serious, perhaps intractable, mind-body problem for modern philosophy and science, the fact that human freedom is part of that problem is much less widely recognized, especially among materialists. Nevertheless, I will argue, we all inevitably presuppose that we have not only consciousness but also (a significant degree of) freedom, so that any acceptable solution to the mind-body problem must also be able to account for our freedom. I have pointed to the equal importance of this issue by including "freedom" in this book's subtitle. Indeed, I consider chapter 9, in which freedom is defended, to be the most important chapter of the book. The earlier chapters, although important in their own right, prepare the way for understanding how the kind of freedom that we all presuppose in practice can be affirmed in theory.*

This book is based on the conviction that a development that has occurred in the intense and extensive current discussion provides an opportunity for a breakthrough with regard to the central metaphysical assumption that has led to the intractability of the mind-body problem, an intractability that has taken the form of a standoff between dualists and materialists. Although dualists were in the majority in the early part of the modern period and materialists have been in the ascendancy since the second half of the nineteenth century, each side has always faced insuperable difficulties. During most of this period, given the assumption that materi-

---

*Jaegwon Kim says, "Mental causation arguably is the central issue in the metaphysics of mind" (*SM,* xv). (Although the affirmation of mental causation is not ipso facto an affirmation of genuine freedom, it is a necessary condition.)

alism (sometimes called physicalism) and dualism were the only serious options, dualists were content to rest the case for their position primarily on the fact that materialism confronted insoluble problems. Materialists in turn rest their case primarily on the insuperable obstacles faced by dualism. Each side, accordingly, largely ignored or at least minimized the problems in its own position. The recent development that has occurred is a much greater willingness by advocates on both sides to admit the deep problems in their own positions.

On the dualist's side, Geoffrey Madell, in *Mind and Materialism* (1988), has been particularly frank about "the difficulties which any dualist position confronts" (*MM,* preface [n.p.]). While arguing that materialism's problems are so great that "interactionist dualism looks to be by far the only plausible framework in which the facts of our experience can be fitted" (*MM,* 135), he admits that "the nature of the causal connection between the mental and the physical, as the Cartesian conceives of it, is utterly mysterious" (*MM,* 2). He also concedes the "inexplicability" of the appearance of consciousness at some point in the course of evolution and in the development of each embryo, prior to which everything was understandable in terms of physical laws alone (*MM,* 140f.). He offers, accordingly, only "a limited and qualified defense of dualism" (*MM,* 9).

Madell's confession of inexplicable mystery was anticipated in 1977 by fellow dualist Karl Popper. In an earlier book, Popper had seemed confident of finding a solution. "What we want," he said, "is to understand how such nonphysical things as *purposes, deliberations, plans, decisions, theories, tensions,* and *values* can play a part in bringing about physical changes in the physical world" (*OCC,* 15). But in the 1977 book he wrote with John Eccles, *The Self and Its Brain: An Argument for Interactionism,* he admitted that understanding *how* interaction occurred between nonphysical mind and physical brain was perhaps impossible. "Complete understanding, like complete knowledge," said Popper, "is unlikely to be achieved"(*SAB,* 105). Popper was not as ready as Madell now is to admit that this constitutes a serious problem for the dualistic hypothesis, but his admission is significant nonetheless.

More remarkable and extensive has been the change in attitude on the part of those who reject dualism in favor of some form of physicalism or materialism.[*] On this side, Thomas Nagel's writings have been especially influential. While rejecting a distinct mind or soul and hence dualistic in-

[*]Throughout most of this book I use "physicalism" and "materialism" interchangeably, in line with widespread practice (e.g., Jaegwon Kim [*SM,* 266n]). Accordingly, I normally refer to the position I advocate, panexperientialism, as an alternative to both dualism and physicalism. In chapter 10 as well as in a few anticipatory references, however, I point out that my kind of panexperientialism could be considered a form of physicalism. This usage implies a distinction between "materialist physicalism" and "panexperientialist physicalism."

teractionism (*MQ*, 182, 190, 211; *VN*, 29), Nagel has said that the drive to develop a physicalist account of mind has led to "extremely implausible positions" (*VN*, 15). Although he is not ready to conclude that physicalism must be false, he does say that "physicalism is a position we cannot understand because we do not at present have any conception of how it might be true" (*MQ*, 176). Colin McGinn, having been stimulated by Nagel, has created a considerable stir by going even further. While rejecting dualism and affirming physicalism more emphatically than does Nagel,* he argues that our present perplexity is terminal, that we will *never* be able to resolve the mystery of how consciousness could emerge from the brain (*PC*, 1–2, 7). William S. Robinson is equally emphatic. Although he thinks that a physicalistic approach can do justice to more mental phenomena than do Nagel and McGinn, he argues in *Brains and People* (1988) that it cannot handle sensations, such as pains. There is no imaginable story, he says, that leads from talk of neurons in the brain to "our seeing why *such* a collection of neurons has to be a pain." And this absence of understanding, Robinson adds, "is not merely a temporary limitation" (*BP*, 29). William Seager, although not ready to declare that physicalism will never solve the mind-body problem, says that the record thus far suggests that this may well turn out to be the case. In spite of holding that physicalism "still deserves our allegiance" (*MC*, 224), he says that "the degree of difficulty in formulating an explicit version of physicalism which is not subject to immediately powerful objections is striking" (*MC*, 4). Reviewing the various types of physicalism (type-identity theory, functionalism, token-identity theory, psychological instrumentalism, eliminative materialism), he says, "Taken as a group they appear as an orderly retreat becoming a rout" (*MC*, 32). The attempt to deal with consciousness in terms of the normal explanatory method of physically resolving higher phenomena into lower elements results, Seager says, in "a 'principled breakdown' of the explanatory scheme," adding that "it remains true, and may forever remain true, that we have no idea whatsoever of *how* the physical states of a brain can constitute consciousness" (*MC*, 195). In a similar vein, Galen Strawson says that the "mysteriousness, for us, of the relation between the experiential and the physical-as-discerned-by-physics is . . . a sign of how much is at present, and perhaps forever, beyond us" (*MR*, 50). Likewise, Jaegwon Kim's 1993 book, *Supervenience and Mind*, concludes with the reflection that the physicalists' attempt to save the reality of the mental seems "to be up against a dead end" (*SM*, 367).

---

*Although (as I know from personal conversation) McGinn would reject physicalism or materialism under one definition, according to which it holds that consciousness is identical with the brain in such a way as also to be a spatial entity or property, he does, like Nagel, accept a two-aspect version of physicalism.

For good measure we can throw in a similar conclusion by an advocate of epiphenomenalism, which, being halfway between dualism and materialism, can be considered an aberrant version of one or the other. Keith Campbell, the second edition of whose *Body and Mind* appeared in 1984, at one time had accepted materialism. But he came to reject it after deciding that phenomenal properties, such as the feeling of pain, could not be properties material objects could have (*BM,* 105–9). His "new epiphenomenalism" says that we do have a spiritual mind, which is produced by the body, but that it does not act back on the body (which allows a physicalist, deterministic account of human behavior, the need for which is a regulative principle for Campbell [*BM,* 125]). Recognizing that his position shares an "embarrassing" question with dualism, namely, how a "spiritual mind"—our awareness with its phenomenal properties—can be "caused by changes in sense organs and brain," he says: "How this is done we do not know. . . . I suspect that we will never know how the trick is worked. This part of the Mind-Body problem seems insoluble. This aspect of humanity seems destined to remain forever beyond our understanding" (*BM,* 131).

This new situation—the recognition by leading advocates on all sides of unresolved and probably unresolvable problems within their own positions—provides an opportunity for a conceptual breakthrough insofar as it has led to the realization that a satisfactory solution will have to move beyond assumptions of long standing. Nagel has again led the way. "The world is a strange place," he says, "and nothing but radical speculation gives us the hope of coming up with any candidates for truth" (*VN,* 10). Suggesting the direction that this radical speculation should take, he says that "any correct theory of the relation between mind and body would radically transform our overall conception of the world and would require a new understanding of the phenomena now thought of as physical" (*VN,* 8).

Strawson* agrees. Saying that "the enormity of the mind-body problem" requires a "radical response," he predicts that a solution, if possible at all, will involve a "revolution" in our conception of the nature of the physical (*MR,* 99, 92). McGinn locates the intractability of the mind-body problem in "our inadequate conception of the nature of the brain and consciousness" (*PC,* 2n). Although doubting that we are up to the kind of radical reconception that would be needed, he does agree that "something pretty remarkable" would be necessary to find a constructive solution to the mind-brain relation (*PC,* 2, 86, 104).

John Searle has been particularly caustic in his treatment of the materialist tradition, saying that the "most striking feature of . . . mainstream phi-

---

*Because I discuss both Galen Strawson and Peter Strawson, referring simply to "Strawson" could be confusing. However, my discussion of Peter Strawson is limited to section V of chapter 9. All references to "Strawson" before that are to Galen Strawson.

losophy of mind of the past fifty years" is how much of it "seems obviously false" (*RM*, 3). It also, Searle suggests, reflects a neurotic-like pattern of behavior:

> A philosopher advances a materialist theory of the mind. . . . He then encounters difficulties. . . . [C]riticisms of the materialist theory usually take a more or less technical form, but in fact, underlying the technical objections is a much deeper objection . . . : The theory in question has left out . . . some essential feature of the mind, such as consciousness or 'qualia' or semantic content. . . . And this leads to ever more frenzied efforts to stick with the materialist thesis and try to defeat the arguments put forward by those who insist on preserving the facts. After some years of desperate maneuvers to account for the difficulties, some new development is put forward that allegedly solves the difficulties, but then we find that it encounters . . . the same old difficulties. (*RM*, 30)

"After half a century of this recurring pattern in debates about materialism," Searle adds, "one might suppose that the materialists and the dualists would think there is something wrong with the terms of the debate. But so far this induction seems not to have occurred to either side" (*RM*, 49). Searle believes that the basic problem is that materialism has accepted the vocabulary and categories of Cartesian dualism, according to which if something is "physical" it cannot also be "mental," and if something is "mental" it cannot also be "physical" (*RM*, 14, 26, 54). A constructive solution will require a reconception in which this "conceptual dualism" (*RM*, 26) is rejected.

Although I do not believe, for reasons I will give later, that Searle's own way of rethinking the relation between physicality and mentality provides the basis for a satisfactory solution, I do believe that his formal recommendations about the kind of radical reconceptualizing that we need, along with those of Nagel, McGinn, and Strawson, point in the right direction. This growing awareness by both dualists and materialists of the inadequacy of their own positions, I have suggested, creates an opportunity for real progress on the mind-body problem, because it reveals the need for more radical reconceptualization. The perception of this need should lead, in turn, to a greater openness to alternative approaches. One philosopher who has especially realized this implication is Strawson. Taking alternative views such as idealism and panpsychism seriously, says Strawson, is part of "a proper response" to the fact that, given standard assumptions about the physical and the mental, the mind-body problem has proved to be intractable (*MR*, 75, 108). My book is an attempt to get a hearing for a particular version of one of these alternative approaches.

As my comments thus far should make clear, I think that the basic problem has been conceptual, which means that the solution must be a philosophical one. This does not mean that I belittle the role science has to play. On the contrary. One of my central purposes is to remove from the back of scientists a false problem with which they have been saddled by bad philosophy, so that they will be free to work without distraction on the properly scientific dimensions of the problem of consciousness. That is, most scientists working in this area have been trying, among other things, to answer a question that is impossible in principle to answer. No amount of empirical research, no matter how brilliant, can answer such a question.

Little progress has been made on the "problem of consciousness," beyond the not unimportant progress of heightening the dissatisfaction with both dualism and materialism, I suggest, for a number of interrelated reasons.

1. Insufficient clarity has been attained on exactly *what problem* is being addressed.
2. Insufficient attention has been given to the role that both *paradigmatic* and *wishful-and-fearful* thinking play in determining our intuitions about regulative principles and data and thereby our theories.
3. The kind of *common sense* that can be overridden by scientific theory has seldom been distinguished from the kind that cannot.
4. Insufficient clarity has been attained about the *regulative principles,* both formal and substantive, that should be exemplified if a theory is to be considered a serious candidate for acceptance.
5. There has been insufficient clarity about the *data* to which an adequate theory should do justice.
6. It is seldom realized that the mind-body problem is rooted even more deeply in the "Cartesian intuition" about the body than in that about the mind.
7. In spite of widespread agreement, especially by nondualists, that "mind should be naturalized," the two fundamental features of mind, *experience* and *self-determination,* have generally not been taken to be fully natural. This has led to the false conclusion that dualism and materialism provide the only realistic options (with "realism" understood as the view that the physical universe really exists, independently of human perception and thought). This false conclusion has meant that the third form of realism, panexperientialism, has been virtually ignored.

These seven problems, I suggest, are the various snarls that together have constituted the world-knot. Unsnarling this knot will require overcoming each of these problems. The first seven chapters of this book deal with these seven problems in turn. Chapters 8 and 9 then provide a solution (begun in chapter 7) to the mind-body problem, focusing on consciousness and on freedom, respectively. Chapter 10 then makes the nature and adequacy of this panexperientialist position clearer by means of a critique of materialist physicalism as articulated in Jaegwon Kim's *Supervenience and Mind*. Interestingly, it turned out that the order of the chapters, although determined in the light of the logical order in which the various issues had to be discussed, also reflected the difficulty of the various issues. Chapters 1 through 9, accordingly, became progressively longer.

ONE

What Is the Problem?

A perusal of books and essays on "the mind-body problem" or "the problem of consciousness" will often reveal that "the" problem being addressed actually comprises two or even more of the following distinguishable problems:

1. How could *experience* (whether conscious or not) arise out of, and perhaps act back on, nonexperiencing things (or events, or processes)?
2. How could a *unified* experience arise out of, and perhaps act back on, a brain?
3. How could *conscious* experience arise out of, and perhaps act back on, a brain?
4. How could *self-conscious* experience arise out of, and perhaps act back on, a brain?
5. How could conscious animal experience have arisen in the evolutionary process out of nonconscious animal experience?
6. How could self-conscious experience have arisen in the evolutionary process out of merely conscious animal experience?

The failure to distinguish among these various dimensions of the overall problem has led to many a confusion. The most serious has been the assumption that Problem 1 is necessarily part of, perhaps even identical with, any or all of the next three problems. This confusion is so serious because Problem 1 is based on a metaphysical assumption that is pure supposition, and one that, on reflection, is revealed to be dubious. After all, an amoeba, like a neuron, is a single-celled organism, and an amoeba shows signs of spontaneity suggestive of some slight degree of experience. If amoebas might have experience, why might not neurons in the brain have experience as well? It is, however, almost universally assumed that they do not, and it is this assumption that lies at the heart of the mind-body problem. For example, on the first page of *The Problem of Consciousness,* McGinn formulates the problem in terms of the question, "How could the aggregation of millions of individually insentient neurons generate subjective awareness?" In any case, whatever one's intuitions or judgments about these matters, it should not simply be assumed that a discussion of Problem 2 (and perhaps Problems 3 and 4) necessarily involves Problem 1.

Making this distinction is especially important if, as I maintain, Problem 1 is insoluble in principle (which Popper, Campbell, Nagel, and Seager have implied and McGinn and Robinson have explicitly asserted). This point has practical as well as theoretical importance: A good deal of money, much of it from taxes, is being spent on research programs in which the first three (and perhaps four) problems are simply equated.

To make this point is not to be antiscience. To the contrary, the point is to distinguish the properly scientific questions, which can in principle be answered by empirical research, from a confused metaphysical question, which cannot be answered. Given Problems 2 through 6, scientists (perhaps in cooperation with philosophers) have a difficult enough assignment without having to do the impossible as well.

Incidentally, although the distinction between Problems 5 and 6, on the one hand, and Problems 3 and 4, on the other, will not play a central role here, I mention it for the sake of completeness and because of its importance. It should not simply be assumed, for example, that an answer to Problem 4, which involves the relation between self-consciousness and the brain, would automatically answer Problem 6, which involves the evolutionary relation of self-conscious experience to prior experience that enjoyed consciousness but not yet self-consciousness. The emergence of distinctively self-conscious experience may have depended on certain social developments rather than, or at least as well as, further neurological changes. This distinction is related to the recent discussion, in physicalist philosophy of mind circles, of the extent to which the content of consciousness is related to "extrinsic" realities beyond the present, "intrinsic" state of one's body.

In summary, the formal point of this chapter is that scientists and philosophers need to become clear about exactly which problem or problems they are seeking to answer. The main polemical point is that Problem 1 is probably a pseudoproblem and should not, in any case, be simply assumed to be involved in any of the other problems. Because it is *the* problem that has made the "mind-body problem" intractable thus far and has led to the growing consensus that it is probably permanently insoluble, separating the other problems from this one is likely to be a precondition for answering them.

TWO

Paradigmatic and Wishful-and-Fearful Thinking

Philosophers and scientists are supposed to be empiricists, in the broad sense of taking into account all the kinds of evidence that are relevant to the question at hand. Various factors conspire, however, to make the reality fall short of the ideal. The most important of these factors are paradigmatic thinking, wishful-and-fearful thinking, and the interaction between them.

Thomas Kuhn's discussion of the role of paradigms in science has led to much greater awareness of the power of paradigmatic thinking, both its inevitability and its dangers. Its chief danger, of course, is that it may blind us to genuine phenomena that do not fit the paradigm or, when these phenomena are forced on our attention, lead us dogmatically to reject them a priori. Although we may be genuinely motivated by the desire for truth, we may become so convinced that our present framework is the one and only route to truth that open-minded consideration of the evidence becomes virtually impossible. Strong social dimensions are also involved: We are usually socialized into a paradigm through our schooling, and the paradigm is more or less subtly enforced by hiring, promotion, and tenure committees, by grant-authorizing committees, by journal editors and referees, by book reviewers, and so on. If there are data that do not fit the currently dominant paradigm, it is very difficult for most philosophers and scientists to take them into account—or at least to do so publicly, so that these data would be brought to the attention of other thinkers.

The phenomenon of wishful thinking is also well known. We tend to believe what we wish to be the case. Equally important is the other side of the dynamic, which I follow Susan Haack in calling "fearful thinking."[1] We tend to reject a priori all those things that we do not want to be true, or at least do not want to be generally believed. For example, some thinkers seem to espouse a dualistic view of the mind-body relation primarily because they want to support belief in life after death, perhaps fearing that a loss of this belief will lead to a general nihilism and loss of morality. Other thinkers, considering belief in life after death pernicious (perhaps the "opiate of the masses"), may adopt a materialistic view primarily to support the impossibility of life after death. The way these two types of thinkers weigh data and arguments may at least be significantly influenced by their respective wishes and fears. In this way, the wish (or the fear) may be the parent of the paradigm.

The causal relation can also work the other way, as there can be paradigm-induced wishful-and-fearful thinking, especially among intellectuals, whose personal as well as professional egos may be very attached to the way they have come to understand the world. John Searle regards this dynamic as essential to understanding why the currently dominant materialistic views are held so widely and so tenaciously, in spite of their implausibility:

> One of the unstated assumptions behind the current batch of views is that they represent the only scientifically acceptable alternatives to the antiscientism that went with traditional dualism, the belief in the immortality of the soul, spiritualism, and so on. Acceptance of the current views is motivated not so much by an independent conviction of their truth as by a terror of what are apparently the only alternatives. (*RM*, 3)

"The deepest motivation of materialism," Searle suggests, "is simply a terror of consciousness" with its "essentially terrifying feature of subjectivity," which most materialists think to be "inconsistent with their conception of what the world must be like" (*RM*, 55).

Of special importance in trying to see through the assumptions that have made the mind-body problem seem insoluble is the evidence, reported by recent historians of science, that the dualistic worldview, which most scientists and philosophers now wish to avoid, was itself significantly a product of wishful-and-fearful thinking. One motive in the seventeenth century for affirming an absolute dualism between soul and body was to support the immortality of the former: In several of the "Renaissance naturalisms," self-motion, which Plato had seen as distinctive of soul, was attributed to *all* natural entities. On this basis, some "mortalists" were arguing that the evident fact that the soul is a self-moving thing is no argument for its immortality, for the body, which is clearly mortal, is also composed of self-moving things. The assertion by René Descartes, Robert Boyle, Isaac Newton, and other founders of the early modern worldview that matter is totally inert and insentient provided the basis for saying that the mind or soul is different in kind from matter, therefore arguably immortal.[2] The view of matter as inert also provided an argument for God: Against those who were arguing for an atheistic, pantheistic, or panentheistic view of the universe as a self-organizing organism, Boyle and Newton used the view that matter is essentially inert to point to the need for an external First Mover.[3] Newton also supported the existence of a transcendent deity by interpreting gravity in the light of the view that matter is devoid of all hidden (occult) properties: Because it is absurd to hold that the power to exert attraction at a distance is inherent in matter, he argued, the phenomenon of gravitational attraction points to the need for a transcendent explanation.[4] This denial to matter of the power to exert influence at a distance was also used by Fr. Marin Mersenne and others to support the notion that the Christian miracles, which had traditionally been taken as divine designations of Christianity as the One True Religion, did indeed point to supernatural intervention. A threat to this belief had been posed by Renaissance naturalists and Hermeticists who, by regarding the capacity to exert and receive influence at a distance as purely natural, described the so-called miracles in the New Testament and the lives of the Christian saints as simply extraordinary but not supernatural happenings, no different in kind from similar types of events in other traditions. To counter this threat, Mersenne chose the Democritean view of matter, recently revived by Galileo and Gassendi, in part because it declared influence at a distance naturally impossible, thereby pointing to the need for a supernatural intervention to account for the Christian miracles.[5] Still another motive behind the view of matter as totally inert and insentient, evident in both Descartes and Boyle, was the desire to be able to use the nonhuman world for human purposes without compunction.*

The mechanistic view of nature was the product of this kind of wishful-and-fearful thinking more than of any direct insight by the seventeenth-century geniuses into the nature of what matter is in itself. Of course, thinking of matter *as if* it were nothing but what could be treated by the method employed by modern science has proved enormously successful for certain purposes in certain areas. But to assume that matter *really is* nothing but this may be a distorting result of another common form of wishful thinking, that of turning a method into a metaphysic.

The awareness that the dualistic paradigm was significantly based on this kind of wishful-and-fearful thinking becomes even more important when we realize that materialism is simply a decapitated version of the worldview created by the dualistic supernaturalists. That is, materialism lopped off God and the soul while retaining that worldview's idea of matter—even though this idea of matter had been constructed in large part precisely to show the necessity for an external deity and a different-in-kind soul.

---

*Descartes's denial of experience to "nature," which included all nonhuman animals, was used to justify exploitative practices such as hunting and vivisection (Leonora Cohen Rosenfield, *From Beast-Machine to Man-Machine* [Oxford: Oxford University Press, 1940], 15–16, 22, 47–48).

McGinn is exactly right, accordingly, in pointing out that materialism is "a comparatively recent innovation" and in surmising that it is connected to "the demise of the divine." He is also right to think that atheistic materialism "would probably have struck the Great Dead Philosophers as an absurd aberration" (*PC*, 48n). Indeed, they assumed that their view of matter *precluded* a materialistic view of the person and an atheistic view of the universe. In thinking that their successors would never, on the basis of this view of matter, move to a wholly materialistic worldview, they underestimated the power of paradigmatic and wishful-and-fearful thinking.*

Materialism, of course, involves the creation of a total worldview out of the method intended by the seventeenth-century thinkers to be used for only a portion of reality; but this is only one of the dimensions of the wishful-and-fearful thinking involved. In any case, one of the reasons why the mind-body problem has seemed so intractable may be that we have failed to be sufficiently aware not only of our own wishful-and-fearful thinking, which limits current thinking about options, but also of the wishful-and-fearful thinking that influenced the seventeenth-century paradigm-establishing ideas of mind and matter.

---

*Strawson, while endorsing (noneliminative) materialism, comments, "It is interesting that modern eliminativists appear to concur with the seventeenth-century view that the physical (matter in motion) cannot possibly be the realizing ground of conscious experience. . . . This led many in the past to believe in immaterial substance as a realizing ground of experience. Now it seems to lead some philosophers to deny the existence of experience. Things have clearly gone downhill in the last three hundred years" (*MR*, 101f.).

THREE

Confusion about Common Sense

Another factor that has made the mind-body problem seem so intractable is confusion about common sense. Philosophers as well as scientists have failed to distinguish between the kind of common sense that science can sensibly reject and the kind that it cannot.

Science has widely come to be understood as a systematic assault on common sense. Common sense said the world was flat; science showed this to be false. Common sense said the sun and the moon were the same size; science showed this to be wrong. Common sense said the Earth was the center of the universe; science showed this to be false. Common sense said matter was solid; science has shown this to be false. And so on. Progress in understanding has come to be seen as the accommodation of common sense to the scientific worldview. As modern philosophers and scientists have dealt with the mind-body relation, accordingly, they have assumed that the same adjustment would occur. As Searle puts it, "the general form of the mind-body problem has been the problem of accommodating our common-sense and prescientific beliefs about the mind to our general scientific conception of reality" (MBWP, 215).

As the above litany of examples illustrates, furthermore, science is seen as successively revealing truths that in area after area show the illusory nature of common sense. Through this portrayal, common sense has come to be regarded as generally mistaken. Through this way of understanding the relation between science and common sense, the fact that a given scientific theory runs counter to our "commonsense intuitions" can be complacently dismissed. In fact, as Searle points out, this discrepancy with commonsense intuitions can be regarded as a point in the theory's favor:

The fact that the views in question are implausible and counterintuitive does not count against them. On the contrary, it can even seem a great merit of contemporary functionalism and artificial intelligence that they run dead counter to our intuitions. For is this not the very feature that makes the physical sciences so dazzling? Our ordinary intuitions about . . . the solidity of the table . . . have been shown to be mere illusions. . . . Could not a great breakthrough in the study of the mind similarly show that our most firmly held beliefs about our mental states are equally illusory? Can we not reasonably expect great discoveries that will overthrow our commonsense assumptions? (*RM*, 17–18)

Searle's criticism of this attitude, his contention that an adequate theory cannot deny "obvious" truths (*RM*, xi, 1, 3, 5), and his employment of "commonsense objections" to identism and eliminative materialism (*RM*, 39, 48) imply a distinction between two quite different meanings of "common sense," which can provisionally be called the *weak* and the *strong* meanings. The idea that not all things called "common sense" are analogous is implicit in Searle's criticism of what he calls the "heroic-age-of-science maneuver" of some eliminative materialists: "They claim that giving up the belief that we have beliefs is analogous to giving up the belief in a flat earth or sunsets" (*RM*, 48). However, Searle does not, to my knowledge, provide a criterion for distinguishing between the weak and the strong meanings of "common sense" and thereby between things that merely *seem* obvious to some people and things that *really are* obvious in the not-to-be-denied sense. This kind of criterion is also implicitly called for by Nagel's principle that, "given a knockdown argument for an intuitively unacceptable conclusion, one should assume there is probably something wrong with the argument" (*MQ*, x). The problem is that "intuitions" notoriously differ. Is there some criterion for distinguishing between those "commonsense intuitions" that are defeasible by a knockdown argument and those that are not?

The conviction that there is such a criterion lay at the root of the "Scottish commonsense tradition" associated primarily with Thomas Reid.[1] The criterion for what is common sense in the strong sense was formulated in various ways, but the basic idea was that there are certain notions that are "common" in the sense of universal—truly common to all people—and that they are such because they cannot be consistently denied: The very act of denying them verbally would involve an implicit affirmation. To deny such beliefs, Reid said, would be "metaphysical lunacy."[2] I have come to refer to common sense in this strong sense as "hard-core common sense,"[3] to distinguish it from common sense in the weak sense, which I call "soft-core common sense." Common sense of the latter sort does *not* refer to truly common or universal notions but merely to parochial notions that *can* be denied without pain of implicit inconsistency. In any case, this tradition fell into disrepute and virtual oblivion in the late nineteenth century. One reason seems to be that proponents came to claim the status of common sense in the strong sense for all sorts of ideas, including reactionary (such as antievolutionary) ones, that did not really match the criterion, a tendency not altogether absent in Reid himself. Another problem was that no naturalistic explanation for the origin of these commonsense notions was offered.* They were, instead, said to have resulted from a supernatural implantation in our souls.[4] With the demise of supernaturalism, accordingly, no explanation of these commonsense notions seemed possible.

The notion of common sense that is not truly deniable reemerged in twentieth-century philosophy. The best-known version of common sensism has probably been that of G. E. Moore; but his version fails to provide a clear criterion for distinguishing between weak and strong meanings of common sense. Better is the "critical common-sensism" of Charles Peirce.[5] But the best version, in my view, is that of Alfred North Whitehead. That Whitehead is a "commonsense" philosopher has not been widely recognized, however, for two reasons (besides the fact that most philosophers today simply do not bother to read Whitehead, probably in large part because they were not introduced to him by their own teachers during the rabidly antimetaphysical period of twentieth-century philosophy). One reason is that he used "common sense" in both the weak and the strong senses but failed to point this out. Second, those passages in which the *criterion* for hard-core common sense is stated do not themselves contain the *term* "common sense." However, by reading Whitehead with this issue in mind, one can ferret out his doctrine without great difficulty. One can also see that this issue is no merely minor theme in his philosophy but that he understands the very task of philosophy to be that of showing how the various hard-core commonsense notions are mutually consistent. A central task of epistemology, furthermore, is to provide a naturalistic explanation as to why we all share these notions.

Whitehead's clearest statement of the criterion for hard-core common sense is contained in a statement of what he calls "the metaphysical rule of evidence," namely, "that we must bow to those presumptions which, in despite of criticism, we still employ for the regulation of our lives" (*PR*, 151). Even this statement is not as clear as it might be. One question is who the "we" indicates: *all* human beings (perhaps all rational beings), or only a limited portion thereof, such as modern Western human beings? I interpret it to mean the former. And when Whitehead says that even if we criticize these notions, we still employ them for the regulation of our lives, does he mean that we *inevitably* do so, so that we could not do otherwise, or only that it is a contingent fact that all people thus far have done so (which would

---

*Reid spoke of these common notions as "those things, which all mankind have believed without being able to give a reason for it" (*IHM*, 12).

leave open the possibility that we could quit doing so, perhaps through sustained self-discipline or through adopting a worldview and self-understanding radically different from anything in the past)? Again, I take him to mean the former. Accordingly, I take his meaning to be that the ultimate criteria for theoretical thought are *those notions that all human beings inevitably presuppose in practice, even if and when they deny them verbally*. This interpretation is consistent with another explicit statement: "[Philosophy's] ultimate appeal is to the general consciousness of what in practice we experience. Whatever thread of presupposition characterizes social expression throughout the various epochs of rational society must find its place in philosophic theory" (*PR,* 17).

The idea that the notions in question are *presupposed in practice* is crucial. The contention that these notions are universal cannot be refuted simply by pointing to the fact that some people have verbally denied them. As the first quotation above indicated, Whitehead is speaking of notions that we continue to use in practice "in despite of criticism." The term "practice," in fact, is used in reference to Hume (*PR,* 81, 133, 242f.), who, denying that we have any direct experience of "causal efficacy" and of an "external world," said that these notions can have no place in our (philosophical or scientific) theory while adding that we must, nonetheless, presuppose them in practice. Against this antirationalism (*PR,* 153), Whitehead says,

> Whatever is found in 'practice' must lie within the scope of the metaphysical description. When the description fails to include the 'practice,' the metaphysics is inadequate and requires revision. There can be no appeal to practice to supplement metaphysics. (*PR,* 13)

On the basis of these explicit formulations of the idea of hard-core common sense, in which the term "common sense" is unfortunately not used, we can locate many passages in which Whitehead *does* use the term with this meaning. He speaks of several notions that cannot "be dropped without doing violence to common sense" (*PR,* 128). He speaks of his "endeavor to interpret experience in accordance with the overpowering deliverances of common sense" (*PR,* 50) or, in a Searle-like statement, of "the obvious deliverances of common sense" (*PR,* 51). He speaks, for example, of the direct experience of actual entities beyond ourselves as a "a presupposition of all common sense" (*PR,* 52).

Whitehead can also, however, use "common sense" in the weaker sense (unfortunately, without a qualifier such as "soft-core" to warn the reader of the very different meaning). For example, he speaks of "the benumbing repression of common sense" (*PR,* 9). In a statement in *Science and the Modern World* in praise of then-recent developments in science, especially relativity and quantum physics, he says that "scientific theory is outrunning common sense" (*SMW,* 114). Elsewhere he says, "It is the part of the special sciences to modify common sense" (*PR*, 17). Indeed, he can even speak of "the general common-sense notion of the universe" that he seeks to modify (*MT,* 129). In these passages, Whitehead is using "common sense" in a nontechnical sense. For example, after saying that science is "outrunning common sense," he explains his meaning: "The settlement as inherited by the eighteenth century was a triumph of organized common sense. . . . It grounded itself upon what every plain man could see with his own eyes, or with a microscope of moderate power. It measured the obvious things to be measured, and it generalized the obvious things to be generalized" (*SMW,* 114).

Once we have seen the distinction in principle between soft-core and hard-core common sense, we can agree wholeheartedly that science not only has falsified common sense of the first type in the past but also will probably continue to do so. We will not, however, conclude from this fact that science should lead us to doubt commonsense ideas of the second type, because they are presupposed by the practice of science itself. *This kind* of common sense provides the "ultimate appeal" to which all theory, including scientific theory, must "bow."

Whitehead has thereby provided, I suggest, the kind of criterion Searle needs to distinguish the "obvious facts" that cannot be overridden by scientific theory from those that can. Whitehead, in fact, formulated his "metaphysical rule of evidence" cited above in response to those who, having "arrogated to themselves the title of 'empiricists,'" have been chiefly employed in explaining away the obvious facts of experience" (*PR*, 145). The *truly* "obvious facts of experience," I suggest, are those that we inevitably presuppose in practice, even if we deny them verbally. One can see, indeed, that eliminative materialists verbally deny a range of notions that Searle rightly regards as obvious. Not having formulated this criterion of obviousness, however, Searle sometimes mixes things that fit it with things that do not. To illustrate: Searle speaks both of "the obvious facts of physics—for example, that the world is made up entirely of physical particles in fields of force," and of "obvious facts about the mental, such as that we all really do have subjective conscious mental states" (*RM,* 3), as if the truth of these two types of assertions were equally obvious and in the same sort of way. But they are not. The so-called obvious facts of physics, unlike the "obvious facts about the mental," involve a long series of sensory observations and (dubious) inferences. Also, one could deny Searle's statement about the physical world without pain of self-contradiction, whereas this would not (as Descartes pointed out) be possible with regard to the statement about conscious experience.

Yet another qualification is necessary with regard to the term "obvious." I have sought to show how this term could be defined so as to make an appeal to obviousness defensible as an ultimate criterion of philosophical and scientific acceptability. It is, however, problematic. The word usually is taken (as by my dictionary) to mean "readily apparent." Now, some of our hard-core commonsense notions, such as the fact that we have conscious experience, *are* readily apparent (some eliminativist arguments notwithstanding), whereas others are less so. For example, it may take some argumentation to convince us, in the face of the great extent to which our behavior is conditioned, that we always presuppose that we have a degree of freedom or, in the face of the evidence for ethical relativism, that we always presuppose the reality of some normative ideals. Given the widespread rejection of both of these beliefs by philosophers and scientists in our time, it would be strange to refer to them as *obvious*. It is better, accordingly, to speak of the "inevitable presuppositions of our practice" or of our "hard-core common sense."

In any case, these hard-core commonsense notions can be seen to supply the kind of criterion Nagel is presupposing in saying that we should assume that there is probably something wrong with any argument that leads to an "intuitively unacceptable conclusion." Whitehead spells out the criterion of the intuitively unacceptable by speaking of "difficulties which take the shape of negations of what in practice is presupposed" (*PR,* 13). Without this criterion, Nagel's recommendation could lead philosophers to feel justified in rejecting any good argument for a conclusion they disliked with the flippant assertion, "It contradicts my intuitions." Whitehead countenances no such appeal to idiosyncratic intuitions: "It is a disease of philosophy when it is . . . merely a reflection of the temperamental presuppositions of exceptional personalities" (*PR,* 17). His appeal is instead to "the *general* consciousness of what in practice *we* experience" (*PR,* 17; emphases added), and he limits the appeal to those notions that *all* of us *inevitably* employ in the regulation of our lives (even if we are not conscious of them and even if we explicitly deny them). It is when a theory, whether called philosophic or scientific, contradicts intuitions in *this* sense that we should assume that something must be amiss.

Using the term "intuitions" for our inevitable presuppositions would be less problematic than speaking of them as "obvious facts." True, this term can be misleading (because it can connote idiosyncratic hunches), but so can the term "common sense," if unqualified. With an adjective such as *inevitable, deepest,* or *universal,* the term "intuitions" can serve to refer to these universal presuppositions of practice.

In this relativistic age, of course, many philosophers, even given the above clarifications, will tend to be suspicious of, if not to reject out of hand, the idea that there are *any* notions or presuppositions that are universal. After realizing that this idea cannot be refuted simply by pointing out that probably *every* "obvious" idea has been denied by *someone*—because the claim is about presuppositions of practice, not explicit, verbal beliefs—many will want to put the burden of proof on those making the positive claim. No universal claim, of course, can be proved by any number of instances. But a universal claim *can* be *disproved* by a single negative instance: As William James said, it takes only one white crow to prove that all crows are not black. So the burden is really on those who would deny the universal claim. They need to come up with at least one instance of someone, perhaps themselves, who can live without presupposing the notion in question. And, with regard to one or more of the notions, they may well succeed, especially with regard to some particular formulation of the notion. If we return to a form of commonsensism, we should, with Whitehead as well as Peirce, combine it with fallibilism. The claim that any particular notion is inevitably presupposed in practice is fallible; the attempt to formulate the notion verbally is even more fallible; and even the idea that there are such notions is fallible.

Insofar as claims for such notions survive all attempts to refute them, however, they should be taken as the ultimate criteria for judging a theory's adequacy, and this for a simple reason: *If we cannot help presupposing these notions in practice,* including the practice of scientific experimentation and theory-building, *we are guilty of self-contradiction if our theory denies these notions.* And the first rule of reason, including scientific reason, should be that two mutually contradictory propositions cannot both be true.

Is this foundationalism? As usually understood, foundationalism says that nonbasic beliefs are to be derived from basic beliefs and that basic beliefs themselves are not supported by nonbasic beliefs. In my position, however, hard-core commonsense beliefs function not as a foundation upon which all other beliefs are to be built but as a compass telling us when we have gotten off course. And part of the reason why we should have confidence in our hard-core common sense, I argue, is that we can understand in a naturalistic way why we have these beliefs (see pages 27 and 133).

One result of this third snarl in our knotty problem—the failure to distinguish hard-core from soft-core common sense—has been that the former has often been denied in the name of the latter. The idea that the units of the physical world, such as electrons and living cells, are "insentient," in the sense of being wholly devoid of experience of every sort, is one of the most widespread "commonsense" notions of the modern West. It does not, however, belong to our *hard-core* common sense: It is not universally accepted; it is not inevitably presupposed in practice; one can deny it without necessarily presupposing its truth in the act of denying it. And yet in the name of this parochial, merely soft-core commonsense idea, many modern philosophers and scientists deny other notions, such as freedom and the reality and efficacy of conscious experience, that do belong to our hard-core common sense. The counter-proposal, that soft-core common sense should never be allowed to trump the hard-core variety, brings us to the topic of the next chapter: regulative principles for theory-construction.

FOUR

Regulative Principles

All discussions of the mind-body relation presuppose various regulative principles. Some of these are formal, such as the principles just enunciated—that a theory should be self-consistent and that in a conflict between hard-core and soft-core common sense, the latter must submit. Others are substantive, such as the principle that a theory should be compatible with the evolutionary origin of human beings. In distinguishing a (substantive) regulative principle from an empirical hypothesis, Seager describes it helpfully as "a view of nature to which particular theories must conform, or else, embarrassed and uneasy, awkwardly await eventual conformation" (*MC*, 5). Regulative principles, by specifying the conditions to which any theory must conform to be potentially acceptable by the author or community in question, indicate the range of theories that can be eliminated a priori. For example, Seager says that when physicalism is accepted as a regulative principle, "a psychological theory which denied the compatibility of its posits with the purely physical nature of the brain or, more generally, demanded the existence of non-physical psychological entities could thus be ruled out *a priori*" (*MC*, 5).

It would greatly increase prospects for consensus on the mind-body relation if authors would state the decisive principles regulative of their theories, insofar as they are conscious of them, as precisely and systematically as possible.* This would facilitate mutual criticism and thereby refinement

*After completing the first draft of this book, I learned that Arthur Lovejoy, the eminent historian of philosophy, had made a similar proposal in 1917. In a presidential address to the American Philosophical Association called "On Some Conditions of Progress in Philosophical Inquiry" (*Philosophical Review* XXVI [1917], 127–63)—which he had thought of calling "What's the Matter with Philosophy?"—Lovejoy suggested that before developing a position

of the principles. Too often many of the crucial regulative principles, especially substantive ones, are left unstated. When some principles *are* stated,
they are usually scattered throughout the writing, making criticism difficult.
Mutual criticism is especially important because even when principles are
explicitly formulated, they are often formulated ambiguously. Searle is ad-
mirable for stating some regulative principles explicitly. However, in stating
his first formal principle—"we ought to stop saying things that are obviously false" (*RM*, 247)—he does not, as I indicated in the previous chapter,
provide any criterion for discerning obvious (from merely apparent) falsity.
One of Daniel Dennett's substantive regulative principles is that "dualism
is to be avoided at all costs" (*CE*, 37). Although Dennett refers here to
dualism "in all its forms," the context shows that dual-aspect theory is not
in view. But this still leaves at least two very different doctrines: (1) the
mind is not only numerically distinct from, but also ontologically different in kind from, the brain and interacts with it, and (2) the mind is numerically distinct in kind from, but *not* ontologically different from, the
brain and interacts with it. Does Dennett mean that the second doctrine
(nondualistic interactionism) is to be avoided as strongly as the first
(Cartesian dualism)? And when he says that dualism is to be avoided "at all
costs," does he really mean that this regulative principle should take priority over all others, such as self-consistency and adequacy to obvious facts of
experience? If so, why?

The possibility of making progress toward consensus has been lessened
by the fact that most discussions of other theories focus primarily on the
theories themselves rather than on the regulative principles lying behind
them. A theory, however, is largely determined by the author's regulative
principles (which are in turn influenced by paradigmatic and wishful-and-
fearful thinking, discussed earlier, and data convictions, to be discussed
below). Criticism of an inadequate theory that does not deal with the
deeper convictions lying behind it will generally result only in another
equally inadequate theory (as in the neurotic-like pattern of behavior discussed by Searle).

A clarification: Although Kant, with whom the notion of "regulative principles" is historically associated, thought of them as unchanging, I am, in
harmony with Seager (*MC*, 6), thinking of them as revisable. Even if some
of the formulations can be thought to reflect eternally valid principles,
the formulations themselves should always be considered fallible attempts,
which might be improved.

Another clarification: Any list of *all* the formal and substantive regulative

---

with regard to some philosophical question, the philosopher should observe "as completely
and exactly as possible . . . the 'considerations' pertinent to this question" (142). I learned of
Lovejoy's proposal from Charles Hartshorne (*DL*, 390).

principles that guide one's thinking would threaten to approach infinity. But no exhaustive list is needed. Most of the principles by which we operate are noncontroversial or practically irrelevant to the subject at hand. We need only to try to state those principles that are both controversial and directly relevant to our approach to the mind-body problem. We will, no doubt, fail to list all such principles. But those that we do list will be out in the open for public discussion; and those that are missing will likely, as we become more adept at mutual "regulative principle criticism," be pointed out by others.

With these clarifications, I will now attempt a formulation of regulative principles—first formal, then substantive—that I think should guide discussions of the mind-body relation.

I. FORMAL REGULATIVE PRINCIPLES

1. We should assume the *unity of truth* and therefore the principle of *noncontradiction*—that no theory that is self-contradictory can be true and that if one theory contradicts another, they cannot both, as stated, be true.

a. An implication is that logical inconsistencies, as Whitehead says, should not be taken to "indicate anything else than some antecedent errors" (*PR*, xiii). They should not, for example, be taken to mean that the universe is inherently inconsistent, or that the truth about some aspect of reality is necessarily forever beyond human grasp. The latter may be true, but we should not jump to this conclusion before we have fully explored the possibility of "some antecedent errors." Here I agree with Nagel that McGinn's pessimism is premature (*NYR*, 40n7).

b. We should distinguish clearly between natural and artificial mysteries. *Natural mysteries* are those that are simply given to us, such as how our universe began, how a spider "knows" how to spin a web, and how our conscious experiences are related to our brains. *Artificial mysteries* are those that are created by the way we have defined an issue, such as why our creator, being benevolent and omnipotent, allows evil, or how the brain, being composed of nothing but insentient bits of matter, could give rise to conscious experience. Before we declare something a permanent mystery, we should see whether the problem lies in a (revisable) definition rather than in reality or our limited cognitive capacity as such.

2. We should not rest content with any theory until it seems to be adequate to *all* the relevant data.

a. We should not let fashionable exaggerations about the "theory-laden nature of all data" blind us to the fact (!) that a distinction between data and theories about them can usually be made. As Seager points out (*MC*, 6), the fact that data notoriously resist our systematizing efforts illustrates the transcendence of data over our perceptual and conceptual filters.

b. While we should strive for self-consistency as well as adequacy, we should not deny any obvious or well-attested data in the interests of a self-consistent theory. Although we should in principle give equal allegiance to self-consistency and adequacy, we should in practice, when forced to choose, give higher allegiance to adequacy. (Searle's principle that "we ought to stop saying things that are obviously false" [*RM*, 247] was appropriately offered as the *first* of his principles.) Anomalous data, if kept in view, may evoke a reconciling theory, whereas simply eliminating recalcitrant data forecloses the possibility of an adequate theory. It is the violation of this principle that constitutes the central formal failure of the eliminative materialists. As Strawson says, "They are simply deciding to leave part of reality out of their scientific account of reality. They are just giving up on the great philosophical-scientific project of giving a unified account of the whole of reality, so far as we are acquainted with it and so far as we are able" (*MR*, 103).

3. The data to which we should give the highest allegiance are our *hard-core commonsense notions*. Again, because such notions are presupposed in all practice, including the practice of discovering facts scientifically and formulating scientific theories, such notions should take priority over any theories from which their falsity would follow. For example, just as we should reject any theory that says that the existence of human beings is impossible, we should reject any theory articulated with the purpose of proving that human purposes are nonexistent or at least without effect.

4. We should distinguish as clearly as possible what we really *know* from what we merely *believe must be the case* because of dubious interpretations of data, perhaps combined with wishful-and-fearful thinking.

a. John Searle has stated this regulative principle: "We ought to keep reminding ourselves of what we know for sure" (*RM*, 247).

b. Searle, however, illustrates that, apart from criticism from those with other points of view, this is easier said than done, as he goes on to say: "For example, we know for sure that inside our skulls there is a brain, sometimes it is conscious, and brain processes cause consciousness in all its forms." In the first place, we need to distinguish between the sense in which we know hard-core commonsense notions "for sure" and the way in which we may know other things "for sure" (beyond a reasonable doubt). With regard to Searle's present list of alleged truths of the second type, I would agree that we know that we each have a brain in our skulls. I would not agree, however, that we know for sure that it is sometimes conscious: We know that *we* are sometimes conscious but not that consciousness is a state, property, or attribute characterizing our brains as such; that is an inference based on the confidence that all forms of interactionism must be false. We also do not know for sure that *every* state of consciousness is *entirely* caused by brain events, which is what Searle means (see *RM*, 92, 111–12, 114, 116, 125).

Some conscious states may be partly caused by previous conscious states (as prima facie seems to be the case in memory); some conscious states may be partially caused by influences that have not been transmitted through the brain (as seems to be the case in moral, logical, and religious experience, not to mention clairvoyance and telepathy); and some may be partly caused by the conscious experience itself (as must be the case if our presuppositions about partial freedom and responsibility are true). So, in accepting Searle's formal principle, we should also remind ourselves of our need for mutual criticism and cooperation in trying to carry it out.

5. We should follow Nagel's formal regulative principle that "pursuit of truth requires . . . the generation and decisive elimination of alternative possibilities until, ideally, only one remains" (*VN*, 9). And in doing so it is essential that we follow two procedures:

a. All alternatives compatible with one's regulative principles must be examined. For example, if one has a substantive regulative principle that narrows the choice to the various theories that are realistic (in the philosophical sense of affirming the reality of the universe apart from our conception of it), then *all* realistic theories must be examined. In practice this means that, given the existence of panexperientialist theories, the choice cannot arbitrarily be narrowed down to dualistic and materialistic theories (barring, of course, some other regulative principle that allows all panexperientialist theories to be excluded a priori).

b. The strongest versions of each of the basic alternatives should be compared, rather than, say, the strongest version of one's personal favorite and the weakest (or a fabricated) version of any of the other alternatives. (These two procedures are so important, and so generally violated, that it is probably no exaggeration to say that the single thing that we could do to improve the quality of philosophy [including the philosophical aspect of science] would be to hold ourselves and each other responsible for abiding by these procedures.)

6. We should try to become aware of our own *wishful-and-fearful thinking* and to overcome its distorting effects as much as possible. This is not to say that wishful-and-fearful thinking necessarily leads to false conclusions; it may happen that our hopes about what is true will coincide with the way things really are. But we should suspect that this will often not be the case.

7. Having recognized the often-distorting effects of subjectivity, one aspect of which is wishful-and-fearful thinking, we should strive for *objectivity* in a more inclusive way, as Nagel says, which means overcoming the distorting effects of other subjective elements, such as prejudices of one's time and place, anthropocentric prejudices, and prejudices based on the distorting nature of sensory perception.

a. As Searle points out (*RM*, 19), objectivity in this epistemic sense must be kept distinct from objectivism in the ontological sense (according to which all truly existing and effective things are devoid of subjectivity, in the sense of awareness, purpose, and point of view). Jacques Monod, for example, simply conflates the two meanings (*CN*, 21).

b. If the world truly contains subjectivity in the sense of points of view (and we know that it does), then a theory that is truly objective in the epistemic sense cannot be wholly objective in the ontological sense.

8. We should combine *boldness with humility.* The need for boldness was enunciated in Nagel's statement that "the world is a strange place, and nothing but radical speculation gives us the hope of coming up with any candidates for the truth" (*VN*, 10). Nagel has likewise expressed the need for humility with his observation that today's practitioners of philosophy "are at a particular and, we may hope, early stage of its development, limited by their own primitive intellectual capacities and relying on the partial insights of a few great figures from the past" (*VN*, 10). Accordingly, he says, "a pervasive skepticism or at least provisionality of commitment is suitable" (*VN*, 69). The need for this formal principle is illustrated by William Lycan's comment (even though it was obviously a deliberate overstatement) that he is prepared "to kill for" his particular (functionalist) solution to the problem of consciousness (*C*, 37). Two other dimensions of humility are pointed to by Whitehead: "Speculative boldness must be balanced by complete humility before logic and before fact" (*PR*, 7). Recent philosophy has given logic its due; (paradigm-threatening) fact has not fared so well, because philosophers practice the wrong kind of boldness: "Failure to include some obvious elements of experience in the scope of the system is met by boldly denying the facts" (*PR*, 6). Whitehead's statement, published in 1929, shows that the eliminative approach is not new.

9. Our *epistemology* should match our *claims to knowledge.* That is, as Nagel says, our conception of the world should include an explanation of "how beings like us can arrive at such a conception" (*VN*, 74).

a. This formal regulative principle is violated if the epistemic capacities ascribed (whether explicitly or only implicitly) to us are exceeded by the author's own assumed claims (whether explicit or only implicit) to knowledge. For example, my claim that we all share various hard-core common-sense notions should be supported by an explanation as to how we know these truths.

b. This principle should also make us suspicious of all claims, à la Locke, Kant, and McGinn, to be able to know the limits of human knowledge. Does not the claimed capacity to discern permanent barriers to human insight imply an epistemic capacity so great that we should be able to discern the truth about the matters said to lie beyond the barriers? As Hegel asked, What kind of reason was Kant using when he described the permanent limitations of human reason?

10. We should accept the formal regulative principle of *simplicity* or

parsimony in this sense: We should, all else being equal, prefer the theory that least multiplies independent principles. Any explanatory principle is stronger to the extent that it can explain apparently disparate phenomena.

11. If the acceptance of some dubious assumption has led to a problem that has remained insoluble for a long time, we should question this assumption. If the problem seems insoluble in principle, we should definitely try another approach. We should, in other words, change a losing game.

II. SUBSTANTIVE REGULATIVE PRINCIPLES

Although my substantive principles are given prior to my discussion of the kinds of data that should especially be taken into account, they are not independent of these data. The general dependence of these principles on data of experience in fact lies behind the point that our accepted list and understanding of such principles should be understood as revisable. In any case, I suggest the following substantive regulative principles.

1. We should accept only a *realistic* theory about the "physical world."

a. This substantive principle rules out all idealisms that deny full-fledged actuality to the "physical world," making its reality dependent on its being perceived or conceived by mind. (This principle would not necessarily rule out various types of "realistic idealism" or "idealistic realism.")

b. A theory is more adequate to the extent that it can provide an intelligible answer to Bishop Berkeley's question—What does it *mean* to say that physical things "exist"?—without succumbing to his idealistic answer that for them "to be" is "to be perceived."

c. To have a realistic view of the physical universe requires, especially given our evolutionary cosmology, a realistic view of time. In particular: How can we conceive of the reality of time apart from animal minds, so that we can speak of billions of years of cosmic and geologic evolution prior to the rise of animal life?

2. A theory should embody the following substantive principles about *causation.*

a. Efficient causation, meaning the influence of one thing (or event, or process) on another, should be understood as real influence (not mere constant conjunction).

b. Efficient causation and actuality should be strictly correlated: All actualities should be assumed to exert efficient causation (the "no-idle-wheels" principle); and whenever efficient causation is discerned, it should be ascribed only to one or more actualities (the Aristotelian dictum dubbed the "ontological principle" by Whitehead), never to mere abstractions (such as "properties").

c. We should assume an *unbroken causal nexus,* according to which all actualities are subject to efficient causation and in turn exert efficient causation.

d. The substantive principle of an unbroken causal nexus, however, does not necessarily imply determinism, because the exertion of self-causation by some actualities is not ruled out.

e. Efficient causation should be understood as temporally structured such that it always goes from the past to the present and the present to the future. There is no retrocausation exerted by the future back on the present, or by the present back on the past. There is also no efficient causation between events that are contemporaries in the strictest sense. Although it may sometimes seem as if the cause and the effect were strictly simultaneous, this would be true only in self-causation. In efficient causation, the cause must always occur before its effect, even if this be less than a billionth of a second. (If causes and effects were simultaneous, it would be arbitrary that one were the "cause" and the other the "effect"; also, assuming a relational view of time, according to which the temporal structure of reality is the result of the causal relations between events, no temporality would be generated if causes and effects were simultaneous.)

3. We should adopt a realist stance on *explanation.*

a. This principle means that we should strive for causal explanations that do in fact correspond significantly with causal relations that exist objectively to our thoughts about them.

b. This "correspondence" of theory with fact need not be thought to express the *whole* truth about the causal factors involved. It needs only to mean, in Jaegwon Kim's words, "that a causal explanation of E in terms of C is a 'correct explanation' only if C is in reality a cause of E" (*SM,* 256).

c. A realist stance does strongly suggest, however, what Kim calls the "principle of causal-explanatory exclusion" (*SM,* 281, 291), which says: "No event can be given more than one *complete* and *independent* explanation" (*SM,* 239). In other words, because an event in all its concreteness* cannot be thought to have two sufficient causes, it cannot intelligibly be given two sufficient causal explanations—such as a mechanistic explanation, in terms of efficient causes, and a purposive, teleological explanation, in terms of final causation in the sense of self-determination in the light of a goal.

---

*It is sometimes urged, against the principle of explanatory exclusion, that an event can be "overdetermined." A common example, mentioned by Kim (*SM,* 252), is that a man may be killed by two assassins whose bullets hit at the same time, although either bullet would have been sufficient to bring about the death. However, to describe the effect simply in terms of the man's death is a great abstraction from the event in all its concreteness. If we move close enough to the concrete effect to mention that the corpse contained two bullets, which had entered the body from different angles, it will be clear that neither bullet by itself was a sufficient cause of the effect.

Either each explanation must be considered insufficient or else the one explanation must exclude the other.

4. Our theory should be *naturalistic*.

a. This substantive regulative principle, which has recently been insisted on strongly by McGinn, entails not only the rejection of any explicit supernaturalism, according to which the natural causal nexus is said to be interrupted; it also entails the rejection of any doctrine that even implies the need for supernatural intervention.

b. Naturalism need not entail physicalism (at least as ordinarily understood). That would be the case only if it were specified that things (or events or processes) that are physical, by virtue of exerting and being subject to efficient causation, are *exhaustively* physical; but naturalism need not be so defined. Naturalism does involve, however, what Nagel calls the valid impulse behind physicalism: the desire "to find a way of thinking about the world as it is, so that everything in it, not just atoms and planets, can be regarded as real in the same way" (*VN*, 16).

c. Naturalism also need not entail determinism (contra McGinn and many others). That would be the case only if it had been specified that efficient causation is the only kind of natural causation; but naturalism need not be so construed (see 2*d*, above).

d. Naturalism also does not necessarily rule out seemingly "paranormal" types of causal influence, such as extrasensory perception and psychokinesis. That would be the case if paranormal events were understood to be "miracles" involving interruptions of fundamental causal principles, but they need not be (and by parapsychologists usually are not) so understood. Naturalism would also rule out such events if it entailed that efficient causation between events occurs exhaustively between *contiguous* events; but naturalism need not dictate this. Naturalism can be relaxed enough to trust empirical research to answer the question of whether causal influence at a distance really occurs.

e. Naturalism also does not necessarily rule out any reference to a divine reality. For example, if a thinker were to refer to energy as divine or as God, this would not make her or him a supernaturalist. Naturalism does not even rule out every conceivable form of theism; it only specifies that theism, if affirmed, cannot be supernaturalistic. Naturalism only rules out supernaturalism.* It rules out, in Whitehead's words, "a *deus ex machina* capable of rising superior to the difficulties of metaphysics" (*SMW*, 156).

---

*In discussing the "naturalization" of mind, Kim distinguishes between a stricter sense, which involves "physicalization" (see 4*b*, above), and a looser sense, "which only requires expulsion of the supernatural, the theological, and the essentially normative-evaluative" (*SM*, 297). Naturalism as I am using it, to refer to a worldview, requires the expulsion only of the supernatural.

f. Naturalism does entail the attempt, as W. D. Hart says, to "naturalize the mind, that is, to fit it into the causal nexus that constitutes nature" (*EOS,* 56). Naturalism does, accordingly, involve the view, as Flanagan says, "that the mind-brain relation is a natural one" (*CR,* xi). It does not, however, necessarily entail his further assertion that "mental processes just are brain processes." That would only follow if it had already been determined that there could not be a naturalistic form of interactionism.

5. A theory of the mind-body relation should embody the substantive principle of *continuity.*

a. This substantive regulative principle follows from the acceptance of evolution in a naturalistic framework, which forbids positing any jumps that would imply some supernatural insertion into the causal nexus. In evolutionary reconstruction, as elsewhere, we must avoid implying, as well as saying, "and then a miracle occurs."

b. The principle of continuity forbids, therefore, any ontological dualism, according to which the mind would be different *in kind* from the entities from which it arose. Being different in kind would include operating according to different causal principles, as if, à la vitalism, final causation (or self-determinism) could emerge in a world that had previously operated in terms of efficient causation alone.

c. The substantive principle of continuity even forbids jumps *in degree* that are too great to be intelligible naturalistically. For example, something as complex as a squirrel could not have emerged directly out of something as simple as a flea.

6. A philosophical theory should be compatible with the scientific worldview.

a. The "scientific worldview" contains all the fairly assured results of scientific discovery, such as atomic theory, the evolutionary nature of our universe, and whatever is truly known about brain function.

b. The scientific worldview does *not* necessarily include all currently dominant scientific theories, such as big bang cosmology, the neo-Darwinian theory of evolution, and the Copenhagen theory of quantum physics. One could question any of these without ipso facto having rejected "the scientific worldview."

c. Still less does it necessarily include the metaphysical worldview of materialism, or physicalism, with which science has been primarily associated for the past century. Science is a matter of method and results, and, just as it has changed its worldview in the past when this change enabled it to make greater progress (perhaps among other reasons), it may find a more

---

It need not necessarily exclude the theological and the essentially normative-evaluative, *if* these can be conceived apart from supernaturalism.

congenial worldview in the future (perhaps in part out of the realization that the current worldview will never be able to solve its mind-body problem). Accordingly, when we speak with Seager of "limits set by the range of models that science provides and accepts as legitimate explanation" (*MC*, vii), we must understand this to refer to science as such, *not* present-day mainline science. As Nagel says, it is scientism "at its most myopic" to assume "that everything there is must be understandable by the employment of scientific theories like those we have developed to date" (*VN*, 9).

d. Even the statement that "science is a matter of method" must be understood in a very general sense, because the worldview adopted by science in a particular period tends to constrain its methods. Also, we have to beware of the temptation to assume that a method that has produced spectacular results with regard to a limited range of phenomena is *the* scientific method, which must be employed in relation to *all* phenomena. As Nagel says, "Too much time is wasted because of the assumption that methods already in existence will solve problems for which they were not designed" (*VN*, 10). The formal regulative principle of humility should warn us against "the bizarre view that we, at this point in history, are in possession of the basic forms of understanding needed to comprehend absolutely anything" (*VN*, 10).

e. The scientific worldview *should*, however, be understood to include any and all hard-core commonsense notions. Because such notions, if they exist, by definition involve notions that are necessarily presupposed in practice, including the practices of observing, thinking, and testing, it would be self-defeating for scientific theories to contradict them.

f. The scientific worldview should also be understood to include, in a somewhat more tentative manner, various regulative principles insofar as they follow from the hard-core commonsense notions in combination with generalizations from empirical discoveries. (The greater tentativeness is appropriate because of our limited capacities for generalizing from empirical discoveries and for discerning and properly formulating hard-core commonsense notions in all their variety well enough to see clearly what principles would "follow from" them.)

FIVE

Data

One reason that contemporary theories of mind vary so greatly is that different theorists are presupposing greatly different ideas about the kinds of data to which a theory must be adequate. Data that one theorist considers fundamental, perhaps devoting a hundred pages to defending, will be dismissed in a sentence by other theorists, if mentioned at all. The likelihood of approaching greater consensus would be increased if, instead of prematurely debating the merits of various theories, we would give more attention to the arguably relevant kinds of data. There has been, to be sure, considerable discussion of certain kinds of data, such as "qualia," "point of view," and "intentionality." But seldom if ever does one find an attempt to provide a somewhat complete list of the kinds of data that should be taken into account. Of course, one reason for this is that the currently dominant philosophy of mind has such a restricted view of what could possibly be experienced that the desire for self-consistency, while good in itself, leads, in Nagel's words, "to false reductions or to outright denial that certain patently real phenomena exist at all" (*VN*, 7). That is, while claiming to be "scientific" and thereby "empirical," these theories in fact allow the authentic data to be dictated by theory rather than by observation. But the formal principle of adequacy should lead us to resist systematizing until we have tried to assemble the various kinds of data that need to be unified. In Whitehead's words, "Philosophy can exclude nothing. Thus it should never start from systematization. Its primary stage can be termed *assemblage*" (*MT*, 2). I can do no full-scale assemblage here, of course, but I will illustrate what I have in mind by pointing to some of the kinds of data that would be most relevant to the contemporary attempt to understand the place of conscious experience in the world.

I. HARD-CORE COMMONSENSE NOTIONS

I list these first because, as argued in chapter 3, they should be regarded as the data to which a theory should primarily be adequate. I will list here several of these notions, which we seem inevitably to presuppose in practice.

1. The reality of "*the external world.*" As Whitehead says, "Hume retained an obstinate belief in an external world which his principles forbade him to confess in his philosophical constructions" (*PR,* 140). Indeed, Hume himself pointed out that although he was a solipsist in theory, he could not be one in practice. This means, however, that we should not accept non-realism even in theory; the theory, as Whitehead says, should be revised so as to include what is presupposed in practice (*PR,* 13). Asserting that the external world exists independently of our perception and conception of it need not imply, of course, that it exists in itself *just as* it appears to our sensory perception or *just as* it is conceived in our sensory-based conceptions. (For one thing, sensory perception may not be our only or even primary way of perceiving the world beyond ourselves.)

2. The reality of *efficient causation understood as the real influence* of one thing (or many things) on another. Again, Hume pointed out (and demonstrated in his historical writing) that he in practice could not help presupposing causation in this sense. None of us can. So we cannot rest content until we have found a way to affirm and conceptualize it in our theories. Real influence, of course, need not mean total determination (and *cannot,* at least universally, if this point is to cohere with the point below about freedom).

3. The reality of the *past* and the future* and therefore of *time.* Full-fledged solipsism would be, in George Santayana's phrase, "solipsism of the present moment."[1] But we all presuppose in practice that there has been a past and that there will be a future. Santayana spoke of these presuppositions as "faith," but that is too weak: We seem to *know* these things as strongly as we know anything.

4. The reality of our *conscious experience* with its emotions, pains, pleasures, perceptions, purposes, decisions, memories, anticipations. Descartes was surely right at least about this, that there is nothing we are more certain of than our present conscious experience and that to deny it (consciously) would be self-contradictory. As Searle says, "if your theory results in the view that consciousness does not exist, you have simply produced a *reductio ad absurdum* of the theory" (*RM,* 8). Strawson points out why this is the

---

*By "the reality of the future," I do not mean that future events already exist, which would imply determinism and the *unreality* of time. I mean only that subsequent events, causally influenced by present events, *will* follow on them and that the anticipation of the future in this sense is a fact about the present.

case. With regard to those eliminativists who "suppose that although it *seems* to one that there is experience—for this cannot be denied—there really isn't any experience," he says: "But this is an immediate reductio ad absurdum. For this seeming is already experience. . . . [These eliminativists] cannot hope to treat experience itself as some sort of total illusion, for illusion presupposes—it is a form of—experience" (*MR*, 51). In a passage on the way in which eliminativists discuss pain, Strawson expresses the principle that common sense (of this type) cannot be sacrificed to a theory based on alternative intuitions:

> I find the suggestion that common sense makes any error about the qualitative or lived nature of pain inexplicable except as an extreme case of theory-driven Procrusteanism. If there is any sense in which these philosophers are rejecting the ordinary view of the nature of things like pain . . . , their view seems to be one of the most amazing manifestations of human irrationality on record. It is much less irrational to postulate the existence of a divine being whom we cannot perceive than to deny the truth of the commonsense view of experience. (*MR*, 53)

5. *Bodily influence on conscious experience,* at least with regard to some pains, pleasures, desires, and sensory perceptions. (Of course, some theories would claim that the body not only *influences* but *completely determines* our conscious experiences, and not only *some* but *all* of them. This claim, however, would go beyond anything inevitably presupposed in practice.) Given the universality of this presupposition, it did not have to wait on recent neuroscience. For example, we know—as Whitehead pointed out in his polemic against Hume's claim that we have no direct experience of causal efficacy—that we *see* by means of the *eyes* (*PR*, 62, 81). This means that there is a touch of exaggeration in McGinn's claim that introspection "tells us nothing about the physical network in which our conscious states are embedded" (*PC*, 73). Our introspectible experience involves what Whitehead calls "the 'withness' of the body" (*PR*, 81, 312).

6. *The unity of our experience.* Including this notion will likely evoke objections. And, indeed, the unity of our experience is subject to several important qualifications. Data from split-brain patients raise deep questions about just how to understand the kind of unity we have, as do some kinds of hypnotic phenomena, various kinds of brain disease, cases of multiple personality, and the relative autonomy of unconscious processes. Even our ordinary experience of ambivalence suggests something less than total unity, as does our capacity for self-transcendence, in which a dimension of the self seems to stand beyond the self. However, after all of these and other qualifications are made, it remains true that, insofar as we "retain our minds" so that we are not merely "human vegetables," there is a significant unity to our experience. We are not simply aggregates of experiential data;

what we call the mind is a *unification* of vast amounts of data into an experiential unity.*

For example, as Searle points out in including "unity" as one of the structures of consciousness (*RM*, 130), at any moment I simultaneously experience sights, sounds, smells, tastes, touches, bodily pains, bodily pleasures, bodily hungers, memories, and so on, while at the time feeling desires and emotions, anticipating the future, making decisions, and so on. Another way to realize the remarkable degree of unity we enjoy, in spite of all needed qualifications, is to recall that the brain is composed of more than 100 billion neurons. No case of multiple personality approaches that number.**

Even if we were to localize conscious experience in one portion of the brain, we would be speaking of unifying data from tens of billions of neurons. Seen from this perspective, our experience, especially our conscious experience, has a remarkable unity, of which we are directly aware. As Nagel says, "the unity of consciousness, even if it is not complete, poses a problem for the theory that mental states are states of something as complex as a brain" (*VN*, 50). This unity is also presupposed in points 7 and 8, below, which involve the active side of our experience. In summary, as Whitehead has observed, "what needs to be explained is not dissociation of personality but unifying control, by reason of which we not only have unified behavior, which can be observed by others, but also consciousness of unified experience" (*PR*, 108).

---

*Stephen Braude has argued convincingly, in *First Person Plural: Multiple Personality and the Philosophy of Mind*, that multiple personality not only is consistent with but also presupposes a unity underlying the multiplicity. Multiple personality disorder (MPD) does, he argues, truly involve the existence of two or more distinct "apperceptive centers," often with radically different personalities and perhaps even physiological conditions (e.g., one may be color blind, or near-sighted, the other not; one may be left-handed, the other right-handed; one may have severe allergic responses, such as rashes, to things to which the other is not allergic). Nevertheless, the alternate personalities tend to overlap in many respects, sharing not only memories but also usually language and many other complex abilities, such as the ability to drive an automobile, shop for groceries, and host parties. Having pointed out that MPD usually follows on a severe trauma (*FPP*, 39), Braude provides an insightful argument against the view, which he says is based on "the principle of compositional reversibility" (a chapter title), that the existence of post-traumatic (or in the case of commissurotomy, post-surgical) multiplicity provides evidence for pre-trauma (or pre-surgical) plurality, as if the disintegration of the personality were a reversal of an earlier process of partially integrating a colony of lower-order selves.

**According to Braude (*FPP*, 41), some recent surveys place the average number of personalities in MPD cases at sixteen, whereas others place it at six. In some cases, however, over a hundred alternate personalities are reportedly manifest. The highest number of reported "alters" is evidently about 4,500. As Braude says, "One can only wonder about the accuracy of such an estimate." Even if such an estimate were credited, however, the unity of the experience of the personality in executive control of the body at any given moment, as well as the memories, linguistic abilities, and other abilities shared by the various personalities, would still require explanation—an explanation that materialism seems unable to provide.

7. The *efficacy of conscious experience* for bodily behavior. The fact that we all presuppose the efficacy of conscious experience in practice is well stated by Ted Honderich, who speaks of the "axiom of the indispensability of the mental." The main recommendation of this axiom, he says, is "the futility of contemplating its denial." In a phrase reminiscent of Charles Peirce's criticism of "paper doubts," Honderich says of epiphenomenalism, "Off the page, no one believes it" (MBSC, 447). Some people do, of course, confess it *on* the page. For example, William Robinson, whose denial that sensations can be understood physicalistically was cited earlier, says that although epiphenomenalism does seem to conflict with common sense, this conflict is only apparent (*BP,* 51). Many other nondualists, however, reject epiphenomenalism. Flanagan, for example, rejects "conscious inessentialism"—the view that any intelligent activity done with conscious accompaniments can in principle be done without them—and thereby rejects epiphenomenalism as implausible, saying that our bodily actions are "individuated in part by the intentions and motives that constitute them" (*CR,* 5–6). Seager says that the "efficacy of consciousness . . . presents the aspect of a datum rather than a disputable hypothesis" (*MC,* 188). Kim suggests a *reductio ad absurdum* of epiphenomenalism: "If our reasons and desires have no causal efficacy at all in influencing our bodily actions, then perhaps no one has ever performed a single intentional action!" (*SM,* 104). The neurophysiologist Roger Sperry, who won a Nobel Prize for his work on split-brain patients, contributed to the current widespread rejection of epiphenomenalism by beginning in 1965, as he continued to do in *Science and Moral Priority* (1983), to speak of "downward causation" from the mind to the brain (*SMP,* 4, 79–81). Searle includes "the reality and causal efficacy of consciousness" (*RM,* 54) among the obvious facts about our minds, endorsing the "commonsense objection to eliminative materialism" that it is "crazy to say that . . . my beliefs and desires don't play any role in my behavior" (*RM,* 48). Indeed, it is worse than crazy. As Honderich says, it is futile, meaning self-refuting, because the very act of denying the efficacy of consciousness, whether by speaking or writing, presupposes it. In Whitehead's sardonic words, "Scientists animated by the purpose of proving they are purposeless constitute an interesting subject for study" (*FOR,* 16).

8. *Freedom, in the sense of self-determination,* which involves a decision among *genuine* alternatives, so that it is true that the agent could have done otherwise. It might be thought that freedom in this sense is implied by the rejection of epiphenomenalism, but this is not so. Freedom in this sense is rejected by most of the authors quoted under the former point. For example, although Sperry affirms downward causation from the mind to the brain, and sometimes on this basis speaks of freedom and self-determination (*SMP,* 27, 39, 69, 112), he in reality affirms universal determinism, according to which the mind is simply one more link in the deterministic

chain of causes and effects (*SMP,* 40, 69, 89). In opposition to Popper, Sperry says that the mind is in no sense a "first cause" or "prime mover." This denial means that it does not *originate* any activity (*SMP,* 89). But it is only if the mind is self-determining in the sense of originating activity, so that it is not totally determined by the efficient causation on it, that we have freedom in the sense that we all presuppose in practice. Whitehead refers to this fact in saying that our own decision, in which we form our purpose in the moment, "is the foundation of our experience of responsibility, of freedom, of emphasis." Against those who would say that this feeling must be an illusion, he adds, "This element in experience is too large to be put aside merely as misconstruction. It governs the whole tone of human life" (*PR,* 47).

Most modern philosophers, however, especially those who reject dualism, do put it aside, more or less explicitly, as a misconstruction. All those who advocate eliminative materialism, of course, include freedom among the "folk beliefs" to be eliminated. But even most materialistic philosophers who generally eschew the eliminative approach conclude that freedom is an assumption that cannot be saved. McGinn, for example, says that "it is much more reasonable to be an eliminativist about free will than about consciousness" (*PC,* 17n).

Some philosophers, however, find that freedom is something that they can consistently neither deny nor affirm. That is, while recognizing that they cannot deny it in practice, they can find no way to affirm it in theory. For example, Nagel finds himself of two minds on this issue: "I change my mind about the problem of free will every time I think about it" (*VN,* 112). On the one hand, he can find no way to give a coherent account of freedom, in part because he (rightly) rejects the view that genuine freedom is compatible with causal determinism (*VN,* 110–17). On the other hand, he sees that he cannot help presupposing freedom in practice: "I can no more help holding myself and others responsible in ordinary life than I can help feeling that my actions originate with me" (*VN,* 123). Searle's position is similar. On the one hand, he states, "Our conception of ourselves as free agents is fundamental to our overall self-conception" (*MBS,* 85). And the kind of freedom in question is *not* compatible with physical determinism, he says, because our sense of freedom is based on our conviction in all sorts of experiences that we *could have done otherwise* (*MBS,* 87, 92, 95). Because of this, we have an "unshakable conviction of our own free will" (*MBS,* 95), so that it is "impossible for us to abandon the belief in the freedom of the will" (*MBS,* 94). On the other hand, Searle argues, "Science allows no place for the freedom of the will" (*MBS,* 92; see also 86, 88, 93). In response to this "philosophical conundrum" (*MBS,* 88), Searle says, "Now, ideally, I would like to be able to keep both my commonsense conceptions and my scientific beliefs. . . . But when it comes to the question of freedom and determinism, I am . . . unable to reconcile the two" (*MBS*, 86).

What makes Searle's position so important is that, as pointed out earlier, he sees the difference between the kind of "common sense" that is revisable and the kind that is not. With regard to such "commonsense beliefs" as the belief that the earth is flat or that the sun literally "sets" in the West,

> it is possible to give up a commonsense conviction because the hypothesis that replaces it both accounts for the experiences that led to that conviction in the first place as well as explaining a whole lot of other facts that the commonsense view is unable to account for. . . . But we can't similarly give up the conviction of freedom because that conviction is built into every normal, conscious intentional action. (*MBS*, 97)

Having clearly stated the distinction in kind between what I have called soft-core and hard-core commonsense beliefs, he makes the further point that the latter, unlike the former, are *inevitably presupposed in practice:* "We don't navigate the earth on the assumption of a flat earth, even though the earth looks flat, but we do act on the assumption of freedom. In fact we can't act otherwise than on the assumption of freedom, no matter how much we learn about how the world works as a determined physical system" (*MBS*, 97).

Because Searle has seen and stated the point so clearly, one might assume that he would reconsider the assumption that "science allows no place for the freedom of the will," because that belief is *not* inevitably presupposed in practice. In fact, if we are speaking about the very *practice* of science—for example, the kinds of efforts that go into trying to make a breakthrough that will win a Nobel Prize—then it is clear that scientific practice, far from presupposing determinism, actually presupposes the opposite. Scientists, for example, often work eighteen-hour days, trying to make the desired breakthrough before scientists in a rival laboratory do. Even with regard to the *entities* that scientists study, it is not the case that scientists necessarily presuppose that they are strictly determined. This is most obviously the case in (human) psychology. But there is also no necessity that ethologists assume that the behaviors of the objects of their study, such as gorillas, dolphins, or even rats, are fully determined. Twentieth-century developments in physics have even cast doubt on the earlier assumption that the ultimate units of nature behave in a fully deterministic (predictable-in-principle) way. There are good grounds, to be sure, both in (soft-core) commonsense observations and in scientific experimentation, to believe that the behaviors of things such as stars, oceans, tectonic plates, billiard balls, and computers are fully determined. And Searle may, along with many others, *think* that this evidence is sufficient to show that *all* composite beings behave in equally deterministic ways, so that the behavior of rats, gorillas, and human beings is as predictable in principle as that of billiard balls and computers (*MBS*, 87). But that extrapolation is far from self-evident. (In chapter 9, I will argue that there is a difference in principle between "aggregational societies," such as billiard balls and computers, and "compound individuals," such as rats and human beings; only the latter are said to have experience and freedom.) In any case, the belief that all composite things behave in a fully deterministic way certainly does not belong to those commonsense beliefs that are inevitably presupposed in practice by all of us. Accordingly, the received view that "science allows no place for freedom of the will" could be challenged.

Searle, however, does not do this. Saying that he sees no good reason to revise physical theory (as he has portrayed it), he affirms a view of the mind-body relation that does not allow for freedom while at the same time saying that "neither this discussion nor any other will ever convince us that our behavior is unfree," so that the problem of freedom and determinism is "likely to stay with us" (*MBS*, 98, 86). Accordingly, in spite of seeing clearly that freedom is one of those commonsense beliefs that cannot be denied in practice, Searle does not allow such beliefs to be decisive for theory. He thus ends up with an admittedly inadequate theory. This kind of inadequacy can only be avoided if we take our *hard-core* commonsense notions as the ultimate criteria for (scientific and philosophical) theory. What often occurs instead, however, is that our hard-core common sense is rejected in the name of merely soft-core commonsense beliefs. This occurs most often in relation to our present topic, freedom in the sense of self-determination in the moment. I will discuss at greater length in chapter 9 the way in which Searle allows widespread but dubitable beliefs to convince him that his unshakable presupposition of freedom must be illusory.

Clearly, freedom is the hard-core commonsense notion that is most challenging to any philosophy of mind that means to be adequate to *all* such notions. Of course, a few contemporary philosophers have defended freedom, but most of them, such as Popper, have affirmed dualism, which violates the principle of continuity and thereby has an insuperable problem of causal interaction. The question is whether a nondualistic philosophy can make sense of the kind of freedom we all presuppose in practice.

9. *Our awareness of norms.* McGinn expresses one aspect of this awareness in including, as one of three major problems for a physicalist account of consciousness, the question of "how a physical organism can be subject to the norms of rationality. How, for example, does *modus ponens* get its grip on the causal transitions between mental states?" (*PC*, 23n). In practice we all presuppose awareness of logical norms, and, more generally, we presuppose that there is such a thing as truth and that knowing or telling the truth is inherently good (which is not inconsistent with believing that its

inherent value may be overridden by other considerations, such as kindness or, less happily, self-interest). We also have presuppositions involving the other two members of the traditional axiological trinity: goodness and beauty. That is, we all presuppose in practice that some modes of behavior and intended outcomes are inherently better than others and that some states of affairs, whether internal or external, are more beautiful, pleasing, fitting, tasteful, or what have you, than others. We may differ in our judgments and even our criteria; but *that* a distinction between better and worse exists we all presuppose. We can, accordingly, expand McGinn's question to ask how to think about our minds so as to understand how they are subject to all such norms.

Having listed some of the hard-core commonsense notions that are most obviously relevant to the treatment of mind and consciousness, I will now mention some other kinds of data that are especially pertinent to the current discussion.

II. EVIDENCE FOR THE EVOLUTION OF LIFE IN GENERAL AND OF HUMAN BEINGS, ESPECIALLY THE HUMAN BRAIN, IN PARTICULAR

Of special importance is the evidence for a positive correlation of intelligence with brain size (in relation to body size) and complexity. Also of special importance, even if we do not quite know what to make of it, is the fact that the great increase in brain size in our ancestors occurred very rapidly by evolutionary standards (as discussed, for example, by Christopher Wills in *The Runaway Brain*). In this book, however, it is only the implications of the more general fact of evolution that will be considered.

III. EVIDENCE FOR THE DEPENDENCE OF (AT LEAST SOME) CONSCIOUS STATES ON BRAIN STATES

Whitehead expressed this fact by pointing out that the external world is in a sense irrelevant to our perceptions, that all the essential events occur in the body: "It is an evident fact of experience that our apprehensions of the external world depend absolutely on the occurrences within the human body. By playing appropriate tricks on the body a man can be got to perceive, or not to perceive, almost anything" (*SMW*, 91). Searle has labeled this idea, that "the relevant causal processes are entirely internal to the brain," the "principle of neurophysiological sufficiency" (MBWP, 221, 229). According to this principle, "whenever a mental phenomenon is present in the mind of an agent—for example, he is feeling a pain, thinking about philosophy or wishing he had a cold beer—causally sufficient conditions for that phenomenon are entirely in the brain" (MBWP, 229).

The difference between Whitehead and Searle is that Searle applies this point to *all* mental states whereas Whitehead is speaking only of our sensory perceptions. Recent studies, while not necessarily supporting Searle's notion that brain states are causally *sufficient* for mental states, and for *all* mental states at that (which is one expression of Searle's denial of self-determination to our conscious experience), do show that all of our capacities, such as memory and rational thought as well as consciousness itself, are heavily dependent on the state of our brains.

In trying to sort out the precise nature of this dependence, however, there is a baffling variety of evidence to account for. On the one hand, various studies, including those of brain-damaged and split-brain patients, suggest a high degree of localization of brain function. On the other hand, other studies suggest more holistic interpretations and a plasticity of the brain allowing for reallocation of functions.[2] Particularly startling, given all that has been assumed about the correlation between human intelligence and brain size, is the evidence from hydrocephalics, popularized by John Lorber, that some people with very little brain matter (having, instead of the normal 4.5-centimeter thickness of tissue between the ventricles and the cortical surface, a mantle of only a millimeter or so, with the total brain weighing perhaps 50 or 150 grams rather than the normal 1.5 kilograms) are completely normal or even above normal in intelligence and social relations.[3]

IV. THE APPARENT CAPACITY OF THE MIND FOR NONSENSORY PERCEPTION

1. In *mathematical* and *logical* experience, the mind seems to be in touch with entities that are not only nonphysical but even nonactual, which the brain's sensory organs are not suited to perceive. Of course, under the pressure of a materialistic worldview—for example, McGinn says that to affirm a causal relation between abstract entities and human minds would be to affirm a nonnatural, even "funny," kind of causation (*PC*, 53)—mathematics and logic can be interpreted as invention rather than discovery. But this interpretation is problematic and certainly does not seem the natural interpretation to many mathematicians and logicians.

2. *Moral* and *aesthetic* experience is also suggestive of apprehension of nonactual entities, whether they be called values, norms,* principles, forms,

---

*Kim makes our awareness of norms (logical as well as moral and aesthetic) central to his rejection of eliminative materialism's program to replace vernacular ("folk") psychology with a purely mechanistic cognitive science: "As long as we think of ourselves as reflective agents

or something else (Nagel discusses the apparent objectivity of values at *VN*, 143–45).

3. The experience of *choosing among possibilities* seems to involve the apprehension of nonactual entities (the counter-factual possibilities).

4. *Memory* can arguably best be understood as direct apprehension by the present experience of the mind's prior experiences. Within a materialistic framework, of course, memory has been understood as based entirely in the brain. But if this were the total truth, it would be hard to understand how we would have the very notion of "pastness": Why would a vivid memory of a scene be qualitatively different from a present sensory perception of that scene, differing precisely in the fact that in the former case we say that we are "remembering" something that happened in the "the past"? Particularly with events that happened a second or two ago, it seems prima facie more likely that the present moment of experience directly perceives a previous moment of experience than that it somehow activates a "memory trace laid down in the brain." Of course, even dualists have usually not thought of memory as a form of (nonsensory) perception, because they have generally thought of the mind as a numerically self-identical "substance" enduring through time. Making a distinction between the mind and the brain, however, does not entail thinking of the mind as a substance in this sense.

5. *Religious experience* is, at least in some cases, prima facie suggestive of perceptual contact with a reality beyond oneself. Much energy in modern times, of course, has gone into giving alternative explanations of such experiences. But such explanations have generally been a priori, based on a materialistic worldview and a sensationist epistemology,[4] no more convincing to those with vivid religious experiences than reductionistic interpretations of mathematical or moral experience are to those with vivid experiences of those types. Religious experience at the least provides one more desideratum against the assumption that we have no contact with realities distinct from our minds except through our physical senses.

6. There is considerable evidence, some of it of quite high quality and some of it vouchsafed by people of otherwise undoubted intelligence and honesty, for *telepathy and clairvoyance*.[5] Current writers about the mind-body relation typically reject the possibility of extrasensory perception in this sense. But their rejections are usually a priori; few of them show signs of serious grappling with the evidence. Some philosophers and scientists who *have* seriously studied the evidence, such as Sir William Barrett, Henri Bergson, David Bohm, C. D. Broad, Alexis Carrel, Sir William Crookes,

---

capable of deliberation and evaluation—that is, as long as we regard ourselves as agents capable of acting in accordance with a norm—we shall not be able to dispense with the intentional framework of beliefs, wants, and volitions" (*SM*, 215).

Hans Driesch, C. J. Ducasse, Camille Flammarion, Sigmund Freud, William James, Pierre Janet, Gabriel Marcel, Gardner Murphy, H. H. Price, Lord Rayleigh, Charles Richet, and Henry Sidgwick,[6] became convinced (some of them, such as Freud, much against their wills) that these experiences sometimes really do involve nonsensory perception. Of all of the kinds of prima facie nonsensory perception listed above, this is the one form that is subject to empirical testing. It has, according to most of the small minority of intellectuals who have seriously examined the evidence, passed that test. To the extent that this evidence is accepted, it provides a scientific basis, by generalization, for also accepting the other forms of prima facie nonsensory perception for what they seem to be.

In any case, unless a treatment of the mind-body relation has dealt with all of these prima facie counterinstances, it is premature to say that we *know* that all mental states are dependent for *all of their content* on brain states. The task *may* be to develop a theory that accounts both for a high degree of dependence in some respects and for partial independence in other respects. Given Nagel's point about the relative immaturity of both our philosophy and our science, it should not be unthinkable that fully adequate theories may need to be far more complex and nuanced than those of current orthodoxy.

V. ALTERED STATES OF CONSCIOUSNESS

Any adequate theory must also not contradict what is known about various altered states of consciousness, such as hypnotic states, multiple personality syndrome, religious ecstasy, and deep meditational trances.[7]

VI. THE APPARENT CAPACITY OF HUMAN EXPERIENCE, UNCONSCIOUSLY AND SOMETIMES CONSCIOUSLY, TO EXERT EXTRAORDINARY CAUSAL EFFICACY

"Extraordinary" here means any influence that apparently conflicts with the received view that the mind can directly influence only its motor-muscular system.

1. The "placebo effect" and the power of our mental attitude to contribute to physical illnesses such as ulcers and cancer are now rather widely accepted, as is the power of a deeply hypnotized mind to produce dramatic bodily changes, such as raising welts on the skin where the person has been told that he or she has been burned.[8] The power of "faith" to bring about dramatic cures is somewhat less widely accepted but well documented.[9] The same is true for stigmata.[10] These effects seem for the most part to be produced unconsciously. But studies involving meditation and biofeedback have shown some ability to produce extraordinary effects through con-

scious intent.[11] Also, although the relation between cause and effect may be debatable, it is interesting to note that in some cases of multiple personality disorder, the different personalities will have differing biochemistries (e.g., the body under one personality may have diabetes but not under the other[s]).[12]

2. Whereas those effects all occur within the body, there is also ample evidence of the power (usually called psychokinesis or telekinesis) of some people, at times, to produce extraordinary effects beyond the body.[13] The most dramatic effects tend to be produced unconsciously (as in "poltergeist" cases),[14] but some significant statistical effects and even some examples of conspicuous psychokinesis have evidently been brought about by conscious intent.

I have, probably to the annoyance of some readers, listed several kinds of data that are especially difficult for a materialistic view of the mind to accommodate. I have done this deliberately, because most recent discussions, among both scientists and philosophers, have weighted the evidence one-sidedly in favor of evidence meant to be embarrassing to views that distinguish mind from brain, especially those that attribute some autonomous powers to the mind. What we need to do, assuming that we are motivated by the concern for truth, not simply by party spirit, is to weigh even-handedly all the relevant evidence. As Whitehead has said, "It is easy enough to find a theory, logically harmonious and with important applications in the region of fact, provided that you are content to disregard half your evidence" (*SMW*, 187). In the current discussion, the tendency has been to stress the evidence that supports a materialistic view and then to look only at that part of the contrary evidence, such as consciousness itself, that is too obvious to everyone to be completely ignored. My discussion has sought to redress the imbalance.

It is very difficult, of course, for philosophers and scientists who have been socialized into one worldview to take seriously data that are, from that perspective, not respectable. Some of the reasons for this were discussed in the section on paradigmatic and wishful-and-fearful thinking. Although it is difficult to transcend these factors so as to give the data a chance to be seen, we can, through becoming aware of the blinding effects of these factors, achieve a degree of transcendence over them.

In any case, we need a theory that takes account of all the relevant facts—those that have been regarded as supportive of materialism, those that have been regarded as supportive of dualism, and those that may count against both materialism and dualism.

SIX

Problems of Dualism and Materialism and Their Common Root

As I discussed in the introduction, there is widespread agreement that both dualism and materialism are inadequate. Of course, materialists have always found insuperable problems in dualism, and dualists have always found equally insuperable problems in materialism. But now members of each camp are admitting deep problems in their own positions, holding these positions not as adequate solutions but only as the least inadequate of the options. This attitude raises the question as to whether another option, perhaps more adequate than either, has been overlooked. I discuss that question in the next chapter. Here, I prepare the way for discussing that option—an option against which the modern mind has been so biased that much preparation is necessary—by pointing out that the problems of dualism and materialism are both rooted in the same source: the Cartesian intuition about matter.

The phrase "Cartesian intuition" has generally been used with regard to Descartes's view of *the mind,* as if it were the basic source of the mind-body problem. His view of the mind is indeed problematic (as I will discuss in chapter 8), but even more problematic is his view of matter. By this I mean his view, not unique to Descartes but associated primarily with him, that matter is completely different in kind from mind. Matter is spatially extended, mind is not. Mind has temporal duration, matter does not (in the sense that it can exist at an "instant," not requiring any temporal duration to be what it is).* Mind has an "inside," consisting of thoughts, desires, feelings, and volitions, and thereby has intrinsic value; it is *pour soi,* something for itself. Matter is all "outside" and is therefore devoid of any

---

*See footnote, p. 49, below.

value for itself; it is only *en soi.* (Descartes expressed this idea by saying that [spatial] extension is the only essential attribute of matter; but other thinkers, while rejecting this reduction of matter to extension, have agreed that matter has only an outside, no inner reality, such as feelings.) Matter exerts causal efficacy only by efficient causation (for Descartes, only by impact; Newtonians would disagree); mind exercises final causation or self-determination.

Searle is right: To be willing to entertain a radically new view of the mind-body relation, we need to see that dualism and materialism, widely supposed to be the only real options, are both false (*RM,* 2–3). To develop an alternative that really solves the problem, however, we need to see what the root cause of the problem has been. Searle moves in the right direction by questioning the "conceptual dualism" inherited from Descartes, according to which if something is "physical" it cannot also be "mental" and vice versa (*RM,* 14, 26, 54). But he does not take this insight far enough. He ends up, accordingly, with simply one more problematic version of materialism, because he continues to assume that *most* physical things are *not* also mental. It is precisely this assumption, I will argue, that creates the insuperable problems of the various dualisms and materialisms alike.

Although I have thus far, like most writers, referred simply to "dualism" and "materialism," as if these terms were unambiguous, I now need to specify more exactly how I use them. "Dualism" I always use in the sense of *ontological* (or *Cartesian*) *dualism.* This doctrine contains a double thesis: (1) that the mind is an actuality numerically distinct from the brain (the quantitative or numerical thesis) and (2) that it is ontologically different in kind from the entities of which the brain consists (the qualitative or ontological thesis).

Many writers use "dualism" as a synonym for *dualistic interactionism.* There are, however, parallelist forms of ontological dualism, which say that the interaction of mind and brain is merely apparent. Some parallelists have explained the appearance by reference to God (Malebranche, Geulincx), whereas those not able or willing to call on supernatural assistance have left the synchronization an even greater miracle. Because most thinkers today employ regulative principles ruling out miracles, whether explicitly supernatural or not, few dualists today are parallelists. Another form of dualism that does not affirm interactionism is full-fledged epiphenomenalism, according to which the mind is a semi-actuality numerically distinct from the brain. It receives causal influence from the brain, and may even be capable of determining some of its own states, but it cannot exert any downward causation back on the brain (which is why it can be considered only a *semi*-actuality). However, although Keith Campbell, quoted in the introduction, is one, there are few confessing epiphenomenalists in this sense today. So for most practical purposes, "dualism" as I intend it *can* be equated with *dualistic interactionism,* and I always use it with this meaning unless indicating otherwise.

A widespread practice that should be avoided, however, is the use of "dualism" to refer to *all* positions that affirm interactionism or, which amounts to the same thing, the use of "interactionism" as a synonym for *dualistic interactionism.* The problem with these practices is that they imply that there could not be a nondualistic interactionism, thereby serving to restrict our thinking about alternatives. To call a position "dualistic" simply because it posits a distinction between brain and mind (the numerical thesis) creates the impression that any such position would necessarily have all the problems of Cartesian (ontological) dualism, and that might not be true.

Finally, dualism in the ontological sense is often called "substance dualism" (to distinguish it from so-called property dualism, which is generally best classified as a form of materialism). I do not use this term, however, partly because the term "substance" suggests its Cartesian meaning of "requiring nothing but itself in order to exist," whereas many ontological dualists today see the mind as dependent on the body for its existence. Also, the term "substance" suggests an entity of long duration, whereas a contemporary ontological dualist might well speak of a dualism of types of "events" or "processes."

By "materialism" I mean *materialistic monism,* which contains the double thesis (1) that there is only one *kind* of actual entities, namely, material or physical ones (the qualitative or ontological thesis), and (2) that what we call the "mind" is somehow numerically identical with the brain (the quantitative or numerical thesis), so that there is no interaction between mind and brain. (The other possible quantitative meaning of "monism," that there is in reality only one actuality, as Spinoza suggested, is not in view. In this respect, contemporary materialism is a form of *pluralistic* monism, being monistic qualitatively but pluralistic quantitatively.) Because this is how virtually everyone today uses the term, the simple use of "materialism" (unlike the simple use of "dualism") occasions no problems. The widespread practice of sometimes using "monism" as a synonym for materialistic monism, however, *is* problematic, because it suggests that there are no nonmaterialistic forms of (pluralistic) monism, and this is false. In any case, by "materialism" I mean the twofold thesis that (1) all actual things are material and (2) there is no mind or soul in the sense of an actuality numerically distinct from brain. In fact, it is a threefold thesis, because the statement that "all actual things are material" must be specified to mean that at least *most actual things,* certainly the *most fundamental* ones, are devoid of any experience. For example, Strawson says that materialists "believe that there was once no experiential reality on earth but plenty of nonexperiential reality, and that experiential reality came to exist as life evolved" (*MR,* 66).

Because of this usage, I classify as materialists some who are sometimes regarded as questioning full-fledged materialism, such as Strawson, Searle, and Nagel (although if Nagel were to turn his flirtation with panpsychism into full-fledged embrace, he might be a proponent of one of the non-materialistic monisms to which I referred above).

With these clarifications, I will now summarize the major problems of dualism and materialism, showing how all of these problems are rooted in the Cartesian intuition about matter. I will divide this discussion into those problems that are unique to dualism, those that are unique to materialism, and those that are common to both dualism and materialism.

I. PROBLEMS UNIQUE TO DUALISM

1. The chief problem of dualism has always been to understand *how two totally different types of things could causally influence each other.* How could that which is spatially extended and embodies physical energy but is devoid of any duration,* therefore of any "inside," therefore of any feelings and desires, and therefore of any intrinsic value, be capable of exerting causal influence on a nonphysical mind? As John Passmore says, according to dualism a "body can only push" (*PRE,* 55). How could a body exert efficient causation on that which takes up no space (at least not in an impenetrable way) and embodies no physical energy (which is one side of the problem suggested by speaking of the mind as the "ghost in the machine")? What would such a body have to offer something that lives in terms of values? Likewise, as Passmore says, according to dualism "the only force the mind has at its disposal is spiritual force, the power of rational persuasion" (*PRE,* 55). How could it exert causal efficacy on something that is constituted so as to be affected by other pushy things (which is the other half of the ghost-in-the-machine problem)? Things with final causation inwardly and the

---

*It may seem that matter as conceived in modern thought is *not* devoid of duration, because it endures through time. What is meant, however (as the ensuing discussion will gradually make clear), is that matter as usually conceived is thought not to require any lapse of time in order to exist, which means that it can exist "at an instant" (with "instant" understood to be a durationless slice in time). In matter thus conceived, in Whitehead's words, "the lapse of time is an accident, rather than of the essence, of the material. The material is fully itself in any sub-period however short. Thus the transition of time has nothing to do with the character of the material. The material is equally itself at an instant of time" (*SMW,* 50). "Matter," accordingly, "involves nothing more than spatiality" (*MT,* 132). Whitehead's contrasting view is that what we call the physical world is made up of events, that "an event in realizing itself displays a pattern," and that "the pattern requires a duration involving a definite lapse of time, and not merely an instantaneous moment" (*SMW,* 124). Put otherwise, each primordial element is "an organized system of vibratory streaming of energy," and such a system is, like a note of music, "nothing at an instant, but . . . requires its whole period in which to manifest itself" (*SMW,* 35).

power of persuasion outwardly, on the one hand, and things with no final causation inwardly and the capacity outwardly to cause and be caused only by pushing power, on the other, are ill-suited for the kind of interaction at which our minds and bodies seem quite good. We can, accordingly, sympathize with Descartes when he finally said, in response to Princess Elisabeth's persistent questioning as to *how* mind and body could interact, that the human mind is not capable of conceiving this very distinctly.[1] We can also understand why other thinkers, given their unquestioning belief in supernaturalistic theism, would assign the interaction, whether real (Reid) or apparent (Malebranche, Geulincx), to God.[2] We can understand, further, why a contemporary dualist reluctant to call on a deus ex machina, such as Popper, would return (as cited in the introduction) to Descartes's confession of ignorance. Popper does try to mitigate the problem by saying that quantum physics has superseded Descartes's idea of causation, according to which bodies push each other around (*SAB*, 483, 499, 510). But then, in explaining what he means by affirming the "ghost in the machine," he says, "I think that the self in a sense plays on the brain, as a pianist plays a piano" (*SAB*, 494f.). How a physical-physical (finger–piano key) relation can be used as an analogy for the psychical-physical (mind-brain) relation is not cleared up by telling us that physical-physical relations are not as pushy as Descartes had thought.

Some dualists have tried to finesse the problem of causal interaction between ontologically unlike things by appeal to Hume's contention that only experience can tell us what in fact can or cannot cause what—in other words, that we have no basis for a priori claims that physical events cannot be the cause of mental events and vice versa. However, Hume's contention presupposed his analysis of (efficient) causation, according to which it refers merely to regularity of sequence ("constant conjunction"), and this understanding of causation was ruled out in the substantive regulative principles: Efficient causation is real influence, not mere constant conjunction. Furthermore, if one returns to a realistic view of causation as real influence, one cannot—philosophers such as C. J. Ducasse and H. D. Lewis to the contrary—validly appeal to Hume's rejection of all a priori ideas about causation.* So the problem of the interaction of ontologically unlike things remains.

2. Dualism also *violates the principle of continuity.* The idea that somewhere

---

*C. J. Ducasse, with an appeal to Hume, says, "The Causality relation is wholly neutral as to whether the cause-event and the effect-event are both physical, or both psychical, or either of them physical and the other psychical" (MMB, 85). And yet Ducasse rejects as "patently invalid" Hume's view of causality as merely empirical regularity of sequence. The term causation *means,* Ducasse insists, that the event called the cause *etiologically necessitates* the effect (MMB, 83). A similar position has been taken by H. D. Lewis (*EM*, 26–29, 123, 173). Neither seems to see that Hume's first point presupposes the second.

late in the evolution of the universe an entirely new type of actuality has sprung into existence would seem either to require a supernatural cause or to constitute an even more incredible miracle. In truth, this problem could be counted as one of the problems shared with materialism, because materialists also affirm an essential discontinuity; and, indeed, I will raise this point below. But it is proper to include the problem here because dualism, in affirming the emergence of a new type of *actuality,* generally with a *new type of causal power* (that of final causation or self-determination), violates the principle of continuity in a particularly egregious way.

3. A third charge against dualistic interactionism is that it apparently *violates the principle of the conservation of energy.* Eccles has regarded this charge as *the* problem to which he as a dualist needed to provide an answer (*HS,* 23, 72, 140, 168). This problem, however, has been greatly exaggerated. For one thing, we do not know the absolute truth of this principle. Do we know, for example, that the energy of the universe has remained constant from the big bang, assuming that there was one, to the present? Do we know that the principle, insofar as it holds absolutely in some domains or contexts, does so in all? We certainly have less reason to be confident of the absolute, universal truth of this principle than we do of the mutual influence of mind and body. So, if forced to choose between them, one should give up the absolute truth of the principle of conservation. But perhaps the dualist need not choose. W. D. Hart has recently argued, in defending dualism, that energy may be conserved in the interactions between mind and body. That is, the principle of the conservation of energy depends on understanding energy as a quantity that is conserved while being converted into various forms, such as mechanical, electromagnetic, thermodynamic, and chemical (*EOS,* 62–64). Perhaps, Hart suggests, the idea of "psychic energy" should be taken literally, so that it would be one more form that would be interconvertible with the other forms (*EOS,* 127, 149, 152, 178, 186n). It may be, accordingly, that Eccles (tragically) devoted much of his life to the solution of a pseudoproblem.

In any case, although Hart properly describes his position as Cartesian dualism, insofar as he speaks of "two basic or fundamental sorts of things" (*EOS,* 1, 8), his resolution, in ascribing energy to both mind and matter, actually moves away from Cartesian (ontological) dualism toward a form of nondualistic interactionism. However, he does not go all the way, so his position still suffers, like that of Eccles and other dualists, from the problems of discontinuity and causal interaction between ontologically unlike things.

Whereas materialists typically use these problems unique to dualism (plus some others, to be mentioned below, that are in fact shared by materialism) to rule out dualism, materialism has even more problems unique to *it.*

II. PROBLEMS UNIQUE TO MATERIALISM

1. One of materialism's problems is that of accounting for our *unity of experience* (as discussed in chapter 5). The idea that there is no mind over and above the brain, which is composed of 100 billion or more neurons, each of which is in turn composed of myriad particles (in which all agency is said finally to be lodged), creates a great puzzle as to why we should enjoy the kind of unified conscious experience we normally do. Dennett tries to mitigate this problem by saying that the unity is a mere appearance (*CE*, 23, 458). But if in reality there are billions of "miniagents and microagents (with no single Boss)" and "that's all that's going on" (*CE*, 458, 459), the very *appearance* of unity is utterly mysterious. Searle is more forthright: After illustrating the unity of consciousness—"I have my experiences of the rose, the couch, and the toothache all as experiences that are part of one and the same conscious event"—he adds, "We have little understanding of how the brain achieves this unity" (*RM*, 130). Dualism is more intuitively adequate here, because it can attribute our *experienced* unity to the *actual* unity of the mind. Eccles, for example, says that "a key component of the [dualist] hypothesis is that the unity of conscious experience is provided by the self-conscious mind, not by the neural machinery" (*HS*, 22). Indeed, dualism could identify the mind with the unification of various influences from the brain—if only it could explain how the mind, being ontologically different from the brain cells, could receive influences from them.

2. The mirror image of this problem is that of accounting for the *unity of our bodily behavior.* How can I pat my head with my hand while beating time to music with my foot while smiling at my wife while thinking about the mind-body problem while . . . ? If there is in no sense a "single Boss," so that all of our behavior, inner and outer, is produced by an aggregate, how can there be such remarkable coordination? Dualism, with its distinction between the (more or less) unified mind and the aggregational brain, again seems better able to handle the phenomena—if only it were not unable to explain how the mind can affect the body at all.

3. Closely related is the problem of *freedom.* If the "mind" is just the brain, or some aspect or function thereof, then it would seem impossible to ascribe self-determining freedom to us. Even if quantum indeterminacy is taken to qualify the older notion of absolute causal determinism, how the indeterminacy of trillions of particles could account for our sense of freedom would be far from clear. In any case, the indeterminacy of the individual particles or events is generally canceled out in aggregates by the "law of large numbers." And, indeed, at least virtually all materialists do deny freedom (as illustrated in chapter 5). In *Elbow Room: The Varieties of Free Will Worth Wanting,* Dennett tries to convince us that freedom in this sense is

not "worth wanting" anyway, ascribing to us only kinds of freedom that are compatible with causal determinism. McGinn, while rejecting Dennett's eliminativism with respect to consciousness, joins him with respect to free will (*PC*, 17n).

Even Searle, after berating most materialists for denying obvious facts of experience, articulates a theoretical position that denies freedom, although he agrees (as seen in chapter 5) that it is "obvious" in the sense of being one of our hard-core commonsense notions. After noting that Howard Gardner's comprehensive summary of cognitive science in *The Mind's New Science* does not contain a chapter or even an index entry on consciousness, Searle comments sarcastically, "Clearly the mind's new science can do without consciousness" (*RM*, 249). But Searle's book *The Rediscovery of the Mind* has nary a chapter or even an index entry on freedom. Clearly, one could retort, the rediscovered mind can do without freedom!

There is no doubt that Searle still denies freedom. (I speak here of his theoretical, philosophical position; as I reported in chapter 5, Searle pointed out in his earlier book [*MBS*] that *in practice* he cannot give up his conviction of freedom.) Although he lists a dozen structural features of consciousness (*RM*, 127–41), he does not include freedom. When Searle does finally mention "free will" in a list of features of consciousness, he puts after it the qualification "(if there is such a thing)" (*RM*, 227). This implicit denial to conscious experience of any capacity for self-determining freedom is made explicit in a passage in which Searle explains in what sense consciousness is and is not an emergent feature:

> A feature F is emergent2 if F is emergent1 and F has causal powers that cannot be explained by the causal interactions of a,b,c. . . . If consciousness were emergent2, then consciousness could cause things that could not be explained by the causal behavior of the neurons. The naive idea here is that consciousness gets squirted out by the behavior of the neurons in the brain, but once it has been squirted out, it then has a life of its own. (*RM*, 112)

Searle then adds, "On my view, consciousness is emergent1 but not emergent2" (*RM*, 112). In other words, consciousness is totally produced by the brain, and, once produced, it has no partially autonomous power by which it could determine some of its own states, such as its desires, attitudes, and volitions, which then might influence the brain with something that had not been simply produced by it. His position is then the same as Sperry's: Nothing goes down that had not first been sent up. Searle, in fact, had explicitly said this in his earlier book: "Top-down causation only works because the top level is already caused by and realized in the bottom levels" (*MBS*, 94).

In short, the datum of freedom, like the data of the unity of experience and the unity of our bodily behavior, favors dualism over materialism—or at least would if the problems of discontinuity and dualistic interaction could be ignored.

4. Whereas the three preceding problems should be felt as real problems by materialists, they have received relatively little treatment. The problem that has received by far the most attention is, not surprisingly, the most obvious one, which is *what it can mean* to say that we, with our conscious experience, are wholly material (or physical) beings. Conscious experience, with all its features, evidently has to be portrayed as somehow reducible to, or somehow resolvable into, purely material stuff, entities, processes, structures, functions, or something that can in principle be adequately described from a wholly externalist, third-person perspective. The basic problem of all of these programs is the simple point raised by Nagel: If the world contains experiences, points of view, beings that it is like something to be— and we know that it does—then every purely externalist description will necessarily leave something out. Most of those materialists who have recognized this point have abandoned the various forms of identity theory and moved to eliminative materialism. They simply eliminate consciousness, experience, points of view, from the list of realities to which a theory must be adequate. As Paul Churchland has said, "If we do give up hope of reduction, then elimination emerges as the only coherent alternative."[3] (If you can't join 'em, eliminate one of 'em.) This is the process that Searle has described as a long pattern of neurotic-like behavior and Seager as "an orderly retreat becoming a rout" (*MC*, 32).

Whereas Seager, however, agrees with Nagel, Robinson, McGinn, and Strawson that no solution is on the horizon, Searle believes that he has produced one. Although he criticizes materialism, his position is still within the materialistic framework, as I have defined it. That is, Searle says that the mind is not an actuality numerically distinct from the brain, that reality is "entirely physical" (*RM*, 54), and that the fundamental units of the world are "material" or "physical" *in the sense* of being devoid of any experience, any "point of view." (Although Searle says "we do not know at present how far down the evolutionary scale consciousness [by which he seems to mean experience of any sort] extends," he is "not inclined to ascribe any consciousness" to amoebas [*RM*, 89, 74]; he asks, "How do unconscious [by which he seems to mean totally nonexperiencing] bits of matter produce consciousness?" [*RM*, 55]; and he says, of objects about which *we* have a point of view, "the objects themselves have no point of view" [*RM*, 31].) He is critical of hitherto dominant forms of materialism insofar as they assume that if something is "physical" it cannot also be "mental," or, more precisely, that "the same phenomenon under the same aspects cannot literally satisfy both terms" (*RM*, 10, 14). He sees this notion, which he criticizes, to be closely related to the assumption that "reality is objective (meaning accessible to all competent observers)" (*RM*, 16), which he sees in turn as closely related to the assumption that "the objectivity of science requires that the phenomena studied be completely objective," which is in turn "based on a confusion between the epistemological sense of the subjective-objective distinction, and the ontological sense" (*RM*, 10, 19). I think Searle is right about all this (except the assumption that the same thing *under the same aspects* can be both physical and mental). But the way that he develops his alternative position is (partly because of that faulty assumption) as problematic as the theories he has rejected.

According to Searle's revisionist materialism, "materialists [can] cheerfully embrace consciousness as just another material property among others" (*RM*, 55). According to Searle's "biological naturalism," more precisely, "the mental state of consciousness is just an ordinary biological (that is, physical) feature of the brain" (*RM*, 1, 13). What can Searle mean in referring to consciousness as "ordinary," as "just another material property among others"? He emphatically does not mean that it, like all others, can be described "objectively" in the sense of "from a third-person point of view." His realization that this is impossible is the basis for his protest against eliminative materialism and most forms of reductionism. He insists that "the actual ontology of mental states is a first-person ontology," that "the real world contains . . . elements that are irreducibly subjective" (*RM*, 16, 19). So what *does* it mean to say that these irreducibly subjective states are entirely physical?

One of the root problems in Searle's book is that although he tells us what he does *not* mean by "physical," he never tells us what he does mean. One common meaning is "devoid of experience"; but Searle is denying that this is a necessary feature of the physical, because he thinks that some physical things (brains) do have experience. Nagel, who does accept this definition of the physical, puzzles over the meaning of Searle's position: "But however great the variety of physical phenomena may be, ontological objectivity is one of their central defining characteristics; and as we have seen Searle insists that consciousness is ontologically subjective" (*NYR*, 40). Another candidate for the meaning of "physical" is "publicly observable"; but Searle also rejects this definition, because our own subjective experience is not publicly observable. If it means neither of these, however, what does it mean? If he were to say, for example, that to be physical is simply to embody energy, he could affirm a truly nonmaterialistic pluralistic monism, in which all units have mental as well as physical features, which would open the way to a resolution of the mind-body problem quite different from the position he has hitherto taken.

In any case, we still need to explore the intelligibility of Searle's claim that conscious states are just another, ordinary physical property, analogous to others. To make this case, Searle offers several analogies. Two of his favorites are liquidity and solidity:

> Consciousness is a higher-level or emergent property of the brain in the utterly harmless sense of 'higher-level' or 'emergent' in which solidity is a higher-level emergent property of H_2O molecules when they are in a lattice structure (ice), and liquidity is similarly a higher-level emergent property of H_2O molecules when they are, roughly speaking, rolling around on each other (water). Consciousness is a mental, and therefore physical, property of the brain in the sense in which liquidity is a property of systems of molecules. (*RM*, 14)

Lying behind Searle's analogy is the notion that at least many features of big systems can be causally explained by the behavior of the little systems of which they are composed: The macrophenomena are explicable in terms of microphenomena (*RM*, 87). He is claiming, then, that consciousness is a surface phenomenon caused by microphenomena in the brain, just as the solidity of ice and the liquidity of water are surface phenomena caused by the microphenomena beneath the surface. He uses the language of "supervenience"* to express this relation: Consciousness is supervenient on neurophysiological states just as liquidity is supervenient on certain molecular states.

Is there a genuine analogy here? Seager, in response to an earlier version of Searle's position, pointed out one reason why this type of analogy breaks down. Seager distinguishes between *constitutive* supervenience, which holds in ordinary physical explanations such as those of solidity and liquidity, and merely *correlative* supervenience, which consciousness seems to exemplify in relation to the brain. In the former, the lower states are somehow constitutive of the supervenient states in a way that allows us to understand why that supervenient state should emerge:

> Roughly speaking, in cases of constitutive supervenience the dual evidence provided by a knowledge of a system's basic components and their link to its behavior is decisive for ascription of the supervenient property. . . . [I]t makes credible the idea that the joint activity of the various components,

---

*For a thorough discussion of the meaning(s) of "supervenience," see Kim's *Supervenience and Mind*. According to the evidently dominant usage, the core meaning is that the observable, macroproperties of an entity are fully determined by its microproperties—although perhaps not reducible to them (*SM*, 275f., 339f.). As Searle's use of "supervenience" in place of "emergence" suggests, the two terms can be considered virtually synonymous. In fact, as Kim points out, one of the early evolutionary emergentists, Lloyd Morgan, used "supervenience" as a stylistic variant of "emergence," and some nonreductive physicalists today speak of their higher-level, supervenient properties as "emergent" (*SM*, 134, 348). I will continue to use primarily the language of "emergence" until discussing Kim's position in chapter 10.

through their own causality, could reasonably be claimed to produce the system's overall behavior. (*MC*, 179)

However, Seager points out, the relation of consciousness to brain states is not like that: Nothing about the behavior and property of the neurons as studied from without would lead us to expect some brain states to produce consciousness. The supervenience remains brute, merely correlative. Seager approvingly cites Simon Blackburn's statement that supervenience of the psychological on the physical is part of the problem, not the solution (*MC*, 180).*

In response, Searle agrees that the kind of supervenience that is relevant to the mind-body problem is *causal* supervenience, not *constitutive* supervenience (*RM*, 125). But then, it would seem, all of the analogies he employs—photosynthesis, digestion, mitosis, electromagnetism, and transparency (*RM*, 90, 104) as well as solidity and liquidity—are of no intuitive help in understanding how consciousness is related to the brain, because they are all cases of constitutive supervenience. The only thing that causal and constitutive supervenience have in common is that in both the higher-level property is said to be "caused" by the lower,** and in the case of consciousness we have been given no clue as to how this "property" *could* have emerged out of its causes. Strawson agrees. With regard to the idea that experiential properties are "reducible to nonexperiential physical properties in a way that is ultimately similar to the way in which the property of liquidity is held to be reducible to van de Waals molecular-interaction properties," he says: "This reduction is very hard—impossible—to imagine" (*MR*, 68). Searle's analogies may at first glance give the appearance of providing a glimmer of intuitive understanding, but on closer examination they are more confusing than helpful. As Nagel has said, "much obscurity has been shed on the [mind-body] problem by faulty analogies" (*MQ*, 202).

---

*Kim agrees, saying that supervenience "is a 'phenomenological' claim, not a theoretical explanation. Mind-body supervenience, therefore, does not state a solution to the mind-body problem; rather it states the problem itself." Kim adds that although the research strategy of explaining psychological functions in terms of the interactions of subsystems conforms to the generally accepted scientific approach, "whether such microstructural explanations really 'explain' mentality in the sense of making mentality, in particular consciousness, intelligible—something that the emergentists despaired of ever attaining—may be another question" (*SM*, 168).

**As Kim portrays it, supervenience is a relation of dependency but not of *causal* dependency. The macroproperties are said to be determined by the microproperties without being *caused* by them. The difference is that the causal relation is temporal—the cause is antecedent to the effect—whereas in supervenience, the determining and the determined are simultaneous (*SM*, 354, 359). As Kim points out, however, this distinction has little import (*SM*, 359), so the language of "causal supervenience" seems to do no violence to anything essential to the idea of supervenience.

Searle's position is not really as different from previous forms of materialism as he suggests. In spite of his emphatic rejection of "property dualism," his position, as Nagel points out (*NYR*, 40), seems to be another variant of it. I will return to Searle's position when I consider the problem of the emergence of experience out of nonexperiencing entities, which materialists and dualists alike share; at that time I will consider Searle's claim that his position is really that of "property polyism" (MBWP, 228).

5. A fifth problem for materialism is that it implies an *epistemology that does not allow us to know various hard-core commonsense notions* (which we all *do* know). I refer here to an epistemology based on the sensationist view of perception (along with assumptions, of course, that prevent us from knowing these things a priori, or through divine revelation, or otherwise transcendentally). This problem *could* be included under the problems that materialism and dualism share, because many dualists in modern times (beginning at least with Locke) have accepted a sensationist theory of perception (although Locke himself could still appeal to supernatural revelation to explain how he knew things he should otherwise not have known). However, dualists *need* not accept a sensationist view of perception, because a mind distinct from the brain might be able to perceive some things directly, without the aid of the brain and its sensory organs. This problem, therefore, is best included under problems unique to materialism.*

Although each of the five examples I will give would be worthy of an entire chapter, if not a book, I can mention them only briefly. Two of them are most closely associated with Hume: knowledge of *efficient causation* and knowledge of *a world external to the mind*. Although there have been enormous efforts to get around Hume's demonstrations, they remain valid: If sensory perception, understood as perception providing only sensory data, were the only mode of perception we have, we should not *know* what efficient causation (in a non-Humean sense) is or that there is a real world to which the sensory data may refer. Likewise, as Santayana showed in an extension of Hume's argument, if this were our only mode of perception, we should not know (as distinct from taking on "animal faith") the *reality of the past*. With no knowledge of the past, furthermore, we would have no knowledge of *time*. Finally, our inexorable presuppositions about *objective norms*, such as truth, goodness, and beauty, are notoriously difficult to ex-

---

*Many modern philosophers simply assume the equation of perception with sensory perception. For example, in the editor's introduction to an anthology entitled *Perceptual Knowledge* (Oxford: Oxford University Press, 1988), Jonathan Dancy simply asserts on the first page that perceptual knowledge is the sort of knowledge we get by "using our senses." Some philosophers, however, state the sensationist position explicitly. Willard Quine, for example, says, "The stimulation of his sensory receptors is all the evidence anybody has to go on, ultimately, in arriving at his picture of the world" (*Ontological Relativity and Other Essays* [New York: Columbia University Press, 1969], 75–76).

plain from within a materialistic, sensationist perspective. (The implicit contradiction that results is illustrated by those philosophers and scientists who support their preference for a materialistic worldview in terms of aesthetic criteria, such as "simplicity" and "beauty," ignoring the fact that such a worldview denies the possible knowledge and even existence of such norms.) A position that could fully allow the genuineness of our knowledge of all these things and that could explain it naturally, without forcing, would be in this respect more adequate than any of the materialistic positions.

6. A related problem for materialists, given the virtual necessity of their restricting perception to that which occurs through the physical sensory organs, is the impressive evidence for *extrasensory perception,* in the sense of telepathy and clairvoyance.[4] D. M. Armstrong, for example, has referred to psychical research as a "small black cloud on the horizon of a Materialist Theory of Mind." Herbert Feigl and Keith Campbell have both said that if the alleged evidence for extrasensory perception were authentic, materialism could not handle it.[5] And many dualists point to the data from psychical research as decisive evidence in favor of dualism.[6] Of course, these alleged data are rejected out of hand by most materialists, such as those just mentioned and McGinn (*PC,* 53), Humphrey (*HM,* 11), and Churchland (*MAC,* 17). However, these rejections generally demonstrate little if any familiarity with the evidence and discussions of it by otherwise reputable philosophers, such as William James, C. D. Broad, C. J. Ducasse, and H. H. Price. (By contrast, Seager, who shows more familiarity with the evidence, is more open to it [*MC,* 188, 241].) These rejections seem to be based more on paradigmatic and wishful-and-fearful thinking, in other words, than on considered judgments, after serious investigation, that good evidence is really lacking.*

*While doing the final revision of this manuscript, I learned that Humphrey had recently written a book, *Soul Searching: Human Nature and Supernatural Belief* (London: Chatto & Windus, 1995), in which parapsychology is extensively discussed. Humphrey does indicate that he has become at least somewhat familiar with the available evidence and knows that some of it is good. He says that "the evidence that has accumulated over the ages [for ESP] is undeniably impressive" (115), and he refers to "the hundreds of experimental studies that over the last century have made strong claims to demonstrate the reality of PK or ESP" (138). He even says that in many cases one who is trying to explain the phenomena in normal terms may be "baffled" (115). However, he studiously avoids an examination of the actual evidence, which, he says, "would be tedious" (116). He instead constructs purely a priori arguments against the reality of extrasensory perception, concluding that, because the phenomena do not meet his "advance expectations" of how ESP would work if it were genuine, he need not take any of the evidence seriously (138). He is thereby able to conclude that parapsychology provides no credible evidence against a "materialism of the strictest order" (36). A more empirical thinker, I suspect, would not escape so unscathed. In any case, Humphrey's book does not provide a counterexample to my statement that few philosophers have evidently arrived at "considered judgments, after serious investigation, that good evidence is really lacking." He in effect admitted that the evidence was too good to be challenged on its own terms.

To the extent that this evidence *is* studied and *is* found convincing, materialism has another count against it.

7. Insofar as materialism rules out the possibility that our mind—our feelings, thoughts, desires, decisions—can have any power to exert causal influence other than that of the brain, it would also not be able to accommodate *psychokinesis*, the direct production by the psyche of changes in the extrasomatic world. And yet good evidence for psychokinesis exists.[7] Insofar as psychokinesis is accepted, this will be another count against materialism's numerical identification of mind and brain. Of course, the inability of materialism here can be regarded as simply a part of its more general inadequacy to the fact, which we all presuppose in practice, that the mind has power of its own with which it acts back on the world (usually first of all its own body). But psychokinesis, when accepted, provides particularly dramatic evidence of this power, more difficult to interpret otherwise than more ordinary phenomena.

To summarize the problems unique to dualism and materialism: Those unique to dualism are all clearly due to the fact that the matter of which the body is composed is said to be different in kind from the mind. The problems unique to materialism can be seen to be due to the fact that, finding *dualistic* interactionism impossible, materialists gave up interactionism altogether, so that the mind is no longer thought to be a numerically distinct actuality (which *could* perhaps account for our unity of experience and of action and therefore our freedom, and which *might* be capable of the various forms of nonsensory perception arguably implied by various data and might even be capable of direct extrasomatic effects on the world). The problems unique to materialism are finally, therefore, traceable to the Cartesian intuition about matter, because it was the resulting problems of dualism that led to materialism's numerical equation of mind and brain. I turn now to problems, originating from the same root, that dualism and materialism have in common.

III. PROBLEMS COMMON TO DUALISM AND MATERIALISM

1. One problem shared by materialists and dualists alike—Campbell also lists this as one of the "embarrassing questions" his epiphenomenalism cannot answer (*BM,* 135)—is exactly *where to draw the line* between experiencing and nonexperiencing things. Given the continuity suggested by the evolutionary perspective and the increasing discovery of continuity where gaps once seemed to exist, any place that is chosen will seem arbitrary. Descartes's decision to draw the line between the human mind and the rest of nature, so that even his dog was said to be an insentient machine, has

seemed arbitrary to most. The most popular position has been to draw the line between those animals with and without a central nervous system, but where exactly is that? Having a central nervous system in borderline cases is a matter of degree.

This point is related to the problem of continuity raised in relation to dualism, but it is different. There the point was the *philosophical* one that any essential dualism seems to contradict the principle of continuity. Here I am raising the additional point that once this essential discontinuity has been accepted (whether by dualists or materialists), then there is the *empirical* problem of specifying a nonarbitrary place where that discontinuity allegedly occurs. Dualists and materialists typically avoid this problem: Because they "know" that the discontinuity *must* have happened somewhere in the evolutionary process, they are content to indicate only vaguely where that might have been. Searle, as I pointed out, thinks amoebas do not experience, but he says that he has no idea whether fleas, grasshoppers, crabs, and snails do (*RM*, 74, 81). Flanagan, while recognizing that scallops and paramecia receive information from and respond to their environments, seems confident that they do not feel or experience anything (*CR*, 35). McGinn supposes that consciousness must have arisen "when some of the fancier models of mollusc took up residence in the oceans, or when fish began to roam the depths. . . . [S]entience reverberated in the seas: awareness was born, quite late in the game" (*PC*, 44). But if these thinkers would try to specify exactly where this magical line is, the arbitrariness of the spot and the disagreement about it would make the problematic nature of the supposition more apparent. For example, evidence has been provided suggesting that bacteria make decisions (of a primitive sort) on the basis of memories (of a primitive sort).[8] If our (soft-core) intuition is that experience and "life" go together, do we attribute experience to prokaryotic as well as eukaryotic life? Furthermore, the virus has some but not all of the features generally regarded as characteristic of living things. If we have included bacteria, do we attribute experience to viruses too? And if we do, then what about the remarkable DNA and RNA macromolecules, which certainly manifest organismic characteristics? And so on. On what basis could one claim to know, for example, that the apparent lack of complete determinism at the level of quantum physics does not reflect an element of spontaneity and thereby experience in subatomic events? Of course, Nagel is sociologically right: "If one travels too far down the phylogenetic tree, people gradually shed their faith that there is experience there at all" (*MQ*, 168). But that there actually is such a place does *not* belong to our hard-core common sense. It belongs at most to our merely soft-core common sense, the type empirical facts and rational reflection can modify.

2. A second problem is that of the *Great Exception*. This problem is generally raised by materialists against dualists. In fact, Michael E. Levin makes

this point "the main positive evidence for materialism," even more important than the problem of dualistic interaction. Appealing to the regulative
principle of simplicity or parsimony, Levin says,

> So far as we know, everything, except possibly the psychological states of sen-
> tient beings, is physical. . . . [Against dualism] it is simply more reasonable to
> think that the properties expressed by psychological predicates will turn out
> to be physical. Given that most of the universe is explicable physicalistically,
> the view which least multiplies independent principles is that the entire uni-
> verse is explicable physicalistically. (*MMBP*, 87)

This point, however, can be turned back against materialism,* especially in
light of the agreement by Nagel, McGinn, Seager, and Searle, not to mention
countless dualists, that conscious experience is *not* "explicable physicalistically." That is, would it not be strange that if human beings and many other
animals (wherever one draws the line) are *not* fully explicable physicalistically (that is, in completely externalist categories), the rest of the universe
would be? Because we *know* that we are not, the only way to avoid the problem of the Great Exception is to rethink the rest of the universe.

   3. Yet another problem for dualists and materialists, because they both
assume that experience arose at some late date in cosmic evolution, is to
explain *how the evolutionary process could have had the time—literally—to have
gotten to the point at which time is said to have emerged.* That is, as most of those
who have thought much about it, such as the archmaterialist Adolf Grünbaum, have realized, time, in the real sense, presupposes experience: Without experience there would be no "now," and without a "now" there would
be no distinction between past and future.[9] (Incidentally, Newton's "absolute time" is usually thought to have been an exception to all relative views
of time, according to which temporality is dependent on some kind of actual events; but, as Milič Čapek has pointed out, this interpretation fails to
recognize that Newton, quite a heretic, held a temporalistic view of deity:
So-called absolute time reflected God's temporal experience.[10]) Assuming
this necessary connection between time and experience, those who believe
that experience arose historically must also hold that time arose at some
point in the evolutionary process. This is the position of J. T. Fraser, who
has probably (along with Čapek) thought and written about time more than
any other thinker in history. This position is reflected in the title of one of

---

*The fact that materialism has the problem of the Great Exception is illustrated by Herbert
Feigl, one of the first formulators of materialistic identism. After speaking of the "identity"
of matter and experience, Feigl clarified that "nothing in the least like a psyche is ascribed
to lifeless matter." This implies that the language of psychology is applicable "only to an extremely small part of the world" ("Mind-Body, *Not* a Pseudoproblem," in *Dimensions of Mind*,
ed. Sydney Hook [New York: New York University Press, 1960], 32, 33).

Fraser's books, *The Genesis and Evolution of Time*. The problem with this po-sition, of course, is that it is circular, because evolution itself presupposes the existence of time. The paradox is expressed in Fraser's assertion that, although we cannot help thinking of several billion years passing between the big bang and the rise of life (which is where Fraser thinks time in the real sense of the word arose, evidently because that is where he dates the emergence of experience), we must say that all the events "prior" to the emergence of life were in truth all "contiguous with the instant of Creation" (*GET,* 132). Of course, the immediate response of most dualists and mate-rialists will be that there must be something wrong with the assumption that time requires experience. (Indeed, the dominant position has been that time originated when there was sufficient organization of matter for entropic processes to begin; but that would only push the problem back: How would there have been time for cosmic evolution to proceed even to *that* stage?) To those who so respond, I would recommend reading Fraser and Grünbaum. If the argument is found convincing, what adjustment should be made? If you are a dualist or a materialist, are you more certain of the reality of time throughout the history of our universe or of the doc-trine that experience as such emerged out of nonexperiencing things?

4. Although all of these problems are serious, perhaps the most serious problem shared by dualism and materialism is *how the emergence of experience out of nonexperiencing entities is conceivable.* I touched on this problem above in pointing to the problem of discontinuity for dualism and the problem of the meaning of the materialist's assertion that we, with our conscious experience, are entirely physical beings. I broached, especially with regard to Searle's position, the problem of the disanalogy between the alleged emergence of experience and the forms of emergence with which it is com-monly compared. But the problem of this disanalogy runs even deeper. I will introduce this problem by citing a provocative statement by the mate-rialist J. J. C. Smart: "How could a non-physical property or entity suddenly arise in the course of animal evolution? . . . [W]hat sort of chemical process could lead to the springing into existence of something non-physical? No enzyme can catalyze the production of a spook!" (M, 168f.). Although Smart directs this comment against dualism, it can be directed back at his own materialism. One can equally well ask, How can an enzyme catalyze the production of even the *appearance* of a spook? Regardless of whether one refers to a mind as a distinct *actuality* or does not (which is the only difference between dualists and materialists once the latter agree that mind, with its point of view and other subjective features, is irreducible to purely externalist description)—that is, whether it is called a real spook or only an apparent spook—*how* a mind could emerge out of enzymes or any-thing else assumed to have only external features is equally mysterious.

Nagel states the issue clearly in "What Is It Like to Be a Bat?" "One cannot derive a *pour soi* from an *en soi*. . . . This gap is logically unbridgeable. If a bodiless god wanted to create a conscious being, he could not expect to do it by combining together in organic form a lot of particles with none but physical properties" (*MQ,* 189). A *pour soi* is something that exists *for* itself, being a subject of experience with feelings; an *en soi*, which is said to exist *in* itself but not for itself (being what Whitehead calls a "vacuous actuality"), is thought to have "none but physical [meaning purely external] properties." An *en soi* has only an "outside," having no features beyond those that are perceivable in principle by others and describable in externalistic language; it is hence nothing but an *object* (for others). A *pour soi*, by contrast, has an "inside," having features that are not externally perceivable by others and describable in externalistic terms; it is thus a *subject* (for itself). A subject or a *pour soi*, in other words, is something about which we can intelligibly ask, "What is it like to be one of those?" Strawson expresses this point by speaking of "the 'what-it's-like-ness' characteristics of experience" (*MR*, 45). Nagel is saying that it is inconceivable that a subject, something that it is like something to be, could arise out of mere objects naturally. *This* type of alleged emergence violates the principle of continuity and thereby implies a violation of naturalism.

Many philosophers, both dualists and materialists, have not yet seen the distinction between this alleged emergence and the nonproblematic types and thereby continue to think of them as analogous. Searle's analogies of experience with emergent properties such as solidity, transparency, and liquidity, considered earlier, provide an example. Searle, as I mentioned then, has described his position not as property dualism but as "property polyism," explaining that "there are lots of different kinds of higher-level properties of systems, and mental properties are among them" (MBWP, 228). This fits, of course, with Searle's attempt to portray "mental properties" as fully "ordinary," just one more example of ordinary physical properties.

We have here a prime example of a *category mistake*. (I use this term, associated with Gilbert Ryle, to articulate a point quite opposed to Ryle's own philosophical behaviorism.)* The alleged emergence of subjectivity out of pure objectivity has been said to be analogous to examples of emergence that are different in kind. All of the unproblematic forms of emergence refer to *externalistic features,* features of things *as perceived from without,* features of *objects for subjects.* But the alleged emergence of experience is not

---

*I refer here to Ryle's position in *The Concept of Mind* as it has usually been interpreted. As either a clarfication or a modification of his position in this early book, Ryle later eschewed behaviorism. For example, while still rejecting Cartesianism, he also said that "no account of Thinking of a Behaviourist coloration will do" (Gilbert Ryle, *Collected Papers,* vol. II: *Collected Essays 1929–1968* [London: Hutchison, 1971], viii).

simply one more example of such emergence. It involves instead the alleged emergence of an "inside" from things that have only outsides. It does not involve the emergence of one more objective property for subjectivity to view, but the alleged emergence of subjectivity itself. Liquidity, solidity, and transparency are properties of things *as experienced through our sensory organs,* hence properties for others. Experience is not what we are for others but what we are *for ourselves.* Experience cannot be listed as one more "property" in a property polyism. It is in a category by itself. To suggest any analogy between experience itself and properties of other things as known through sensory experience is a category mistake of the most egregious kind.

In describing this confusion, which can be called the *emergence category mistake,* I am simply trying to drive home Nagel's point about faulty analogies. Although most contemporary commentators on the mind-body problem have accepted Nagel's point about the indispensability of including points of view in our world-pictures, many have evidently not seen the full force of his point about faulty analogies. Nagel says,

> Every reductionist has his favorite analogy from modern science. It is most unlikely that any of these unrelated examples of successful reduction will shed light on the relation of mind to brain. But philosophers share the general human weakness for explanations of what is incomprehensible in terms suited for what is familiar and well understood, though entirely different. (*MQ*, 166)

In a passage only parenthetically cited earlier, Nagel says that "much obscurity has been shed on the [mind-body] problem by faulty analogies between the mental-physical relation and relations between the physical and other objective aspects of reality" (*MQ*, 202). Although Nagel does not use the term "category mistake," the thought is there.

Once alerted to the emergence category mistake, we can see it committed all over the place, by dualists and materialists alike. For example, Eccles, from a dualist standpoint, says, "Just as in biology there are new emergent properties of matter, so at the extreme level of organized complexity of the cerebral cortex, there arises still further emergence, namely the property of being associated with conscious experience" (*FR*, 173). Conscious experience is spoken of as simply one "further emergence," no different in kind from all others. Popper, coauthor with Eccles of *The Self and Its Brain,* almost shows recognition of the difference in kind, saying that the "incredible" invention of consciousness (out of wholly insentient neurons) "is much more incredible than, for example, the invention of flight" (*SAB*, 560). This recognition of incredibility does not, however, lead Popper to be incredulous.

The recognition that we have no real analogies for the alleged emergence of experience out of wholly insentient entities is what lies behind the recent turn by McGinn to pessimism about ever finding a solution to the mind-body problem. McGinn is more explicit than most writers about the principle that no solution can require supernatural causation, even implicitly: "It is a condition of adequacy upon any account of the mind-body relation that it avoid assuming theism" (*PC*, 17n). But he also sees that no naturalistic explanation of the emergence of conscious experience out of "insensate matter" is possible (*PC*, 46). He is certain that this emergence is *not* "inherently miraculous" (*PC*, 2). He is equally certain, however, that no one can *show* that it is not.* "The difficulty," says McGinn, "is one of principle: we have no understanding of how consciousness could emerge from an aggregation of non-conscious elements" (*PC*, 212). In that passage, he is discussing the possibility of strong AI;** but he makes the same point with regard to the brain, saying that we also cannot "see how an entity constructed naturally from mere matter can be conscious" (*PC*, 205). Supernaturalism, accordingly, cannot be *shown* to be unnecessary.

McGinn compares the fact of conscious experience with the fact of complex organisms. Both could at one time have reasonably been pointed to as evidence for supernaturalism. The theory of evolution, however, "undermined the theism required by the creationist thesis." But no such explanation for consciousness is available or even on the horizon: "In the case of consciousness the appearance of miracle might also tempt us in the 'creationist' direction, with God required to perform the alchemy necessary to transform matter into experience. . . . We cannot, I think, refute this argument in the way we can the original creationist argument, namely by actually producing a non-miraculous explanatory theory" (*PC*, 17n). McGinn goes on to say, "But we can refute it by arguing that such a naturalistic theory must *exist*." This, of course, is simply a confession of faith, not a real argument.

Another passage in which McGinn continues this comparison states the problem so clearly that it is worth quoting in full, partly because it embodies the recognition that it would be a category mistake to regard the emergence of sentience as analogous to the emergence of life, as if no greater violation of the principle of continuity were involved.

> A basic continuity between the inorganic and the organic can . . . be demonstrated. No miraculous jump in the fortunes of the universe need be ruefully

---

*Strawson expresses a similar view: "Insofar as we are committed to naturalistic no-miracles materialism, we seem obliged to hold that the appearance of radical disconnection between experiential properties and nonexperiential properties is a kind of illusion. . . . But it won't go away, and it constitutes a vivid proof of the limitations on our understanding of reality" (*MR*, 75).

**"Strong AI," for Strong Artificial Intelligence, is a term for the position of those who believe that the "artificial intelligence" of computers could involve consciousness.

,accepted. The Soft Rustle could therefore have occurred without the benefit of God's intervention. But in the case of consciousness we have no such understanding: we do not know how consciousness might have arisen by natural processes from antecedently existing material things. Somehow or other sentience sprang from pulpy matter, giving matter an inner aspect, but we have no idea how this leap was propelled. . . . One is tempted, however reluctantly, to turn to divine assistance: for only a kind of miracle could produce *this* from *that*. It would take a supernatural magician to extract consciousness from matter, even living matter. Consciousness appears to introduce a sharp break in the natural order—a point at which scientific naturalism runs out of steam. (*PC*, 45)

McGinn adds in a note:

I do not know if anyone has ever tried to exploit consciousness to prove the existence of God,* along the lines of the traditional Argument from Design, but in this post-Darwinian era it is an argument with more force than the usual one, through lack of an alternative theory. It is indeed difficult to see how consciousness could have arisen from insentient matter; it seems to need an injection from outside the physical realm. (*PC*, 45n)

This recognition that the alleged emergence of experience is sui generis, without analogy to anything else, is the basis for McGinn's agnostic physicalism. He compares his position to that of Locke's "idea that our God-given faculties do not equip us to fathom the deep truth about reality. Locke held . . . [that] only divine revelation could enable us to understand how 'perceptions' are produced in our minds by material objects" (*PC*, 4n).

Not all physicalists agree with McGinn's agnosticism, of course. Flanagan, in fact, offers his book as a response to McGinn's view that consciousness is "terminally mysterious" (*CR*, xi–xii). "The gap between the subjective and the objective," Flanagan argues, "is an epistemic gap, not an ontological gap" (*CR*, 221). McGinn, of course, agrees with that. But Flanagan goes on to argue, against Nagel and McGinn, that "we do understand how physicalism can be true":

It can be true if every mental event is realized in the brain. Those of us who believe that all mental events . . . are tokened in the brain do not believe that the theory that eventually explains *how* they are tokened will capture "the true character of the experiences" as experiences. The whole idea that the qualitative feel of some experience should reveal itself in a theoretical de-

*The answer to McGinn's query is Yes. His former Oxford colleague Richard Swinburne, for example, argues in chapter 9 of *The Existence of God* (Oxford: Clarendon, 1979) that God is needed to explain consciousness. Swinburne summarizes this argument in *The Evolution of the Soul* (Oxford: Clarendon, 1986): "The ability of God's action to explain the otherwise mysterious mind-body connection is just one more reason for postulating his existence. . . . God, being omnipotent, would have the power to produce a soul thus interacting" (198–99).

scription of how that experience is realized fails to acknowledge the abstract
relation between any theory and the phenomena it accounts for. (*CR*, 93)

No language, Flanagan says, can "convey phenomenal feel!" (*CR*, 99). But
surely McGinn and Nagel understand *that*. Their point is quite a different
one—that a theory couched entirely in externalistic (third-person) language is the wrong *kind* of theory for referring to conscious states. Of
course, to describe my wife, or my neighbor's cat, as "feeling pain" does not
convey the phenomenal feel of their experience. But it at least indicates
that I think there is some phenomenal feel (some "what-it's-like-ness")
there, whereas the language of chemical processes or neuron firings does
not. Flanagan has simply missed the main point. That this is so is shown by
the fact that, even after reading Nagel and McGinn, he proceeds to commit
the emergence category mistake:

> If we operate with more sensible standards of intelligibility, several credible
> stories can already be told to explain how such things as sensory qualia su-
> pervene on certain patterns of neural activity. Just as ordinary water *is* H_2O
> and is caused by H_2O, so too are experiences of colors, tastes, and smells
> identical to and caused by activity patterns in certain brain pathways. (*CR*,
> 221)

His solution, in other words, is essentially the same as Searle's. It does not
provide any basis for considering McGinn's agnosticism baseless. Strawson
sees this point clearly:

> As an acting materialist, I . . . assume that experiential phenomena are real-
> ized in the brain. . . . But this assumption doesn't solve any problems for ma-
> terialists. . . . [W]hen we consider the brain as current physics and neuro-
> physiology presents it to us, we are obliged to admit that we do not know how
> experience—experiential what-it's-like-ness—is or even could be realized in
> the brain. (*MR*, 81)

One temptation, whenever there is an alleged gulf between ontological
unlikes to be spanned, is to assume that unlike things can be connected if
we posit a sufficient number of intermediaries in between, so that the gulf
need not be spanned in one leap. The transition can be made gradually.
For example, many theological worldviews, positing an absolute difference
between the ultimate divine reality (e.g., as totally timeless) and the world
as we know it (e.g., as fully temporal), portray a hierarchy of intermediate
realities. The one at the top is virtually godlike, sharing many divine attributes (e.g., being virtually timeless) and having only a hint of worldliness
(e.g., being slightly temporal). The next one down has a little less divinity
and a little more worldliness, and so on, until the nature of the lowest intermediary is so like that of the world that interaction between them does
not seem too miraculous to swallow. That lowest intermediary can likewise

interact with its immediate superior, and so on, so that, finally, interaction between the divine and the world seems possible, in spite of their absolute heterogeneity.

Contemporary physicalists, being as human and therefore as unresistant to temptation as their forebears who operated out of a theological paradigm, sometimes employ a similar strategy. Dennett provides a good example. In his chapter "The Evolution of Consciousness," he begins by stating clearly the assumption that at one time there was no experience: "In the beginning, there were no reasons [i.e., final causes]; there were only [efficient] causes. Nothing had a purpose . . . ; there was no teleology in the world at all. There was nothing that had interests" (*CE,* 173). Dennett's task is to get from that starting point to us, with our reasons, purposes, and interests. And, like McGinn, he makes clear that the explanation must not require, even implicitly, a supernatural injection somewhere in the process. He states repeatedly, even to the point of including a cartoon, that one of the steps in the explanation cannot say, in effect, "then a miracle occurs" (*CE,* 38, 239, 255, 455). Unlike McGinn, however, he thinks that an explanation devoid of miracle can be given. Let us see.

After millennia, Dennett says, simple replicators emerged. Did they have purposes? Dennett's answer is ambiguous: "While *they* had no inkling of their interests, and perhaps properly speaking had no interests, we . . . can nonarbitrarily assign them certain interests—generated by their defining 'interest' in self-duplication" (*CE,* 173). Has he said that things with final causes (reasons, interests, purposes) have (miraculously) emerged out of things that operate mechanically, by efficient causes alone? No, at least not yet: In spite of his weasel word "perhaps," he seems to grant that the replicators "properly speaking had no interests," and he uses scare quotes in speaking of their assigned "defining 'interest' in self-duplication." Dennett explains his meaning, furthermore, by saying, "*If* these simple replicators are to survive and replicate . . . , their environment must meet certain conditions" (*CE,* 173). No miracle, evidently, has occurred. But then he continues:

> Put more anthropomorphically, if these simple replicators want to continue to replicate, they should hope and strive for various things; they should avoid the 'bad' things and seek the 'good' things. When an entity arrives on the scene capable of behavior that staves off, *however primitively,* its own dissolution and decomposition, it brings with it into the world its 'good.' That is to say, it creates *a point of view.* (*CE,* 173–74; emphases added)

Although Dennett begins this statement with the disarming assurance that it is "put anthropomorphically," which seems to mean that it is a purely *as-if* account, by the end it seems that the miracle has *really occurred:* Replicators really do, "however primitively," have a point of view and hence interests, purposes. Teleology has emerged out of pure mechanism. Once Dennett has, thanks to his quiet little miracle, crossed this divide, he can account for human consciousness in terms of greatly increased complexity alone: "The point of view of conscious observers is . . . a sophisticated descendant of the primordial points of view of the first replicators who divided their worlds into good and bad" (*CE*, 176). But even if the miracle occurs long before the rise of human consciousness, it is no less a miracle (unless, of course, Dennett is giving a purely externalist, and thereby wholly inadequate, account of a "point of view").

Humphrey provides a similar explanation based on tiny steps. He says, "Before life emerged . . . there were presumably no minds of any kind at all. It follows that four thousand million years ago the world was totally unexperienced. . . . [E]verything . . . in nature was insentient" (*HM*, 16, 217). Humphrey's task is to get from there to the existence of animals, for whom, "whether at the level of an amoeba or an elephant," there is a boundary wall between "me" and "not-me" (*HM*, 18). His story describes "how present-day sensory activities could have developed step-by-step from primitive beginnings, starting with a local 'wriggle of acceptance or rejection' in response to stimulation at the body surface" (*HM*, 180f.). (Note how externalist language ["wriggle"] and internalist language ["acceptance or rejection"] are combined, just as in theological accounts the intermediaries embodied both divine and worldly features.) What occurred first, according to Humphrey, was a slight degree of "sensitivity" (*HM*, 18), which at first could be understood in purely externalist categories. But then natural selection selected for this sensitivity, so that it became more sophisticated. Pretty soon, an inner, phenomenal life of sorts emerged: "The phenomenology of sensory experiences came first. Before there were any other kinds of phenomena there were 'raw sensations'—tastes, smells, tickles, pains, sensations of warmth, of light, of sound and so on" (*HM*, 21). At some point, then, "certain events were being responded to *as* good or bad . . . , *as* of significance to 'me' " (*HM*, 19). Subjectivity had emerged out of pure objectivity.

Humphrey thinks this explanation has answered McGinn's problem: "A seeming miracle? No, as close to a real miracle as anything that ever happened. The twist may be that it takes only a relatively simple scientific theory to explain it" (*HM*, 219). The theory is indeed simple; but it is deceptively simple. The deception is that an infinite step has been made to seem a tiny one.* No matter how tiny, far back, and innocuous one tries to make

---

*After writing this, I learned that McGinn had addressed this issue in an earlier book, *The Character of Mind*. There he argues that although life admits of borderline cases, such as bacteria and organic molecules, which can be considered partly living and partly not, this is not the case with experience: Either there is "something 'inner,' some way the world appears *to*

it, however, it is still a miracle. For McGinn, the task is "to take the magic out of the link between consciousness and the brain" (*PC*, 2). This is because, for him, the question "How is it possible for conscious states to depend on brain states?" is assumed to be identical (see my list of problems at the outset of chapter 1) with the question "How could the aggregation of millions of individually insentient neurons generate subjective awareness?" (*PC*, 1). But if we assume that experience emerged earlier, perhaps with single-celled organisms such as amoebas, we would have the "experience-organelle problem," that is, the problem of how "to take the magic out of the link between" an amoeba's experience and its organelles. In other words, magic is implicit regardless of the level at which the first emergence of experience is said to occur.

This concern about magic, incidentally, is not new. At a conference on evolution in 1974, the great evolutionist Sewall Wright, a panexperientialist, declared in his paper, "Emergence of mind from no mind at all is sheer magic" (PS, 82). Theodosius Dobzhansky, an equally great evolutionist, replied, "Then I believe in magic!" Dobzhansky's reply, delivered in his thick Russian accent, brought the house down; but it also brought out the apparent trilemma: panexperientialism, supernatural intervention, or (Dobzhansky's choice) natural magic. McGinn, however, believes that there is another alternative. But this alternative is nothing but physicalist piety.

McGinn's "nonconstructive solution" (*PC*, 31) to the mind-body problem is simply to assert that there must be something purely natural about consciousness and therefore the brain that accounts for the relation between them, but that we are so constructed that we will never be able to know what this is. This *must* be the truth, he says, or else naturalism would be threatened: "The radical emergence of mind from matter has to be

---

the creature," or there is not. Accordingly, whereas with life "we have to do with a gradual transition from the plainly inanimate to the indisputably living," with regard to experience "we cannot take such a gradualist view, admitting the existence of intermediate stages." The emergence of experience "must rather be compared to a sudden switching on of a light, narrow as the original shaft must have been." We must, therefore, think of the lowliest minds "as consisting in (so to speak) a small speck of [experience] quite definitely possessed, not in the partial possession of something admitting of degrees" (*CM*, 14). Although McGinn couches his argument in terms of "consciousness," I have phrased it in terms of "experience," because I do not, unlike McGinn, equate the two, and because I, thinking of consciousness as a very high-level type of experience, do believe that it can emerge gradually. With regard to the fundamental issue, however, which is that an entity must either have an inner aspect or not— regardless of what term is used for this inner aspect—he seems absolutely right. The problem that McGinn's clarity on this point creates for a materialist, of course, is precisely the problem that Dennett and Humphrey are trying to circumvent: If an inner aspect *suddenly* emerges in things that previously had been completely devoid of any such aspect, the miraculous character of this alleged emergence, and thus its seeming impossibility within a naturalistic framework, is driven home.

epistemic only, on pain of accepting inexplicable miracles in the world" (*PC*, 6). Then, having thereby confessed that his position is based on paradigmatic and wishful-and-fearful thinking, he proceeds to speak as if he *knows* it to be true. For example, having stated that we cannot refute a creationist account of consciousness "by actually producing a non-miraculous explanatory theory," he says that "we can refute it by arguing that such a naturalistic theory must *exist*" (*PC*, 17n). How does this response differ from that of the traditional Christian theologian who, speaking "from faith to faith" to fellow sharers in the orthodox paradigm, argues that although we cannot actually refute the charge of self-contradictory nonsense by producing an account of how Jesus was fully divine and yet fully human, we can refute the charge by arguing that such an account *must exist*? McGinn begins his book by telling us that his solution has given him a great sense of relief, one that he tries to induce in his readership (*PC*, vii). But this sense of relief rests entirely on faith. "The philosophical problem," he says, "arises from the sense that we are compelled to accept that nature contains miracles." But, he continues, "we do not need to accept this: we can rest secure in the knowledge that some (unknowable) property of the brain makes everything fall into place" (*PC*, 18). (Believers commonly gain a sense of security by thinking of their faith as knowledge.) McGinn says that a proposal is adequate to the degree that it avoids the seeming necessity to choose between eliminativism and accepting a miracle, and proclaims his own proposal a success because "it allows us to resist the postulation of miracles" (*PC*, 18n). All it really does, however, is declare that no miracle occurred while giving not a hint as to how the feat was accomplished without one. Having pointed out that we do not know how to reduce consciousness to the brain, McGinn explains: "We need to distinguish being able to *give* a reduction from knowing that a reduction *exists*" (*PC*, 31n). But McGinn's position here is similar to that of reductionists who base their present confidence in physicalism on promissory notes about the future glories of neuroscience—except that McGinn gives no such note, saying instead that we will never be able actually to give a reductionistic explanation.

Indeed, in calling his position "agnostic realism" (*PC*, 120), McGinn recognizes that he is similar to an "agnostic theist" (*PC*, 119). In answering the question as to how he can so enthusiastically believe in something about whose nature he can say nothing, he claims that we "can know that something exists without knowing its nature. We can assert that a gap is filled without being able to say how it is filled" (*PC*, 119). His comparison with agnostic theism is apt. One of the main reasons for rejecting theism is the problem of evil: Why, critics ask, if God is both omnipotent and good, is there such horrendous evil in the world? One of the most popular answers today, employing a combination of claimed knowledge and agnosticism analogous to McGinn's, goes something like this: "Because we know that

God exists, and because we know that God is perfect in wisdom and goodness, we can know that God must have a perfectly good reason for allowing all these evils. We can know this without having the slightest inkling as to what that reason might be. In fact, we can see that it is perfectly reasonable, given our finite natures, that we should not be able to figure out what that reason is." This kind of argument, of course, is viciously circular: The so-called knowledge is based entirely on faith—a faith, in fact, that is insulated from the possibility of falsification.

In spite of all his talk of knowledge, McGinn does finally admit that it is something less. Of his naturalism, which he describes as "the thesis, metaphysical in character, that nothing that happens in nature is inherently anomalous, God-driven, an abrogation of basic laws," he says: "It is, I suppose, an article of metaphysical faith" (PC, 87).* One can sympathize with Flanagan and others for not finding the relief that McGinn had hoped his "solution" would provide. Blind faith is blind faith whether it be of the supernaturalistic or the naturalistic variety, and blind faith does not provide a secure resting place for most intellectuals.

I am not at all, given my regulative principles, objecting to McGinn's naturalistic faith; I share it myself. But it should be a faith seeking understanding. Just as I hold that a theistic faith is not reasonable unless it can provide an intelligible and persuasive theodicy, which for me means rejecting supernaturalism in favor of a version of naturalistic theism,[11] so any form of naturalism is precarious insofar as it cannot provide an intelligible and persuasive account of the mind-body relation. This account must be more than simply a restatement of faith.

McGinn's position is meant to be based, to be sure, not simply on faith but also on an argument. This argument, however, involves a fallacy, which can be dubbed the *actual-possible fallacy*. The best way to show that something is possible is to show that it is actual. Actually going to the moon settled all the doubts as to whether it was possible. That part of the argument is unassailable. Insofar as we take a particular paradigm for granted, however, we are apt to insinuate theoretical inferences into our statement of empirical fact. Some theists, for example, have answered the question as to whether an individual could be both fully human and fully divine by pointing to Jesus: Because it happened, it is obviously possible.** Likewise,

---

*Strawson sees this point more consistently. "Belief in the truth of materialism is a matter of faith," he says, adding: "My faith, like that of many other materialists, consists in a bundle of connected and unverifiable beliefs" (MR, 43, 105).

**Millard J. Erickson provides an example: "We sometimes approach the incarnation the wrong way. We define deity and humanity abstractly and then say, 'They could not possibly fit together.' . . . If, however, we begin with the reality of the incarnation in Jesus Christ, we . . . recognize that whatever [the two natures] are, they are not incompatible, for they once did

in response to questions as to whether it is possible for a purely spiritual being to act upon a material world (an aspect of the mind-body problem writ large), one would commit the actual-possible fallacy if one pointed to the world as God's creation as proof. To a physicalist, these theistic examples of the fallacy are obvious, but physicalists are then likely to commit their own versions. For example, McGinn says, "It is just as hard to see how an entity constructed naturally from mere matter can be conscious as it is to see how an intentionally created material object can be. But we know that the former is possible, because we have seen it done" (*PC*, 205).

This argument may seem unobjectionable until we recall the theoretical idea packed into the term "mere matter," which entails that the "grey matter" of the brain is composed entirely of "individually insentient neurons" (*PC*, 1). It is one thing to say that we know that it is possible for conscious states to arise out of a brain, because it actually occurs. It is something entirely different to say that we know that it is possible for conscious states to arise out of *a brain composed of neurons that are individually insentient*, because it has actually happened. This we do not know; it is pure supposition. This actual-possible fallacy, I suspect, provides the basis for McGinn's twofold conclusion that the relation between the brain and consciousness is a purely naturalistic relation, meaning one consistent with physicalism, but that we will never be able to understand this relation.

The actual-possible fallacy with regard to our question is not at all rare; in fact, it seems to be committed by a good share of dualists and materialists alike. It goes back to Descartes, who was persistently questioned by Princess Elisabeth as to how mind and body, if they were totally different, could interact. After it was clear that reference to the pineal gland at best answered only the question of *where*, not that of *how*, Descartes finally admitted that he did not know how. He added that this is not very important, however, because it is empirically obvious that they *do* interact.[12] It evidently did not occur to him that this empirical fact counted against his own characterization of the body, or the mind, or both. This same fallacy is committed by the contemporary Cartesian H. D. Lewis. In response to John Passmore's question, cited earlier, as to how minds, capable of only rational persuasion, can affect bodies, capable only of pushing and being pushed, Lewis says,

> It seems quite evident that my purposing to put on my spectacles or wave my hand is not itself a physical state or process. . . . But if we find that this non-spatial purpose does in fact normally bring about a physical change, how can we possibly question this just because it defies further explanation? . . . [W]e must accept [the world] however remarkable it may seem to be in some respects. (*ES*, 34)

---

coexist in one person. And what is actual is of course possible" (*Christian Theology* [Grand Rapids, Mich.: Baker, 1985], 737).

Lewis, like Descartes, fails to distinguish between the "evident" facts and his theoretical construal of them. In response to Bernard Williams, Lewis says,

> We may indeed admit that there is "something deeply mysterious about the interaction which Descartes's theory required between two items of totally disparate natures." . . . But there is a limit to explanation and a point where we just have to accept things as we find them to be. . . . [W]ould it not be better for philosophers, rather than trying to explain away or discredit extraordinary facts of experience, to stop and wonder at them and their possible further implications? (*ES*, 38f.)

Lewis, having so deeply internalized the dualistic paradigm, evidently fails to consider that there may be nothing "extra-ordinary" about the facts of experience at issue, but that it is only the dualistic construal that makes them seem so, and that what at least some critics are doing is discrediting that construal, not the facts. Nor does he evidently consider that, having accepted interaction of mind and body, the "possible further implications" are that the Cartesian construal of mind or body or both is erroneous.

I return now to materialistic examples of the actual-possible fallacy, beginning with one provided by Dennett: "How could a complicated slew of electrochemical interactions between billions of neurons amount to conscious experience? And yet we readily imagine human beings to be conscious, even if we can't imagine how this could be" (*CE*, 433). Ergo, the conclusion is, consciousness has arisen out of insentient neurons. Humphrey makes a similar move, contrasting the problem of turning water into wine, which he considers unsolvable in principle, with the problem "of getting consciousness into the brain." The "interesting difference" between them, he says, is that "while the former has never been known to occur, the latter occurs all the time" (*HM*, 6). The latter part of that statement is certainly true, but Humphrey assumes that this fact carries with it the fact that consciousness has arisen out of a "foam of insensate matter." (It is, incidentally, puzzling that both Dennett and Humphrey, after having given an evolutionary sketch according to which an elementary form of sentience is present in amoebas, which are single-celled organisms, persist in thinking of neurons, which are single-celled organisms, as insentient.) Humphrey does not *know*, however, that consciousness has arisen out of brains composed of insentient neurons; he only believes this. What he knows, at best, is that conscious experience has arisen out of brains.

By recognizing the actual-possible fallacy for what it is, we can overcome the widespread assumption that we know that conscious experience has somehow emerged out of insentient matter, an assumption on the basis of which thinkers, both philosophic and scientific, set themselves the impossible task of trying to figure out where and how this occurred. We can thereby realize more clearly that the problem is simply that of trying to figure out how conscious experience arose out of brains, a problem whose solution may require us to modify our inherited assumptions about the components of those brains.

The main purpose of this chapter has not been simply to rehearse the problems of both dualism and materialism; those are known well enough (although it is usually not appreciated how many problems they have in common). The main purpose has been to show that all of those problems are rooted in the same intuition: the Cartesian intuition about matter. As Whitehead points out, almost all schools of thought have "admitted the Cartesian analysis of the ultimate elements of nature" (*SMW*, 145). This was an analysis that completely excluded mind from nature. What is suggested, accordingly, is that a solution to the mind-body problem may need to be based on a philosophy that would regard mind as fully natural, thereby rejecting the Cartesian intuition about bodies. This is the topic of the next chapter.

SEVEN

Fully Naturalizing the Mind

The Neglected Alternative

I. THE EXCLUSION OF THE PANEXPERIENTIALIST ALTERNATIVE

As the previous chapter has shown, the philosophical aspects of the mind-body problem (as distinct from its empirical aspects) are due to the assumption that what we normally call the physical or material world, at least below some level, is wholly devoid of experience, of any "within." Once this is seen, the long-standing standoff between dualism and materialism over the "world-knot" can be seen for what it is: a family quarrel. It is a squabble, apparently interminable, among those who have accepted early modernity's absolute exclusion of all experiential features from the basic units of nature. As pointed out earlier, the naturalistic materialism of late modernity simply eliminated God and the nonphysical soul from the dualistic supernaturalism of early modernity, leaving intact its view of nature as insentient matter. To bring out the similarity between the two positions even more, we can say, with Searle, that materialism is "really a form of dualism," insofar as it has accepted the dualistic analysis of the meaning of "physical" and "mental" (*RM*, 26). Charles Hartshorne, from a different perspective, argues that materialism is really dualism in disguise (*CSPM*, 9, 27). His point is that materialists must in some sense acknowledge the existence of experiencing things, because they are examples thereof; they, accordingly, implicitly affirm that the universe contains two metaphysically different types of actual things: experiencing and nonexperiencing.

If their common Cartesian intuition about matter is the basic reason why neither dualists nor materialists can provide an adequate account of the mind-body relation, the way forward in the discussion would seem obvious: Let's try out the version of realism that they excluded from the family, panpsychism—or, better, panexperientialism. "Panpsychism" is the term that has generally been used for this position. "Panexperientialism" is preferable, however, for two reasons: (1) The term "psyche" suggests that the basic units endure through long stretches of time, whereas they may be momentary experiences; and (2) "psyche" inevitably suggests a higher form of experience than would be appropriate for the most elementary units of nature.* Nevertheless, I will in this chapter sometimes use "panpsychism," because it is the term used by the various authors I quote.

To affirm panexperientialism would be finally to carry through the regulative principle that mind should be naturalized, because it would involve attributing the two basic features that we associate with mind—experience and spontaneity—to all units of nature.** As Searle has pointed out, when materialists talk about " 'naturalizing' mental phenomena, they mean reducing them to physical phenomena" (*RM*, 2). What this reduction implies is that those aspects of the mind that do not fit the materialist paradigm, the mind's experience and spontaneity, are not really natural. The early modernists' dualism between natural matter and supernatural mind is still assumed.

This assumption is revealed in McGinn's discussion of why he locates the unknowable property that explains the relation between consciousness and the brain in the hidden structure of consciousness, not merely in the brain. He says,

> It is consciousness that cries out for naturalistic explanation, not cerebral matter. Consciousness is the anomalous thing, the thing that tests our naturalistic view of the world. It is what threatens to import . . . weird properties that cannot be instantiated by physical objects. . . . Consciousness needs to have a nature that renders it incorporable into a world whose fundamental constituents are physical particles and the forces that govern them. . . . The stigma of the occult must be removed from consciousness. (*PC,* 68)

(Although McGinn speaks of consciousness here, not merely experience, he typically does not distinguish them, using "consciousness" inclusively for

---

*Although Hartshorne, after long using the term "panpsychism," replaced it with "psychicalism," he has recently said that he sees advantages in the term "panexperientialism" ("General Remarks," in *Hartshorne, Process Philosophy and Theology,* ed. Robert Kane and Stephen H. Phillips [Albany: State University of New York Press, 1989], 181). I first (to my present knowledge) proposed "panexperientialism" as the preferable term in *MN,* 97–98.

**The term "units" implies a distinction between true individuals and aggregational organizations of such, which I will explain in the following chapters. For now the point is that panpsychism or panexperientialism does *not,* in spite of a host of detractors wishing to be able to dismiss it in a phrase as obviously ludicrous, necessarily imply (for example) that "rocks have feelings." The "pan" in the panexperientialism to be advocated here refers not simply to all *things* but only to all genuine *units* or *individuals.* This means that experience is *not* attributed to aggregational things, such as rocks and chairs, as such.

all forms of experience.) How unnatural experience seems to one who has imbibed the physicalist version of naturalism is brought out by the fact that "properties that cannot be instantiated by physical objects" are considered "anomalous," even "weird" and "occult." Although physicalists—for example, Flanagan (*CR*, 1f.)—typically regard dualists as supernaturalists for affirming the existence of a nonphysical mind, they no more than dualists regard the mind's experience and spontaneity as fully natural, as present to some degree in all natural units.* Panexperientialism is hence the only form of realism that truly regards the mind as natural. As Whitehead says,

> Any doctrine which refuses to place human experience outside nature, must find in descriptions of human experience factors which also enter into the descriptions of less specialized natural occurrences. If there be no such factors, then the doctrine of human experience as a fact of nature is mere bluff. . . . We should either admit dualism . . . , or we should point out the identical elements connecting human experiences with physical science. (*AI*, 185)

Materialistic monism's inability to solve the mind-body problem, in spite of ostensibly rejecting dualism, is due to the fact that its claim to naturalize human experience has been "mere bluff." A panexperientialist monism might be able to do better. We should at least give it a try.

The panexperientialist or panpsychist option has, however, been virtually ignored in most discussions. Almost all authors write as if there were only two realistic options, dualism and materialism. For example, Dennett, saying that he will defend a functionalist form of materialism, contrasts materialism with the "other idea" that "conscious thoughts and experiences cannot be brain happenings, but must be . . . something in addition, made of different stuff. . . . The idea of mind as distinct in this way from the brain, composed not of ordinary matter but of some other, special kind of stuff, is dualism, and it is deservedly in disrepute today" (*CE*, 33). The idea that there might be a third option, according to which the mind is distinct from the brain but *not* composed of a different kind of "stuff," does not come up. Dualists also generally keep the discussion within the family. For example, Geoffrey Madell writes in the preface to *Mind and Materialism* that he has sympathy with "the underlying motivation behind materialism" because of "the difficulties which any dualist position confronts." He concludes, however, that the difficulties of materialism are even greater, so that there is no alternative but to return to dualism, in spite of its serious difficulties (*MM*, 9, 135, 145). The idea that there might be a third option is not se-

---

*It should be noted that I am generalizing *experience* to all individuals; *consciousness*, by contrast, is understood as a very high level form of experience, a way of focusing a light, as it were, on a few ingredients of experience; more on this in the next chapter. In speaking of *spontaneity*, I refer to an at least rudimentary anticipation of what becomes *self-determination* in high-grade individuals.

riously considered. The books by Dennett and Madell provide only two of countless writings in which we are told time and time again that the choice must be between dualism and materialism (sometimes phrased as dualism and monism, with the assumption that monism means materialism). These writers will sometimes explore two or three varieties of dualism and even more varieties of materialism (the large number of which reflects what Searle calls the neurotic-like pattern of behavior based on the assumption that *some* version of materialism *must* be true). But much more time will be devoted to each of those versions of dualism and materialism than to all the versions of panexperientialism or panpsychism combined.

If panpsychism is even mentioned, it is usually dismissed in a paragraph, if not a sentence. For example, Madell devotes one sentence to it, dismissing it with the statement that it does not have "any explanation to offer as to why or how mental properties cohere with physical" (*MM,* 3). But against *which version* of panpsychism this complaint is lodged he does not say; he does not even show evidence of having studied any actual author advocating panpsychism. Humphrey, after having said that "there was a time in history when consciousness existed nowhere," adds this parenthetical comment: "(The alternative idea, that consciousness has always been inherent in every particle of matter, sometimes called 'panpsychism', is one of those superficially attractive ideas that crumbles to nothing as soon as it is asked to do any sort of explanatory work.)" (*HM,* 193). Besides the fact that most forms of panpsychism do *not* attribute *consciousness* (as distinct from experience, feeling, sentience, or protoconsciousness) to particles of matter, the reader is left to take on faith Humphrey's declaration that when it is asked to do any explanatory work it "crumbles to nothing." Again, no reference to any actual version of panpsychism is given. Seager, as usual more open-minded than most about unorthodox ideas, says that panpsychism does not seem "outright impossible" (*MC,* 106). And he states (in an endnote) that panpsychism *might* make sense of the relation between consciousness and the brain. But, he adds, "I am not sure that such a theory is even intelligible and I am certain it *is* implausible" (*MC,* 241–42n). He at least gives a hint as to the kind of panpsychism he has in mind, namely, one that "maintained that high level mental features were assembled from 'mental atoms' in some way similar to that relating micro-structure to macro-structure in the physical realm." I agree that such a panpsychism would be implausible. But the unknowing reader would be left with the impression that this is what "panpsychism" is, although this doctrine is not referred to any actual philosopher and, in fact, no philosophers are mentioned who have actually developed any form of panpsychism.*

---

*Up to this point, I have been referring to Seager's position as stated in his 1991 book, *Metaphysics of Consciousness*. However, after reading an earlier version of my manuscript for this

If philosophers take seriously the regulative principle that when arguing for the truth of one position by eliminating all alternatives but one, *all* alternatives must really be examined, then in their examination of realistic, naturalistic philosophies they cannot simply ignore panpsychism or dismiss it as obviously false without examining any actual examples of it. A second aspect of the principle is that the strongest version of each basic option should be examined, not one of the weaker versions (and certainly not a made-up caricature). This second aspect of the principle, of course, introduces a matter of judgment, but Whitehead and Hartshorne, both of whom have been included in the "Library of Living Philosophers," are clearly the two most distinguished twentieth-century philosophers who have developed versions of panpsychism. It would not be unreasonable, accordingly, to assume that they have developed the strongest versions. My own treatment draws on what I consider the best ideas in both.

Nagel, who explicitly advocates the principle of seeking truth by excluding all alternatives but one, was evidently the first contemporary analytic philosopher dealing with the mind-body problem to take panpsychism seriously. (His discussion, in fact, seems to be the source of the brief comments about panpsychism made by several other contemporary philosophers.) Nagel is puzzled by panpsychism. On the one hand, he sees that some version of panpsychism (a two-aspect version) seems to follow from realism combined with the denial of a soul, the nonreducibility of experiential states to nonexperiential properties, and the fact that a *pour soi* cannot be formed (naturalistically) out of entities devoid of experiential states (*MQ,* 181–82, 188, 192). On the other hand, he finds this conclusion "unsettling" (*VN,* 49), perhaps in part because he is describing himself when he says that "if one travels too far down the phylogenetic tree, people gradually shed their faith that there is experience there at all" (*MQ,* 168). Another difficulty is puzzlement as to what the protomental properties of an atom could be (*VN,* 49–50). The *chief* problem, however, seems to be the thought that panpsychism is "perhaps unintelligible," because it seems impossible to understand how "a single self [could] be composed of many selves." The reason for this is that the only concept of a part-whole relation we have, he believes, is a physicalist one, such as "how a muscle movement is composed of myriad physico-chemical events at the molecular level" (*MQ,* 194; *VN,* 50). But Nagel is not dogmatic: After saying that this model will not work and that we lack the concept of "a mental part-whole relation" that would do justice to the experienced unity of consciousness, he adds

---

book, Seager articulated a version of panpsychism with features that, he says, "ameliorate its implausibility" (CIP, 283n14). While offering "a defence of it only with great diffidence" (CIP, 279), Seager says that "the philosophical objections against panpsychism [can] be answered" (CIP, 284). I will discuss Seager's version later.

that he may be working with "false assumptions about the part-whole relation" (*VN,* 51).

The weakness of Nagel's discussion, bold as it is given modern prejudices, is that it is not based on an examination of any actual panexperientialist position developed by a twentieth-century philosopher. In particular, it does not come close to the form articulated by Alfred North Whitehead, who was called, in the (hostile) article on panpsychism in the 1972 *Encyclopedia of Philosophy,* "the most distinguished champion of panpsychism in the twentieth century" (see Sec. III, 7 below). Nagel, accordingly, has not fulfilled his own principle of examining the strongest version of each of the basic options. Insofar as it is any particular view of panpsychism that he discusses, it seems to be a kind deriving from Spinoza, which is how Nagel describes his own dual-aspect theory, according to which "mental phenomena are the subjective aspects of states which can also be described physically" (*NYR,* n6). No one would think, however, that exploring Descartes's version of the mechanistic view of matter, or Hobbes's version of materialism, would fulfill the principle of exploring the strongest version of each position. In any case, I will suggest in chapter 9 that Whitehead and Hartshorne have provided an experiential concept of the part-whole relation (which Hartshorne calls a "compound individual") that is quite different from the aggregational concept quite rightly considered inadequate by Nagel and others following him.

One of these is McGinn, who devotes a little more attention to panpsychism than do most contemporary philosophers. This is not true of his 1991 book, *The Problem of Consciousness,* however. Only a few brief references to panpsychism are scattered throughout this collection of essays. In a footnote, McGinn says, "Attributing specks of proto-consciousness to the constituents of matter is not supernatural in the way postulating immaterial substances or divine interventions is; it is merely extravagant" (*PC,* 2n). This is on the same page, incidentally, on which he says that "something pretty remarkable is needed if the mind-body relation is to be made sense of." If we take these two assertions to constitute a formal regulative principle, McGinn has given us a difficult assignment: Our solution must be "remarkable" and yet not "extravagant." In any case, McGinn concludes this note by saying he will "be assuming that panpsychism, like all other extant constructive solutions, is inadequate as an answer to the mind-body problem." In another note, McGinn says that if neurons had conscious or protoconscious states, it would be "easy enough to see how neurons could generate consciousness" (*PC,* 28n). This is a startling statement from one who is arguing that the mind-body problem is permanently insoluble. Should we not explore this alternative, the reader might wonder, before succumbing to pessimism prematurely? But McGinn blocks this path of inquiry, assuring the reader that this view of neurons is, in a word, "false." Actually, his main objection (the objection that it is false is inserted parenthetically) is that this view of neurons "just pushes the question back . . . : for how do these conscious properties of neurons arise from their physical nature?" This is a good question, being, in fact, the question I raised above about the attempts by Dennett and Humphrey to speak of "points of view" arising out of purely insentient material particles. McGinn, however, knows that there is another possibility, which is that experience, like the lady's turtles, goes all the way down. McGinn gives a three-word parenthetical response to this possible answer: "(Panpsychism now threatens.)"

Exactly *what* panpsychism threatens is not explicitly stated, but the answer seems implicit. What is threatened is the rock-bottom ontological premise of the modern paradigm, which is that the fundamental units of nature are material or physical in the sense of being devoid of all experience. Having inherited the early modern dualists' idea of matter, late modern materialists, in rejecting the dualism of their elder siblings, are not content simply to espouse a nondualistic or monistic view according to which all actual things would *embody* physicality. They insist that the fundamental units of nature must be physical not only in this broad sense but also in the sense established by their elders—that they be wholly devoid of all experience whatsoever. This love-hate relationship with dualism is what prevents materialism from being truly monistic. Even though panpsychism might solve modernity's central philosophical problem, it is seen as a threat, not an opportunity, because it would solve the problem by rejecting what has probably become the most deeply ingrained soft-core commonsense notion of the modern mind, so deeply ingrained that many are willing to sacrifice several hard-core commonsense notions to carry through its implications. Paradigms are powerful.

McGinn's rejection of panpsychism is particularly interesting in the light of his unearthing a passage suggesting that Kant assumed a panpsychist solution to the mind-body problem. Here is the passage (from the First Critique) quoted by McGinn (*PC*, 81):

> The difficulty peculiar to the problem consists . . . in the assumed heterogeneity of the object of inner sense (the soul) and the objects of the outer senses, the formal condition of their intuition being, in the case of the former, time only, and in the case of the latter, also space. But if we consider that the two kinds of objects thus differ from each other, not inwardly but only in so far as one appears outwardly to another, and that what, as thing in itself, underlies the appearances of matter, perhaps after all may not be so heterogeneous in character, this difficulty vanishes, the only question that remains being how in general a communion of substances is possible.[1]

Kant suggests, in this remarkable passage, that the soul, as we know it from within, and objects of sensory perception, as they are in themselves, may

not be different in kind, that they may *appear* to be thus different only because we know them in different ways: The soul knows itself from within
but knows an outer object only insofar as that object "appears outwardly"
to it. That some kind of panpsychist position should be assumed by Kant,
even if not trumpeted after he took his critical turn, should not be surprising in light of the fact that before that turn he had held a somewhat Leibnizian viewpoint. That this is the view alluded to here is suggested by the
assertion that the only remaining question is "how in general a communion
of substances is possible": Leibniz, of course, given his monadology, had no
special problem with mind-body interaction but, given his views on the self-
identity of enduring substances, described his monads as "windowless," as
he could allow no genuine "communion" (efficient causation) between his
substances. (The present passage discovered by McGinn corresponds to a
footnote in Kant's *Dreams of a Ghost-seer* [Pt. I, chap. 1, n1], in which Kant
says that we must either remain agnostic about what the objects of our sensory perceptions are in themselves or else agree with Leibniz that they are
psychical entities of a nonhuman kind, but that, if we were to adopt the
latter course, we could not understand how they could interact to form a
cosmos.)

What is McGinn's response to this discovery? On the one hand, he says
that Kant diagnoses a "sort of error we are prone to make: mistaking the
phenomenal for the noumenal" (*PC*, 84). On the other hand, he resists
Kant's solution. Formulating the issue in terms of "heterogeneity" and "homogeneity," McGinn suggests, is "too restrictive" and perhaps "the wrong
way to think about it" (*PC*, 82). McGinn himself, however, later asks: "How
can consciousness be physically governed . . . and yet be so utterly unlike
that which governs it?" (*PC*, 100). His real objection to Kant's suggestion
is that Kant "attributes the problem-resolving hidden structure to matter,
not to mind" (*PC*, 82). We have already seen that McGinn is loath to give
up his Cartesian intuition about matter and that he thinks that it is mind,
not matter thus construed, that is anomalous. He goes right back, accordingly, to contrasting his own experience, as known from within, to his brain,
as known from without, saying, "I should be amazed that this vivid experience of red could result from chemical perturbations in that little bit of wet
cortex" (*PC*, 85).

Even his discovery that Kant still took panpsychism seriously after his
critical turn, then, does not lead McGinn to take it seriously. In any case,
although McGinn evidently did not think it important enough to mention in *The Problem of Consciousness,* he had, in an earlier book, devoted
about two pages (*CM*, 31–33) to refuting panpsychism. However, as indicated in the preface (*CM*, v), the version he there treats is the one articulated by Nagel. Although McGinn seems to think that his refutations apply
across the board, to every possible version of panpsychism, this is not the

case. For one thing, although the Whiteheadian-Hartshornean version of panpsychism emphasizes the distinction between compound individuals and aggregational societies, McGinn assumes that all visible entities must exemplify essentially the same type of whole-part relation. Combining this assumption with his own assumption that to have experience is necessarily to have conscious thoughts, he indicts panpsychism for holding the absurd view that rocks have thoughts (*CM,* 32). Also, McGinn's approach to panpsychism is heavily colored by his twofold assumption that experience must be wholly derivative from ("supervenient upon") the purely physical properties of things and that the behavior of all things, including electrons and animals as well as rocks and billiard balls, must be amenable to description and prediction in terms of scientific laws, whereas the Whiteheadian-Hartshornean version of panexperientialism is largely devoted to showing why this twofold assumption, which leads to the rejection of our hard-core commonsense beliefs about freedom, need not be accepted.* After having developed this version of panexperientialism in more detail, I will, in an interlude in chapter 9, show more fully why McGinn's attempted refutations miss the mark.

I have been documenting the exclusion of the panexperientialist form of realism and suggesting that the main reason for this exclusion is that it is dictated by the Cartesian intuition about matter at the root of the modern paradigm, shared by dualists and materialists alike, according to which the elementary units of nature must be devoid of both experience and spontaneity. Although modern philosophers have by and large been unphilosophical in their exclusion of panexperientialism from consideration, this exclusion is understandable. Philosophy is a human enterprise, carried on by fully human beings, and paradigmatic thinking and the associated wishful-and-fearful thinking are part and parcel of the human condition. People who become professional philosophers, furthermore, are probably even more prone than most people to think paradigmatically. The criticism of the fact that panexperientialism has been ignored, accordingly, is not meant to be an indictment of any individual or the mainline philosophical community in general. It is meant only to emphasize the point that there is another alternative, an alternative that may point the way forward. Although we are all paradigmatic and wishful-and-fearful thinkers to a great extent, we are not, in spite of claims to the contrary by some extremists, completely at the mercy of such factors. Although they do greatly color our interpretation of data, they do not completely determine it: The "stubborn facts" retain some of their transcendence over theory. We are, accordingly,

---

*The problems that arise from the standard physicalist account of "supervenience," along with the way in which the mind can be said to be supervenient on the brain in panexperientialism, will be discussed at more length in relation to Kim's position in chapter 10.

able to objectify our own theories, including the paradigmatic intuitions they embody, and come to see their inadequacies and to consider alternatives. That this is currently happening, among dualists and materialists alike, is what stimulated my own writing of this book: The time seems to be ripe for a presentation of the panexperientialist alternative. In the next section I summarize the main reasons why this alternative should be given serious consideration by contemporary philosophers.

Before moving to that discussion, however, I will briefly examine the position of one materialist philosopher who has already seen that panexperientialism should be given careful consideration, Galen Strawson. Recognizing that discussions of the mind-body problem cannot avoid metaphysics and that the metaphysical task is to give a unified account of all of reality (*MR*, 48, 79, 103), Strawson says that what stands in the way of this unified account is the mind-body problem, which is essentially the problem of "the relation between *experience* and *matter*" (*MR*, 44). "Serious materialists" cannot deny the reality of experience, he says, because "it is still, after many centuries of philosophy, the thing of which we can be most certain," and they must also, by virtue of holding that reality is entirely physical, say that "all experiential properties are themselves entirely physical properties" (*MR*, 57). In saying this, however, they must admit that they really do not know what they mean: "We don't understand how experience itself can be a physical thing, given our current physics" (*MR*, 180).

Nevertheless, the recognition that experience must be a purely physical property, if materialism is true, means that the inherited language must be changed. "Serious materialists, then, . . . cannot talk of the physical *as opposed to* the mental or experiential at all. If they do talk like this—and they do all the time [indeed, Strawson himself continues to do so at times]— they can only really mean to talk of the nonexperiential physical as opposed to the experiential physical" (*MR*, 58). This linguistic reform, however, does nothing to mitigate the mind-body problem, which is now how to understand the relation between the physical that is experiential and the physical that is not.

The problem, more precisely, is "the relation between the experiential or mental, on the one hand, and the physical *as conceived of by current physics*, on the other" (*MR*, 58). It seems impossible to integrate them into a unified account because experiential predicates and the predicates employed in the descriptive scheme of current physics are not "theoretically homogeneous," due to the fact that the descriptive scheme of current physics makes no reference to experiential qualities: "We have an atomic physics . . . , but we don't have a qualitative-character-of-experience physics at all" (*MR*, 88, 89). The integration of these two realms, which "seem radically disparate in their intrinsic character," would, therefore, "require a kind of theoretical homogenization that seems at present unimaginable" (*MR*, 75,

89). Thus far Strawson sounds very much like McGinn. In fact, he even suggests that McGinn may be correct, saying that "perhaps we experience and conceptualize the nonexperiential physical in such a way that the existence of the experiential physical will always appear mysterious or inexplicable, relative to our conception of the rest of the physical" (*MR*, 89). Strawson's position is different from McGinn's, however, on a crucial point. McGinn, as we saw, believes that the hidden structure that would resolve the mind-body problem, if only we were privy to it, belongs to the mind, not to matter. He rejects the Kantian suggestion as to the way to overcome heterogeneity, accordingly, because it "attributes the problem-resolving hidden structure to matter, not to mind" (*PC*, 82). Strawson, however, has the opposite intuition. He is well aware that "the [conventional] notion of the physical is usually accepted as an untroublesome terminus for thought," so that "the majority view in contemporary philosophy of mind [is] that the principle cause of the intractability of the problem lies in the defective nature of our existing concepts of the mental or experiential" (*MR*, 32, 104). According to this dominant viewpoint, the "mental notions will give way," with the result that "we will be able to give, at least in principle, a full and satisfactory account of the general nature of reality using only those notions that we already deploy in 'contemporary physical science' " (*MR*, 100; citing Dennett, *CE*, 40). But, says Strawson, "this view seems astonishing. It is a very great act of faith" (*MR*, 100).

Much more likely, holds Strawson, is the opposite view, "that all the blame for the intractability of the mind-body problem should be laid on the inadequacy of our current conception of those phenomena that are traditionally called 'physical,' " which means that "it is the descriptive scheme of physics that will have to change dramatically if there is to be an acceptable theoretical unification with the mental scheme" (*MR*, 99, 104). Strawson bases this minority view on his conviction that "we cannot be as wrong about the mental, and in particular the experiential, as we can be about the physical." With regard to the experiential character of pains, for example, "how they seem is how they are. There is no room for error of the sort envisaged [by those who think that we are *entirely* wrong about the nature of pains and other experiences]" (*MR*, 50–51). By contrast, there is plenty of room to be "very wrong about the nature of the physical" (*MR*, 1). Strawson, in fact, considers "unjustified" the "modern faith that we have an adequate grasp of the fundamental nature of matter at some crucial *general* level of understanding" (*MR*, 105). Indeed, he says, "this cannot be right if materialism is true" (*MR*, 105). This is so because, to repeat, the materialist must hold "that experiential phenomena just are physical phenomena. But if they are, then it seems that we must be ignorant of the nature of the physical in some fundamental way, for experiential phenomena . . . just do not show up in what we think of as our best account of the nature of the physical: physics (or physics plus the sciences that we take to be reducible to physics)" (*MR*, 47).

Of course, one can, as an act of faith, simply *declare* that experience is fully physical, while recognizing that its properties remain different in kind from the properties ascribed to the rest of the physical by our current science of the physical. One remains, accordingly, without even a glimmer of understanding as to how these two kinds of properties—the experiential and the nonexperiential—can both belong to the same thing. This train of thought leads Strawson to affirm "agnostic materialism," which means affirming that everything is fully physical or material as an act of faith while holding that "we must be radically ignorant about fundamental aspects of the nature of the physical," which means assuming that "our current conception of the physical is fundamentally incomplete" (*MR*, xii, 43, 98).

That Strawson's agnosticism differs from McGinn's by assuming our fatal ignorance has to do with the nature of matter, instead of the nature of mind, leads to a second difference: Whereas McGinn assumes our ignorance to be permanently invincible, Strawson evidently believes it might be overcome. This second difference follows from the first, in that McGinn evidently embodies what Strawson calls the modern faith that the conventional view of matter is adequate "at some crucial *general* level of understanding," whereas Strawson, not sharing this faith, believes that we might eventually develop an adequate conception at this level. He holds, in any case, that if we are ever to solve the mind-body problem, we will need a "revolution" in physics, meaning a "radical and currently unimaginable extension or modification of the descriptive scheme of current physics, of a kind that would bring it into theoretical homogeneity with experiential predicates" (*MR*, 92, 99).

This modification of the descriptive scheme would have to hold "at least some experiential properties to be fundamental physical properties" (*MR*, 60). Some of his fellow materialists, Strawson is aware, "will think this very alarming" (*MR*, 61). But this is either because they "are not really realists about experiential properties" or because they have not realized that, if they are, they have only two choices: "either these experiential properties are reducible to other, nonexperiential physical properties, and do not feature as fundamental in an optimal physics; or they are not reducible to nonexperiential physical properties, and at least some of them feature as fundamental in an optimal physics. There is no other possibility" (*MR*, 61). Because there are only these two possibilities (Strawson rightly says), and because there is good reason to believe that the first one is false, materialists must hold the second one to be true, which means that an optimal physics will attribute experiential properties to the most fundamental physical entities or processes. Expanding on the notion that there is not a third possibility, which would reject this conclusion and yet affirm nonreducibility,

Strawson says: "Some have been lulled into thinking that there is a comfortable and strictly materialist middle position that combines rejection of the idea that any experiential properties are fundamental physical properties with endorsement of the idea that they are in principle irreducible to nonexperiential properties" (*MR*, 62). Once it is seen that no such comfortable middle position exists, it follows that if the mind-body problem is ever to be solved, we must look forward to a conceptual revolution that will show how some experiential properties can be fundamental physical properties.

This solution would seem to involve panexperientialism. Indeed, Strawson says: "In theory a *panpsychist* version of materialism could handle the idea that experiential properties might be fundamental physical properties" (*MR*, 62). And although Strawson does not endorse panpsychism, he also presents no argument against it and, in fact, says that "the problem of the relation between the experiential and the nonexperiential is so difficult that panpsychism deserves to be taken seriously" (*MR*, 75).

As we have seen, panexperientialist views have generally *not* been taken seriously. This tendency not to take them seriously, by either ridiculing or simply ignoring them, was especially strong in those who believed that some version of dualism or standard materialism could solve the mind-body problem. The recent flurry of attention to the problem of consciousness, however, has created a growing suspicion that such a solution may be impossible in principle. It is likely, furthermore, that a growing number of philosophers will come to share Strawson's double insight—that the source of the intractability is less the conventional view of mind than the conventional view of matter, and that the problem is not our ignorance about certain details, which might be remedied by further scientific discoveries (about, say, quantum physics or the nature of the brain), but involves the received *general* conception of matter, which makes it seem different in kind from experience. Accordingly, Strawson's book, which appeared only after I had completed the first draft of the manuscript for this book, provides the strongest support yet of the hunch leading to my decision to write it—that the growing awareness of the unsatisfactoriness of the standard solutions would create a climate in which this alternative solution could be taken more seriously than would have been likely in earlier decades. In any case, I turn now to a discussion of just this point: why panexperientialism, especially of the type advocated here, should be given serious consideration.

II. REASONS TO CONSIDER PANEXPERIENTIALISM

Some of the reasons listed here summarize points made above. Others anticipate points to be developed later.

1. Panexperientialism *truly naturalizes mind,* conceiving of it as fully natu-

ral. From a panexperientialist standpoint, accordingly, our own conscious experience, which is the aspect of the world that we know most immediately—the only aspect that we know from within, by identity—no longer needs to be considered either supernatural or even "anomalous." Conscious experience therefore can, as Searle hopes, be studied as "a worthy topic in its own right," not simply as "an annoying problem" (*RM*, 250).

2. Panexperientialism is, as McGinn has pointed out (*PC*, 2n), a *naturalistic* form of realism. Of course, those who have absorbed the physicalistic version of naturalism tend to consider the assertion that experiences are actual things a violation of naturalism; but that merely shows how far they are from truly naturalizing mind. Indeed, as the examination of McGinn's reflections suggests, it is only from a panexperientialist standpoint that a constructive solution without (an at least implicit) supernaturalism is possible.

3. Panexperientialism is *truly monistic* (in the qualitative sense). It thereby fulfills what Nagel calls the valid impulse behind physicalism: "to find a way of thinking about the world as it is, so that everything in it, not just atoms and planets, can be regarded as real in the same way" (*VN*, 16). Panexperientialism, unlike physicalism itself, allows that impulse to be carried out.

4. Panexperientialism *can handle Berkeley's question*—"What is matter in itself?"—without resort to idealism, whether explicit or implicit. Berkeley's idealistic answer, that for matter "to be" is "to be perceived," has been verbally ridiculed but implicitly accepted by dualists and materialists alike insofar as they described matter in purely externalist terms. Panexperientialists, by contrast, can say that just as for us "to be" is "to experience" as well as "to be experienced," the same is true for natural units (true individuals) all the way down. Panexperientialism thereby further fulfills the urge of both realism and monism to regard all levels of the actual world as real in the same sense.

5. Panexperientialism would thereby provide a new *basis for the ontological unity of science,* a dream that under the physicalist paradigm has, as Seager says, come to be widely considered a "hopeless pipedream" (*MC*, 11). There would still be a *practical* division between true individuals (whether simple or compound) and aggregational societies of individuals, in that the latter as such have neither experience nor spontaneity, so that purely externalistic and deterministic descriptions would apply. But philosophers and scientists would be aware of an underlying ontological unity with regard to individuals, for which internalist and externalist accounts would be combined. By thereby assigning both experiential and objective (externalist) predicates to all individuals, from quarks to humans, we would have the "theoretical homogeneity" that Strawson sees to be necessary for a unified account of reality (*MR*, 99).

6. A careful examination of varieties of panexperientialism, especially those that appear strongest, is necessary to fulfill the philosophical *obligation to examine all the alternatives,* at least those not eliminated by the criteria of naturalism and realism. The criterion of continuity, which suggests qualitative monism, should lead philosophers, furthermore, to take panexperientialism more seriously than dualism.

7. While philosophical self-respect alone should lead to the examination of the strongest versions of panexperientialism, this examination should today also be motivated by growing awareness of the fact that *the failure of the approaches built on the Cartesian intuition about matter,* which have been tried for several hundred years, *appears to be terminal.* If philosophy is, as some claim, a kind of game, it should follow the regulative principle accepted by all winners: *Always change a losing game.* The old game plans involved trying to relate our conscious experience to something utterly alien or else, as Nagel says, trying to beat the mind into the shape of the physical, understood in externalist categories (*VN*, 15). Panexperientialism suggests that we try a new strategy: Begin with experience, which we *know* exists, and see if we can understand the various phenomena we call "physical" in terms of various degrees, organizations, and external perceptions of *it.* Trying this strategy should not hurt: We have nothing to lose but our mind-body problem.

8. Panexperientialism provides *a concrete example of the "radical speculation" and "radical conceptual innovation"* that Nagel (*VN*, 10) and McGinn (*PC*, 104) have respectively perceived to be necessary if the mind-body impasse is to be overcome. Of course, it is common for a thinker to call formally for radical innovation and then, when being confronted with a substantive exemplification thereof, to reply, "I didn't mean *that!*" It is, indeed, hard to see how a proposal could be "remarkable" without at first looking "extravagant." As Whitehead says, "almost all really new ideas have a certain aspect of foolishness when they are first produced" (*SMW*, 47). In any case, as Searle says, the long standoff between dualists and materialists suggests that "there is something wrong with the terms of the debate" (*RM*, 49). He has in mind, in particular, the very meanings of "physical" and "mental" assigned by dualism and accepted by materialism. Panexperientialism, giving new meanings to those terms, changes the terms of the debate, thereby providing the "entirely new conceptual tools" for which Nagel calls (*VN*, 52) and, in particular, an example of the "revolution" in the conception of the physical for which Strawson has called. Recognizing this fact, Strawson has listed panpsychism as one of the few "appropriately radical responses to the enormity of the mind-body problem" (*MR*, 99). Seager introduces his own recent defense of panexperientialism (see fn., p. 80, above) by saying: "The generation problem [of explaining why and how experience

is generated by certain peculiar configurations of physical stuff] seems real to me and sufficiently difficult to warrant fairly untrammeled speculation" (CIP, 279).

9. The most important reason for trying a panexperientialist position, of course, is that it *provides hope of actually solving the mind-body problem.* Promising in this regard is that it avoids the problems that plague both dualism and materialism. By rejecting ontological dualism, it *avoids all the problems that are unique to dualism,* namely, discontinuity, interaction between ontologically unlike actualities, and (possibly) the violation of the conservation of energy (more on this later). It also *avoids the problems common to dualism and materialism:* It does not have to decide at what arbitrary place to draw a line between experiencing and nonexperiencing individuals. It does not have to think of experience as the Great Exception. (*Conscious* experience is a great exception, but it is so only by virtue of the fact that it is conscious, not merely by being experience.) It avoids the problem of how evolution could have occurred before time emerged, because panexperientialism implies pantemporalism.[2] And it avoids the problem of how experience could have been generated by nonexperiencing entities, events, or processes.* The way in which *panexperientialism avoids the problems unique to materialism,* all of which involve materialism's numerical identification of mind and brain, depends on the adoption of a (nondualistic) interactionist form of panexperientialism. This form of panexperientialism, which is made possible (although not necessitated) by the rejection of the Cartesian view of the body, will be discussed in chapters 8 and 9.

III. SOME COMMON OBJECTIONS TO PANEXPERIENTIALISM

Panexperientialism, as we have seen, is usually dismissed in a sentence or two, if not simply a phrase. I deal here in summary form with the most common objections, including for the sake of relative completeness some that have already been mentioned.

1. The objection that panexperientialism is *not naturalistic.* I have already dealt with this charge, quoting McGinn's recognition that panexperientialism does not involve supernaturalism and pointing out that it, in fact, seems the only constructive position capable of avoiding supernaturalist implications.

2. The objection that panexperientialism is *a form of vitalism.* The charge

---

*Seager, saying that "the acceptance of the reality of the generation problem and the subsequent perception of its extreme difficulty leads quite naturally . . . to the idea that consciousness is a *fundamental* feature of the world," suggests that "panpsychism is the most natural way to incorporate consciousness as *truly* fundamental" (CIP, 286). I would speak of experience, not consciousness, as fundamental.

of "vitalism" is one that some philosophers and scientists throw at any doctrine that violates their physicalist assumptions, but it does not apply here. Vitalism is the doctrine that nature, prior to the emergence of life, operated solely in terms of mechanistic principles, but that with life an entirely new causal force emerged. This kind of dualism is an example of exactly what panexperientialists want to overcome. Whitehead, for example, explicitly rejects vitalism because it "involves an essential dualism somewhere" (*SMW*, 79). Strawson, besides seeing that panpsychism is a form of monism, even says that there can be a "panpsychist version of materialism" (*MR*, 62). In chapter 10, I will develop this idea, except for calling it a version of physicalism (instead of materialism).

3. The objection that panexperientialism is *a form of idealism*, therefore not realistic. This charge has recently been made by Gerald Edelman, who thinks that panpsychism is a version of Berkeleian idealism, which he also misunderstands, thinking that Berkeley held that we autonomously create the physical world by perceiving it (rather than by having sensory data impressed on our minds by God). On the basis of this double confusion, Edelman refutes panpsychism with a *reductio ad absurdum* based on evolution: It would be impossible to see how the environment and the bodies that give rise to animal minds could also be mental events wholly dependent on those minds (*BABF*, 35, 212). That is, an evolutionary worldview says that the existence of animal (including human) minds depends on their bodies and the more general physical environment, whereas panpsychism (in Edelman's misunderstanding of it) says that what we call physical things, including our own bodies, depend on our minds! This is a good objection, but it should be directed toward those physicists who make all quantum events dependent on conscious observation, not toward panpsychists (or, for that matter, personal idealists, who have their problems but are not guilty of *this* silliness).

4. The objection that panexperientialism is *implausible*. I have dealt with this charge above, showing that it can hardly mean "as compared with dualism or materialism": Their forms of implausibility only seem more acceptable because familiarity breeds contentment. If this charge is not simply an autobiographical report that the speaker personally finds it implausible, but is the claim that "no intelligent person acquainted with scientific facts and philosophical standards of acceptability could believe it," one can cite many examples to the contrary (including Leibniz, Fechner, Lotze, James, Bergson, Peirce, Montague, Whitehead, Hartshorne, Wright, Waddington, Rensch, and Bohm).[3] It is interesting to note that Seager, after having earlier summarily dismissed all versions of panpsychism as implausible, quickly changed his mind after giving serious consideration to an actual example of panexperientialism and comparing its advantages and difficulties with those of dualism and materialism. While still saying that the assertion that

atoms have experience "remains undeniably implausible," he now holds that there is "a coherent view of panpsychism" that can sufficiently "ameliorate" this implausibility so that, all things considered, panpsychism of this sort seems less implausible than any version of dualism or materialistic physicalism (CIP, 282, 283n14, 286). Seager's example suggests that the widespread dismissal of panexperientialism as implausible is based more on a prejudgment than on an actual examination of any of the strongest extant versions of this alternative and the advantages thereof. Seager's experience was to "find it remarkable that a number of issues involved in the question of consciousness get a surprisingly unified treatment under panpsychism" (CIP, 286), meaning that it scores well on parsimony.

5. The objection that panexperientialism might be *unintelligible*. This objection, as we have seen, has to do primarily with the question of whether there can be a conception of an *experiential part-whole relation* that is different in kind from the ordinary physical part-whole relation, which surely provides no model for how myriad low-level experiences could be constitutive of a high-level experience. Seager, calling this "the combination problem," considers it "the most difficult problem facing any panpsychist theory of consciousness" (CIP, 280). It is important, of course, that this objection, articulated by Nagel and repeated by others, is that panexperientialism (panpsychism) *might be* unintelligible. It leaves open the possibility that some concrete version of panexperientialism might provide an intelligible conception of an experiential part-whole relation. And, indeed, Seager's version of panpsychism involves a type of part-whole relation in which the whole is different in kind from aggregations of physical things that are "just the sum of their parts" (CIP, 284). This issue will be at the center of the discussion of "compound individuals" in chapter 9.

6. The objection that panexperientialism *violates our intuitions* about the physical world. Popper cannot attribute experience any further down than single-celled animals (*SAB*, 79f.), evidently because he shares "with old-fashioned materialists the view that . . . solid material bodies are the paradigms of reality" (*SAB*, 10). Of course, Popper knows that although we continue to speak of elementary *particles*, the entities of quantum physics are *not* analogous to billiard balls and other "solid material bodies." Indeed, Popper himself assigns "propensities" to them (*SAB*, 79f.). If the entities, events, or processes at the quantum level have spontaneity and propensities, why should it be counterintuitive to think of them as having experience as well? Popper's statement about his intuitions returns us to the question of whether we are to give priority to our soft-core common sense or to the implications of our hard-core common sense. That is, the (sensory-based and culturally influenced) soft-core commonsense intuition has been that the ultimate units of nature are analogous to rocks, being devoid of experience and spontaneity. But this assumption leads to violations of various

hard-core commonsense intuitions, such as those involving mind-body interaction and freedom, or else to a contentment with mystery. Should we
allow our "intuition" that the ultimate units of nature are devoid of experience and internal spontaneity stand in the way of developing a worldview
that is both intelligible and adequate to the ideas that we inevitably presuppose in practice? That this would be foolish seems especially evident given
the fact that most of our (soft-core) "intuitions" about the ultimate units
of nature, based on analogy with "solid material bodies" such as rocks, have
already been violated, insofar as we have been forced to give up ideas of
solidity and determinism and have even been led to speak of "propensities."
Why should the remaining intuitions—that the ultimate units of nature
lack experience and internal spontaneity—be considered inviolate, when
all the other intuitions with which it was associated have been mistaken?

7. The most prevalent version of the previous objection is based on the
claim that panexperientialism *implies that things such as rocks and telephones
have experiences.* This is probably the most common charge made by those
interested in an easy *reductio.* For example, Popper and Eccles both dismiss
panpsychism on the grounds that it implies that things such as telephones
and minerals have feelings (*SAB,* 55, 517). This *is* true of those forms of
panpsychism, such as Spinoza's, Fechner's, and Rensch's,[4] that do not distinguish in principle between true individuals and aggregational composites of such individuals. But it is not true of versions, such as those of Leibniz, Whitehead, and Hartshorne, that make a big point of this distinction.
Hartshorne, indeed, says that in making this distinction, "Leibniz took the
single greatest step in the second millennium of philosophy (in East and
West) toward a rational analysis of the concept of physical reality" (PP, 95).*
So, in spite of thousands of one-line dismissals to the contrary, such as
McGinn's quoted above, panpsychism does not necessarily say that rocks
have consciousness, or even feelings. (I may perhaps be forgiven for over-

---

*The main difference between my position and the version of panpsychism developed by
Seager involves this point. Discussing the idea that quantum coherence could be at least a
partial explanation of the consciousness of humans and other animals, he suggests that living
brains would be quantum coherent systems, in which quantum properties would be *preserved*
(I would say *amplified*), whereas computers would not sustain quantum coherence but would
instead *deamplify* quantum effects, so that they could not support unified states of consciousness. This distinction would, Seager suggests, be "a modern reincarnation of an old idea, which
goes back at least to Leibniz, distinguishing unified entities, or what Leibniz called *organisms,*
from mere aggregates" (CIP, 285). So far so good. But he then concludes that any quantum
coherent system, such as liquid helium, would support a unified experience. He seeks to mitigate the strangeness of this idea by suggesting that because the structure of liquid helium,
compared with that of a living brain, is "informationally impoverished," it would have "an
extremely primitive state of consciousness" (CIP, 285). My alternative suggestion would be
that insofar as quantum coherence is crucial, we should think of it as a necessary but not
sufficient condition of the emergence of a unified experience.

stressing this point. The charge in question is really made ad nauseam, even in spite of attempts to forestall it. For example, in a recent edited volume in which I discussed panexperientialism in the introduction, I went to reasonable lengths, I thought, to make clear the distinction between true individuals and aggregational entities, pointing out that I attribute experience and spontaneity only to the former and distinguishing my position from some contributors in the volume who did not accept that distinction. Indeed, at the conference out of which the book arose I had argued, against some of the participants, that failure to make the distinction would lead panexperientialism to be dismissed out of hand. Nevertheless, *the* criticism of the book leveled by a reviewer was that Griffin thinks rocks have feelings.[5] So, now I'm trying the tack of going to *unreasonable* lengths to forestall this misunderstanding.)

It is with regard to this issue that philosophers hostile to panpsychism are most likely to violate the principle that we, in assessing the intelligibility of some opposing doctrine, are obligated to examine the strongest, not the weakest, version of that doctrine. An example is provided by the article on panpsychism in Paul Edwards's *Encyclopedia of Philosophy*, which he assigned himself to write.[6] In an evaluative section entitled "Is Panpsychism an Intelligible Doctrine?" he examines primarily the version of panpsychism articulated by F. C. S. Schiller, who argued that rocks have feelings. The other panpsychist to whose position Edwards devotes the most attention is Fechner, who also did not make the Leibnizian distinction between aggregational composites and true individuals, on which Whitehead and Hartshorne insist. Having left the reader with no doubts about the unintelligibility of panpsychism, Edwards then says in a note in small print:

> Little was said in this article about A. N. Whitehead, probably the most distinguished champion of panpsychism in the twentieth century, chiefly because his views on the subject could not have been discussed without consideration of other features of his difficult system. Whitehead would have disagreed with many other panpsychists about the "units" that are regarded as bearers of psychic life. These, he held, are not stars and stones but the events out of which stars and stones are constituted and which Whitehead called "occasions." . . . Panpsychist views strongly influenced by Whitehead are put forward by Charles Hartshorne.[7]

Given the recognition that Whitehead is the century's "most distinguished champion of panpsychism" and therefore, one could assume, probably presents the strongest version of it, surely a stronger version than those of Fechner and Schiller, should Edwards not have at least *tried* to summarize this version? His failure to deal with Whitehead himself instead of these earlier and less precise thinkers is especially irresponsible in the light of the fact that Edwards's main basis for considering panpsychism unintelligible—the idea that things such as stars and stones are experiencing units—is lifted up as the main point on which Whitehead differed from these other panpsychists. Edwards would surely be irate if someone were to write a critique of materialism in an analogous way. If he really thought Whitehead's position too complex and difficult for him to summarize, should he not have assigned the article to someone able to do so, or at least have discussed the position of Hartshorne—which is similar and yet much less difficult—before implying that panpsychism (in all its forms) is unintelligible?

8. The objection that panexperientialism is *a form of parallelism,* so that, in denying true interaction between mind and brain, it *does not allow for human action to be genuinely free.* This charge, which is made by Popper (*SAB,* 53–55, 516) and Eccles (*HS,* 5), amounts to saying that panpsychism forces us to swallow a difficult pill that produces no real benefits. But this charge, again, applies only to some versions of panpsychism—in general the same ones to which the previous objection applied. That is, those versions of panpsychism that take the "pan" to mean that literally *all* things have experience, making no distinction in this regard between genuine individuals and aggregational or nonindividuated things, tend to think of the "physical" and "mental" features of things as simply parallel aspects, or at most of the mental aspect as somehow dependent on the physical but not vice versa. In any case, these versions allow for no causal influence of the mental as such on the physical.[8] But those forms of panexperientialism that do distinguish between aggregational societies and compound individuals can speak, in relation to the latter, of causal interaction between the "dominant" experience and the lower-level experiences. Of course, Leibniz, although he distinguished between the "dominant monad" and the rest, did not allow for any real causal interaction between them, only for the appearance of such. But Whitehead and Hartshorne installed windows in the Leibnizian structure (by conceiving of enduring individuals, such as minds, cells, and electrons, as "temporally ordered societies" of momentary "occasions of experience," each of which begins by receiving influences from the environment into itself [as will be explained in chapters 8 and 9]). There is, accordingly, interaction in this view, which provides the basis for affirming freedom (assuming that the dominant experience, or mind, is assigned some power of self-determination). Of course, the charge that panexperientialism does not allow for freedom would not be a mark against it for many philosophers, given the widespread assumption that causal determinism reigns in nature generally, so that a view that naturalizes the mind would necessarily acquiesce in causal determinism for the mind-body relation. But freedom is, after all, a hard-core commonsense notion, so it is a condition of adequacy that a theory show the possibility of freedom.

9. The objection that panexperientialism *violates the objectivity required*

by science. This charge is sometimes based on a confusion, as Searle has stressed, between epistemological or methodological objectivity (overcoming wishful-and-fearful thinking and other distortingly subjective prejudices on the part of the scientist), which science does indeed require, and objectivity or objectivism in the ontological sense (according to which the entities studied by scientists must be said to be devoid of all subjective experience), which science does not require.* The supposition that science does require ontological objectivism is what led to behaviorism in psychology—which psychologists now generally agree, even increasingly with regard to nonhuman animals,[9] to have been a big mistake. It is now widely recognized that psychology requires discussion of both the within and the without of things, the inner experience and outer (including neuronal) behavior, trying to correlate the two as best we can. Once the necessity of this dual perspective is recognized in two scientific domains (ethology as well as human psychology), there is no reason in principle why it could not be extended all the way down. Nothing about science, in other words, would prevent the replacement of the dualistic and materialistic paradigms by panexperientialism as the dominant paradigm of the scientific community and the development of a dual-perspective methodology thereon (remembering, of course, that this dual perspective would apply only to individuals and hence would not change geology, astronomy, classical dynamics, and other sciences dealing only with aggregational societies).

There are still some more objections to panexperientialism that have been raised by McGinn, which I will treat when I discuss McGinn's attempted refutation of panpsychism in chapter 9. At this point, however, I will deal with a potentially more serious objection, which is implied by McGinn's position.

IV. ARE WE INCAPABLE OF RADICAL CONCEPTUAL INNOVATION?

This further objection to panexperientialism, which could be constructed from *The Problem of Consciousness,* can be put this way: (1) Panexperientialism purports to provide a constructive solution to the mind-body problem. (2) But we have good reason to believe, not simply from the intractability of the problem thus far (although this is suggestive) but primarily from an examination of our concept-forming capacities, that we simply are incapable of providing a constructive solution. (3) Therefore, panexperientialism, which purports to give a constructive solution, must be wrong. McGinn

---

*I have discussed the confusion between these two kinds of objectivity in the introduction to *The Reenchantment of Science: Postmodern Proposals* (Albany: State University of New York Press, 1988), 3–4, 26.

does not explicitly offer this type of a priori argument against panexperientialism. But something like this seems implicit (as when he says that he will "be assuming that panpsychism, like all other extant solutions, is inadequate as an answer to the mind-body problem" [PC, 2n]). In any case, I have constructed this somewhat artificial objection for a purpose: I believe that McGinn's insightful analysis of why our concepts lead us astray provides the most helpful clue in the current discussion to the kind of solution we need. McGinn did not mean to be doing this, to be sure, but just the opposite: to show why we *cannot* come up with a constructive solution. He has, however, been even more helpful than he intended. I will conclude this chapter, thereby preparing the way for the next one, by examining McGinn's argument.

McGinn's reason for thinking the mind-body problem to be permanently insoluble involves a twofold point: (1) Solving the problem would require radical conceptual innovation, but (2) we are simply incapable of that innovation. I will suggest that McGinn's attempt to show why this is so actually takes us part of the way toward precisely the kind of radical conceptual innovation that is needed and that, by transcending some dubious assumptions behind McGinn's analysis, we can see how to go the rest of the way.

McGinn begins by suggesting, sensibly enough, that the source of the mind-body problem lies in "our inadequate conceptions of the nature of the brain and consciousness" (PC, 2n). We have had inadequate conceptions of the "essential nature" of both body and mind (PC, 20). If this is the problem, one might say, then the solution would be to get better conceptions. McGinn believes, however, that this is just what we cannot do. The problem is that our conception-forming capacities are biased away from finding the correct explanatory theory (PC, 5). We have two bases for forming conceptions about things. On the one hand, we have sensory perception, which forms the basis for conceptions about outer objects (including the brain as known from without). On the other hand, we have introspection, which provides the basis for conceptions about mind or consciousness. I will begin with McGinn's analysis of conceptions based on sensory perception.

The problem with our senses, says McGinn, is that Kant was right about them, that "the form of outer sensibility is spatial" (PC, 12). The problem, in other words, is that "the senses are geared to representing a spatial world; they essentially present things in space with spatially defined properties. But it is precisely *such* properties that seem inherently incapable of resolving the mind-body problem" (PC, 11). Because of this feature of outer perception, "our faculties bias us towards understanding matter in motion, but it is precisely this kind of understanding that is inapplicable to the mind-body problem" (PC, 18). However, we might protest, our thinking about nature need not be based on ordinary sensory perceptions. For one thing, we can use microscopes and other perception-enhancing instruments. Second, and more important, we can develop hypotheses based on conceptions that radically transcend perceptually based conceptions. McGinn agrees with the first point but rejects the second. With regard to it, he does not argue that *perceptual* closure to the secret of the mind-body relation in itself entails *cognitive* closure (*PC*, 12). But he does argue that our concept-forming capacity is *severely constrained* by our perceptions (whether raw or enhanced). Rejecting what he calls a "magical emergentism with respect to concept formation," he argues that theoretical concepts are formed only by "a sort of analogical extension of what we observe" (*PC*, 13). That is, although we can extend our concepts some distance beyond our perceptual starting points, "we cannot prescind from them entirely" (*PC*, 27). So, after we "receive sensory inputs by directing our senses onto the brain as a physical object in space," we then "use our theoretical faculty to reason about what is received." The resulting conception of the brain is necessarily "a perception-based conception" (*PC*, 60). This conception leaves us without a clue as to how consciousness could emerge from the brain. Through perception-based conceptions we understand whole-part relations in terms of spatial composition; but this (as Nagel had pointed out) provides no model for understanding the relation of brain parts to conscious experience (*PC*, 79).

Introspection, our faculty for learning about mind or consciousness, is also biased. The problem here is that introspection generates "isolationist illusions" by insinuating the autonomy of consciousness (*PC*, 77n, 107), suggesting that it is isolated, only contingently related to the rest of the world (*PC*, 106). This critical observation about consciousness raises what turns out to be the key issue in McGinn's analysis: Is introspection *more* or *less* distorting with regard to its object than sensory perception is with regard to *its* objects? In one place, McGinn seems to say that introspection is more reliable with regard to its object (*PC*, 66). His dominant position, however, is that introspection is even less privileged with regard to giving a complete science of its object than unaided sensory perception is with regard to its material objects (*PC*, 79). Although introspection does tell us something about consciousness, it gives us only the tip of the iceberg (*PC*, 64, 78). What introspection leaves completely in the dark is the "physical network in which our conscious states are embedded" (*PC*, 73): "Events in the nervous system constitute the predominant causal background to events in consciousness, but all of that whirring background is concealed from introspection. You can introspect religiously from dawn till dusk and you will not figure out the physical causes of the conscious events you experience" (*PC*, 74).

At this point, one might protest: We can grant that Descartes thought about both matter and mind in these ways and that the Cartesian intuitions about both matter and consciousness have had a tremendously constraining influence on subsequent modern thought. But now that we understand what happened and that this way of thinking of both matter and mind leads to an impasse, we can change our concepts of both, revising both radically enough to show how consciousness can arise from the brain. McGinn's claim, however, is that the concepts that block the way to a solution are not simply culturally and therefore contingently constrained, so that with sufficient energy and ingenuity we could transcend them. Rather, he argues, they are constrained by our very natures, the way we are: "the enemy lies within the gates" (*PC*, 19).

> Our concepts of matter and consciousness are constrained, respectively, by our faculties of perception and introspection—and concepts so constrained will not be capable of explaining the psychophysical link. Our perceptual access to material things, including the brain, sets limits on the way we can conceive of these things; and our introspective access to consciousness sets limits on the way we can conceive of it. We need a manner of conception that abstracts radically away from these two fundamental ways of apprehending the world, but we simply have no such manner at our cognitive disposal. We have no faculty that would enable us to form concepts of consciousness and the brain capable of solving the mind-body problem. (*PC*, 120f.)

Now that we have before us McGinn's analysis, must we not ask a question similar to Hegel's question about what kind of reason Kant was employing in diagnosing the permanent limitations of human reason? Given all that human imaginative reason can do, including this type of analysis of its own limitations, must we not wonder whether we are as constitutionally incapable of radical conceptual innovation as McGinn has proposed? I would at least think that we should tentatively accept an alternative construal—that McGinn's analysis does indeed tell us about strong constitutional *tendencies* that people in all cultures have had, which have made an ontological dualism between matter and consciousness a quite widespread "folk philosophy"; but that these universal tendencies have been strengthened by contingent historical developments in the West, especially from the seventeenth century to the present. According to this analysis, the "enemy within the gates" would be one that has in part been put there by our ancestors, and to whose presence we have continued to acquiesce. According to McGinn's *wholly* constitutional analysis, "given the way we form our concepts, we cannot free ourselves of the conceptions that make the problem look insoluble" (*PC*, 29). But with the alternative analysis, which combines constitutional tendencies with historical accidents, so that the problem of the "we" we are diagnosing is not simply human nature as such but a cultural exaggeration of universal tendencies, we might be able, with effort, to break free from inadequate concepts of both brain and mind. We should at least explore this possibility.

And indeed, having referred to Kant, we can recall that McGinn himself discovered a passage in which Kant suggested a solution (although McGinn declined the assistance), which we can construe in the following way: Communion between mind and body seems impossible because they seem to be different in kind. On the one hand, the mind knows itself to have experience, which essentially has temporal extensiveness (duration) but does not seem to be spatial, at least not in the sense in which the objects of sensory perception (especially vision and touch) seem to be spatial. On the other hand, these objects of sensory perception, while being spatial, show no sign of being temporal, in the sense of requiring some minimal duration in order to be what they are;* and if they have no inner duration, they could not conceivably have experience. However, this appearance of absolute opposition may be mere appearance, due to different modes of apprehension. Through what is sometimes called our "inner sense," we know our own minds as they are *in* themselves. And what we know thereby is that they are something *for* themselves (which is the basis for an ethic of treating all other people as ends in themselves). Through our "outer senses," however, we are knowing not ourselves but other things. We are, therefore, not knowing them from within, by identity, but from without: We are knowing them *as they appear to us from without*. Not only that, we do not even know them from without directly, but indirectly, through a very complicated bodily sensory system. (I leave aside the question whether this realistic interpretation of the body is consistent with Kant's general interpretation of the physical world.) Accordingly, we need not assume that our purely spatial and externalistic conceptions of these objects exhaust what they are in themselves. In particular, we need not assume that they are devoid of internal duration. And, if they have an inside, with duration, then this would need to be "filled" with something. The clue to what this is can come from our knowledge of our own mind, which is the one part of the world that we know from within. By analogy, in other words, we can suppose that what outer objects are in themselves is analogous to what we are in ourselves: experiencing things. *In* themselves they are, like our minds, something *for* themselves. (This insight, carried through, could have led Kant to an ecological ethic.) The apparent heterogeneity between mind and body is, accordingly, mere appearance, so that it constitutes no problem to intercommunion. We do not have to ask how an *en soi* and a *pour soi* can relate. The only problem, Kant concludes, is how to understand enduring experiencing things (which he called "substances") such that mutual influence is conceivable.

*See fn., p. 49, above.

The question of how much of this argument can be attributed to Kant (as he was in and for himself) I leave to Kant scholars. My point is that we can at least read into his suggestive comment the first step of a radical conceptual innovation that would overcome the mind-body problem. McGinn suggests that there is not "any road we can travel in forming our concepts of the brain" that would explain how consciousness could emerge from it (*PC*, 28). Perhaps Kant pointed out the entrance to that road, even if he himself did not take it.

McGinn's analysis of our introspection of our mind and our sensory perception of physical objects leads him to a reasonable conclusion: "We must therefore be getting a partial view of things" (*PC*, 28). But he thinks that we are stuck with our heterogeneous concepts about mind and body because we can derive conceptions about the mind only from introspection and concepts about the body only from sensory perception. Why should we assume, however, that we are *this* constrained? The suggestion I have read into Kant is that, beginning with what we know about the mind from introspection and assuming a pluralistically monistic form of realism, we could, through imaginative generalization, use this knowledge to fill in and thus correct our concepts of "physical objects." We could perhaps also, to take the suggestion a step further, use what we know about things through sensory perception to fill out and thus correct our concepts of our minds. I used "fill in" in the former case and "fill out" in the latter deliberately: What we do not learn from sensory perception of outer objects is what they are like inside, or even if they are like anything; what we do not learn about our minds by introspection is how they "appear" to others—how, for example, they exert causal influence on neurons. In any case, by taking what we know from our two approaches, we could thereby perhaps partially overcome the "partial view" of each, at least enough to see how they can commune with each other.

McGinn provides an opening to this possibility: "These two faculties—sense perception and introspection—have different *fields*, meaning by this that they take different kinds of object of apprehension. . . . (Alternatively, if we want to make room for some kind of monism, we can say that they present the same reality in different *ways*, from different perspectives.)" (*PC*, 61). After making the dualistic-sounding statement about "different kinds of object," McGinn notes parenthetically that we may want "some kind of monism." We certainly do: The regulative principles of realism, continuity, and naturalism seem to commit us to a pluralistic monism, in which there are multiple instances of one kind of actuality. This could be taken to mean that minds and neurons are of the same ontological type, so that we could use what we know of each (from introspection and perception, respectively) to enlarge our view of the other. But McGinn cannot adopt the approach I suggest, because he presupposes physicalism's *quantitative* meaning of monism, according to which mind and brain must somehow be numerically one. This is one of the dubious assumptions leading McGinn to the view that introspection and sensory perception both fall *hopelessly* short of discerning the true nature of their objects.

Consider how the situation looks to McGinn, given his assumption that the terms "mind" and "brain" finally refer to the same entity. The knowledge that the mind has of itself has to seem extremely superficial. I quoted earlier the passage in which McGinn says, "Events in the nervous system constitute the predominant causal background to events in consciousness, but all of that whirring background is concealed from introspection" (*PC*, 74). It would be easy to read this passage in an interactionist or at least epiphenomenalist sense, according to which the brain as one entity provides the "causal background" for the mind as another entity. But if mind and brain were one and the same entity, all of that "whirring background" would actually be part of the mind itself. This is what McGinn means in saying that introspection provides only the tip of the iceberg. (He does *not* mean, by contrast, that introspection knows so little of the mind because most of it is unconscious experience not open to conscious introspection; he rejects the idea of unconscious experience.) McGinn's meaning is reflected in an adjacent passage: "[Introspection] tells us nothing about the physical network in which our conscious states are embedded. . . . Introspective data do not (by themselves) provide us with information about the condition of our nervous system. Introspection does not deal in physical concepts" (*PC*, 73). From this perspective, we can see why McGinn says that introspection does not even give us the *essential nature* of the mind, let alone the whole truth about it. After all, if the mind is numerically one with the brain—and if the brain is known to be composed of insentient neurons— then introspection, in giving us conscious experience, is giving us very superficial stuff. "Superficial" is, indeed, the term McGinn uses. In rejecting the view of those eliminativists who think of "folk psychology" as a primitive theory employing inferential entities to provide underlying causal explanations, McGinn says, "Folk psychology is . . . not a naive and pitiful attempt to carve out the natural kinds and laws that obtain at the hidden level; its business is strictly superficial" (*PC*, 125). McGinn's criticism of folk psychology eliminators is on target. But McGinn "defends" introspective psychology only by saying that it is so superficial that it does not even provide the *essential nature* of the mind. This is why McGinn says that introspection provides an even less privileged access than does sensory perception with respect to giving us a true science of the mind/brain (*PC*, 79).

According to McGinn, to be sure, sensory perception provides only limited information. It does, at least when magnified, give us much that introspection does not, providing knowledge about "the underlying causal machinery," such as "the theory of the neuron and its electro-chemical processes" (*PC,* 75). But it does not, as we have seen, give us the slightest clue as to why the brain should have conscious experiences. That is, given the assumption that the brain and the mind are numerically one, so that it is correct to say, as most physicalists do, that "the brain is conscious," then conceptions based on sensory perception must leave us woefully ignorant of the true nature of the brain.

The reason, in short, that we cannot use concepts from either introspection or sensory perception to correct the partial view provided by the other, according to McGinn, is that *neither* view tells us about the *essential nature* of what anything is in itself. It is not, as my wishful-reading of Kant suggested, that introspection provides the essential nature of the mind, which could then be generalized to objects of sensory perception (such as brain neurons) as they are in themselves. Indeed, McGinn reverses Kant's suggestion, believing instead that if either approach comes closer to providing the essential nature of things, it is conceptualizing on the basis of sensory perceptions. For example, in an essay entitled "Consciousness and Space," McGinn says:

> I am presupposing here a robust form of realism about the natural world. The constraint to form our concepts in a certain way does not entail that reality must match that way. Our knowledge constitutes a kind of 'best fit' between our cognitive structure and the objective world; and it fits better in some domains than others. The mind is an area of relatively poor fit. (CS, 230)

The implication is that our sensory-based concepts of matter correspond to reality better than do our introspection-based concepts of consciousness.

We here see another crucial distinction between the agnosticism of Strawson and that of McGinn. Strawson, in asking whether conscious experience can be radically wrong about its own nature, grounds his claim on phenomenology, observing that, with regard to the what-it's-like-ness of experience itself, there is no basis for a distinction between appearance and reality. He concludes that insofar as the mind-body problem implies that we must be radically ignorant about something, that something must be the nature of matter. McGinn, by contrast, allows a purely speculative belief— that mind and brain are numerically identical—to distort the seemingly indubitable deliverances of a phenomenological analysis of experience. So, even though his own analysis of the conventional view of matter, showing it to be rooted in our spatializing sensory perception, could provide strong grounds for Strawson's radical agnosticism about the true nature of matter, McGinn concludes that the mind-body problem is overwhelmingly due to our radical ignorance about the nature of consciousness—which perhaps leads to impatience with views that suggest radically new ideas about matter.

McGinn's form of agnosticism, which implies a permanent inability to solve the mind-body problem, follows in part from his *lack* of agnosticism about the numerical relation between mind and brain. McGinn simply takes it for granted that these terms refer to one and the same entity (which is illustrated by the fact that of the unknown property that is postulated to account for the link between brain and consciousness, he says that "it cannot be a property of the brain and *not* a property of consciousness" [*PC*, 68]). Let us, however, tentatively assume the other possibility, that mind and brain are numerically *distinct* (which would be a possibly helpful thesis to explore, given that all of the problems distinctive of materialism in our earlier discussion were due to its numerical equation of mind and brain). In that case we could return to our suggestion built on Kant's cryptic comment: While it is true that sensory-based conceptions do not describe the essential natures of things—what they are in themselves as distinct from how they appear to us through our sensory apparatus—what we sometimes call introspection does give each of us, as Strawson says, the essential nature of one actuality in the world, our own mind. That is, we know that this actuality is experiential in nature.* In Berkeley's language, *to be*, for the mind, is *to perceive*. As will become clearer, I think of "perception" in a very broad sense: Besides not assuming most perception to be conscious, I also do not assume most of it to be sensory. For this double reason, I certainly agree that conscious introspection reveals only the tip of the iceberg (to use that externalist metaphor). But just as we can assume that the iceberg is ice all the way down, so that in knowing the tip we know the essential nature of the iceberg (although things get dark and sometimes frightening beneath the surface), so in knowing the superficial part of our experience we know the essential nature of our mind: We can assume that it is experience (devoid of the light of consciousness, of course) all the way down. (This notion, incidentally, implies Searle's antifunctionalist statement that "the mind consists of qualia, so to speak, right down to the ground" [*PC*, 20].) This is the interpretation I would put on McGinn's statement that "omniscience does not follow from inerrancy" (*PC*, 63): It is fully consistent with the recognition that we are *far* from omniscient about the contents and workings of our minds to hold that our direct knowledge by acquaintance—nay, stronger: by identity—of our mind is inerrant about its essential nature. At least this is true insofar as we take this to be *experience*, not *conscious* experience.

---

*Strawson says that "there is a sense in which we cannot be wrong about experience that has no parallel in the case of the nonexperiential" (*MR*, 103). The only difference between our views on this issue is that whereas I distinguish between *conscious* experience and experience as such, Strawson equates them (*MR*, 3), which would certainly make it more difficult to adopt the panexperientialist position that experience goes *all* the way down, to the most elementary units of nature.

That distinction points to a further dubious assumption behind McGinn's belief that there is an epistemically unbridgeable gap between mind and brain: Finding no metaphysical problem with the Cartesian intuition that he has inherited, he speaks of consciousness, rather than simply experience, as the stuff of the mind: "Logically, 'consciousness' is a stuff term, as 'matter' is; and I see nothing wrong, metaphysically, with recognizing that consciousness *is* a kind of stuff. At any rate, I shall persist with the intuitive use of the term 'consciousness' without fretting unduly over its proper interpretation" (*PC,* 60n). One can wonder, however, how much fretting might be *due,* given our location almost one hundred years not only after Freud but also after William James's article "Does 'Consciousness' Exist?" in which he denied its existence precisely in the sense of a stuff (suggesting instead that consciousness is a particular function of experience). In any case, to persist in thinking of consciousness as the stuff of the mind creates at least two problems with regard to the mind-body connection. On the one hand, it is arguably the mind's identification of itself with its *conscious* experience that creates the illusion of the mind's isolation from the world, about which McGinn rightly complains; more on this in the next chapter. On the other hand, thinking of consciousness (rather than experience) as the stuff of the mind provides us no notion that can be generalized to lower-level entities, so as fully to naturalize mind. I would agree with every rejecter of panpsychism that we cannot think of neurons, let alone molecules, as conscious. One of the reasons for preferring the term "pan-experientialism," as I said earlier, is that it less readily suggests the extension of *conscious* experience to all individuals. The relation between experience and consciousness will be discussed in the next chapter. For now I will stress the difference by saying that experience essentially involves *feeling,* not consciousness.*

According to McGinn's analysis, we have two approaches to trying to find the link between mind and brain. One is the "top-down strategy," in which we reason on the basis of concepts derived from introspection. The other is the "bottom-up strategy," in which we reason on the basis of conceptions derived from perception (*PC,* 60). McGinn's conclusion is that neither strategy gets very far toward the middle, so that an epistemically unbridgeable gap remains. We have seen that two dubious assumptions lie behind McGinn's conclusion that the top-down strategy does not take us

---

*It is interesting that Strawson, who also equates experience with *conscious* experience, says that the "problem of experience in its entirety" is raised by a worm, "if worms can feel" (*MR,* 83). He is absolutely right about the point he is making. But does his use of the language of "feeling" here not also suggest that although we can meaningfully and plausibly suppose that worms have experience of a sort (so that it's like something to be a worm), the attribution to them of *consciousness* would be less plausible?

very far down: the assumption that mind and brain are numerically identical and the assumption that the stuff or essence of the mind is consciousness. We now need to look at McGinn's bottom-up strategy, to see if it also contains a dubious assumption that prevents this approach from taking us very far up.

I have talked glibly about generalizing experience to the objects of sensory perception—not the objects qua perceived, of course, but as they are in themselves. McGinn's point, however, is that sensory perception gives us no basis whatsoever for such a move. Here we must recall McGinn's crucial point about our physical senses, that "they essentially present things in space with spatially defined properties." And, as McGinn rightly adds, "it is precisely *such* properties that seem inherently incapable of resolving the mind-body problem" (*PC*, 11). Given that point, plus his (correct) conceptual empiricist point that concepts to be meaningful must be based on perceptions, he concludes that we can have no concepts of the physical world that provide a link to conscious experience. Here is his fullest analysis:

> We can, it is true, extend our concepts some distance beyond [their perceptual] starting-points, but we cannot prescind from them entirely. . . . [O]ur concepts of the body, including the brain, are constrained by the way we perceive these physical objects; we have, in particular, to conceive of them as spatial entities essentially similar to other physical objects in space, however inappropriate this manner of conception may be for understanding how consciousness arises from the brain. . . . [I]t is precisely the perceptually controlled conception of the brain that we have which is so hopeless in making consciousness an intelligible result of brain activity. No property, however inferential the ascription, seems capable of rendering perspicuous how it is that damp grey tissue can be the crucible from which subjective consciousness emerges fully formed. (*PC*, 27)

In other words, the Cartesian definition of matter as consisting of spatial extensiveness is not arbitrary but is based on the fact that that is how sensory perception (especially vision) portrays the world to us: as spatially extended. If we can think of it only in such terms, however, we cannot attribute experience, even conceived as simple feeling, to it. This is why, McGinn would say, we cannot generalize experience from our introspection to outer objects of sensory perception. And, because we must interpret our brain in the same terms as we interpret all other objects of sensory perception, we cannot attribute experience to neurons either. Hence the permanent mystery: How can insentient neurons generate conscious experience?

Although this analysis seems exactly right, given its presuppositions, one of those presuppositions—that perception of the world through our external sensory organs is our only way of perceiving things beyond ourselves—

is arguably false, because it ignores two other types of perception: proprioception and nonsensory perception. I will begin with the former.

Sensory perception is of two types: perception of the world beyond the body, which originates in receptor cells called "exteroceptors," and perception of various parts of one's own body, which originates in internal receptor cells ("proprioceptors") of basically the same type. In one respect, these two types of sensory perception are the same: The information originates in receptor cells in various parts of the body and is conveyed to the brain by means of routes of nerve cells. In another respect, however, these two types of sensory perception are significantly different.

This difference is most obvious in relation to those proprioceptions that result in pain and pleasure. Such perceptions provide the basis for very different conceptions of the physical world than do our sensory perceptions, especially visual and tactile, of the extrasomatic world. For example, in feeling the pain in my back, I do, it is true, conceive the pain in spatial terms: I can say pretty clearly where the pain is and indicate, more or less clearly, the spatial extensiveness of the pain. But this twofold spatial nature (location plus extensiveness) of the pain is hardly its dominant feature: This dominating feature is that it is *pain,* that it hurts! We have, accordingly, another "property" aside from spatiality to attribute to bodily parts: We have to say, at least, that they are the kinds of things that can produce pain. And, having said that, it would not seem a great inferential leap to think of them as things that can *feel* pain. (After all, in thinking of a ball as something that can cause a perception of roundness, we suppose that the reason the ball can cause this perception is that it itself is round.) Of course, the leap *does* seem too great to most philosophers, inheritors as they are of an almost four-centuries-old distinction between primary and secondary (and sometimes tertiary) qualities. The primary qualities—which are really *quantities*—such as shape, are really out there, says this tradition, whereas secondary qualities—which really *are* qualities—such as colors, are not, being somehow created by the perceiving mind out of purely quantitative elements, such as wavelengths. Pains fit into the category of secondary (or, in some analyses, the even more mind-dependent *tertiary*) qualities.

There are at least two prima facie reasons to entertain the possibility that this distinction is false. First, there is the well-known but usually ignored fact that the clear-thinking Bishop Berkeley argued persuasively that so-called primary and secondary qualities are all in the same epistemic boat, so that if the one category is mind-dependent, so is the other. The good bishop used this argument, to be sure, to bolster his idealist view of nature. Insofar as we cannot refute the argument but are convinced of the need for a realistic view of nature, we may need to consider the possibility that nature is *not* reducible to matter in motion with none but quantitative properties. The second reason to entertain dubiety about the primary-secondary distinction is that it is based precisely on the dualism of mind and matter that generated the mind-body problem in the first place. The fact that the problem has proven intractable, given the seventeenth-century distinction between the physical and the mental, is good reason to become skeptical of that very distinction, as Searle suggests. Part and parcel of that skepticism should be skepticism about the primary-secondary distinction based on that physical-mental distinction.

In any case, to employ the primary-secondary distinction to reject the possibility that bodily parts feel pain is circular, because it is to presuppose precisely the Cartesian intuition about matter that the panexperientialist, in saying that bodily parts feel pains, is denying. So, I ask the reader for a temporary suspension of disbelief (or, put otherwise, suspension of *belief*— in the Cartesian intuition) while the alternative hypothesis is sketched.

Let us assume, for the sake of entertaining a possible solution to the mind-body problem, that bodily cells feel pain and that *we* feel pain—unless an anesthetic, hypnotic trance, or some other inhibitor prevents it—because we perceive our bodily parts sympathetically. Let us, from the standpoint of this hypothesis, look back at McGinn's argument regarding perception-based conceptions. Here are the final two sentences of the lengthy passage quoted above:

> It is precisely the perceptually controlled conception of the brain that we have which is so hopeless in making consciousness an intelligible result of brain activity. No property, however inferential the ascription, seems capable of rendering perspicuous how it is that damp grey tissue can be the crucible from which subjective consciousness emerges fully formed. (*PC*, 27)

Now that we have distinguished between two kinds of sensory perception, this passage no longer seems so self-evident. What if, even with regard to sensory perception, we have *two* types of "perceptually controlled" conceptions—those based on sensory perceptions of external objects and those based on perceptions of our bodily states? From the second type, we have seen, we can make the not-too-wildly-inferential ascription of pain-feelings to at least some bodily cells. This would mean, of course, that bodily cells experience. We would no longer have to wonder, accordingly, how insentient neurons could give rise to our conscious experience: They could not; but we, fortunately, have sentient ones.

At this point, however, an obvious objection arises: How can we conceive of cells as having experience of any kind, such as feeling pains and pleasures? More pointedly, given the fact that cells have no sensory organs, how could we conceive of some cells as somehow perceiving the pain of other cells and then passing along this pain-feeling to still other cells higher up in the nervous system? The assumption behind this argument, of course, is that our own perceptual experience is essentially sensory perception. Given this assumption, the analogical extension of the notion of experience to entities devoid of sensory organs would be implausible.

The assumption that perception is essentially sensory perception, however, is dubious. As I pointed out in chapter 5, there is good evidence for extrasensory perception, in the sense of telepathy and clairvoyance. Also, one can argue, as I will in the following chapter, that memory should be considered a form of nonsensory perception, in which one moment of experience, understood as an actual entity, directly perceives ("prehends") a prior moment of experience, understood as another actual entity. For now, however, I will speak only of a third example: our direct perception of our own brains. Sensory perception, whether of the external or proprioceptive sort, presupposes this kind of nonsensory perception. For example, in seeing a tree by means of my eyes, the information about the tree is gathered by the exteroceptors in my eyes and then transmitted to my brain. But all of this would do me no good unless I had the power to perceive my brain. I am not referring to the kind of perception of the brain with which McGinn deals, in which one, by means of a mirror, can see one's own brain after a surgeon has opened up one's skull. That external sensory perception of one's own brain from without presupposes the internal perception of the brain to which I refer.

I do not, of course, have any sensory organs between my experience (my mind at the moment) and my brain with which to *see* it: I simply perceive it in a direct, nonsensory way. By analogy, some philosophers have recognized that all bodily action, through which one acts on the outer world, presupposes a direct, "basic action," in which one acts directly on the brain (given an interactionist view). Likewise, we can say, all sensory perception, which is indirect, presupposes a "basic perception," in which one directly perceives the brain. This nonsensory perception, in being presupposed by sensory perception, is more basic than it. If our basic form of perception is nonsensory, the idea that it cannot be generalized to individuals devoid of sensory organs is not self-evident. That it *can* be generalized will be argued in the following chapter.

As a materialist, of course, McGinn might well resist talk of the mind as *perceiving* its brain, because this talk seems, by presupposing that the mind is distinct from the brain, to beg the question. But McGinn himself speaks of the brain as *causing* conscious experience ("Brain states cause conscious states, we know" [*PC*, 6]). And perception can be understood as simply the reverse end of the causal relation: My perception of the tree is, from the tree's end, the result of its causal influence on me. So, if the brain exerts causation on the mind, then the mind perceives the brain. Insofar as the body in general exerts causal influence on the mind, the mind perceives the body. In any case, we are trying out the hypothesis that mind and brain *are* numerically distinct, so that this talk of the mind's (nonsensory) perception of its brain is not ruled out in principle.

By refusing the equation of perception with external sensory perception, accordingly, the bottom-up strategy will take us up far enough to meet the descent of the top-down strategy in the middle of the supposed gap. By combining reasonable inferences from proprioception and evidence for nonsensory perception, we can say that mind and body have *experience* in common, with experience understood fundamentally in terms of *feeling*, not consciousness. This feeling-experience is the hidden feature that McGinn seeks—the feature *partially* hidden by introspection, with its tendency to focus on consciousness, and *totally* hidden by sensory perception of the extrasomatic world. By challenging the equation of perception with external sensory perception, we can carry out the solution at which Kant hinted.

Mention of Kant, however, reminds us that we have moved too fast. We have overlooked the key point of McGinn's analysis, that the purely spatial cannot be thought to have experience of any sort. What reason do we have for thinking of the objects constituting nature as having some kind of temporal extensiveness, as having duration analogous to that of our own experience, so that we can think of them also as having some degree of experience? Our bodily parts are analogous to physical things outside the body; in fact, everything inside was once outside. We cannot assume a magical transformation on entry (and another one on exit). What good reason is there to think of the basic units of nature in general as having temporal as well as spatial extensiveness?

One argument is from the very fact that our bodily members do seem, as argued above, to be capable of experience. This provides a reason in itself for supposing that they, internally, have duration, insofar as experience and duration seem to presuppose each other. Then, from the fact that things within and without the body must be similar, we can infer that all natural units are temporal as well as spatial units. As Whitehead has argued,

> It is the accepted doctrine in physical science that a living body is to be interpreted according to what is known of other sections of the physical universe. This is a sound axiom; but it is double-edged. For it carries with it the converse deduction that other sections of the universe are to be interpreted in accordance with what we know of the human body. (*PR*, 119)

Whitehead's statement in context applies the point to the notion of causation (which will be discussed in the next chapter). But we can use it also to argue for the idea that nature in general is composed of spatiotemporal units.

However, if this were the only reason to ascribe inner duration to natural units, with everything else pointing to the physical world as purely spatial, it would carry little weight. This could have seemed the case in Kant's time, so that there would have been little basis for carrying out his suggestion systematically. Then as well as now, of course, there is another consideration: If we take a relative (rather than absolute) view of time, according to which time arises from relations among things, then those "things" must be events that have a temporal as well as spatial dimension, or we would have a purely spatial, timeless world. Unless the world is composed of units with a temporal dimension, in other words, it is hard to see why time exists: A billion trillion times nothing is still nothing. Of course, many thinkers, including Einstein, *have* thought of the world as essentially timeless, considering time an illusion. One of many problems with this view, however, is that we all in practice presuppose the reality of time. (As Einstein admitted, time is a *stubborn* illusion.)* Also, it is hard to see how an essentially timeless world could generate even the illusion of time. We can understand, however, that this consideration would not have weighed heavily on Kant: Part of his soft-core common sense was traditional (supernaturalistic) theism, according to which God, who is the ultimate reality, is essentially timeless, which implies that reality as such is essentially timeless. With the shift to a naturalistic worldview, however, there no longer exists this basis for overriding our hard-core commonsense presupposition as to the ultimate reality of time. We must, accordingly, think of the world's ultimate units such that time as we presuppose it could be derived from them.[10] This gives us a second reason for ascribing duration to the fundamental individuals of the world (and, of course, any *compound* individuals formed out of them).

Advances in science that had not been provided by the science of Kant's time provide further reasons for thinking of the fundamental units of nature as temporal. A third reason is that quantum physics suggests that there is a minimal time period for events. The world as infinitely divisible temporally is an abstraction. In the actual world, there is no "nature at an instant." It seems to take a certain minimum time to be. This suggests that the ultimate units of nature are durations, that is, that they have a temporal as well as a spatial dimension.[11]

This same conclusion, that nature is composed of spatiotemporal events, is suggested by relativity physics as well, with its notion that space and time are inseparable, so that we must speak of space-time, or time-space.[12] If this is so, and if we hold a relative view of both space and time, then it would

*Einstein's statement, "For us believing physicists, the distinction between past, present and future is only an illusion, even if a stubborn one," is quoted in Banesh Hoffman (with Helen Dukas), *Albert Einstein: Creator and Rebel* (New York: Viking Press, 1972), 258.

seem that the units from which space-time are derived must be temporal as well as spatial. This is a fourth reason for ascribing some minimal duration—which could be less than a billionth of a second—to the ultimate units of the world.

To the degree that this is a plausible hypothesis, it is no longer unthinkable that these units would enjoy experience, to at least some slight degree. A brief duration can be taken as a sign of a slight experience.

The method employed thus far has been that of taking what we know from our own experience—which is precisely that we *have* (or *are*) experience—and then asking whether there are bases for using this knowledge, by means of imaginative generalization, to fill in those conceptions of the physical world that are based on sensory perception alone. This is only half of the complete method, however, which is that of mutual enrichment. The other half is to take what we know of nature through sensory perception and natural science to fill out and even modify our introspection-based conceptions of our own minds. If we think, for example, of physical things, such as electrons, as composed of rapidly repeating momentary units with very brief durations,* as suggested above, then we could generalize this idea to think of the mind as composed of a series of momentary experiences, rather than simply as a single, enduring actuality, numerically one through time. This might be one way in which we would come to see conceptions based on introspection alone as partially illusory, rather than privileged in all respects. Soft-core common sense could be modified in the light of science, as long as we honor whatever hard-core commonsense intuition of self-identity through time is shared by all of us (including, for example, Buddhists). I will develop further in the next chapter this twofold method of mutual enrichment and modification.

My conclusion in this section is that in spite of the brilliance of McGinn's analysis, he has, because of dubious assumptions, been premature to deny

---

*It might be objected that quantum physics gives us no basis for thinking of electrons and other subatomic entities in this or any other way. This is true of the dominant, orthodox (Copenhagen) interpretation. But now, thanks to David Bohm and Basil J. Hiley's *The Undivided Universe* (1993), we have, as the subtitle indicates, *an ontological interpretation of quantum theory*, which does describe the behavior of particles apart from our observations of them. This interpretation, furthermore, is consistent with the Whiteheadian view of particles. The fact that Bohm's realistic interpretation has finally been presented in a reasonably complete form is, incidentally, relevant to Strawson's point that we need a satisfactory understanding "of the relation between experiential and nonexperiential phenomena" (*MR*, 87). A possible objection to this claim, he points out, could be based on the observation "that quantum mechanics, often called the most successful theory in the history of science, notoriously fails to provide us with the feeling that we can really explain or understand why things happen as they do at the quantum level" (*MR*, 87). The desire for this kind of understanding was precisely what motivated Bohm and Hiley to present their ontological interpretation (*UU*, 1–5).

that there is "any road we can travel" that will lead us to the clue to unsnarling the world-knot. I have been implying, in fact, that Whitehead has already blazed the trail.

It is not surprising that many philosophers today do not know of Whitehead's pioneering work, given the almost complete disregard of his philosophy, with its radical conceptual innovations, during a period when Anglo-American philosophy was largely content with either the conceptions of "ordinary English" (which was, in fact, heavily shaped by Cartesian-Newtonian intuitions) or the conceptions of a more-or-less sophisticated scientism. Given this contentment, Whitehead was ahead of his time. But now that this dual contentment is dissipating, in large part because of the intractability of the mind-body problem to either approach, philosophers who were not introduced to Whitehead by their contented professors may want to take a look. A large percentage of each of Whitehead's books in his last (American, metaphysical) period, from *Science and the Modern World* to *Modes of Thought*, can, in fact, be described as sustained reflections on the mind-body problem.* Prior to this metaphysical period, he had written what he called the philosophy of natural science, by which he meant trying to understand nature without taking mind into consideration.** Having decided that this project could not finally succeed, he moved to a metaphysical approach, which meant including the human mind in the overall description. His whole enterprise, in other words, was to naturalize the mind. His ideas were partly based on the works of others: Bergson, for example, made the breakthrough of overcoming the dualism of individuals with and without duration;*** and James ultimately came, more or less clearly, to see the enduring mind as a series of momentary drops of experience. But the position was developed most fully and adequately by White-

*Whitehead's books in this period, in order of appearance, are *Science and the Modern World* (1925), *Religion in the Making* (1926), *Symbolism: Its Meaning and Effect* (1927), *Process and Reality* (1929), *The Function of Reason* (1929), *Adventures of Ideas* (1933), and *Modes of Thought* (1938). Another volume, *Essays in Science and Philosophy* (1947), is, as the title suggests, a collection of his essays.

**The books in this earlier period of Whitehead's thought were *The Organisation of Thought* (1917), *An Enquiry Concerning the Principles of Natural Knowledge* (1919), *The Concept of Nature* (1920), and *The Principle of Relativity* (1922). *The Aims of Education*, published in 1929, also contains essays from this earlier period. Whitehead's distinction between the "philosophy of natural science," which is limited to nature as that which we know through sensory perception, and "metaphysics," which "embraces both perceiver and perceived," is found in *The Concept of Nature*, 28.

***For an account of Bergson's overcoming of his early dualism between inner duration and outer spatiality, see Pete A. Y. Gunter, "Henri Bergson," in Griffin et al., *Founders of Constructive Postmodern Philosophy*, 133–63, esp. 135–41.

head, with some further refinements made by Hartshorne. I will spell out the position in more detail in the following chapters, giving special attention to the question of consciousness, the way in which the "compound individual" provides a conception of a part-whole relation that is unlike sensory-based physical conceptions, and how this conception allows for freedom of action.

EIGHT

Matter, Consciousness, and the Fallacy of Misplaced Concreteness

The crux of the mind-body problem is that, given what is assumed to be the scientific conception of nature and therefore the human body, including the brain, it is impossible to understand how our conscious experience, which we know exists, could arise out of the body, and also how this experience could have the dual capacity for self-determining freedom and for employing this freedom in directing the body, which we all presuppose in practice. We are confronted by a paradox: What we in one sense know to be the case seemingly cannot be. The solution to be suggested here is based on Whitehead's proposal that "the paradox only arises because we have mistaken our abstraction for concrete realities" (*SMW*, 55).

Whitehead's statement occurs in the midst of his historical-philosophical examination of the effects on modern Western thought of its "acceptance of the [seventeenth-century] scientific cosmology at its face value" (*SMW*, 17). What was accepted at "face value" was "scientific materialism," which "presupposes the ultimate fact of an irreducible brute matter, or material, spread throughout space in a flux of configurations," material that is "senseless, valueless, purposeless . . . following a fixed routine imposed by external relations which do not spring from the nature of its being" (*SMW*, 17). The view of nature articulated by this "scientific materialism," which is still widely presupposed, lies at the root of the mind-body problem—a fact illustrated by Searle's statement of the problem: "We think of ourselves as conscious, free, mindful, rational agents in a world that science tells us consists entirely of mindless, meaningless physical particles" (*MBS*, 13). This view of nature, Whitehead suggests, results from "the fallacy of misplaced concreteness."

Whitehead connects his own philosophical reconstruction, which is devoted to explaining and overcoming this fallacy, directly to the mind-body problem:

> The living organ of experience is the living body as a whole. . . . In the course of [its] physical activities human experience has its origin. The plausible interpretation of such experience is that it is one of the natural activities involved in the functioning of such a high-grade organism. The actualities of nature must be so interpreted as to be explanatory of this fact. (*AI*, 225)

We need, in other words, a philosophical cosmology that explains the fact that our minds seem to be fully natural. The reason a cosmology based on scientific materialism cannot provide such an explanation is that the abstraction on which this materialism is based involves precisely the removal of mind from nature. The science that has provided the most help toward a reinterpretation of the actualities of nature, Whitehead suggests, is physiology, because "the effect of physiology was to put mind back into nature" (*SMW*, 148). Whitehead is not naive: He knows that physiologists "are apt to see more body than soul in human beings" (*AI*, 189). What he means is that physiology has had the effect of overcoming the dualism of mind and body formulated by Descartes and Locke and that overcoming this dualism will require us to reconceive the nature of the body as well as the mind.

In this chapter I lay out the various kinds of evidence and argument employed by Whitehead in justifying his reconstrual of both mind and body. Because it contains my answer to the question of the relation of "matter" and "consciousness," and because this answer will be presupposed in the following chapter (on freedom), this is the key chapter in the book. Unfortunately, however, it is also the most difficult one. There are three reasons for this difficulty. First, the mind-body problem is inherently a difficult one, as more than three centuries of discussion have demonstrated. Second, this chapter is where the radical conceptual innovation called for by several thinkers, and promised in the introduction, is encountered. Now, it is one thing to call formally for radical reconceptualization; it is something quite else to encounter an example of it in which deeply ingrained ways of thinking are challenged, new words (such as *prehension*) are employed, and old words (such as *feeling, physical,* and *mental*) are given new meanings. One will probably find it difficult to keep the meanings straight, and the new way of looking at things may seem so odd that one will wonder if it is worth the effort. Third, this chapter's argument is developed in the form of an exposition of Whitehead's thought, and I quote rather extensively from Whitehead's own statements, which sometimes, especially when containing technical terms and taken out of context, are not as clear as one might like. I use this method, in spite of the added difficulty it creates, because one of my purposes is to show that, although this fact has not been widely appreciated (even among Whitehead scholars), Whitehead's philosophy can best be read as an extended solution to the mind-body problem. Also, exactly what the various elements in his solution are, and how they fit together, have not been widely understood (again, even among Whitehead scholars), so it is necessary to show, by means of extensive quotation, that the points I make really are Whitehead's points. I hope thereby to contribute not only to a viable solution to the mind-body problem but also to a much wider appreciation of the power and relevance of Whitehead's thought, now that philosophy is emerging from its antimetaphysical slumbers.

Before moving to the heart of this chapter, which is an exposition of Whitehead's new understanding of both mind and body, I need to discuss the fallacy that he sees as lying at the root of modernity's mind-body problem.

I. THE FALLACY OF MISPLACED CONCRETENESS

What is common to all forms of the fallacy of misplaced concreteness is the "error of mistaking the abstract for the concrete" (*SMW*, 51)—of assuming an abstraction from a concrete reality to be the totality. The version of this error most germane to our topic is that of assuming nature as it actually is to be composed of matter understood as having "simple location." For a bit of matter to be "simply located" would mean that it could properly be said to be right *here* in space and time in a way that required no essential reference to other regions of space-time (*SMW*, 49). In other words, the concrete units of nature would have no essential reference either to the past or to the future.

This notion of nature creates obvious difficulties. As Hume pointed out, it makes the justification for scientific induction difficult.

> For [Whitehead says], if in the location of configurations of matter throughout a stretch of time there is no inherent reference to any other times, past or future, it immediately follows that nature within any period does not refer to nature at any other period. Accordingly, induction is not based on anything which can be observed as inherent in nature. (*SMW*, 51)

Thinkers in the early modern period were not bothered by this fact, because they held that matter obeyed rigorous laws imposed by its creator; even Darwin retained a deistic form of that belief. But what is the justification for induction in a naturalistic framework? It is freeloading to keep the imposition while rejecting the Imposer. It seems that we are again presupposing something in practice for which orthodox theory provides no basis. Also, if nature's units have no reference to the past, our own memory, given the assumption that we are fully natural, would be difficult to explain (*SMW*, 51).

A second feature of the materialistic view of the concrete units of nature, besides simple location, is the notion that they can exist at an *instant*, in the technical sense of an idealized slice in time completely devoid of duration. According to this view, "if material has existed during any period, it has equally been in existence during any portion of that period. In other words, dividing the time does not divide the material" (*SMW*, 49), which means that "the lapse of time is an accident, rather than of the essence, of the material. . . . The material is equally itself at an instant of time" (*SMW*, 50). There is, accordingly, no inner motion, no internal becoming; the only kind of motion ascribable to the units of nature is locomotion, motion through space. Combining this second feature with the first, we get the notion of the "simple location of instantaneous material configurations" (*SMW*, 50).

A third feature of this view of matter is that because the concrete units of nature are assumed to have no inner duration, they are assumed to have no intrinsic reality whatsoever, which means that they are assumed not to have any intrinsic *value*, not to be things that exist for their own sakes. They are "vacuous actualities" (*PR*, 167), meaning actualities totally devoid of experience. "Nature is thus described as made up of vacuous bits of matter with no internal values, and merely hurrying through space" (*MT*, 158).

According to this view, the units of nature, being completely timeless, are totally different from our conscious experience as we know it immediately. We have memory, whereas natural units are said to have no reference to the past. We experience a present duration, in which we enjoy intrinsic value and make choices among possible values, whereas the reality of the units of nature is said to be exhausted by their outer features. Finally, our present experience, with its purposes, includes an anticipation of the future, whereas nothing analogous is said to occur in the units of nature. Our experience is temporal through and through; the units of nature are purely spatial.

The idea that our experience could arise out of natural units thus conceived is indeed paradoxical. But this paradox only arises, Whitehead says, because we have committed the fallacy of misplaced concreteness. Employing Bergson's term to express the nature of the error involved, he says that we tend to "spatialize" the objects of sensory perception (*SMW*, 50; *PR*, 209). This tendency is so strong because it arises from the conjunction of at least three factors: (1) We cannot perceive contemporary events while they are becoming; we can perceive events only when they are past, after their internal becoming is finished. (2) Objects of sensory perception are aggregational societies of large numbers of individuals and, as such, *are* predominantly spatial entities. (3) Conscious sensory perception itself spatializes its data, removing in the process any inherited affective tone. The meaning of these three points will be filled out in the ensuing discussion;

for now, the point is the old one of being suspicious of appearances. Modern philosophy, in stressing the illusory nature of sensory appearances, has congratulated itself on having fulfilled its duty to be suspicious by distinguishing between primary and secondary qualities while accepting unquestioningly the deeper illusion: the notion of instantaneous bits of matter simply located in space (which lay behind the distinction between primary and secondary qualities). Whitehead is much more suspicious than McGinn of the conception of matter based on spatializing sensory perceptions.

Philosophy's task, Whitehead suggests, is to be "the critic of abstractions." By playing this role, it can be helpful to society, including society's science (*SMW,* 59, 87). For a period, of course, society in general and science in particular were not interested in this help, thanks to the "narrow efficiency" of the scheme of ideas based on scientific materialism. That is, this scheme of ideas was extremely successful in directing attention to, and getting relevant knowledge about, "just those groups of facts which, in the state of knowledge then existing, required investigation" (*SMW,* 17). This scheme of ideas was *efficient* precisely because it was *narrow,* suitable only for a particular range of facts that needed to be considered first, namely, the "simplest things" (*MT,* 154). The great success of this method made it impervious to philosophical criticism, such as that of Berkeley and Hume (*SMW,* 59, 66). Because of "its expulsion by science from the objectivist sphere of matter," philosophy "retreated into the subjectivist sphere of mind," thereby losing "its proper role as a constant critic of partial formulations" (*SMW,* 142).

Now, however, Whitehead says, this scientific materialism, with its abstractions, has become too narrow for science itself, "too narrow for the concrete facts which are before it for analysis. This is true even in physics, and is more especially urgent in the biological sciences" (*SMW,* 66).

Whitehead's attempt to provide a "wider basis for scientific thought" (*SMW,* 67) has, of course, been largely ignored. Like previous philosophical critics of the abstractions that the scientific community has inherited from the dualists of the seventeenth century, Whitehead has until now been left crying in the wilderness. However, the present attempt to develop a science of mind or consciousness, which requires putting mind back into nature, provides the context in which Whitehead's analysis of misplaced concreteness may get a hearing. The attempt to produce a fully naturalistic science of mind makes abundantly obvious—even more so than does biology, including physiology—that the received ideas are "too narrow for the concrete facts which are before [science] for analysis." This is the recognition behind the dissatisfaction of Madell, the perplexity of Nagel, the agnosticism of Strawson, and the pessimism of McGinn, Robinson, and Campbell. The basic reason for the problem, as these thinkers more or less clearly recognize, is the one Whitehead gave—that this scheme of ideas "provides none of the elements which compose the immediate psychological experiences of mankind. Nor does it provide any elementary trace of the organic unity of a whole" (*SMW,* 73).

Whitehead bases his criticism of these abstractions, as well as his own proffered replacements, on the conviction that although the tendency to spatialize the objects of sensory perception is a very general tendency, it is not, as McGinn's analysis seems to suppose, an inherent necessity of the intellect (*SMW,* 51; *PR,* 209). He rejects the idea that "the abstractions of science are irreformable," offering his own program of reform "in the interest of science itself" (*SMW,* 83).

Besides hindering the progress of science, Whitehead says, the fallacy of misplaced concreteness, resulting in the idea of instantaneous matter with simple location, has been "the occasion of great confusion in philosophy" (*SMW,* 51). This confusion has not been limited, however, to the abstract view of matter. The usual notion of the mind, as consisting essentially of consciousness and distinctively mental operations, is also a high abstraction (*SMW,* 58). This twofold abstraction lies behind the reason that neither the top-down strategy nor the bottom-up strategy, as described by McGinn, could go very far toward overcoming the gap between matter and mind. Closing the apparent gap requires overcoming both parts of the twofold abstraction. That is, although my Whiteheadian approach agrees with Strawson that the *primary* reason for the intractability of the mind-body problem has been the received view of the physical body, not, as the majority view holds, the received notion of conscious experience, my approach holds that this notion of consciousness shares some of the blame—partly because it contributes significantly to the false view of the body.

The mind-body problem has been generated, Whitehead suggests, because the bits of matter that enter into scientific description, as well as the conscious minds thought to be doing the observing and describing, are entities "of a high degree of abstraction" resulting from "a process of constructive abstraction" (*SMW,* 52, 58). Unlike extremists on this point, Whitehead does not say that the very notion of matter is a complete fiction, created out of whole cloth, with no correspondence to reality. Nor does he, unlike other extremists, say this about consciousness. Rather, he says, " 'matter' and 'consciousness' both express something so evident in ordinary experience that any philosophy must provide some things which answer to their respective meanings" (*SMW,* 143). To speak of them as abstractions is to say that, rather than being simply fictions, they are "simplified editions of immediate matters of fact" (*SMW,* 52). Overcoming the twofold abstractness of *vacuous bits of matter* and *consciousness as the stuff of mind* can be described as the central purpose of Whitehead's philosophy.

The fallacious view of matter resulting from misplaced concreteness, Whitehead believes, can be overcome by starting from the bottom, with physics, or at the top, with human psychology, supplemented by physiology. The "organic realism" toward which he is heading (*PR*, 309) could also be reached, he says, by beginning in the middle, with biology, which most readily suggests the concept of *organism* in place of mechanism (*SMW*, 41, 103) and which, with its doctrine of evolution, demands a doctrine of elementary units that are capable of evolution (which the aboriginal stuff of the materialistic philosophy is not [*SMW*, 107]). But he devotes most of his attention to psychological and physiological studies of human beings and to physics, reporting that he in fact arrived at his own convictions by means of an analysis of fundamental notions in physics (*SMW*, 152). Part of what he means can be learned from chapters 1 through 10 of *Science and the Modern World* or, more briefly, from chapter 7 of *Modes of Thought*.

Developments in modern physics, he argues in these chapters, have undermined all the elements on which the materialistic view of nature was based. In the new view, in particular, "there is no nature at an instant" (*MT*, 146), and the notion of passive, enduring matter has been undermined: "Matter has been identified with energy, and energy is sheer activity" (*MT*, 137). Physics as such, to be sure, does not completely overcome the dualism between experience and matter, because of the limited interests of physics: "In physics there is an abstraction. The science ignores what anything is in itself," that is, its *intrinsic* reality, considering its entities only with regard to their *extrinsic* reality, and only certain aspects of this, namely, the modifications of spatiotemporal specifications of other things (*SMW*, 153).* Also, although the notion of energy as fundamental is an advance on the older idea of matter, "the physicists' energy is obviously an abstraction" (*SMW*, 36). But, in sweeping away the Cartesian-Newtonian "essential distinction between matter at an instant and the agitations of experience," the new

---

*I quoted earlier Strawson's statement that physics provides "what we think of as our best account of the nature of the physical" (*MR*, 47). Although Strawson's statement can be accepted as a sociological statement about the dominant view today in scientific and philosophical circles, from Whitehead's analysis it follows that we emphatically *should not* think of (present-day) physics as performing this role. To do so involves doubly misplaced concreteness, given the double abstraction involved in the conceptions provided by (present-day) physics. Of course, Strawson's statement does not mean that he himself is guilty of this fallacy, given his assertion that the account of the physical provided by present-day physics must, at a general level, be radically incomplete. It does seem, however, that by and large scientists and philosophers reinforce each other in this fallacy of misplaced concreteness: Most philosophers seem to think that the materialistic view of nature's ultimate units is vouchsafed by physics, whereas most physicists, generally being aware that, because they deal only with abstractions, they are not in a position to settle philosophical questions about the nature of nature, seem to assume that the materialistic view of their realm is based on good philosophical reasoning (whether of professional philosophers or of fellow physicists functioning as their own philosophers). If philosophy would, as Whitehead proposes, recover its role as the critic of abstractions, this vicious cycle might be broken.

physics now at least allows "bodily activities and forms of experience [to] be construed in terms of each other" (*MT*, 115). That is, we can add content to the notion of "bare activity" by fusing experience and nature (*MT*, 166).

The bottom-up approach from physics, however, can only take us part of the way. Bridging the apparent gap requires supplementation from the top-down approach. That approach, however, faces great obstacles, especially given inherited modes of thought. I turn now to this approach.

II. OVERCOMING MISPLACED CONCRETENESS WITH REGARD TO BOTH MATTER AND MIND

The abstract understandings of matter and mind are mutually supportive. Overcoming misplaced concreteness with regard to one will, therefore, require overcoming it with regard to the other. While this is true, it is also the case that the most important direction is from mind to matter. While overcoming the fallacious view of matter will help overcome the fallacious view of the mind, *getting a correct understanding of the human mind, especially the status of its sensory perception and consciousness, is essential for overcoming the erroneous view of matter.*

Whitehead's argument, especially how the various elements in it are related, is not always as clear as one might wish. A careful reading, however, reveals that there are six major dimensions of his contention that *we can generalize from our own experience to understand what matter is in itself.* I have organized this section in terms of these six dimensions.

A. The Status of Human Experience in Nature

The first dimension of Whitehead's argument is that we know our own experience, which we normally refer to as our "mind," as a fully natural actuality. Accordingly, what we know about it from within can be generalized to other actualities, which we know only from without.

Regarding the idea of the mind as fully natural: As we saw earlier, Whitehead accepts what he calls the "plausible interpretation" of human experience, according to which it is "one of the natural activities involved in the functioning of . . . a high-grade organism" (*AI*, 225). He even refers to it as the "total bodily event" (*SMW*, 73). By this he means not that it is simply the numerical sum of the bodily happenings but that it is the *experiential unification* of those happenings: "It has its own unity as an event" and exists as "an entity for its own sake" (*SMW*, 148). This fact, however, does not make it different in kind from other things: Whitehead takes it to be, except for its unusual complexity, "on the same level as all other events" (*SMW*, 73). He bases this conclusion not only on general philosophical and scientific considerations, such as the evolutionary origin of humans, but also on direct experience: "We seem to be ourselves elements of this world in the same sense as are the other things which we perceive" (*SMW*, 89).

Included in that statement is the notion that we are not only natural but also actual. To be an *actual* entity is to be able both to receive and to exert causation, and we directly experience both sides of the causal relation. On the one hand, a large portion of our experience is of the overwhelming degree to which our experiences, such as our pains, pleasures, and sensory perceptions, are caused by our bodies. On the other hand, as discussed in chapter 5 and more fully in chapter 9, we are also directly conscious of, and constantly presuppose, the efficacy of our experience for our bodily actions.

Taking, then, my own experience to be simply one of the many actualities in nature, a unique feature of it is that it is the one that I know from the inside, by identity. Referring to our experience, which unifies various bodily activities into a totality, Whitehead says that its knowledge is simply "the reflective experience of a totality, reporting for itself what it is in itself as one unit occurrence" (*SMW*, 148). Because I perceive myself in this unique way, I may tend to think of myself as different in kind from the other things I perceive, but this conclusion need not follow: "The private psychological field is merely the event considered from its own standpoint" (*SMW*, 150). Whitehead here expresses the point made by Kant in the passage discussed by McGinn.

On the assumption that my own experience is one natural actuality among others, no different in kind from others, my self-knowledge gives me an inside viewpoint on the nature of nature. I can then generalize what I thereby know about the nature of natural units to other such units (*SMW*, 73), taking due account, of course, of the fact that most of them (all except other human experiences, as far as we know) are evidently less complex.

This first dimension of Whitehead's argument will be met by two immediate objections. In the first place, our experience is constituted by consciousness and sensory perception. How can one possibly generalize our experience to amoebas, let alone to electrons? In the second place, even if the most primitive dimensions of human experience could be understood so as to make this suggestion not seem completely absurd, what empirical foothold do we have for making such a generalization? That is, what is there about our experience of physical things that could provide the slightest excuse for attributing even the lowliest type of experience to them? These are formidable questions. The remaining five points will be devoted to Whitehead's answers to them.

B. The Status of Consciousness in Human Experience

The first precondition for Whitehead's generalization from our own experience to the intrinsic reality of other things is his repudiation of the "implicit assumption of the philosophical tradition . . . that the basic elements of experience are to be described in terms of one, or all, of the three ingredients, consciousness, thought, sense-perception." In Whitehead's philosophy, "these three components are unessential elements in experience," belonging to a derivative phase of experience "if in any effective sense they enter at all" (*PR,* 36). I will deal with consciousness and thought in this point, saving sense perception for the next.

Whitehead specifically connects the derivative nature of consciousness with the program to generalize. Just after saying that, because of analogies, "bodily activities and forms of experience can be construed in terms of each other," he adds:

> This conclusion must not be distorted . . . [by] a distorted account of human experience. Human nature has been described in terms of its vivid accidents, and not of its existential essence. The description of its essence must apply to the unborn child, to the baby in its cradle, to the state of sleep, and to that vast background of feeling hardly touched by consciousness. Clear, conscious discrimination is an accident of human existence. It makes us human. But it does not make us exist. It is of the essence of our humanity. But it is an accident of our existence. (*MT,* 116)

This notion means that the unity of a moment of experience—the unity of reception, enjoyment, and action—is not dependent on conscious operations. With regard to a moment of experience's reception of causal influences from its body, Whitehead uses the term "prehension," which means a *taking account* that may or may not be conscious, or cognitive (*SMW,* 69). Whitehead is here pointing to the most basic form of the operation that lies behind what philosophers, following Franz Brentano, have called "intentionality," meaning "aboutness." By using the term "prehension," however, Whitehead means no merely external reference but the way an experience "can include, as part of its own essence, any other entity" (*AI,* 234). Accordingly, in speaking of a moment of our experience as a "unit occurrence," he says: "This total unity, considered as an entity for its own sake, is the prehension into unity of the patterned aspects of . . . the various parts of its body" (*SMW,* 148f.). One point of this description is "to edge cognitive mentality away from being the necessary substratum of the unity of experience" (*SMW,* 92), because that unity occurs prior to, and perhaps without the accompaniment of, consciousness or cognition.

> Cognition discloses an event as being an activity, organizing a real togetherness of alien things. But this psychological field does not depend on its cognition; so that this field is still a unit event as abstracted from its self-cognition. Accordingly, consciousness will be the function of knowing. But what is known is already a prehension of aspects of the one real universe. (*SMW,* 151)

As Whitehead put the point more concisely later, "consciousness presupposes experience, and not experience consciousness" (*PR*, 53). Whenever I speak of the mind, accordingly, the reader should understand this "process of unification," which Whitehead puts in place of "mind" as usually understood in philosophy (*SMW*, 69).

If consciousness is not the substratum of experience, what status does it have? In discussing this question, Whitehead refers to James's essay "Does 'Consciousness' Exist?" Whitehead accepts James's rejection of consciousness in the sense of an "aboriginal stuff . . . , contrasted with that of which material objects are made, out of which our thoughts of them are made" (*SMW*, 144; quoting James). He also accepts James's view that consciousness is a particular *function* of experience. (Note that consciousness is said to be a function of *experience* [which *is* an "aboriginal stuff," although *not* one "contrasted with that of which material objects are made"] rather than a function of the brain.) This function (as indicated in the extract above) is the function of *knowing* or (as indicated in the previous extract) the function of clear discrimination of the prehended objects.* Whitehead later works out this view more technically, defining consciousness as the "subjective form" of an "intellectual prehension." To clarify this definition will require a discussion of Whitehead's account of the phases of a moment of experience.

Whitehead also accepts James's idea (although he had evidently come to it independently) that one's experience, although it may seem like a "stream," consists literally of "buds or drops of perception," which "come totally or not at all" and in that sense are not divisible (*PR*, 68). Such a "drop" has the internal duration stressed by Bergson. Whitehead's technical term for these "drops" is "occasions of experience." This term involves a further specification of his other technical term for an actual entity, "actual occasion," which is used to indicate the temporal and spatial extensiveness of an actual entity (*PR*, 77). He thereby overcomes the dualism between physical entities as having spatial but not temporal extension and minds as having temporal but not spatial extension. His view is that *all* actual entities are actual occasions, thereby having both spatial and tempo-

---

*Given this distinction between distinctively *conscious* experience and experience itself (which essentially involves prehensions, which may not clearly discriminate among any of the prehended objects), it would be implausible in the extreme to attribute consciousness to amoebas, let alone atoms and electrons. Those philosophers who insist that all experience is conscious experience, such as McGinn, Seager, and Strawson, must be presupposing some very different notion of consciousness. Of course, there is no "right" way to define consciousness. However, it is puzzling that, so many decades after Freud, Jung, and others have provided extensive evidence of unconscious experience in human beings, many philosophers still define their terms in such a way that, as Strawson puts it, "the expression 'conscious experience' is, strictly speaking, pleonastic" (*MR*, 3).

ral extension, and that all actual occasions are occasions *of experience*. But that is to anticipate. For now the focus is on a *human* occasion of experience.

An occasion of experience consists entirely of prehensions. A prehension always involves—besides the occasion of experience that is the *subject* of the prehension—two aspects: (1) the *object* that is prehended and (2) the *subjective form* with which it is prehended. The most basic kind of subjective form is emotion, but there are other subjective forms as well. Every prehension has both an objective datum and a subjective form. There can be no "bare" grasping of an object, devoid of subjective feeling. (This position, incidentally, agrees with McGinn's view that "the subjective and the semantic are chained to each other" [*PC*, 30] so that there cannot be content without subjective experience.) Given this twofold meaning of prehension, Whitehead uses as a virtual synonym* the term "feeling," which suggests both that *something* is felt and that it is felt *with affective tone* (*AI*, 233). The term "feeling" suggests the operation of "passing from the objectivity of the data to the subjectivity of the actual entity in question" (*PR*, 40). Prehensions or feelings can be simple or they can be more or less complex, involving integrations of simpler feelings.[1]

An occasion of experience, although not divided or divisible in fact, can be divided intellectually into phases. Each phase has different types of prehensions. The first phase consists of *physical prehensions*, which are prehensions whose objects are *other actualities*, that is, other occasions of experience or groups thereof. To speak of a "physical feeling," accordingly, does not necessarily mean that the object is some portion of one's body. The only requirement is that the object be an *actuality*, not a mere possibility. Feelings of one's body are, however, of overwhelming importance in one's physical experience. (To speak of "physical experience," of course, is to challenge the dualistic use of these two words, which put them in opposition: To be "physical" was to be devoid of experience, whereas to have "experience" was to be mental.) In any case, all higher forms of experience presuppose physical experience.

Physical prehensions stand in contrast with *mental* (or *conceptual*) prehensions, in which the object is a possibility, an ideal or abstract entity (what is often called a "mental object," meaning an object of mental apprehension). These conceptual feelings occur in the second phase of an occasion of experience, being derivative from physical feelings. For example, out of a particular set of physical feelings originating from a red object, I may lift out redness as such, in abstraction from its exemplification in this particular object. The feeling of redness itself is a conceptual feeling; it is mentality.

---

*There is a technical difference, in that there are both *positive* prehensions, which are termed feelings, and *negative* prehensions, which exclude their data from feeling (*PR*, 23). For our purposes, however, the terms "prehension" and "feeling" can be used interchangeably.

Mentality, however, does not necessarily involve consciousness and, in fact, in this second phase *cannot*. (As we will see, consciousness cannot arise prior to the fourth phase.) Mentality is essentially *appetition*, either for or against some possible form of experience. It can be a blind urge to realize, or avoid, some form of feeling. In any case, conceptual feeling is derivative from physical feeling, with which experience originates.

This account of the relation between the physical and mental types of experience agrees, then, with Hume's claim that experience originates with "impressions," not "reflections"; but it disagrees with Hume's opinion that the *data* of these "impressions" are mere universals, such as sense data, rather than actual entities (*PR,* 160). For Whitehead, perceptual experience begins with the direct perception of other *actualities,* such as those comprising our bodies. This is the ground of our realism, our knowledge that we exist in a world of other actual things. This Whiteheadian view agrees, therefore, with McGinn's view that "physical facts [rather than "mental items" in the sense of abstract objects] are the basic kind of intentional object" (*PC,* 48n), except that what McGinn refers to as "mental states" would be included among the "physical facts," that is, among the actual entities that can be the objects of physical prehensions. For example, in "remembering" what I meant to say when I started this sentence a few seconds ago, my present occasion of experience is prehending some earlier occasions of experience. This perception of those prior "mental facts" is an example of a physical prehension, because the data are prior actualities, not mere possibilities. In any case, the basic point is that mental experience, which in its most sophisticated forms may *seem* to be completely detached from the actual world, always in fact arises out of physical experience,* with the body being the most powerful source of physical experience.

In the third phase of experience, there is an integration of prehensions from the first two phases, resulting in *propositional feelings,* which are prehensions whose objects are propositions. A proposition is a union of an actuality (from a physical feeling) and a possibility (from a conceptual feeling). An example is "this stone is grey." Of course, the conscious judgment that "this stone is grey" would belong to the fourth phase, in which intellectual feelings arise. But the proposition involving the stone could constitute part of the *content* of such a feeling. Other examples would be "my body is tired" and "my back is painful," both of which happen at the moment to be true. More important in a sense are untrue propositions, such as one in which I imagine my back as not painful. Such a counterfactual proposition, which may lead me to take remedial action, best illustrates the basic role of propositions in experience, which is to serve as lures for feel-

*This point is the basis for calling panexperientialism of this sort a species of "physicalism," which I do in chapter 10.

ing. (To serve as objects of "judgment" is simply a highly intellectualized version of this role.) This description of their role depends on the previous point that mentality is basically appetition: A proposition serves to lure its experiencer either toward or away from the conjoining of some particular possibility with some particular fact(s). Propositional feelings, then, are feelings in which such propositions are entertained.

This description of propositions as basically "lures for feeling," rather than as essentially objects of intellectual judgment, allows their functioning to be generalizable to nonhuman occasions of experience, by virtue of minimizing the sophistication of the mentality needed to entertain them. Even with this definition, however, propositional feelings in their full-fledged form could not be generalizable to the lowest types of occasions of experience. In a propositional feeling, the possibility, such as redness, is lifted up as such, that is, as a possibility, in abstraction from its presence in the immediate feeling. That operation takes considerable sophistication. Whitehead, accordingly, distinguishes propositional feelings in this full-fledged sense from "physical purposes," in which this abstraction from the present feeling is only latent.* In a physical purpose, the possibility embodied in the physical feeling is felt with blind appetition, either positive or negative. Even in human experience, most of the feelings in the third phase would seem to be mere physical purposes rather than full-fledged propositional feelings. In any case, "propositional feelings" should here be understood to include "physical purposes."

In the fourth phase, if it occurs, there is an integration of a propositional feeling (from the third phase) with primitive physical feelings (from the first phase). The result is an *intellectual feeling*. A peculiarity of intellectual feelings is that their subjective forms involve consciousness. One species of intellectual feelings, in fact, is that of "conscious perceptions" (*PR*, 266f.). But intellectual feelings also include judgments, which would cover most of what is usually meant by "thought," including that kind of thought that we are inclined to call knowing or cognition.

Whitehead's point is that consciousness, as a subjective form of a feeling, can occur only in a feeling that has an adequate datum or content (*PR*, 241f.). His notion that this datum must involve a synthesis of a proposition and a fact connects his position with the widespread agreement that consciousness is always associated with *negation*. Whereas experience always in-

---

*Another difference between a "physical purpose" and a "propositional feeling" is that, in the latter, the actual entity that was physically felt in the first phase is reduced to a bare "it" in becoming the logical subject of the proposition (*PR*, 261). This twofold difference between physical purposes and propositional feelings is especially important in indicating (as I do below) how organisms as simple as neurons, which presumably cannot entertain propositions, can nevertheless experience an *incipient* intentionality, in the sense of aboutness.

volves some minimal awareness of *what is,* we should not speak of consciousness unless there is also awareness of *what is not:* "Consciousness is the feeling of negation: in the perception of 'the stone as grey,' such feeling is in
barest germ; in the perception of 'the stone as not grey,' such feeling is in
full development. Thus the negative perception is the triumph of consciousness" (*PR*, 161). More precisely, consciousness involves the *contrast* between
what is and what might be, between fact and theory. It involves awareness
both of something definite and of potentialities "which illustrate *either* what
it is and might not be, *or* what it is not and might be. In other words, there
is no consciousness without reference to definiteness, affirmation, and negation. . . . Consciousness is how we feel the affirmation-negation contrast"
(*PR*, 243). This is the kind of datum that consciousness presupposes, without which it cannot be provoked into existence.

This account of the phases of a moment of experience, culminating in
the conscious entertainment of an intellectual feeling, constitutes an explanation of the rise of what has come to be called conscious *intentionality*, in
the sense of "aboutness." Whitehead's account, describing consciousness as
the way in which an intellectual feeling (the contrast of a proposition and
an alternative possibility) is entertained, agrees with the widespread doctrine that consciousness is always consciousness *of something*. One virtue of
the account by Whitehead is that, rather than implying that conscious intentionality somehow emerged in full-blown form out of wholly noninten-
tional objects (such as neurons as conventionally understood), he portrays
it as emerging out of experience that involves intentionality but not consciousness. That is, in the third phase of a moment of experience, there are
numerous propositional feelings, only a few of which, if any, will become
full-fledged intellectual feelings and thereby be entertained consciously.
To be sure, this point by itself would not be relevant to the mind-brain relation if neurons are too simple even to entertain propositional feelings. However, propositional feelings, as I have indicated, can be regarded
as simply more sophisticated versions of "physical purposes," which neurons (by hypothesis) *do* have. So, neurons, while (presumably) being devoid
of conscious intentionality, are not devoid of intentionality, or at least an
incipient intentionality, altogether. This is one way of explaining how this
kind of panexperientialism, in portraying minds and neurons as different only in degree, avoids (ontological) dualism while affirming interactionism.

This summarizes Whitehead's technical account of his view that thought,
consciousness, and cognition are "unessential elements in experience." Far
from being foundational, they are not even necessary. When they do occur,
they are surface elements, being derivative from the basic operations of an
occasion of experience. In most occasions of experience, the fourth phase
does not occur, or is latent at best. Without the integration of integra-

tions that can occur only in that phase—that is, without intellectual pre-hensions—consciousness, which is the subjective form of an intellectual prehension, cannot arise. It is provoked into existence only by the right kind of experiential content. In a sense, then, Whitehead would agree with Dennett's functionalist claim that content is "more fundamental than con-sciousness" (*CE*, 455). However, Dennett here seems by "consciousness" to mean any subjective experience whatsoever, not simply consciousness as a very high-level form of experience. Whitehead would, as I indicated ear-lier, support McGinn's antifunctionalist point that subjective experience and content are inseparable.

In any case, one of the implications of Whitehead's view of consciousness as a "function" is that *consciousness is not a preexistent stuff lying in waiting, as it were, to be filled by this content or that.* That assumption, which Whitehead rejects, has led to the related *assumption that those elements that are most clearly lit up by consciousness must be the elements that actually arise first in experience.* The opposite is, Whitehead insists, more nearly the case. That is, because "consciousness only arises in a late derivative phase of complex integra-tions," it tends to illuminate the data of that late phase, not the data that were in the first phase, except for those relatively few elements that are carried into the late phase (*PR*, 162). From this point follows Whitehead's criticism of what he considers the basic error of modern epistemologies:

> Thus those elements in our experience which stand out clearly and distinctly in our consciousness are not its basic facts; they are the derivative modifica-tions which arise in the process. . . . [T]he order of dawning, clearly and dis-tinctly, in consciousness is not the order of metaphysical priority. (*PR*, 162)

It should be recalled that we are exploring Whitehead's claim that the ordinary (especially in modern times) notions of "mind" and "matter" as stark opposites arise from mistaking the abstract for the concrete. I have just reviewed much of his explanation as to why the common understand-ing of the "mind" as consisting essentially of "consciousness" and "thinking" involves such a mistake. I will now, building on this account of conscious-ness, do the same for the notion that perception is essentially *sense* percep-tion. That will provide the basis, in turn, for explaining his related idea that the ordinary notion of matter is derived from a process of constructive abstraction rather than from any truly primary elements in our experience.

C. The Status of Sensory Perception in Human Experience

The assumption that sensory perception is a primary element in our expe-rience follows from the equation, false from Whitehead's perspective, *of primacy in consciousness* with *genetic primacy in experience.* Sensory perception is a derivative form of perception, resulting from an integration that occurs in a late phase of experience. It thus tends to get clearly illuminated by consciousness. That sensory perception gets lit up clearly follows not from the fact that our perceptual experience *begins* with sensory perception but from the fact that it does *not.*

Sensory perception, in Whitehead's analysis, is derivative from two simpler modes of perception. The first of these is called "perception in the mode of causal efficacy." Perception in this mode has already been discussed, because it is simply *physical prehension* described in the language of perception.

It is through perception in the mode of causal efficacy that we know most of those things that we inevitably presuppose in practice, which I have called *hard-core commonsense notions.* Modern philosophy has had difficulty explaining *how* we knew them, thereby relegating them to the category of "practice," "faith," "*a priori* forms of intuition," or even "dispensable common sense," because it has not recognized this more primal mode of perception underlying sense perception. It is through this more basic mode of perception, for example, that I have the category "other actualities besides myself" and know that there is an *external world* beyond my own experience, because I directly prehend other things, such as my bodily actualities. This is the basic reason why we are all realists in practice: "Common sense is inflexibly objectivist. We perceive other things which are in the world of actualities in the same sense as we are. Also our emotions are directed towards other things, including of course our bodily organs" (*PR,* 158).

This same mode of perception is, likewise, the basis for our knowledge of the reality of *causation as real influence;* this point is implicit in calling it "perception in the mode of causal efficacy." In prehending my body, for example, I prehend some of its parts as causally efficacious for my own experience. This applies not only to various pleasures and pains but also to external sensory perception itself. In opposition to Hume's claim that "impressions" arise in the soul "from unknown causes," Whitehead points out that Hume reveals elsewhere "his real conviction—everybody's real conviction—that visual sensations arise '*by* the eyes.' The causes are not a bit 'unknown,' and among them there is usually to be found the efficacy of the eyes [although sometimes it may be alcohol]. . . . The reason for the existence of oculists and prohibitionists is that various causes *are* known" (*PR,* 171). "The notion of causation arose," Whitehead adds, "because mankind lives amid experiences in the mode of causal efficacy" (*PR,* 175).

It is through this mode of perception that we also know about the *past* and therefore the *reality of time.* I mentioned earlier that memory is an example of a physical prehension, because the present occasion of experience prehends prior experiences. This explains why we are not in practice afflicted by Santayana's "solipsism of the present moment." This prehension of our own past occasions of experience also provides an explanation for our sense of self-identity through time—which *needs* an explanation in any philosophy such as that of Buddhism, Hume, and Whitehead in which the notion of a soul or mind as a numerically self-identical substance through time is denied (*AI*, 184, 186, 220f.; *MT*, 117f., 160ff.).

Perception in the mode of causal efficacy, which is a nonsensory mode of perception more basic than sensory, also serves to explain another assumption presupposed in the mind-body problem: our close *sense of identification with our bodies*. In a statement expressing a fact so obvious as to be seldom noticed, Whitehead says,

> Nothing is more astonishing in the history of philosophic thought than the naive way in which our association with our human bodies is assumed. . . . [The body] is in fact merely one among other natural objects. And yet, the unity of "body and mind" is the obvious complex which constitutes the one human being. . . . [O]ur feeling of bodily unity is a primary experience. It is an experience so habitual and so completely a matter of course that we rarely mention it. No one ever says, Here am I, and I have brought my body with me. (*MT*, 114)

Whitehead's explanation: "There is . . . every reason to believe that our sense of unity with the body has the same original as our sense of unity with our immediate past of personal experience. It is another case of nonsensuous perception" (*MT*, 189). This sense of unity arises from what I in the previous chapter called "basic perception," in which one prehends one's own brain and through it the remainder of one's body.

I might add here that although Whitehead's method is certainly based on what can be called "introspection" in a broad sense, he is critical of introspection as it has typically been practiced by philosophers.

> The attitude of introspection . . . lifts the clear-cut data of sensation into primacy, and cloaks the vague compulsions and derivations which form the main stuff of experience. In particular it rules out that intimate sense of derivation from the body, which is the reason for our instinctive identification of our bodies with ourselves. (*AI*, 226)

The reason the *top-down approach* has not gotten very far in overcoming the gap between mind and body is that it has *usually started too far up,* with the superficialities of human experience rather than with its essential ingredients. It has started with what makes our minds human, not with what makes them actual. I move now toward that higher level of superficialities.

The second mode of perception, derivative from the first, is called "perception in the mode of presentational immediacy." It is thus named because in this mode the data are immediately present, in themselves telling no tales of their origin. Taken by themselves, sense data, such as those constituting the yellow round shape before me, arise, in Hume's words, from "unknown causes." In fact, when they are considered in isolation, we should not even call them *sense data,* because this term implies that we do know that they are derived from the senses. If this kind of perception were our only mode of perception, as Hume's theory held, then we would not even have the idea of causal influence: "Hume's polemic respecting causation is," Whitehead says, "one prolonged, convincing argument that pure presentational immediacy does not disclose any causal influence" (*PR*, 123). Pure presentational immediacy also does not disclose other actualities, a past, time, or much of anything else. Insofar as it gets reduced to visual data, as it often does (*MT,* 168), it gives us nothing but space, shapes, and colors. Given the modern tendency to equate perception with perception in this mode of presentational immediacy, it is no wonder that modern philosophy has had epistemological problems (such problems, in fact, that many philosophers want to give up the whole epistemological enterprise).

These problems have arisen because of *the false assumption,* discussed earlier, *that those elements that are primary in consciousness must be primary in the perceptual process.* After the passage in which Whitehead argues that "those elements of our experience which stand out clearly and distinctly in our consciousness are not its basic facts; they are the derivative modifications which arise in the process," he writes:

> For example, consciousness only dimly illuminates the prehensions in the mode of causal efficacy, because these prehensions are primitive elements in our experience. But prehensions in the mode of presentational immediacy are among those prehensions which we enjoy with the most vivid consciousness. These prehensions are late derivatives in the concrescence of an experient subject. (*PR,* 162)

"Most of the difficulties of philosophy," Whitehead continues, are due to assuming the opposite: "Experience has been explained in a thoroughly topsy-turvy fashion, the wrong end first" (*PR,* 162).

What, then, is sensory perception? It is a synthesis of these two more primitive forms. It is thus a form of "perception in the mode of symbolic reference," because data from one of the two former modes (usually presentational immediacy) are used to interpret data arising from the other mode (usually causal efficacy). To continue the example begun above, I use the yellow round patch that is immediately present to my mind to interpret the feeling of causal efficacy from my body, particularly my eyes. I say, accordingly, that I am seeing the sun. I may be wrong about that. I cannot be wrong about experiencing the yellow shape; and I cannot be wrong about feeling the causal efficacy (although I may be wrong in thinking that it originated from the eyes). In those two pure modes of perception, there is simple givenness. But perception in the mode of symbolic reference introduces interpretation and thereby the possibility of error (*PR,* 168, 172).

The fact that sensory perception includes perception in the mode of causal efficacy explains why we are all realists about sensory perception. We do not, as Whitehead says, begin dancing with sense data and then infer a partner (*PR*, 315f.). However, the fact that presentational immediacy generally far outweighs causal efficacy in consciousness, especially when one is involved in philosophical introspection, has led most philosophers simply to equate sensory perception with presentational immediacy. Some of the problems of this equation have already been mentioned. Another problem—which I touched on in the previous chapter—is the resulting *assumption that entities without sensory organs can have no perceptual experience at all.* This assumption lies behind the fact that most philosophers and scientists, even if they will allow some form of experience to most animals, draw the line at the point where there seem to be no sensory organs. However, *if presentational immediacy and therefore sensory perception are derivative forms of perception even in us, then it is not impossible in principle to generalize some kind of perceptual experience to all individuals, however primitive.* This point is the basis for Whitehead's generalization:

> The perceptive mode of presentational immediacy arises in the later, originative, integrative phases of the process of concrescence. The perceptive mode of causal efficacy is to be traced to the constitution of the datum by reason of which there is a concrete percipient entity. Thus we must assign the mode of causal efficacy to the fundamental constitution of an occasion so that in germ this mode belongs even to organisms of the lowest grade; while the mode of presentational immediacy requires the more sophistical activity of the later stages of process, so as to belong only to organisms of a relatively high grade. (*PR*, 172)

Besides taking as primary a mode of perception that could not possibly be generalized to all levels of the actual world, the "topsy-turvy" interpretation of our experience also ignores, or takes as secondary, those dimensions of our experience that in principle *could* be generalized. The fallacious assumption that the notion of causation depends on vivid sense data, I have just argued, rules out the generalizability of perception in the mode of causal efficacy. Other relevant dimensions of experience are our emotions and purposes. In fact, just after the "topsy-turvy" sentence quoted above, Whitehead says: "In particular, emotional and purposeful experience have been made to follow upon Hume's impressions of sensation" (*PR*, 162). If we think, instead, of our experience as consisting most fundamentally of emotional, appetitive, and purposive (recall the discussion of "physical purposes") responses to physical feelings of other things, most basically our body and our own past of a split second ago, then we have elements some faint analogy to which can less implausibly be ascribed all the way down.

This completes my formulation of Whitehead's response to the first question, raised at the end of the first point in this section, regarding the plausibility of generalizing any aspect of human experience to the simplest actualities. Because much skepticism will surely remain, let me recall White-head's challenge:

> Any doctrine which refuses to place human experience outside nature, must find in descriptions of human experience factors which also enter into the descriptions of less specialized natural occurrences. If there be no such factors, then the doctrine of human experience as a fact within nature is mere bluff. . . . We should either admit dualism, . . . or we should point out the identical elements connecting human experience with physical science. (*AI*, 185)

Assuming that the threat of (ontological) dualism is sufficient to prod even the most skeptical of my antidualist readers into continuing, I will proceed to the second question, which asks *what basis there is in experience* for thinking of the units of nature as the kind of entities to which primitive emotions, appetites, and purposes could be ascribed.

D. The Spatializing Nature of Sensory Perception's Presentational Immediacy*

The general thesis of the remainder of this section is that "among the primary elements of nature as apprehended in our immediate experience" there is no element that is experienced as simply located or vacuous, with "vacuous" understood to mean *void of all experience* (*SMW*, 58; *PR*, 29, 167). The points below (E and F) treat the positive side of this thesis, which is that the truly *given* elements of experience are all given so as to suggest just the opposite—that the units of nature contain experience and references to the past and the future. The present point treats the negative side of the thesis, which is that the conception of matter as having the twin characteristics of vacuity and simple location is based on *constructed,* not *given,* elements in experience.

In this discussion, I will, as the above head indicates, be thinking of sensory perception in terms of its dimension of presentational immediacy (which is overwhelmingly dominant in it and with which it is usually simply equated). The main point is that the view of nature on which scientific materialism is based, in which matter is seen as having none but spatial properties, is a result of the spatializing nature of presentational immediacy. Because of the prominence of presentational immediacy in sensory

---

*I distinguished, in the final section of chapter 7, between two kinds of sensory perception: perception of things external to one's body and "proprioception" of parts of one's own body. In this section, I distinguish between sensory perception as such, but especially of external things, and perception in the mode of causal efficacy.

perception, the perceptual mode of causal efficacy, which suggests a quite different view of nature, is virtually if not totally ignored. By misunderstanding the status of presentational immediacy within sensory perception, we are led to construct a false view of nature.

The point that presentational immediacy is a derivative, not a direct, mode of perception has already been made. Whereas nonsensory prehension of our own body is perception of nature as directly *given* to experience, in sensory perception that provides information of things beyond the body we have nature as constructed, not simply given. This is a point on which our usual epistemological assumptions should be partly corrected by our science: "Unless the physical and physiological sciences are fables, the qualitative experiences which are the sensations, such as sight, hearing, etc., are involved in an intricate flux of reactions within and without the animal body" (*MT*, 121). Sense data, in other words, are produced by an amazingly complex, indirect process. Philosophers tend to give lip service to this fact and then continue to think of nature in terms of the purely spatial matter that is a product of (external) sensory perception.

One respect in which sensory perception is illusory—we now know, thanks to modern physics, chemistry, and biology, with their atomic, molecular, and cell theories—is that sensory perception hides the true individuals composing material things. A stone, for example, is composed of billions of individuals engaged in energetic activity. Sensory perception, however, gives us a single, passive, enduring substance, numerically one both temporally and spatially (*MT*, 154; *PR*, 77). Even when we know better, we may continue, with Popper, to take "solid material bodies" as the paradigms of reality.* Historically, what happened was that the characteristics originally attributed to the stone were reassigned to the molecule and the atom. In Whitehead's words, "The metaphysical concepts, which had their origin in a mistake about the stone, were now applied to the individual molecules. Each atom was still a stuff which retained its self-identity and its essential attributes in any portion of time—however short, and however long" (*PR*, 78). When it became clear that the concept of passive, enduring matter did not apply to the atom, its application was shifted to the (revealingly named) "elementary particles." Even though quantum physics suggests that the whole concept is a mistake, it continues to be assumed. This

---

*Even Strawson seems to continue this practice. Although he says that experience must be taken to be fully natural and to be as real as any other properties or phenomena of physical things, emphasizing that the reality of experience is "the thing of which we can be most certain" (*MR*, 57), he nevertheless, when naming "paradigm cases of physical phenomena," names "rocks, seas, neurons, and so on" (*MR*, 110). The logic of his argument would seem to require him, instead, to take human beings, especially himself as known from within, as paradigmatic.

is the power of the perception-based conceptions suggested by perception in the mode of presentational immediacy.

Whereas the former point is well known (even if its implications are usually ignored), Whitehead's further point about the constructed nature of sensory data is among his most original and, to conventional ways of thinking, most challenging ideas. It is also one of his most important ideas, lying behind his greater suspicion (compared with McGinn) about the adequacy of our conceptions based on sensory perception with its tendency to "spatialize" its objects. The idea in question is that the transition from the perceptual mode of causal efficacy to that of presentational immediacy involves an *inversion* of emphasis, so that the features that were prominent in the data as received in physical prehension are radically played down by presentational immediacy, whereas other features, which were only faintly present in the primal perceptual mode, are greatly emphasized in the derivative mode. Let us deal with a case of visual perception, in which I perceive the early morning sky as red. I, as the prehensive unification of the relevant activities in my brain at that moment, receive, in the perceptual mode of causal efficacy, both a sensum and certain geometrical relationships to the environment (*PR*, 171, 312). In that mode of perception, the sensum is strongly felt in terms of its primary status in the nature of things, which is as a qualification of affective tone (*AI*, 245). Whitehead knows that this is not the conventional view about sensa: "Unfortunately the learned tradition of philosophy has missed their main characteristic, which is their enormous emotional significance" (*AI*, 215). In a physical prehension, it is this aspect of the sensum, in this case red, that is primarily felt.

> In their most primitive form of functioning, a sensum is felt physically with emotional enjoyment of its sheer individual essence. For example, red is felt with emotional enjoyment of its sheer redness. In this primitive prehension we have aboriginal physical feeling in which the subject feels itself as enjoying redness. (*PR,* 314f.)

The geometrical relationships that I inherit from the feelings transmitted through the brain from the optic nerve, however, are only vaguely felt in this mode of perception; they are ill-defined, having only faint relevance to any particular region. The sensum is felt with strong emotion, accordingly, but is "unspatialized" (*PR*, 114, 172).

In the perceptual mode of presentational immediacy, by contrast, this relationship is inverted. The geometrical relationships are lifted into prominence, with the result that the sensum is projected onto a contemporary region of space (which may or may not be the locus from which the red originated). In this process, the sensum is transmuted from being primarily a qualification of affective tone into being primarily a qualification of an external region (*PR*, 172; *AI*, 215, 245). The sensum has, accordingly, been "spatialized." Here is a summary statement:

> The more primitive types of experience are concerned with sense-reception, and not with sense-perception. . . . [S]ense-reception is 'unspatialized,' and sense-perception is 'spatialized.' In sense-reception the sensa are the definiteness of emotion: they are emotional forms transmitted from occasion to occasion. Finally in some occasion of adequate complexity, [a transmutation] endows them with the new function of characterizing nexūs.* (*PR*, 114)

This spatializing nature of presentational immediacy is of its essence: "presentational immediacy is the mode in which vivid feelings of contemporary geometrical relations, with special emphasis on certain 'focal' regions, enter into experience" (*PR*, 324).

We have now arrived at Whitehead's explanation as to how sensory perception tends to lead us astray in ontology, once more because of our tendency to mistake an abstraction for the real thing. "The separation of the emotional experience from the presentational intuition," he says, "is a high abstraction of thought" (*PR*, 162f.). We are so accustomed to thinking about the world in terms of high abstractions, such as "the tree as green," furthermore, that "we have difficulty in eliciting into consciousness the notion of 'green' as the qualifying character of an emotion" (*PR*, 162). Although more than one reader is probably having that difficulty right now, we do have some reasons from ordinary experience to think that colors are, down deep, emotional in nature. If sensa had no tendency to evoke affective, aesthetic responses, it would be difficult to explain how art is possible (*PR*, 162; *AI*, 216). Also, many people experience irritation in the presence of red (*PR*, 315). There is further support for Whitehead's view, I might add, in recent studies demonstrating the differing emotional and behavioral responses of people depending on whether they are in red rooms or green rooms.

Whitehead's position on sensa does agree with the orthodox view that, for example, colors as we see them are "secondary qualities," which as such do not inhere in the objects onto which we project them. But Whitehead's view has quite different consequences. The orthodox view is that these secondary qualities have arisen, mysteriously, out of so-called primary qualities, which are, in fact, purely *quantitative* factors. It is generally held, for example, that colors are "really" nothing but wavelengths, which are said to be turned into colors by one's mind (often in spite of its being assigned purely epiphenomenal status, so that a miracle is performed by an illusion). Whitehead's view is that secondary qualities are produced by the mind out of values, or emotions. Recalling that such things are sometimes spoken of

---

*"Nexūs" is the plural of "nexus."

as "tertiary" qualities, we could say that secondary qualities are produced in the mind out of tertiary qualities that are in the body and even nature in general. From Whitehead's standpoint, however, these terms need to be reapplied, because what was tertiary in the dualistic view is primary in the panexperientialist view: "Value" is the term Whitehead applies to the intrinsic reality of every actual entity (*SMW*, 93). The qualities called primary in the dualistic and materialistic views are for him simply features of things as viewed from without. For example, in the transmission of light, the events intrinsically are "pulses of emotions," while from the outside these appear as "wave-lengths and vibrations" (*PR*, 163). Lest this seem an idea that could not be reconciled with "real physics," it should be recalled that before turning to metaphysics Whitehead produced an alternative interpretation of relativity physics.[2]

In any case, the central point of the foregoing discussion is that the idea of matter as devoid of any inherent values, and as instead consisting of purely spatial features, is a result of misinterpreting the status of presentational immediacy within sensory perception, especially the fact that it "spatializes" the data as received in the more primal mode of perception, thereby submerging their emotional significance by turning them into qualifications of geometrical regions. The perception of matter that leads to the notion of vacuous actuality, accordingly, does *not* arise from nature as immediately given to human experience but from nature as constructed by a derivative mode of perception. The building of a worldview (with an insoluble mind-body problem) on the basis of this type of perception is the result of failing to see that the prominent side of sensory perception, the perceptual mode of presentational immediacy, gives us an artificial, constructed view of the world. We have failed to see the deeper significance of the fact that our sensory perception in respect to its "prominent side of external reference is very superficial in its disclosure of the universe" (*MT*, 153). It is implicit in that statement, however, that there is another side to our sensory perception: its "bodily reference." The next points will deal with that other side, in which nature is perceived more concretely. These points involve overcoming philosophy's tendency to concentrate on *visual* feelings to the neglect of *visceral* feelings (*PR*, 121).

E. Implications of the Bodily Origin of Sensory Perception

"How do we observe nature?" Whitehead asks. "The conventional answer to this question," he says, "is that we perceive nature through our senses" (*MT*, 158). We are likely, he adds, to narrow this down to sight. However, he points out, we should be suspicious of this answer. (For all their talk about suspicion, most philosophers who think of themselves as "postmodern" have remained true believers in this respect.) This suspicion should follow from what Whitehead has called the "physiological attitude" (*SMW*, 148). Besides the fact that we are directly (if only vaguely) aware of the intervention of the body even in visual perception,

> every type of crucial experiment proves that what we see, and where we see it, depend entirely upon the physiological functioning of our body. . . . All sense perception is merely one outcome of the dependence of our experience upon bodily functionings. Thus if we wish to understand the relation of our personal experience to the activities of nature, the proper procedure is to examine the dependence of our personal experiences upon our personal bodies. (*MT*, 158f.)

The most *direct* way to *observe* nature, in other words, is to observe it working in ourselves, as it influences our own experience (which is, we recall, as much a part of nature as anything else). If we are empiricists, we should draw our conclusions about the nature of nature from our best vantage point: "The human body provides our closest experience of the interplay of actualities in nature" (*MT*, 115). Of course, many today have adopted a "physiological attitude" with respect to the mind-body relation. The dominant approach, however, interprets the physiological and psychological evidence in externalist categories derived from sensory perception. Whitehead means something quite different: *an approach that interprets what we know from physiology in terms of what we know about the body from within*. This approach, while including an introspective element, is not a return to introspective psychology in the old sense. First, as pointed out earlier, the introspective element here does not focus on the high-level, superficial aspects of our experience, even its medium-level mentality, but on the truly fundamental, originating, *physical* dimension of our experience, in which it takes its rise largely from bodily activities. Second, it involves a coordination of this internal observation of nature in action with the information acquired from the external physiological approach.

The moral of Point D must not be forgotten. The purely external, purely physiological approach to the study of the body is an approach in which "all direct observation has been identified with sense-perception" (*AI*, 217). But *the central lesson of physiology itself is that sense perception is not direct observation of its objects*. The physiologist looking at my brain is not directly observing my brain cells. As Whitehead repeatedly stresses, "unless the physicist and physiologist are talking nonsense, there is a terrific tale of complex activity" that occurs between my brain cells and the brain cells and conscious experiences of the observing physiologist (*MT*, 121). It is simply credulous to accept the results of sense perception (even if magnified by instruments), accordingly, as giving us direct information, and indeed the only kind of relevant information, about the nature of brain cell activity. Sensory perception gives very *indirect* information, mediated through billions of events and then modified by the constructive and abstractive processes of one's own unconscious and conscious experience. Although I from within am not consciously aware of my individual brain cells and their "firings" (all this kind of knowledge must come from physiology) and am not even directly aware of the existence of a brain in my head (except perhaps when I have a headache), I do in effect observe the brain insofar as I am directly aware of *the kinds of influences that flow into my own experience from it.* And I *am* conscious of receiving influences from various other portions of my body, such as my eyes, my hands, my skin in general. The purpose of the present point and the next is to see what can be learned from this direct observation that can be used to interpret the more indirect findings of physiology.

In speaking of (external) sensory perception thus far, I have for the most part been assuming the equation of it with its dimension of presentational immediacy, which conveys information about the world external to the body. This information, albeit highly abstract, is still information (when all goes well) about that external world. As I took pains to stress in Point D, however, sensory perception involves an integration of the perceptual mode of presentational immediacy with that of causal efficacy. If we attend to that other mode, then even (external) sensory perception tells us something about the body. The remainder of the present point explores *implications* of the fact that sensory perception does arise out of our perception in the mode of causal efficacy of our own bodies. Points F and G will then explore the information directly learned from that mode.

One thing that an examination of our own sensory perception tells us is based on the recognition that the human body is the "self-sufficient organ of human sense-perception" (*AI*, 214). Although generally, to be sure, the body in producing sensory perceptions in us does convey information transmitted through the body from the outside world, this need not be the case: By doing various things with the body, such as with drugs or electrodes, the same kinds of sensory impressions can be generated; and our dreaming activity shows most clearly that the body can be quite self-sufficient in producing sensory imagery. The pertinent question from this realization is: *What does this fact, plus the fact that waking sensory perception normally does convey information about the world external to the body, tell us about the bodily parts themselves?* Whitehead's answer: It tells us that *our bodily units must incorporate within themselves aspects of the world beyond themselves.*

> Your perception takes place where you are, and is entirely dependent on how your body is functioning. But this functioning of the body in one place, exhibits for your cognisance an aspect of the distant environment. . . . If this cognisance conveys knowledge of a transcendent world, it must be because the event which is the bodily life unifies in itself aspects of the universe. (*SMW,* 91–92)

For example, if my sensory perception of the sun arises completely from my prehension of my brain cells and yet my sensory data *in some sense* correspond to the sun itself (and who really doubts *that?*), then my brain cells must in some sense incorporate aspects of the sun into themselves. This recognition implies that the notion of these cells as "simply located" is false. The functioning of the brain cells in conveying this information suggests that each cellular event contains a reference to the past world, in this case the events that occurred on the surface of the sun eight minutes ago, and to the future, in this case to my experience that comes immediately after the neuronal events. (If you doubt that a temporal distinction can be made here, simply think about the cellular events in the eye: They certainly occur prior to the mind's sensory perception based on data received from them, so in this case the temporal relation is clear.) Each event seems essentially to prehend aspects of past events and to pass on aspects to future events, which prehend *it.* What we know from sensory perception by combining inner and outer knowledge, accordingly, is that *bodily cells are analogous* to our own experiences, at least in respect to being *prehenders.* And if they are prehenders, they *cannot be purely spatial entities:* They must have an inside, into which the prehended material is taken before it is passed along to subsequent prehenders. Having an inside would mean that they have an *inner duration,* which is the time it takes each event to occur—the time between its reception of information and its transmission of this information to subsequent events. Looking at sensory perception from *this* perspective, accordingly, gives us a much different idea of the nature of nature than we get simply from the sense data of presentational immediacy alone.

In light of this idea, I will pause to look at a particularly interesting part of McGinn's argument, which I passed over before. In discussing intentionality, he says that the most fundamental question is not the nature of its content but "what this directedness, grasping, apprehension, encompassing, reaching out ultimately consists in" (*PC,* 37). It is this feature of our own experience that leads McGinn, given his assumption that the mind is ontologically reducible to the brain, to despair of ever solving the mind-body problem in physicalist terms (which would require an epistemic reduction). "Phenomenologically, we feel that the mind 'lays hold' of things out there, mentally 'grasps' them, but we have no physical model of what this might consist in." To make the point vivid, he says: "If I may put it so: how on earth could my *brain* make that possible? No ethereal prehensile organ protrudes from my skull!" (*PC,* 40).

In light of Whitehead's analysis, we can give a twofold answer. First, we need not think of the brain as somehow having the ontological unity to prehend other things into the unity of experience that we know directly ("phenomenologically"). By distinguishing between the brain as a multiplicity and the mind-event as a unification of aspects of brain events into an experiential unity, we can attribute that unifying capacity to the mind. Second, we *can,* however, think of each brain cell event as indeed having a grasping or prehensive capacity, by which it unifies aspects of what it has received from beyond itself into an (albeit much less complex and sophisticated) experiential unity. This means, of course, that we must think of the remainder of the bodily cells in a similar way; for example, those constituting the remainder of the central nervous system must be able to prehend and be prehended so that the information from the surface of the body can be transmitted to the brain cells.

In any case, besides learning from this dual mode of observation that our bodily units must be prehensive events, we learn that they must embody, to use the current jargon, "qualia." This conclusion follows from the same kind of reasoning, being already implicit in the analysis of "secondary qualities" in the previous point. Sensory qualities such as *red as we see it,* it is agreed on virtually all sides, do not exist in external nature; for example, the molecules in a red ball are *not red as we see it apart from someone's seeing it,* and *they* certainly do not *see* red. But *we* do see red, and this sensory quality surely arises out of our bodily activities. It is impossible to understand how, apart from supernatural intervention, this could be so if these bodily activities were purely quantitative in nature, devoid of all qualia. A naturalistic perspective leads to the inference that our bodily cells must embody qualia of some sort, even if they do not experience them in the same way that we experience them in conscious sensory perception. That is, cells surely do not enjoy *red as we see it.* But perhaps red for them is an emotion. Perhaps red as it exists throughout most of nature is a subjective form of immediate feeling, whereas it is only in the conscious presentational immediacy of animals with sensory organs that that subjective form is turned into an objective datum projected onto outer things. "Red as seen," then, would be a transmutation effected by more or less high-level experiences out of "red as felt." This is a kind of transmutation that requires no supernatural assistance.

This suggestion, of course, will be widely repudiated out of hand. Many philosophers will respond angrily, or at least smile knowingly, muttering, "This suggestion violates common sense." That is true: It violates soft-core common sense based on an uncritical acceptance of the deliverances of sensory perception reinforced by several centuries of dualistic thinking and language. Most philosophers (including scientists qua philosophers) have become so strongly enculturated with this soft-core commonsense perspective that they are willing to carry out its implications, to violate several of our *hard-core* commonsense convictions, even though this leaves them with a violent contradiction between their theories and the presuppositions of their practice, including the practice of formulating theories. Alternatively, they are willing to countenance an unintelligible dualism, to accept a magical emergentism, or to proclaim the mind-body problem permanently insoluble. Is Whitehead's suggestion, in spite of its violation of long-standing soft-core prejudices, not both more rational and more empirical? Do we not indeed have good reason to be suspicious of the conceptions of matter based on (sensory) perception-based categories alone? Has Whitehead not provided good reason to reject the notion that entities in nature in themselves have only the spatial properties that we assign them on the basis of perception in the mode of presentational immediacy? Has he not provided good reason to think, instead, that bodily events involve prehension and therefore an inside? And does that not remove one of the basic reasons for assuming that cells could not experience subjective forms such as emotions of a lowly sort? This is a defensive paragraph, but I do know from experience what kind of response to expect from the suggestion that colors are emotions and that cells could experience them. My response is an appeal to Searle's regulative principle that we constantly remind ourselves of what we know for sure. This carries with it the negative principle that we keep reminding ourselves of what we do *not* know. We do not know directly that cells do not feel emotions, and we do not know anything from which this could be deduced. However, we do know a lot of things that this idea helps us make sense of.

The present point is based on inference: We derive such and such from our brain, therefore the brain's units must embody such and such. The next point appeals to direct experience.

F. Information about Nature Derived from Direct Prehension of Our Bodies

The recognition that our bodily members are not simply located objects can be based not simply on inference, as above, but also on our experience of being causally influenced by them in our physical experience. To provide the basis for this argument, we can begin with the relation between my present experience and previous occasions of my own experience. In illustrating physical prehension (nonsensory perception of other actualities), Whitehead, in an argument against the Humean view that our experiences are completely separable one from the other, uses the example of a speaker saying "United States."

> When the third syllable is reached, probably the first is in the immediate past; and certainly during the word 'States' the first syllable of the phrase lies beyond the immediacy of the present. . . . As mere sensuous perception, Hume is right in saying that the sound 'United' as a mere sensum has nothing in its nature referent to the sound 'States', yet the speaker is carried from 'United' to 'States', and the two conjointly live in the present, by the energizing of the past occasion as it claims its self-identical existence as a living is-

sue in the present. The immediate past as surviving to be again lived through in the present is the primary instance of non-sensuous perception. (*AI*, 182)

The point here is that our own experience certainly does not have the property of simple location. The present moment is *essentially* constituted by its prehension of the previous moment. And that previous moment has (at least) a twofold existence: It existed in the past, and yet it is here in the present occasion. One might argue that this example provides no example of one actuality's being present in another, because our mind as enduring through time is a single entity. Whitehead's response:

[The former experience] is gone, and yet it is here. It is our indubitable self, the foundation of our present existence. Yet the present occasion while claiming self-identity, while sharing the very nature of the bygone occasion in all its living activities, nevertheless is engaged in modifying it, in adjusting it to *other* influences, in completing it with *other* values, in adjusting it to *other* purposes. The present moment is constituted by the influx of *the other* into that self-identity. (*AI*, 181)

In other words, although in one sense my present experience and that earlier experience are parts of one (enduring) individual, the unity over time is not that of an *individual in the strictest sense,* because the present occasion incorporates not only that prior experience but also many other influences. One of those influences, for example, might lead the speaker to reject the earlier occasion's intention to follow "United" with "States of America" by saying instead "States of Europe." With such different purposes, we could hardly say that the two or more experiences constituted a single individual in the strictest sense. This example, accordingly, presents an instance of our direct awareness of former actualities existing and energizing in a present actuality, thereby showing that simple location does not, at least, characterize all actualities. And it provides a model for inferring that the same is true for our bodily members.

Whitehead argues, in a passage partly quoted earlier, that our sense of identity-with-difference in relation to the body is similar:

Our dominant inheritance from our immediately past occasion is broken into by innumerable inheritances through other avenues. Sensitive nerves, the functionings of our viscera, disturbances in the composition of our blood, break in upon the dominant line of inheritance. In this way, emotions, hopes, fears, inhibitions, sense-perceptions arise, which physiologists confidently ascribe to the bodily functioning. So intimately obvious is this bodily inheritance that common speech does not discriminate the human body from the human person. Soul and body are fused together. . . . But the human body is indubitably a complex of occasions which are part of spatial nature. It is a set of occasions miraculously coordinated so as to pour its inheritance into various regions within the brain. There is thus every reason to believe that

our sense of unity with the body has the same original as our sense of unity
with our immediate past of personal experience. It is another case of non-
sensuous perception. (*AI,* 189)

This unity with our body, however, is no more strict identity than is our
unity with our own past experience. Rather: "The body is that portion of
nature with which each moment of human experience intimately cooper-
ates. There is an inflow and outflow of factors between the bodily actuality
and the human experience, so that each shares in the existence of the
other" (*MT,* 115). In other words, because there is mutual efficient causation between the body and our experience, they cannot be understood as
strictly (numerically) identical. The body is in this sense composed of *others*—that is, of entities that are distinct from our experience or mind as
such: "Actuality is the self-enjoyment of importance. But this self-enjoyment
has the character of the self-enjoyment of others melting into the enjoyment
of the one self" (*MT,* 117f.). Precisely because self and body are not one in
the strictest sense, the intimate relationship between them provides us with
direct observational evidence against the idea that "spatial nature" is *purely*
spatial, being capable of only external relations. My bodily experiences are
internally related to my experience, being partly constitutive of what it is.
The activities constituting my body must therefore have a twofold existence: an existence in themselves (which is perhaps an existence *for* themselves) and then another kind of existence in my experience.

Furthermore, once we have fully accepted the idea that our own experience is fully natural, therefore an (especially high-grade) example of
natural events generally, we can generalize, saying that this twofold mode
of existence must be true of the interactions within the body generally.
Furthermore, realizing that the body is simply one more part of nature, we
can generalize even further, saying that this twofold mode of existence must
apply universally. Just as my present experience prehends previous experiences of mine and bodily events into itself and then is in turn taken up by
later experiences, all events in nature must prehend past events into themselves and then get prehended into later events. Simple location, in other
words, must not characterize *any* of the units comprising the universe. *All*
unitary events must include the past in themselves and then get included
in future events. This generalization suggests the correlative one, that *all
unitary events must have an inside* with a duration (even if less than a billionth
of a second in the most primitive types of events). And this generalization
suggests the final one: *All unitary events must have experience* (however
trivial).

The inference that at least bodily cells have experience is supported by
our direct experience of the body. The main point is contained in the statement
quoted two paragraphs above, that our direct experience includes "the self-

enjoyment of others melting into the enjoyment of the one self" (*MT,* 117f.). Whitehead seems to be saying that *we directly experience the fact that the body has its own experiences.* That indeed is his claim. "Among our fundamental experiences," he says, is the "direct feeling of the derivation of emotion from the body" (*MT,* 159f.). This is our primal relationship to our body:

> The primitive form of physical experience is emotional—blind emotion—received as felt elsewhere in another occasion and conformally appropriated as a subjective passion. In the language appropriate to the higher stages of experience, the primitive element is *sympathy,* that is, feeling the feeling *in* another and feeling conformally *with* another. (*PR,* 162)

This primal experience can also be discussed in terms of experiences of worth and value:

> At the base of our existence is the sense of "worth." Now worth essentially presupposes that which is worthy. Here the notion of worth is . . . to be construed in . . . the sense of existence for its own sake. . . . [O]ur experience is a value experience, expressing a vague sense of maintenance or discard; and . . . this value experience differentiates itself in the sense of many existences with value experiences . . . and the egoistic value experience. (*MT,* 110)

It should be stressed here that Whitehead is engaged in phenomenology, trying to state what is directly given to experience. But his analysis of the given is radically different from that of Edmund Husserl, who spoke of "essences"—which for Whitehead are abstract products of construction and simplification. Husserl's essences are the objects of perception in the mode of presentational immediacy. What is really given to our primordial mode of perception, according to Whitehead's phenomenological analysis, are other actualities, rather than abstract essences, and these as laden with their own feelings. The contrast is brought out by Hartshorne, who had read Wordsworth and then studied with Husserl before coming under Whitehead's influence. In commenting on the fact that both he and Whitehead had independently been influenced by Wordsworth, Hartshorne says,

> [Wordsworth] was describing nature so far as given to our direct intuitions. . . . The 'ocean of feelings' that Whitehead ascribes to physical reality is not only thought; so far as our bodies are made of this reality, it is intuited. What is not intuited but only thought is nature as consisting of absolutely insentient stuff or process. No such nature is directly given to us. . . . Wordsworth was doing a phenomenology of direct experience far better than Husserl ever did. . . . Wordsworth seems to have influenced Whitehead much as he did me. He saved us from materialism and even dualism. Both result from an inadequate phenomenology and now an antiquated physics.[3]

Saying that his own "chief quarrel with Husserl . . . was over his [Husserl's] dualism of sensation and feeling," Hartshorne adds that after Whitehead heard Hartshorne's talk on Husserl for the philosophy department at Harvard in 1925, he "expressed surprise concerning Husserl's stress on essences. . . . Clearly, he felt as I did that Husserl never understood the fully concrete phenomena."[4]

In any case, from Whitehead's analysis of one's direct experience as arising from one's body (along, of course, with the other considerations mentioned earlier), he concludes that "the body is composed of various centres of experience imposing the expression of themselves on each other. . . . [T]he animal body is composed of entities, which are mutually expressing and feeling" (*MT,* 23).

Having reached this conclusion, he then applies his double-edged axiom that just as "a living body is to be interpreted according to what is known of other sections of the physical universe," so "other sections of the universe are to be interpreted in accordance with what we know of the human body" (*PR,* 119). We must assume, by the principle of continuity, that *the same kinds of causal interactions that occur within the body occur without,* especially in light of the twofold fact that the body interacts with the rest of the universe and that we cannot precisely say where the body begins and "external nature" ends (*AI,* 189; *MT,* 21, 161). We must conclude, accordingly, that *the universe in general is comprised of actualities that experientially prehend prior actualities, thereby including aspects of those former actualities within themselves and doing so with subjective form.*

To summarize: Whitehead's overall thesis on this issue is that the notion of mere bits of matter understood as vacuous actualities with simple location is not supported by any truly concrete, direct observations of nature but results instead from misinterpreting the status of high abstractions. I have distinguished six points within this overall argument. The first is that our own experience, taken as an instance of a natural fact, suggests that the units of nature are characterized by prehensive experience. The second and third points support the generalizability of our experience to other individuals by arguing that both consciousness and sensory perception should be regarded as derivative, not foundational, aspects of human experience. The fourth point argues that the materialistic idea of matter is rooted in an aspect of conscious sensory perception that spatializes the data received from the body while stripping it of most of its emotional nature. The fifth point is that the information that we do receive from sense perception can be most naturally interpreted as implying that our bodily activities are, analogously to our own experience, activities of feeling (prehending) other things with emotional form. The sixth point argues that in our primal communion with our body we directly experience it as composed of centers of feeling. In all of these ways, Whitehead argues that our most concrete observations, far from suggesting a materialistic view of the body and thereby the world beyond, suggest just the opposite.

III. FROM INNER PHYSICS TO HUMAN PSYCHOLOGY: SUBJECTIVE UNIVERSALS

Nagel argues that we need to be able to think objectively about subjectivity, which requires having "an objective concept of mind" (*VN*, 18). This would allow us to "think of mind as a phenomenon to which the human case is not necessarily central" (*VN*, 18). An objective concept of mind, however, "cannot abandon the essential factor of a point of view" (*VN*, 20). Rather, this factor must be generalized. Doing so would involve characterizing experience "in terms of certain general features of subjective experience— subjective universals" (*VN*, 21).

It is implicit in my foregoing exposition that Whitehead's philosophy is built around just such a concept of subjective universals. This concept is implied by his statement that unless we can "find in descriptions of human experience factors which also enter into the descriptions of less specialized natural occurrences," then "the doctrine of human experience as a fact within nature is mere bluff." Either we must "admit dualism," he adds, or else indicate "the identical elements connecting human experience with physical science" (*AI*, 184f.). What he means here by "physical science," of course, is the *entities studied* by physical science. The result would be what we could call "inner physics," because it would involve thinking imaginatively about what such entities are in themselves, as we do when we imagine what other people must be going through, or when we engage in cognitive ethology. Although Whitehead himself did not use the term "inner physics," he did suggest the need to complement the "physical physiology" practiced thus far with a "psychological physiology" (*PR*, 103). This notion of an inner physics answers to Strawson's call for "a qualitative-character-of-experience physics" (*MR*, 89).

The subjective universals are meant to apply to all subjects, understood as momentary occasions of experience, from the human level to the actualities studied by physics. This does *not* include all identifiable entities in the world, of course, because many of these, such as rocks, lakes, and computers, have a merely aggregational, not a subjective or experiential, unity. The subjective universals apply only to all genuine individuals, whether simple or compound individuals (to be discussed in the following chapter). *Which* things are to be considered true individuals is an empirical question, to be decided in terms of whether the behavior suggests a unity of responsive action that involves an element of spontaneity (meaning that the response does not seem fully explainable in terms of efficient causation from prior events). Whitehead himself evidently supposed humans, most other animals, eukaryotic cells, molecules, and atoms to be compound individuals, with subatomic (elementary) particles thought of as primary individuals. My supposition is that today the list of likely candidates for compound individuals should also include prokaryotic cells, organelles, macromolecules, and perhaps the previously designated "elementary particles," with that status perhaps now assigned to quarks. But nothing of metaphysical import hinges on the correctness of all these suppositions. If the empirical study of atoms and molecules, for example, suggests that they are best understood as mere aggregational societies, with no overall spontaneity, that would not affect the validity of the philosophical position as such. All it requires is that some degree of partially spontaneous experience be present in human beings and other animals, in the ultimate units of nature, and in some individuals at an intermediary level. In any case, the question is: What features exemplified in our own experience can we think to be subjective universals, exemplified in all experience and therefore (by hypothesis) all individuals?

Lying behind Whitehead's list of subjective universals is his conception that *creative experience* is the ultimate reality, the "universal of universals" (*PR*, 21). Creative experience as such is not an actuality but that which is exemplified in all actualities. This conception of the "category of the ultimate" replaces Aristotle's category of "primary substance" or "matter," eliminating "the notion of passive receptivity" (*PR*, 21, 31). Whitehead's own term for it is simply "creativity," but I, following Hartshorne (*PCH*, 690, 720), have added the term "experience" to emphasize this aspect of the ultimate. The ensuing list of subjective universals is simply an explication of what is implicit in the idea that all individuals embody creative experience. I will list nine such universals, indicating very briefly the meaning of each.

1. *Feeling in the sense of physical prehension.* All experiences begin with feelings or prehensions of other actual things, in which they grasp aspects of those things. This prehension of actualities lies at the root of what philosophers call "intentionality" (aboutness) in our experience.* This physical prehension, which is an experience's orientation to the past, provides (among other things) the basis for memory, which in low-grade entities may extend back no farther than a fraction of a second.

*See Nicholas F. Gier, "Intentionality and Prehension," *Process Studies* 6, no. 3 (Fall 1976): 197–213. In saying that the (physical) prehension of prior actualities, with which an occasion of experience begins, *lies at the root* of intentionality (rather than simply being equatable with it), I am presupposing my discussion above, in which I equated "intellectual feelings" with conscious intentionality, "propositional feelings" with intentionality as such, and "physical purposes" with incipient intentionality.

2. *Causal feeling.* Each experience begins with the experience of the efficacy of other things (for good or ill) for itself. This is simply an aspect of physical prehension but is listed as a separate universal because it is a distinguishable and overwhelming aspect of physical experience.

3. *Feeling in the sense of conceptual prehension.* Conscious human experience is "conscious of its experient essence as constituted by its internal relatedness to the world of realities, and to the world of ideas" (*SMW*, 152). This statement, which summarizes both types of "intentionality," states in terms of human experience the inclusion by all experiences of ideality as well as actuality. In the most elementary experiences, this conceptual experience, or mentality, is no more than a slight appetition to repeat or attenuate forms (in-formation) transmitted from prior experiences. This initiation of the "mental pole" of an experience is the beginning of whatever self-creativity it exercises. The idea that electrons and other subatomic entities have a "mental pole" may, incidentally, seem a purely speculative idea, posited to avoid an unintelligible emergence of freedom out of entities lacking any degree of spontaneity. This is, indeed, an important reason for the affirmation. Beyond this, however, David Bohm and B. J. Hiley's ontological interpretation of quantum theory depends crucially on the notion that "even an electron has at least a rudimentary mental pole, represented mathematically by the quantum potential" (*UU*, 387).

4. *Feeling in the sense of emotion.* Both physical and mental prehensions are felt in a certain way, with particular "subjective forms" (which is Whitehead's technical term for the subjective universal in question). In the highest experiences the subjective forms may include consciousness, but emotional forms are included in experiences of all levels.

5. *Final causation or self-determination.* This feature is the integrative exercise of the experience's power for self-creation, in which it reconciles any tensions that may have existed between various appetitions at the outset of the mental pole. In being partly *causa sui*, the experience does not create itself out of nothing, of course, but out of the physical experiences imposed on it by its past. This element of self-determination may be trivial, as it is in the most elementary experiences, extremely important, as in conscious purposes, or anywhere in between. Whitehead's technical term for this universal is "subjective aim."

6. *Anticipation.* This dimension is the future orientation of an experience, its anticipation of exerting creative influence on future events. The anticipation may be directed toward events a thousandth of a second or thousands of years in the future. (This anticipation, which is the necessity that the experience lays on the future by its very existence, is the ground for induction [*AI*, 193].) An experience's subjective aim, accordingly, involves an aim at the future (however limited) as well as at creating itself for its

own sake. (The altruism that can occur in high-level experience, accordingly, is an extreme exemplification of a subjective universal.)

7. *Value experience.* This universal is best described in Whitehead's own words: "The element of value, of being valuable, of having value, of being an end in itself, of being something which is for its own sake, must not be omitted in any account of an event as the most concrete actual something. 'Value' is the word I use for the intrinsic reality of an event" (*SMW,* 93).

8. *Duration.* This dimension is the time, the epoch, the arrest between an experience's two transitions: its arising from past influences and the perishing of its own subjectivity in the transition to future experiences. The duration, which from the outside might constitute less than a billionth of a second in the lowest-grade experiences, is the event's experienced time to be, its time of "enjoyment."

9. *Perspectival location.* Every experience is from some perspective in relation to other things, both spatially and temporally: Experience is always *here* and *now.* This point and the previous one together reflect the fact that all actual occasions are both temporally and spatially extensive.

These subjective universals flesh out the notion that creative experience is, in Whitehead's phrase, the "universal of universals" (*PR,* 21), in the sense of "the ultimate behind all forms" (*PR,* 20), the dynamic "stuff" in which all abstract forms are embedded in actual things. The meaning of the idea that creative experience is the ultimate reality, and what this implies in terms of revising the materialistic view of nature (which materialism and dualism share), can be made clearer by comparing "creative experience" with "energy" as understood in physics.

I referred earlier to Whitehead's assertion that the physicists' energy is an abstraction (*SMW,* 36). Such an assertion by itself, he recognizes, is all too easy to make: "The mere phrase that 'physical science is an abstraction', is a confession of philosophical failure. It is the business of rational thought to describe the more concrete fact from which that abstraction is derivable" (*AI,* 186). So, what is the energy as described in physics an abstraction from? Whitehead's answer: "The notion of physical energy, which is at the base of physics, must . . . be conceived as an abstraction from the complex energy, emotional and purposeful, inherent in the subjective form of the final synthesis in which each occasion completes itself" (*AI,* 186). In other words, the widespread idea that *energy* (as conceived in physics) is the ultimate reality embodied in all actual things is an example of the fallacy of misplaced concreteness. This concept of energy points to something real, but it has the reality of an abstraction from full-fledged creative experience, which is always emotional and purposeful. In this regard, we can recall Whitehead's assertion (based on his own days as a mathematical physicist) that physics abstracts from "what anything is in itself"—that is, its intrinsic reality. Furthermore, even in dealing with the extrinsic reality of things—

meaning their aspects in other things—it abstracts still further, paying attention to these external aspects only "as modifying the spatio-temporal specifications of the life histories of those other things" (*SMW*, 153). In saying this he is not criticizing physics. He is only saying that insofar as human beings (including physicists) try to think about how the world really is, we should not assume that physics, given the abstractions it makes for its limited purposes, describes the full reality of the most elementary types of actual events at the base of nature. To get a fuller account of what these actual events are in themselves, we need to engage in imaginative generalization, through which we can develop what I call an "inner physics." The development of the subjective universals is part and parcel of that imaginative generalization.

From this perspective, one of the problems often raised against any form of interactionism, the charge that it would violate the principle of the conservation of energy, is not a problem. I had referred in chapter 6 to W. D. Hart's suggestion that we could think in terms of a form of "psychic energy" that would be embodied in minds. Such an enlargement of the concept of energy would be simply the latest in a long string of enlargements that have been necessary to preserve the principle of conservation. Psychic energy would be added to the forms of energy, such as mechanical, electrodynamic, chemical, and thermodynamic, into which energy as such is interconvertible. I pointed out that this suggestion, although proposed by Hart as a solution to a problem of dualistic interaction, actually moves toward a *nondualistic* interactionism. The Whiteheadian position developed here completes that movement, thereby making Hart's proposal even more viable.

In enlarging the notion of energy, it is a purely terminological matter whether we come to speak of "creativity" (as Whitehead usually does), of "creative experience" (as I have), or of a more "complex energy" (as Whitehead does in the passage quoted above). The substantive point is that there are two phases to the embodiment of energy in any event: the subjective phase and the objective phase. The idea of "psychic energy" has seemed purely metaphorical, referring to something that could not conceivably be interconvertible with the forms of energy thus far acknowledged by science, because all those forms involve energy in its objective or extrinsic phase, whereas the psychic energy known in our own experience is energy in its subjective or intrinsic phase. (This point will be explained more fully in the next section.) The development of an inner biology of cells (what Whitehead called a "psychological physiology"), as well as an inner physics, will involve positing a subjective as well as an objective phase of the embodiment of energy in *all* unified events. This means that the transition from intrinsic or psychic energy to *extrinsic* energy will be assumed to be going on all the time. The conversions occurring in the interaction of mind and brain will be exceptional with regard to the level at which they occur, but they will have multiple analogies with interconversions of energy at lower levels, such as that going on within the cell between the molecules and the cell as a whole. (This point will be explained more fully in the discussion of "compound individuals" in chapter 9.)

This enlargement of the notion of energy is at the heart of Whitehead's construction of a cosmology in which the mind-body relation will no longer automatically be thought of as the mind-body *problem.* "The key notion from which such construction should start," he says, "is that the energetic activity considered in physics is the emotional intensity entertained in life" (*MT,* 168).

The difference between Whitehead's "organic realism" and the materialistic realism presupposed by most science and philosophy in the modern period, at least with respect to the "physical world," can be clarified still further by reflecting on the meaning of the idea that physics studies the "simplest things" in nature. The usual assumption is that the so-called elementary particles, such as photons, protons, neutrons, and neutrinos, or now perhaps quarks, *as described by physics,* are the simplest actual things, of which more complex things are composed. Whitehead disagrees, saying that the simplest *actual* things are the simplest occasions of experience, of which the "elementary particles" as described by physicists are abstractions. Whitehead does say, it may be recalled, that the Cartesian separation of body and mind allowed "the simplest things to be studied first," which might seem to imply that the simplest actual things are physical things wholly devoid of experience. But Whitehead immediately corrects that possible misapprehension, saying that "these simplest things" are the most "widespread habits of nature," by which he means what have been called "laws of nature" (*MT,* 154f.). The term "laws" reflects the assumption that the regularities at issue resulted from supernatural imposition. The term "habits," which Whitehead shares with Peirce and James,[5] reflects a naturalistic interpretation of these regularities. In any case, to describe a thing's *habits,* especially in externalist terms, is clearly to describe not the thing in its concreteness, as it is in itself, but a gross abstraction therefrom. Not even the crudest behaviorist would make that mistake with regard to a rat, let alone a human being. An analogous mistake, even if on a lesser scale, has been made, Whitehead suggests, with regard to the entities studied by that level of behaviorism that we call modern physics.

This switch from thinking of laws as imposed (at least in effect) to thinking of them as habits is important not only for overcoming the fallacy of misplaced concreteness but also for understanding how freedom is possible—the central concern of the next chapter, which centers around the concept of the compound individual. Before turning to compound individuals, however, I need to offer a brief explanation of the nature of simple enduring individuals, which will include an explanation of an issue just mentioned, the relation between the subjective and objective embodiments of creative energy.

IV. SUBJECTS, OBJECTS, AND ENDURING INDIVIDUALS: FROM PHOTONS TO PSYCHES

We saw above one of the fruits of Whitehead's reversal of late modern methodology: Rather than try to understand mind in terms of objective features assumed to be universal, we enlarge our understanding of matter by conceiving it in terms of subjective universals as well as in terms of objective features. However, as I have indicated now and then, given a pluralistic monism, the generalization from mind to matter can be complemented by the reverse generalization. What can be learned from physics that can be applied, by analogy, to our minds?

By far the most important generalization Whitehead makes from physics is the notion, derivable from both relativity and quantum physics, that the world studied by physics is composed of spatial-temporal *events*. We have already seen one implication he draws therefrom: the notion that each unit of nature has a certain minimal duration, which means that there are no actual infinitesimals and therefore no "nature at an instant." A second implication is that the apparently enduring things, such as electrons and photons, are in reality *temporally ordered societies* of events, in which events with essentially the same form follow on one another rapidly (sometimes a billion or more per second): "The real actual things that endure are all societies. They are not actual occasions" (*AI*, 204). Although this notion can be derived from reflection on one's own experience—both Buddhists and William James, with his notion of "drops of perception," seem to have done so—Whitehead evidently derived it primarily from twentieth-century physics, then generalized it to our own stream of experience, concluding that the apparently continuous stream actually comes in drops, or occasions, of experience. The generalization of this notion lies at the root of that aspect of his philosophy that is, along with his inversion of the sensationist doctrine of perception, his most original contribution to our understanding of both mind and matter and their interconnection.

The idea that our own experience is in reality a series of discrete drops of experience provides the basis for answering the primary philosophical question about causality: How are efficient and final causation (in the sense of self-determination in terms of an ideal end or *finis*) related? "One task of a sound metaphysics," Whitehead comments, "is to exhibit final and efficient causes in their proper relation to each other" (*PR*, 84). A solution has been impossible as long as the ultimate units—the "substances" in the sense of the most fully *actual* entities—were assumed to be enduring individuals. As such, they could seem to be capable of only one of the two kinds of causation—material bodies could exert and be affected only by efficient causation, whereas minds, as illustrated most clearly by Leibniz's windowless monads, could exemplify only final causation—or else efficient and final causation could, mysteriously enough, run parallel to each other. There was no way to conceptualize what our experience seems to suggest, that efficient causation conditions final causation, which then becomes the basis for another act of efficient causation. For example, my present experience is conditioned by causation both from my body and from past states of my own mind. These efficient causes, however, do not totally determine my present experience: I still can, and in fact must, decide precisely how to respond to those conditioning causes—those bodily cravings, those promises made, those plans, those sensory percepts. When I do make my decisions, they seem to exert causal efficacy on my bodily states and my own subsequent experiences, and so on. The idea that our *stream* of experience is really composed of momentary *occasions* of experience, each of which begins with physical experience and ends with a mental reaction thereto, explains how efficient and final causation can be interwoven.

Whitehead provides a conceptuality for this interweaving of efficient and final causation by retrofitting Leibnizian monads with windows. Each such monad begins as an open window to the past world, into which aspects of previous events stream. This is the physical side of the monad, its physical prehensions. This is the efficient causation of the past world on it. Then it has its mental side, in which it responds not just to actuality but also to ideality, drawing possibilities out of what was received and then deciding just how to respond thereto. This is the monad's self-determination, its exercise of final causation. When this decision has been made, the subjective phase of that monad is completed: Its subjectivity perishes. But *it* does not perish. The end of its existence as a subject of experience means the beginning of its existence as a cause on, and thereby an object in, the experience of subsequent subjects. This is why it is not simply located in one place. It exerts efficient causation on subsequent subjects, hurling aspects of itself into *their* open windows (*AI*, 177). In this way Whitehead's monads are subject to and exert efficient causation and thereby have the physicality that Leibniz's monads did not (*PR*, 19). This is made possible by making the monads momentary events, rather than enduring substances. With that switch, of course, it is better to give up the term "monads," precisely because of its association with enduring units that cannot really prehend other actual things.

Enduring individuals had traditionally been conceived as numerically self-identical substances enduring through time, for which relations to other things were "metaphysical nuisances," being at best construed as "accidents" (*PR,* 79, 137). Enduring individuals are reconceived by Whitehead to be temporally ordered *societies* of momentary occasions of experience, in which there is a *perpetual oscillation* between subjectivity and objectivity, final causation and efficient causation. Each occasion's "activity in *self*-formation passes into its activity of *other*-formation" (*AI*, 193).

Having generalized the idea of momentary events from physics to the psyche, Whitehead can then generalize this notion of the perpetual oscillation between subjectivity and objectivity to all enduring individuals, including those of physics. Each event is a subject for itself before it is an object for others. All things other than our own experience *appear* to be mere objects, rather than subjects, because by the time they can be prehended they *are* objects; their subjectivity has perished. This is the very precondition for their being objects for our perception, or for their exerting any efficient causation whatsoever. This is one of the several interrelated explanations as to why, if the universe is *really* composed exhaustively of active subjects, it *seems* to be composed primarily of passive objects. It is *not* composed exhaustively of things that are *simply* subjects (as was the Leibnizian universe); it is composed of subjects-that-become-objects. So, we are right to think that everything that we perceive is an object—in the ontological as well as the epistemic sense of the term. We are only wrong to think of them as *mere* objects. Some of them, the true individuals (as distinct from the aggregational societies), are objects-that-were-first-subjects. They are, accordingly, the kinds of objects that can pass on values to us, because in their phase of subjectivity they had themselves experienced values. Furthermore, they are usually objects that are parts of enduring individuals with subjects who are now contemporaneous with us, subjects with their own intrinsic value.

It is through this idea that Whitehead's philosophy provides the basis for what Strawson calls a "qualitative-character-of-experience physics" through which the "theoretical heterogeneity" of the predicates of physics and those of experience can be overcome (*MR*, 88f.). The physical predicates refer to actualities (and aggregational clusters thereof) in their objective or superjective mode of existence, in which they exist for others, and in which their *esse* is *percipi*. The experiential predicates apply to actualities in their subjective mode of existence, in which their *esse* is *percepere*. This gives us theoretical homogeneity for all individuals, from photons to cells to human beings. It does not do this as idealists have traditionally tried, by making the physical predicates less real than the experiential. And it does not do it as materialists have tried, by making the experiential predicates less real than the physical. It does so by saying that every actual entity has two modes of existence, a subjective mode, in which it has none but experiential properties, and an objective or superjective mode, in which it has none but objective properties (which can be equated with publicly observable properties if the notion of "public observability" is not limited to properties observable through *sensory* perception). Because both modes of existence belong equally to the essence of what it is to be an actual entity, both types of predicates are equally necessary to describe it.

This position involves a modified acceptance of Strawson's sense that an integrated position would need to say that experiential phenomena "are just one more variety of physical phenomenon," so that, for example, "the experiential is as much of a physical phenomenon as electric charge" (*MR*, 41, 58). Indeed, Strawson himself suggests that panpsychism, at least of one type, says that "being experience-involving is a fundamental property of existing things on a par with extension, rest mass, or electric charge" (*MR*, 77). My Whiteheadian panexperientialism does say that experiential features belong to all actual entities as fully as do those objective features that are usually called "physical." In this sense they are "on a par" with them. But it can be misleading to suggest that experiential phenomena are "just one more variety" of physical phenomena, as this could suggest that they belong to the actualities *in the same mode of existence*. Trying to think of experiential qualities as "on a par" with properties such as mass, charge, and spatial extension *in this sense*, however, is precisely what is impossible. To make the idea of their equal reality intelligible, we must say that the experiential predicates apply only to the actual entity in its subjective mode of existence, when it exists in and for itself, whereas the other predicates apply to it only in its objective or superjective mode of existence, when it exists for others (as an efficient cause on them). One comes closer to this idea by saying (as do panpsychists in the Spinozistic tradition) that the experiential and the objective properties are identical, in the sense that the former simply represent the inside (first-person) view of the latter. The idea that the experiential and the objective features of an actual entity exist *simultaneously,* however, is problematic, perhaps impossible to conceive consistently. It would, for example, make the relation between final causation (self-determination) and efficient causation unintelligible: How could an actual entity already be exerting efficient causation on others while it was still determining exactly what it is to be? (And, indeed, Spinozistic panpsychists are generally determinists, as they cannot attribute any degree of self-determining power to any individuals.) The Whiteheadian view espoused here, in any case, is that the objective mode of an actual entity, with its objective properties, exists only after the subjective mode has come to completion.

This view includes that idea, already intimated, that the type of causality we experience in relation to our own past experiences and our bodily members can also be generalized to other things. The way in which our present experience prehends immediately previous occasions of our own experience, incorporating their basic character and continuing their projects and subjective forms, can be used to understand the continuity of enduring individuals in the worlds of biology and physics. At the same time, my present experience is not *simply* a continuation of my past experiences, with their emotions and purposes, but is constantly broken into by multiple routes of causation from my bodily members, some of which carry causal influence from things beyond the body. This fact can be generalized to understand many-termed causal relations in nature in general, the relations that generate space as well as time (*AI*, 184–89, 221; *MT*, 160–63).

Furthermore, on the principle that our own experience is part of nature as much as anything else, we can generalize from our own distinctively mental experience, in which we grasp possibilities as such with appetition, to the notion that all unitary events have a mental dimension to their experience, hence at least some slight degree of final causation. Whitehead's justification for this inference is again his genuine nondualism. Materialists provide reductionistic explanations of the later products of evolution in terms of the earlier ones. But this is a one-sided application of the implications of nondualism. In a discussion limited to living things (he elsewhere extends the point to the inorganic realm), Whitehead asks: "But why construe the later forms by analogy to the earlier forms? Why not reverse the process? It would seem to be more sensible, more truly empirical, to allow each living species to make its own contribution to the demonstration of factors inherent in living things" (*FOR*, 15). Besides being more sensible and empirical, understanding the earlier in terms of the later (as well as vice versa) is also pragmatic: It helps us avoid an essential dualism somewhere in the process, whether explicit or camouflaged.

One final dimension of Whitehead's overcoming of dualism between the human mind and the enduring individuals comprising even the most elementary levels of nature needs to be brought out explicitly. This is, in fact, one of the basic dualisms with which we began—that between minds as temporal but nonspatial and physical things as spatial but not essentially temporal. Whitehead overcomes the vicious dualism between these two types of actual things by putting a duality within each actual entity. I mentioned earlier that he uses the term "actual occasion" to connote the fact that all actual entities are both spatially and temporally extended. But he explains that general statement more precisely. The distinction between the actualities with and those without duration can be understood as the distinction between the subjective and objective modes of existence of each actual occasion. Qua subject, an actual occasion enjoys duration; qua object for later subjects, it is purely spatial, with no duration left. We know ourselves from within, hence as having duration, and other things from without, hence as devoid of duration. To translate this epistemic duality into an ontological dualism between two different kinds of actualities—those that are always subjects and those that are always objects—is to commit a category mistake (as Kant recognized in the passage discussed in the previous chapter): The mistake is to contrast things as known from within with things as known from without and to conclude from this *epistemic* contrast that they are *ontologically* disparate.

The other side of the traditional dualism was that between physicality as spatial and mentality as nonspatial. Whitehead turns this dualism into a duality within each actual occasion as subject: "Each actuality is essentially bipolar, physical and mental, and the physical inheritance is essentially accompanied by a conceptual reaction. . . . So though mentality is non-spatial, mentality is always a reaction from, and integration with, physical experience which is spatial" (*PR*, 108). (The physical pole is spatial in that it is composed of prehensions of things in the spatiotemporal world; the mental pole is not spatial because its distinctive objects belong to the realm of possibility, not actuality. Whitehead likewise says that whereas the physical pole is "in time," the mental pole is "out of time" [*PR*, 248], because its objects are eternal. These points refer, however, to the *objects* of the mental pole. The *prehensions* of those objects are fully parts of the spatiotemporal occasion.) Accordingly, although Whitehead agrees that the physical is spatial and the mental nonspatial, he avoids a vicious dualism between two different types of actual things. That "vicious dualism," he says, results from "mistaking an abstraction for a final concrete fact" (*AI*, 190). His doctrine of momentary occasions of experience, each of which is both subject and object and thereby both with and without duration, and each of which as subject is both physical and mental and thereby both spatial and nonspatial, is his way of overcoming the fallacy of misplaced concreteness and its resulting vicious dualism between mind and matter, soul and body.

The next chapter builds on this understanding of enduring individuals to show how compound individuals with varying degrees of freedom can arise. This discussion of compound individuals also deals with the major question about panexperientialism and consciousness raised in chapter 7 but not addressed in the present chapter, which Seager calls "the combination problem": How can a unified experience emerge out of a multiplicity of neurons, even assuming that each of them has some experience of its own? In other words, can Whiteheadian panexperientialism provide an intelligible understanding of a whole that is more than the sum of its parts and, in particular, a whole with the kind of unity we know our own conscious experience to have?

NINE

Compound Individuals and Freedom

As we have seen, freedom is the hard-core commonsense notion that is most often denied. Even Searle, after castigating others for doubting "obvious" facts of our experience, says that even though we cannot in practice doubt the reality of freedom, it must be an illusion. To be sure, one reason that freedom can be denied by Searle, McGinn, and many others, none of whom would dream of adopting an eliminativist strategy with regard to consciousness, is that freedom is not *as* obvious as consciousness. The denial that we have a degree of freedom is not prima facie as absurd as the denial that we enjoy a degree of conscious awareness. However, the denial of freedom does involve one in self-contradiction just as surely, because it denies a hard-core commonsense belief, meaning one that we all inevitably presuppose in practice. Whitehead pointed to this self-contradiction with the example of professors who write papers with the purpose of proving that purposes play no causal role in human behavior (*FOR,* 14). Some philosophers, to be sure, admit the causal role of purposes while denying freedom, saying that the purposes are themselves fully determined by antecedent causes. Whitehead's point, however, is that in practice we presuppose that our purposes are *not* thus fully determined. As Searle points out, "The experience of freedom, that is to say, the experience of the sense of alternative possibilities, is built into the very structure of conscious, voluntary, intentional human behaviour" (*MBS,* 98).

The problem of freedom and determinism is one of the two central dimensions of the mind-body problem (the other being, of course, that of how conscious experience could arise from the body). It has not, however, been portrayed as central in most treatments of the mind-body problem in recent times, except by some dualists. This is an aspect of our wishful-and-fearful perceiving: If we have no solution for a problem, we tend not to perceive it *as* a genuine problem. But a problem it is. Whitehead illustrates the nature of the contradiction between theory and practice in these terms: "The enterprises produced by the individualistic energy of the European peoples presuppose physical actions directed to final causes. But the science which is employed in their development is based on a philosophy which asserts that physical causation is supreme, and which disjoins the physical cause from the final end" (*SMW,* 76). Whitehead then adds: "It is not popular to dwell on the absolute contradiction here involved." It is not popular because we do not like to be confronted with contradictions in our own thinking, especially if we can see no way out.

Considerable energy has been devoted to this question by some philosophers. If they are not dualists, however, their solutions generally reduce to variants of one of two strategies: (1) denying that we have freedom or (2) redefining freedom such that it is compatible with our actions, even our beliefs and attitudes, being completely the products of deterministic (or, allowing for a degree of quantum indeterminacy, virtually deterministic) efficient causation. The second solution (compatibilism), however, finally reduces to the first, because *freedom as we presuppose it* in practice is, as Searle has stressed (*MBS,* 87, 92, 95), freedom in the sense of a *choice among alternatives in the moment.* In looking back at our own actions with pride or shame, or in responding to the actions of others with praise or condemnation, we presuppose that the agent at that moment, with all the antecedent conditions just as they were, could have done otherwise. Compatibilism denies this and thereby, as Searle points out (*MBS,* 89), denies freedom as we presuppose it.* (The question of whether moral responsibility really implies metaphysical freedom, as I here imply, is discussed in Section V, below.)

The conflict between our intuitions supporting freedom and those supporting determinism has been one of the chief cultural problems of modern times. Whitehead, in pointing to this fact as one of the effects of scientific materialism on the modern world, describes two inconsistent attitudes:

> A scientific realism based on mechanism, is conjoined with an unwavering belief in the world of men and of the higher animals as being composed of self-determining organisms. This radical inconsistency at the basis of modern thought accounts for much that is half-hearted and wavering in our civilisa-

---

*Sometimes compatibilism involves, instead of a Pickwickian definition of freedom, simply the claim that explaining our action in terms of a genuinely free decision among alternatives is not incompatible with also explaining it in a fully reductionistic, mechanistic way. But such a position runs afoul of our regulative principle of causal-explanatory exclusion, affirmed in chapter 4. That is, if the state of our bodily atoms fully determines the state of our minds, including our apparent decision among alternatives, it is not intelligible also to refer to "free choice" as an explanation.

tion. It would [not]* be going too far to say that it distracts thought. It enfeebles it, by reason of the inconsistency lurking in the background. (*SMW,* 76)

Whitehead illustrates this enfeeblement in terms of Tennyson's *In Memoriam.* On the one hand, one line in the poem alludes to the problem of mechanism: " 'The stars,' she whispers, 'blindly run.' " On the other hand, although Tennyson deals with many other religious and scientific problems, he does not directly face this one. His problem, Whitehead suggests, is this: "There are opposing visions of the world, and both of them command his assent by appeals to ultimate intuitions from which there seems no escape" (*SMW,* 77). One intuition is that we are significantly free. The other, which is implicit in Tennyson's poem, is explicated by Whitehead thus: "Each molecule blindly runs. The human body is a collection of molecules. Therefore, the human body blindly runs, and therefore there can be no individual responsibility for the action of the body" (*SMW,* 78).

The perplexity resulting from this conflict between two "opposing ultimate intuitions" has been widespread and of long standing. Whitehead, in fact, describes the nineteenth century as "a perplexed century" (*SMW,* 82). The perplexity was not, as with most previous issues, simply that of the onlooker, confused by the seemingly intractable opposition between warring camps: "Each individual was divided against himself." Most philosophers in our time have not admitted to this perplexity, at least publicly. But Nagel and Searle are two exceptions.** As we saw earlier, Nagel says that he changes his mind about the problem of freedom every time he thinks about it (*VN,* 112). This internal division is described in terms of conflicting intuitions. On the one hand, "in ordinary life" he cannot help holding himself and others responsible. On the other hand, given seemingly inescapable intuitions about the nature of the world and of persons within it, he can find no way to make rational sense of freedom. Searle describes the conflict as a "philosophical conundrum," which can be formulated as follows:

---

*The "not" is not in the text. That it should be is shown by Whitehead's reference on the next page to "this distracting inconsistency."

**A third is Kim, who says that the "central issue of the mind-body debate" is, "how can the mind exert its causal powers in a world constituted by physical stuff and governed by physical law?" (*SM,* xv). Although Kim characteristically describes the problem in terms of the reality of "mental causation," not of freedom as such, the former is clearly a necessary condition of the latter. The tension between Kim's two basic assumptions—the truth of physicalism and the reality of mentality and thereby of mental causation—is at the heart of my analysis of his position in the next chapter.

> On the one hand, a set of very powerful arguments force us to the conclusion that free will has no place in the universe. On the other hand, a series of powerful arguments based on facts of our own experience inclines us to the conclusion that there must be some freedom of the will because we all experience it all the time. (*MBS,* 88)

Although Searle would like to be able to reconcile his scientific beliefs and his belief in freedom, he is unable to do so. His "solution" is to affirm a position that excludes freedom, while adding that no arguments against freedom, including his own, could possibly convince him that his behavior really is unfree.

A precondition for a real solution, as I suggested in chapter 5, is to recognize that of the "opposing ultimate intuitions," the intuition about genuine freedom is more ultimate. That is, it is a hard-core commonsense intuition. The intuitions that seem to lead dialectically to its negation are less ultimate, being at most merely soft-core commonsense intuitions of late modernity. They, accordingly, are the ones to examine. Searle, as the above extract indicates, assumes the opposite. That is, he says that the arguments from science "force us" to conclude that there can be no freedom in the universe, while the series of arguments from our own experience merely "inclines us" to think that we really must have freedom. In constructing his position, accordingly, he allows the former arguments (based on soft-core common sense) to outweigh the latter (based on hard-core common sense), concluding that although his belief in freedom is "unshakable," it must, nevertheless, be an illusion (*MBS,* 5, 94). In examining this paradoxical conclusion, he says, "For reasons I don't really understand," evolution has built the experience of freedom "into the very structure of conscious, intentional human behavior" (*MBS,* 98). His statement that he does not understand the reasons for this implies that the reason is *not* that we are genuinely free. However, if we cannot really give up our intuition about freedom, because it is inevitably presupposed in practice, we should instead turn our critical eye to those (soft-core) intuitions that *seem* to "force us" to deny freedom in our scientific and philosophical theories.

I. FIVE PRINCIPLES PRESUPPOSED IN THE DENIAL OF FREEDOM

The first step in working toward a real solution is to see what those latter intuitions are. The various presuppositions behind the denial of human freedom in our time seem to be the following.

1. The behavior of physical entities, such as atoms and molecules, is entirely determined by the laws of physics and chemistry and is therefore fully deterministic. (Even if there be ontological [not merely epistemic] indeterminacy with regard to individuals at the

quantum level, it is canceled out in aggregations of such individuals by the "law of large numbers.")

2. The human body is composed entirely of atoms and their subatomic constituents.
3. There is no "mind" distinct from the brain.
4. Even if (*per impossibile*) there were a mind distinct from the brain, it would not be capable of self-determining freedom. (This would be complete epiphenomenalism.)
5. Even if (*per impossibile*) there were a distinct mind capable of self-determining freedom, it would be capable of determining only some of its own states, not those of the body. (This would be partial epiphenomenalism.) The reasons for this conclusion are the following.
   a. Being different in kind from physical matter, such a mind would not be able causally to affect it.
   b. Even if the problem created by Principle 5a could be avoided by reconceiving mind and/or matter so as to affirm a nondualistic interactionism, such interaction would violate the law of the conservation of energy.
   c. Even if the problem created by Principle 5b could be solved by enlarging the notion of "energy" so as to include the mind with its "psychic energy" as part of the closed system of nature within which energy is conserved, there would still be the fact, enunciated in Principle 1, that atoms and subatomic particles within the body obey the same physical and chemical laws as they would outside the body, so that their behavior could not be partly determined by a mind. If there were a "ghost in the machine," it would, like all ghosts, be impotent.

From these five principles, taken as premises, it follows that, even if we could squeak out an affirmation of partial internal freedom so that we would be partly responsible for our beliefs and attitudes, our outer, bodily behavior would be as fully determined by a chain of efficient causation, stretching back into the indefinite past, as is the behavior of the stellar masses. Indicting a thief for stealing would, to use an example of Whitehead's, be like indicting the sun for rising (*FOR,* 14).

Searle's argument that the "contemporary scientific view" does not allow for human freedom (*MBS,* 93) can be seen to be based on these five principles. With regard to the first principle: Although Searle knows better than to say that the behavior of everything is determined by "laws" (MBP, 144), he does assume that the behavior of all more or less complex things, from molecules to human bodies, is determined by events at the microlevel (MBP,

141, 144). Scientific explanation, according to Searle, is in terms of "bottom-up causation," which means that the features of every aspect of nature "are determined at the basic microlevels of physics" (*MBS,* 93). Searle recognizes, to be sure, that contemporary quantum physics "allows for an indeterminacy at the level of particle physics," but he argues (with an implicit appeal to the "law of large numbers") that it provides no support for "any indeterminacy at the level of objects that matter to us" (*MBS,* 86f.).

With regard to the second principle—that the human body is composed entirely of molecules and their atomic and subatomic constituents—Searle believes it to be one of "the obvious facts of physics" that "the world consists entirely of physical particles in fields of force" (*RM,* xii), of "atoms in the void" (MBWP, 225).

With regard to the third principle—that there is no "mind" distinct from the brain—Searle says of the human head that "the brain is the only thing in there" (*RM,* 248) and that "consciousness is just an ordinary biological, that is, physical, feature of the brain" (*RM,* 13). Whereas we might think that human beings, or any other animals—especially those with central nervous systems—are *structurally* different from things such as pieces of glass or bodies of water, Searle says otherwise. Having said that "we explain the behaviour of surface features of a phenomenon such as the transparency of glass or the liquidity of water, in terms of the behaviour of microparticles such as molecules," he says that "the relation of the mind to the brain is an example of such a relation" (*MBS,* 93).

Searle's acceptance of the fourth principle—that if there *were* a distinct mind it would not be capable of self-determining freedom—is shown by his rejection of the idea that "consciousness gets squirted out by the behavior of the neurons in the brain, but once it has been squirted out, it then has a life of its own" (*RM,* 112).* Leaving no doubt, Searle says of the mind that "like the rest of nature, its features are determined at the basic microlevels of physics" (*MBS,* 94). This (allegedly necessary) feature of science, that it explains all surface features in terms of bottom-up causation from the microlevel of nature, is why science allows no place for free will (*MBS,* 93).

---

*In denying that consciousness has any independent causal power, Searle is denying the position sometimes known as "radical emergentism," which holds that, in Seager's words, "some assemblages of physical parts have causal powers that don't depend entirely upon the causal powers of those parts" (CIP, 276). My Whiteheadian panexperientialism affirms radical emergentism in this sense; to deny it is to deny the possibility of genuine freedom. What my position denies, by contrast, is *magical* emergentism, in which parts wholly devoid of spontaneity could be assembled in such a way as to have spontaneity. Given the premise that all "parts" are wholly devoid of spontaneity, accordingly, radical emergentism would be magical emergentism, so that its denial would be fully rational. What is less than fully rational is to rest content with the premise leading to that conclusion.

The fifth principle—that even if the mind had self-determining freedom it would not be able to direct the body—is also affirmed by Searle. That particles are only statistically determined, he argues, is no reason to think that "there is or could be some mental energy of human freedom that can move molecules," causing them to "swerve from their paths" (*MBS,* 87). His reasoning here is based on the assumption that if there were a mind distinct from the brain, it would be an ontologically different kind of thing, so that the problem of dualistic interaction would arise (Principle 5a):

> If our thoughts and feelings are truly mental, how can they affect anything physical? . . . Are we supposed to think that our thoughts and feelings can somehow produce chemical effects in our brains and the rest of our nervous system? How could such a thing occur? Are we supposed to think that thoughts can wrap themselves around the axons or shake the dendrites or sneak inside the cell wall and attack the cell nucleus? (*MBS,* 17)

Searle, to be sure, does affirm that consciousness can cause behavior. But this is, as he puts it, because "thoughts are not gaseous and ethereal" but are instead "physical states of the brain" (MBWP, 227). As such, thoughts are not at all self-determining but are fully determined by neuronal activity.

I do not know whether Searle somewhere buttresses his argument against this kind of mind-brain interactionism by appeal to the conservation of energy (Principle 5b). But he does clearly assume that particles within the body are determined by the same kinds of forces as those outside (Principle 5c). For example, in stating that quantum indeterminacy is irrelevant to the issue of human freedom because all indeterminacy is canceled out at the level of objects that matter to us, he specifically includes human bodies (*MBS,* 87). So, because one can say neither that the brain itself, being composed of trillions of particles, has freedom nor that there is a distinct, self-determining mind that influences the brain, freedom of bodily behavior is ruled out. Although in practice we cannot help presupposing that we have freedom, we must in our theory conclude that freedom is an illusion.

The crucial assumption in Searle's position is that *all part-whole relations are structurally the same.* The fact that the macrolevel behavior of some wholes, such as rocks and bodies of water, is fully determined by events at the microlevel, accordingly, implies that this principle of bottom-up determinism holds universally. This assumption depends, in turn, on Searle's presupposition—criticized in chapter 8 as flowing from the fallacy of misplaced concreteness—that the ultimate units of nature are insentient particles wholly devoid of experience and spontaneity, because such ultimate units *would* be capable of forming only the kind of aggregational wholes that can be understood entirely in terms of the causality of their tiniest parts.

Searle has said to eliminative materialists, "If your theory results in the view that consciousness does not exist, you have simply produced a *reductio ad absurdum* of the theory" (*RM,* 8). Because Searle, however, agrees that freedom as well as consciousness is inevitably presupposed in practice, it would seem that by implying that freedom is illusory, he has produced a *reductio ad absurdum* of his own theory.* When we have a *reductio,* of course, the implication is that at least one of its premises must be faulty. Indeed, Searle himself has said, "I am confident that in our entire philosophical tradition we are making some fundamental mistake, or a set of fundamental mistakes in the whole discussion of the free will problem" (MBP, 145). My argument is that *all five* of the above premises are faulty, that they together constitute the "set of fundamental mistakes" that has made the problem of freedom and determinism seem insoluble.

Many scientists and others who have imbibed the scientific orthodoxy of late modernity summarized in the above five principles do not, of course, think through the implications of these principles sufficiently to realize that they, taken together, imply that the behavior of human beings is fully determined. But the contradiction between these principles and our presuppositions about our own freedom is there, lurking beneath the surface, waiting to be evoked into consciousness by an inconsiderate philosopher. I had the experience of being such a philosopher a few years ago. In a lecture I gave at a conference in which the other participants were all scientists, I dwelt on this problem of the contradiction between scientists' presuppositions about their own freedom, even in their scientific activities, and the implications of their philosophic-scientific theories. Later that evening, another participant—one of the world's leading scientists in his field—struck up a conversation with me, saying that he did not really feel the force of my argument. I proceeded to go through the various steps. "You assume, don't you," I asked, "that the physical processes you study are all fully determined by antecedent causes?" He said, "Yes, I assume that they are all influenced by previous events." "Influenced? Isn't that too weak?" I asked. "Don't you assume that they are fully determined?" He replied that that

---

*One could maintain that it is not necessarily self-contradictory to believe that all of one's behavior and beliefs are strictly determined while admitting that one necessarily acts in practice as if one had freedom. After all, one could believe that we are *determined to believe that we are free.* (Some suggest, for example, that the belief in freedom had been selected for in the course of human evolution, because this belief increases the chances of survival.) But such a move would itself have self-defeating implications: If we once say that we have been programmed to believe a false proposition, why should we not become suspicious of all the other propositions whose truth we in practice cannot help presupposing? We could, for example, conclude that although we cannot help believing in the principle of noncontradiction, it is simply a helpful illusion. This conclusion, however, would undermine the basis for all arguments. Even if one declared purely logical truths, such as the principle of self-contradiction, exempt from this skeptical treatment, one could still apply it to the substantive premises used to lead to any conclusion—such as the conclusion that determinism must be true.

indeed is what he assumed. I then said that I presumed that he was not a dualist, that he did not believe in a nonphysical soul or mind. He said that he absolutely was not a dualist. "Does the combination of those two principles," I concluded, "not imply that your own behavior is as fully determined as that of the physical processes you study?" At this point he turned white, saying that he had never thought of that.* Our conversation then drifted to other matters, but at the end of the evening he said, "I don't think I'm going to sleep very well tonight. You've really bothered me." At the close of the conference the next day, as we were all saying our farewells, he suggested that if I were ever in his city I arrange to come by so that we could talk more about this problem.

As this story illustrates, even if the problem is not widely acknowledged (in part because, as Whitehead says, it has not been popular to dwell on it), there is an absolute contradiction between the freedom that we all presuppose in practice and the implications of ideas that are widely accepted as established scientific fact. Philosophy can have no higher calling than to try to resolve this contradiction at the heart of contemporary culture. Whitehead's philosophy was devoted in large part to doing precisely this. The widespread neglect of his alternative by philosophers has meant that his suggested solution has been largely unknown to scientists and others to whom it might prove helpful.

II. WHY THE FIVE PRINCIPLES PRESUPPOSED IN THE DENIAL OF FREEDOM SHOULD BE REJECTED

In any case, the next step in a solution to the problem of freedom and determinism is to ask whether all of the above five principles behind determinism are really as inescapable as they have generally seemed. On the basis of the alternative understanding of both matter and mind developed in the previous chapters, I will suggest that in fact all five principles are to be rejected.

I have already, in the previous two chapters, explained the grounds for rejecting Principles 5a and 5b (which assume that interactionism would necessarily imply dualism). Still needing discussion, at least more than I have offered thus far, are Principle 3 (which denies the existence of a mind numerically distinct from the brain), Principle 4 (which denies the possi-

*A philosopher who read this account in manuscript form wrote, "The guy turning white is a bit much," adding that the example seems contrived and that "the only way to save it is to *name* the guy." The story, however, is entirely true (at least to the extent that I could correctly reconstruct the actual words). And "the guy" *did* blanch. Because it was a private conversation, however, I did not feel at liberty to give his name in print. And, partly because it is my one real-life example, I was loath to give it up.

bility of self-determining freedom), Principles 1 and 5c (which claim that ultimate constituents of the body, being completely determined by physical laws, could not be affected by a distinct mind, even if there were one), and Principle 2 (which says that the human being is composed exhaustively of atoms and their constituents). I will discuss these four issues in this order, beginning with Principle 3.

Why Think of the Mind as a Distinct Actuality?

Given the previous discussion of enduring individuals from photons to psyches, the idea of the mind as an actuality must be understood to mean a *temporal society* of "occasions of experience," with those occasions being the actualities in the strictest sense. The old notion of the mind as an actuality that is numerically one through time, having various essential attributes in itself and being only accidentally related to the body, exaggerates its distinctness from the brain and the rest of the world. The Whiteheadian idea of the mind as composed of successive occasions of experience, each of which begins as an open window and is essentially constituted by its prehensions of aspects of other things into itself, allows us to conceptualize the *social* or *ecological* nature of our minds (and, by analogy, all enduring individuals). Because of this revision of what an enduring individual is, the notion of the mind as a distinct enduring individual does not belie the intimacy of its relation to the body. In any case, in speaking of the mind as a distinct actuality, the meaning is that it, as an enduring individual, is numerically distinct from the highest-level enduring individuals (the neurons) constituting the brain as such. The question before us is why we should think of our minds in this way.

One answer would be that our minds do seem to be causally affected by, and to exert causal efficacy back on, our bodies and that whatever is part of the universal nexus of cause and effect is by definition an actuality.* Although this is a good answer, the critic could still ask why we should interpret this experience, even if we take it at face value, as indicating that the mind is an actuality distinct from the brain. Why not just say that what we are experiencing is one part of the brain, known from within, receiving causal influence from, and exerting causal influence back on, other parts of the brain? In other words, why is a two-aspect view of the relation of mind to brain not adequate?

A good reply to this query could be based on the unity that our conscious experience has, which was discussed in chapter 5. There are billions of

---

*One could thereby even accept a physicalist criterion of actuality, according to which whatever is actual is physical, because each occasion of the mind's experience has a physical pole, just as does every neuronic occasion. I develop this possibility in the next chapter.

neurons in the brain and, in fact, in any distinguishable part of it. The unity of experience we enjoy, even if it is not complete, suggests that our experience is something distinct from the aggregational brain or any portion thereof. In response, however, the critic could suggest that this apparent unity may have the same status as do other apparent unities: illusion. That is, a rock appears to be a single actuality, but modern science has taught us that it is composed of billions of distinct individuals. Our phenomenological unity may be as illusory as the phenomenal unity of the rock. I can reply that we should associate agency with actualities and that our experience can *act* as a unity, whereas the rock, by contrast, cannot decide to roll up the hill. But, the critic could point out, the rock as such can exert a kind of agency that none of its individuals can: A rock falling from a cliff can crush a skull, whereas a single atom cannot. Nevertheless, I reply, the rock's emergent causal powers qua aggregational society can be explained in terms of the combined effects of its constituents: The gravitational force causing the rock to fall operates on its individual atoms, not on the rock as such. The critic could say, however, that is just the point: The rock in falling can appear to seek a state of rest; the folk physics of Aristotle taught that it actually did. But now we know that the apparent unity of action is an illusion generated by the behavior of billions of constituents. A similar illusion may lie behind the folk psychology that thinks of the mind as having a unity of action. However, I reply, there is a crucial difference between the two cases, alluded to earlier: I am directly aware of my own experience as exercising agency with a purpose not completely forced on my present experience by past causal conditioning. This kind of agency based on self-determination, which was not attributed to a rock even by Aristotle, must be taken to portend actuality. But, the critic can respond, that move brings final causation in the sense of self-determination into the definition of actuality, and that violates almost all previous conceptions of actuality. Besides, the *sense* that we exercise self-determination may well be one of the illusions behind folk psychology that it is the task of science to dispel.

With regard to the idea that our self-concepts known from self-consciousness constitute a folk psychology analogous to the folk physics of yesteryear, I could appeal to the distinction between hard-core and soft-core common-sense notions, which shows that two sets of ideas conjoined as "folk" are really different in kind.* Having already made this point at length in previous chapters, however, I will here move on to another reason for thinking of the mind as an enduring individual distinct from the brain or any of its parts.

---

*A more common way of making the point, as by David Chalmers (FU, 208f.), is that the ideas rejected as "folk physics," such as phlogiston, were explanatory posits, whereas our conscious experience, with its sense of self-determination, is phenomenologically given, not simply posited to explain something else.

At the root of the difference between Whiteheadian panexperientialism, on the one hand, and materialistic and dualistic views, on the other, is the standard of actuality employed. The objects of sensory perception provide the standard for materialists and one of the two standards for dualists. It might even provide the more important standard for present-day dualists: I quoted earlier Popper's statement that he shares "with old-fashioned materialists the view that . . . solid material bodies are the paradigms of reality" (*SAB*, 10). Of course, dualists and materialists know that rocks and other "solid material bodies" are composed of billions of microentities that do not have some of the properties of macro-objects as they appear to our senses. But they still think of the microentities in the purely externalist categories applied to such macro-objects. Whitehead argues that this notion of actuality is rooted in a failure to be sufficiently empirical in our starting point. Becoming fully empirical, he argues, would lead us to take a moment of our experience as "its own standard of actuality" (*PR*, 145).

Whitehead's argument begins with the assertion that an empiricist should "start from the immediate facts of our psychological experience" (*SMW*, 73). On this there is much agreement. The critical question, however, is what those "immediate facts" are. Most science or philosophy that considers itself empirical begins with Popper's solid material bodies, such as "this stone as grey." An empiricism that starts here, which might be called *folk empiricism*, leads straight to materialism.

Another analysis, leading to Humean phenomenalism, takes "awareness of sensation of greyness" (deriving perhaps from "unknown causes") to be the immediate fact. This latter option at least recognizes the advance made by the "subjectivist bias" introduced by Descartes, who enunciated the regulative principle that "those substances which are the subjects enjoying conscious experiences provide the primary data for philosophy, namely, themselves as in the enjoyment of such experience" (*PR*, 159). But Hume, like Descartes, missed the full implication of the change, which is that, in the case at hand, the primary fact is neither simply "this stone as grey" nor "awareness of greyness" but "my perception of this stone as grey." That is, besides explicitly acknowledging that a correct description of some experience cannot simply refer to a *datum* of this experience but must mention my *experiencing* of this datum, this description must also refer to the experience of a concrete object (the stone), not simply a quality (greyness). In Whitehead's words, "Descartes' discovery on the side of subjectivism requires balancing by an 'objectivist' principle as to the datum for experience." The result is "the reformed subjectivist principle" (*PR*, 160). Without it, solipsism threatens.

However, even this description of experience, which often leads straight to Cartesian dualism, is not sufficiently concrete. As we saw in the previous chapter, "this stone as grey" is the objective datum of a very derivative type of perception. A more concrete description of experience would be "my perception of the stone as grey by means of my prehension of my eyes." And, of course, at the same time that I am aware of this complex perception, I am aware (even if not with full consciousness) of other sensory perceptions, of emotions, pleasures, and pains arising from other parts of my body, and also of the presence of my own past experiences energizing in my present experience.

Accordingly, the correct analysis of our experience requires acceptance of the subjectivist bias introduced by Descartes and emphasized by Berkeley: What is immediately given to us for analysis are not simply such-and-such data of conscious experience, whether taken to be actualities or mere universals; what is given are *our conscious experiences of such-and-such data*. We never come upon an unexperienced thing; we never catch things as they are apart from being experienced. This fact, while much discussed, has not penetrated the ontologies of materialists and dualists, who still describe the units of nature as if the fact that we never encounter those units except as experienced by ourselves were a negligible incidental. They continue to think in categories that assume that *things as they enter into our perception*—our *sensory* perception no less—can safely be taken as the clue to the *essential nature of what things are in themselves*. This is surely a greater credulity, especially given the complex and very indirect nature of sensory perception (as analyzed in the previous chapter), than many of the beliefs that are generally mocked by these thinkers as credulous.

Whereas the subjectivist bias introduced by Descartes must be accepted, Whitehead says, a correct analysis of experience requires a rejection of the purely subjectivist interpretation of the datum of experience. We obviously have here a good and a bad type of "subjectivism."[1] Subjectivism in the good sense is the recognition that our own subjective experience is what is most immediately given to us and as such should be the starting point of our analysis of what actual things are really like. Subjectivism in the bad sense is solipsism, the belief that our conscious experience as immediately given does not include the experience of *other actual things as actual*. Subjectivism in this bad sense involves the belief that our experience begins with the perception of universals, such as grey and red shapes, and thereby with distinctively *mental* experience. Whitehead's ontology and epistemology, built around the notion that every occasion of experience begins with a *physical* prehension of other *actualities* (out of which mental prehensions of universals are derived), is his explicit repudiation of that analysis of the datum of our experience. Accordingly, he says (to repeat): "Descartes' discovery on the side of subjectivism requires balancing by an 'objectivist' principle as to the datum for experience" (*PR*, 160), which results in the *reformed* subjectivist principle.

Now for the relevance of this analysis to the question of the mind as a distinct actuality. On the one hand, the implication of subjectivism in the good sense is that on the basis of a thoroughgoing empiricist starting point, we have no basis for taking as actualities anything other than experiences themselves. We have no direct experiential basis for saying that there are any vacuous actualities, actualities devoid of experience. We do not even have any empirical basis—back to Berkeley's point—for assigning a *meaning* to the assertion that there are actual things devoid of experience, because we can give no hint as to what they might be *in themselves*. (To describe them, for example, as "permanent possibilities for sense perception" does *not* do this.) Once we realize this, we have removed one of the major bases for not thinking of our own stream (or temporal society) of experiences, our own minds, as actualities. In fact, we are virtually compelled to do so, if we are to have any actualities at all. This point does not mean, to be sure, accepting Berkeley's idealism, in which human experiences are the only actualities on this earth. What it does mean is that all other actualities affirmed must be conceived by analogy with a moment of our own experience. In other words, "the percipient occasion is its own standard of actuality" (*PR*, 145).

The full implication of this assertion, however, depends on bringing in the reformed dimension of this subjectivism, according to which the "percipient occasion" unifies into itself prehensions of other actual things. "Experience," as interpreted in line with the reformed subjectivist principle, *means* the "self-enjoyment of being one among many, and of being one arising out of the composition of many" (*PR*, 145). If our own experience is our very standard of actuality, then every actuality is to be conceived as a *unification of a given multiplicity into an experiential unity*. If this is what it *is* to be an actuality, then our own experience, in being a unification of aspects from many other things deriving from the brain and the larger world, obviously should be taken as an example of an actuality.

This argument is finally circular, of course: We have concluded that our mind as a series of moments of experience is a distinct actuality by taking any such moment as our standard of actuality. But any ontology is built on a similar circularity: Something is taken as the paradigm case of actuality, from which it follows that that something is an instance of actuality. What Whitehead has done is to provide at least a fourfold argument for taking our own experience as the standard for actuality as such: (1) the argument from empiricism concerning subjectivism, summarized above; (2) the negative argument from empiricism summarized in the previous chapter, which points out that "solid material bodies" are not immediate data of experience; (3) the positive argument from empiricism summarized in the previous chapter, which shows that the immediate data of experience—not only one's own past moments of experience but also one's bodily parts—are felt as contributing emotion to our own experience, suggesting that in themselves they enjoyed subjective experience of a sort; (4) the pragmatic argument, which is that conceiving actualities in general by analogy with our own experience *works,* in that it solves the mind-body problem and many related problems, such as those involving time, causation, and the very meaning of the realist affirmation that nature is actual apart from our perception and conception of it. Whitehead's procedure is, therefore, not circular in a vicious sense.

On the basis of this point and the previous discussion on which it is based, we can now directly address what Seager calls "the most difficult problem facing any panpsychist theory of consciousness," which is the "combination problem" of "explaining how the myriad elements of 'atomic consciousness' can be combined into a new, complex and rich consciousness such as that we possess" (CIP, 280). Believing that "the single most concentrated and insightful attack on panpsychism" is perhaps found in James's *Principles of Psychology,* Seager quotes the following passages:

> Take a sentence of a dozen words, and take twelve men and tell to each one word. Then stand the men in a row or jam them in a bunch, and let each think of his word as intently as he will; nowhere will there be a consciousness of the whole sentence. . . . Where the elemental units are supposed to be feelings, the case is in no wise altered. Take a hundred of them, shuffle them and pack them as close together as you can . . ; still each remains the same feeling it always was, shut in its own skin, windowless, ignorant of what the other feelings are and mean. There would be a hundred-and-first feeling there, if, when a group or series of such feeling were set up, a consciousness *belonging to the group as such* should emerge. And the 101st feeling would be a totally new fact; the 100 original feelings might, by a curious physical law, be a signal for its *creation,* when they came together; but they would have no substantial identity with it, nor it with them. (*POP,* 160)

Seager's response to this argument is to see it as "no more than a reasonable generalization of the mereological reductionism of which the world provides so much evidence," but which, Seager says, "we know to be false." Seager sees James, in other words, as holding the same assumption as Searle, McGinn, and most other materialists, that all apparent wholes embody the principles of "mereological composition," according to which the apparent whole is really just the sum of its parts. "The most startling revelations" of the error of this assumption, says Seager, occur in quantum mechanics: Summarizing his substantial discussion thereof, he says: "Quantum wholes are not just the sum of their parts" (CIP, 284). From this he concludes that "there is no argument from general principles against the panpsychist's combinations of elemental mental units into distinctive mental wholes" (CIP, 284).

Although, I agree, the appeal to quantum physics can indeed provide reason to doubt the widespread assumption that part-whole conceptions derived from middle-scale objects of sensory perception must be the standard for thinking of all part-whole relations, there are also other responses to the James passage. In the first place, this passage, published in 1890, did not prevent James himself from embracing panpsychism at a later time. For example, in lectures delivered in 1901–02, James said (in a passage that anticipates Whitehead's account of an occasion of experience):

> A conscious field *plus* its object as felt or thought of *plus* an attitude toward the object *plus* the sense of a self to whom the attitude belongs—such a concrete bit of personal experience may be a small bit, but it is a solid bit as long as it lasts. . . . It is a full fact . . . of the *kind* to which all realities whatsoever must belong. (*VRE*, 499)

In his outline for a course on the philosophy of nature for 1902–03, furthermore, James wrote that "pragmatism would be his method and 'pluralistic panpsychism' his doctrine," explaining that by the latter he meant that "material objects are 'for themselves' also" (*WJP*, 77). Although it has been a widespread view that, after briefly flirting with panpsychism, James left it behind in 1904 (in *Essays in Radical Empiricism*), Marcus Ford has shown beyond a reasonable doubt that James gave it up only partly and briefly, clearly reaffirming it again from 1905 until his death in 1910 (*WJP*, 75). For example, Ford quotes (*WJP*, 84) James's 1905 assertion that "our only intelligible notion of an object *in itself* is that it should be an object *for* itself, and this lands us in panpsychism and a belief that our physical perceptions are effects on us of 'psychical' realities." In 1909 James refers favorably to "the great empirical movement toward a pluralistic panpsychic view of the universe, into which our own generation has been drawn" (*PU*, 270).

For my purposes, however, an even more important response to James's 1890 argument is to see that he was *not* rejecting the kind of "compounding" involved in the Whiteheadian-Hartshornean notion of a compound individual. As James later made clear in *A Pluralistic Universe*, his target had been the kind of identity between the parts and the whole suggested by "pantheistic idealism," according to which "a collective experience" is regarded as "logically identical with a lot of distributive experiences" (*PU*, 218). James's point was that the more inclusive experience is a *new* experience, numerically distinct from the more limited experiences it includes—as shown by James's statement that, if out of 100 feelings "a consciousness *belonging to the group as such* should emerge," it would be a "101st feeling." James's argument, then, counts only against the identist form of panpsychism, according to which our unified conscious experience is supposed to be strictly (numerically) identical with the much more restricted experiences of the billions of neurons in the brain. I would argue, in agreement with the early James, that that kind of "compounding" of experience is logically self-contradictory (even if the later James withdrew his objections by rejecting the "intellectualistic logic" on which it is based).

Accordingly, James's early argument poses no difficulty for the panex-perientialist theory of consciousness advocated here, because the White-headian view is not that the many *are* one but that "the many become one, and are increased by one" (*PR*, 21). That statement, in fact, is Whitehead's summary statement of his "category of the ultimate," which involves the three ultimate notions—"creativity," "many," and "one"—involved in the concept of a "being." The agreement with James's argument that "the 101st feeling would be a totally new fact" is brought out even more clearly by Whitehead's complete statement:

> The ultimate metaphysical principle is the advance from disjunction to con-junction, creating a novel entity other than the entities given in disjunction. The novel entity is at once the togetherness of the 'many' which it finds, and also it is one among the disjunctive 'many' which it leaves; it is a novel entity, disjunctively among the many entities which it synthesizes. The many become one, and are increased by one. (*PR*, 21)

With regard to the relation of the brain to consciousness, this position sup-ports the numerical distinction stressed above: The brain at any moment is composed of billions of neuronic occasions of experience, whereas our conscious experience at any moment belongs to a "dominant" occasion of experience, which is a new, higher-level "one" that is created out of the "many" neuronic experiences (being partly created by them—by their ef-ficient causation on it—and then partly self-created).

There is a no self-contradiction involved in saying that the many *become* one, because of the fact that a physical prehension—the prehension by one actual occasion of another one—is always of an *antecedent* occasion of ex-perience. The many neuronic occasions of experience exist first for them-selves, as subjects of their own experience. It is only after their own moment of subjective immediacy has perished that they enter into, as objectified experiences, the dominant occasion of experience. This double point—that each enduring individual, such as a brain cell or a mind, is a temporally ordered society of momentary occasions of experience and that each occa-sion exists first as a subject for itself and then as an object in subsequent experiences—allows Whitehead to speak of the compounding of experi-ences without, with the later James, rejecting the "logic of self-identity," according to which "to call a thing and its other the same is to commit the crime of self-contradiction" (*PU*, 219). The reason James believed he had to reject this logic is implicit in his formulation of the question: "How can many consciousnesses be at the same time one consciousness?" The fatal assumption was that they have to be both "many" and "one" *at the same time*.

That James did literally mean "simultaneously" is shown by other passages (*PU,* 255, 261). He did indeed have to flout logic to affirm this, because it means affirming, for example, that an experience both knows and does not know X, or that it is both unconscious and conscious. James thereby violated the law of noncontradiction, which, carefully stated, says that something cannot *in the same respect at the same time* be both X and non-X. Whitehead, by distinguishing between the subjective and objective modes of existence of each occasion of experience, avoids this contradiction, because the contrary attributes are not assigned to the same thing at the same time or in the same respect. The many neuronic experiences that happen more or less simultaneously in one moment are, in their subjective mode of existence, truly many, with no windows to each other (contemporary occasions are independent of each other); it is only in their objective mode that they are a "many becoming one."

With this position, we have the basis for a very different understanding of a part-whole relation than that based on our sensory perception of what are usually thought of as "solid material bodies," such as rocks and animal bodies. It should be recalled that Nagel, in saying that philosophers have lacked the conception of "a mental part-whole relation" that would do justice to the experienced unity of consciousness, added that they might be working with "false assumptions about the part-whole relation" (*VN,* 51). An essential part of Whitehead's attempt to provide a more adequate conception is this idea that, in experiential wholes, the whole is a prehensive unification, in which a multiplicity becomes a unity, and that the relation between the whole and the parts is a *temporal,* never merely a spatial, relation: The whole arises out of parts that were, in their own subjective mode of existence, prior to it. This twofold idea—that an experiential whole is a process and that it is always temporally subsequent to the actual entities that constitute its parts—comprises two of the main contributions of Whitehead's "process philosophy" to a conception of a part-whole relation that does justice to our experienced unity of consciousness. (The other main contribution is the notion of a "compound individual," which presupposes this twofold idea and will be discussed below.)

This part of Whitehead's philosophy, far from being a peripheral element, is at its very center: As already mentioned, the ultimate in this philosophy is creativity, which involves a many becoming a one, which is then part of a new many to be creatively unified into a new one, and so on. Accordingly, a moment of human experience, in which the billions of neuronic experiences are unified into an experience that may involve consciousness and even self-consciousness, in an instance of ultimate reality. That this is the case is no surprise, of course, because Whitehead explicitly uses a moment of human experience—the only actuality the nature of which we know from the inside—as the very standard of actuality, in terms of which to understand other actualities. The part-whole relation exemplified in a moment of human experience is, accordingly, not unique to it but is exemplified in all other entities that are true individuals in the strictest sense. However, it is very different from the part-whole relation involved in aggregational societies devoid of a dominant member (such as sticks and stones), especially as known through vision and touch, in which the "whole" is simultaneous with its parts and nothing more than the sum of its parts, thereby not in any sense an entity or process distinct from them.

In any case, the importance of thinking of our own series of experiences, our mind, as a distinct actuality cannot be overestimated. All the problems with regard to the mind-body relation that are unique to materialism, as I argued in chapter 6, are due to materialism's numerical equation of mind and brain. These problems, which are insuperable—and even greater in number than the problems unique to dualism—have provided the major argument in favor of a return to dualism (as Madell's *Mind and Materialism* illustrates). By affirming the numerical distinctness of the mind as a distinct level of actuality in its own right, we obviate the perceived need to return to dualism. To be sure, an identism based on panexperientialism would not have *all* the problems of a materialistic identism. But it could do justice to neither the unity of our experience and behavior nor, the central topic of this chapter, our freedom. The argument for thinking of the mind as a distinct actuality (thereby rejecting Principle 3) is one element in showing how an interactionist panexperientialism can make sense of our presupposed freedom.

Is Self-Determining Freedom Really Possible?

A second element involves answering the objection (of Principle 4) that, even if the mind is distinct from the brain, there is no good reason to think it capable of self-determining freedom. It might simply be an epiphenomenal by-product of the brain's activity. As such it would account for our unity of experience but would not validate the sense of self-determining freedom, which may well be an illusion. The very conception of self-determining freedom, the objection could continue, may be incoherent, for it would imply that something is *causa sui,* cause of itself: How can something be both cause and effect of itself?

One widespread reason for rejecting freedom is that the old conception of causation based on the impact of billiard balls is still widely accepted. Even McGinn, for example, seems to take "billiard-ball causation" as paradigmatic for all intelligible kinds of causation (*PC,* 55). This objection has already been answered insofar as we have seen the unempirical character of taking "solid material bodies," such as billiard balls, as paradigm cases of actuality. Within the panexperientialist conception, in any case, efficient causation is understood by analogy with the causation of our bodily parts and our own past experiences on our present experience.

One might reply, however, that this model in itself does not necessitate genuine freedom. Even if the brain's effect on the mind is not analogous to the impact of one billiard ball on another, it is still efficient causation. The mind is said to be a many-becoming-one. This would seem to imply that what the "one" or mind is at any moment is fully determined by the "many" constituting the brain.

This second objection is based on the assumption that *efficient* causation, in the sense of the causal efficacy of one thing on another, is the only kind of *effective* causation. Indeed, this restricted meaning of "efficient causation" is distinctively modern: Efficient causation formerly included the self-determining activity of an agent out of which that agent then exerted causal influence on other things. In any case, having accepted this restricted meaning, Whitehead then uses "final causation" as a synonym for the "self-causation" or "self-determination" exercised by an actual entity in response to the many efficient causes on it. Whitehead accepts what he calls the "ontological principle" (on which deterministic analyses are often based), according to which all explanations are to be traced to actual things. In defining the ontological principle causally, however, he defines it as "the principle of efficient, and final, causation" (*PR*, 24). In other words, every actual entity exercises *two* effective types of causation: efficient causation (in the narrow sense) and final causation (in the sense of self-determination). Efficient causation is the type of effective causation that occurs *between* two or more actual entities; final causation is the type of effective causation that occurs *within* a single actual entity, that is, within a moment of experience.

This reconception of effective causation is part and parcel of the view that energy as treated in physics is an abstraction from creativity (or creative experience), understood to be the ultimate reality embodied in all actualities. Because physics abstracts from the intrinsic reality of its entities, dealing only with certain aspects of their extrinsic reality, the physicists' energy is, naturally, restricted to that which occurs *between* events. This fact, combined with modern scientism, has led to the assumption that effective causation is limited to efficient causation, the assumption that implies determinism. Included in the enlargement of the concept of energy, discussed earlier, is the addition of final causation as a second type of effective causation. This enlargement of the concept of the ultimate is one of the chief implications of taking our own experience as the paradigm case of actuality: *If we use our own experience as the key to the nature of the ultimate reality exemplified in all actual things, then we are led to the notion of a creative energy that has two moments: the moment of efficient causation exercised by the many and the moment of final causation exercised by the unifying process that arises out of that many.* The affirmation of freedom over against the widespread modern denial of it, then, follows from a different analysis of experience, thereby of actuality, and thereby of ultimate reality.

The theoretical conviction that freedom is unintelligible, however, has many bases. Another one is the conviction that experience grows entirely out of the actual world: Not only is experience said to be rooted in actuality (with which Whitehead agrees), but it is also widely thought to draw *every-thing* it has from those actualities out of which it arises. If the second part of that statement were true, then it would follow that the experience of freedom must be an illusion, because the contents and even the subjective forms of an experience would be entirely dictated by those actualities out of which the experience arose. The role that any particular event played in one's experience would be determined by the relative weight or intensity of that prior event; nothing would be left to be decided by any self-deter-mination on the part of the present experience itself. There might be "men-tality" in the sense of appetition, but the nature and strength of that appe-tition would be settled by the relative strength of the various bodily appetites.

This objection to genuine freedom follows from the widespread convic-tion among philosophers, supported by materialism, that reality contains no realm in which possibilities exist *as possibilities.* This nominalist bias did not impress Whitehead, who spent much of his professional life explor-ing mathematical and logical relations among pure possibilities, which he called "eternal objects" (because they exist outside of time and are eternally objects, never subjects). But Whitehead did not follow Johannes Kepler and other modern thinkers in limiting eternal objects to those purely quantita-tive ones instantiated in so-called primary qualities, which Whitehead calls "eternal objects of the objective species." He affirms as well "eternal objects of the subjective species," which include possibilities such as colors, emo-tions, life, and consciousness (*PR,* 291f.). These eternal objects of the sub-jective species are as real as those of the objective species. The mental pole of an experience involves the (conceptual) prehension of eternal objects or possibilities. These possibilities are either possibilities that were already ingredient in the prehended actualities *or closely related possibilities.*

An experience's freedom, accordingly, is greatly restricted by the actual world out of which it arises, but it is not completely limited to it. The way in which the unification is effected is not totally determined by the actual elements taken up into the unification; the elements also include genuine possibilities among which to choose. There is something, therefore, for the self-causation of the experience itself to do. This is Whitehead's explana-tion for the freedom we presuppose in practice, as when we attribute moral responsibility to ourselves and others: "The point to be noticed is that the actual entity, in a state of process during which it is not fully definite, determines its own ultimate definiteness. This is the whole point of moral responsibility" (*PR,* 255).

Yet another objection may arise from this very notion of self-causation. Is not the concept of something that is *causa sui* self-contradictory? Does it not violate one of our hard-core commonsense notions to speak of one and the same thing as both cause and effect of itself?

It would be incoherent, to be sure, to think of something as completely cause of itself, as if it were responsible for the very fact that it exists. Something may be able to put an end to its own existence, but the idea that something could create itself completely ex nihilo is nonsense. This intuition lies behind the notion that *something actual* must always have existed. Actuality could never have emerged out of a state in which there was nothing actual, not even if (*per impossibile*) a realm of possibility could have preexisted all actualities.* What the Whiteheadian notion of self-causation affirms, however, is quite different. It says that the fact that a particular occasion of experience exists is due to the activities of prior actualities. It is *their* efficient causation that gives birth to a new occasion of experience (*AI,* 179). However, once the occasion of experience has been given its start, meaning its physical pole, then it, in its mental pole, takes control of its own becoming, deciding just how to unify the various elements imposed on it by its past. "To be *causa sui* means that the process . . . is finally responsible for the decision by which any lure for feeling is admitted to efficiency. The freedom inherent in the universe is constituted by this element of self-causation" (*PR,* 88).

How the experience's power to complete its process of unification arises in the process of unification itself, so that an actuality can act before it is itself fully complete, is, to be sure, something for which we have no model outside experience itself. The question of how such power arose historically does not arise: This power is posited to be part of the ultimate reality of the universe of which all actualities are instances. To complain that this is no answer is to fail to remember that every position must assume that reality is ultimately just some way. To posit the ultimate reality of creative experience is no more arbitrary than to posit the ultimate reality of matter or energy. To say that creative experience is the ultimate reality instantiated in all actualities is to say that it is just the nature of actualities to have the power for partial self-creation (as well as the power then to serve as part-creators of future experiences).

*One philosopher who thinks otherwise is Nicholas Rescher. In *The Riddle of Existence: An Essay in Idealistic Metaphysics* (Lanham, Md.: University Press of America, 1984), he rejects the "hoary dogma" that *ex nihilo nihil fit,* arguing instead that actual things could have emerged out of a realm of pure possibility. I have reviewed Rescher's book in *Canadian Philosophical Reviews,* December 1986: 531–32.

One more objection might involve the degree of self-determination possible: Even if we grant the intelligibility of the notion that creative experience is the ultimate reality, so that every actual entity exercises a degree of self-determination on the basis of what is determined for it by the efficient causation of the past, what is the basis for saying that human experience has enough of this self-determining power to account for the kind of freedom presupposed by human practice? The human psyche is said to be analogous to a photon, but we certainly do not hold photons responsible for their behavior. What is the basis for attributing significantly more power of self-determination to human occasions of experience? Answering this question will require developing the notion that Hartshorne has called the "compound individual."[2]

Compound Individuals, Higher Degrees of Freedom, and Freely Directed Bodily Behavior

This discussion of compound individuals will answer two questions: (1) What is the theoretical basis for saying that the outer behavior of humans and other animals is any less determined by rigid laws than the behavior of other things composed of billions of molecules, such as billiard balls? This discussion responds to Principle 2, which says that the human being is composed exhaustively of the entities studied by physics, and Principles 1 and 5c, which say that the physical entities in the body, being completely determined by physical laws, could not be affected by a distinct mind with freedom, even if there were one. (2) Assuming the first question can be answered, what is the theoretical basis for attributing more freedom to humans and other higher animals than to other individuals? Answering this question completes the response to Principle 4 begun in the previous section. This discussion of compound individuals will also be relevant to the question of whether computers could possess consciousness and freedom.

At the close of the previous chapter, I discussed the notion of enduring individuals as societies that are purely temporal, meaning that there is only one actual occasion at a time. Most of the things that we encounter, however, are *spatiotemporal* societies, in which many enduring individuals are combined. Much of the confusion in modern thought about the possibility of freedom is the failure to see that there are two basic ways in which spatiotemporal societies can be organized, different organizations that lead to diverse modes of functioning. Of course, this failure has been rooted in turn in materialistic notions of the ultimate constituents of nature, which did not allow for these diverse types of organization. The previous chapters, in discussing the transition from a mechanistic to a panexperientialist view of those ultimate constituents, have prepared the way for seeing the possibility of these diverse types of spatiotemporal societies.

One type of spatiotemporal society can be called aggregational. The point of this term is that the society as a whole, such as a rock, does not have any overall experiential unity that allows it to feel and act as an individual. The term "aggregational" should not be taken to mean that the thing in question is a mere aggregate, like a pile of sand, that has no real cohesive unity. A rock or a billiard ball is an aggregational *society,* thereby having properties that no mere aggregate would have. Nevertheless, it is like a pile of sand in having no experiential unity and thereby no power to respond to its environment as a unity with even the slightest degree of freedom. The behavior of a billiard ball is fully predictable in principle in terms of the efficient causation on it. There are, by hypothesis, individual spontaneities in its individual members. But there is no dominant member of the society to coordinate these individual spontaneities into any organized result. Accordingly, these spontaneities are averaged out so that in terms of the observable behavior of the ball itself, they may as well not exist. Even if epistemic indeterminacy at the quantum level betokens ontological indeterminacy, it can be ignored in most calculations involving things such as billiard balls because of the "law of large numbers."

Not all spatiotemporal societies, however, are of this organizational type. Some are *compound individuals,* in which there *are* experiences of a higher and more inclusive type that give the society as a whole an overall experiential unity. These higher-level experiences can be called *presiding, regnant,* or *dominant,* because they exercise greater power over the society as a whole than do any of the other members, thereby giving the society as a whole a unity of response and action in relation to its environment. Animals with central nervous systems are the most obvious examples of compound individuals. Out of the activities of billions of neurons arises that temporal society of dominant occasions of experience that is the mind or soul of the animal. But this emergence is not unique in nature. Out of the organelles in the living eukaryotic cells (by hypothesis) emerge the living occasions of experience that give the cell an experiential unity and capacity for unified response. Likewise the organelles themselves may be supposed to be compound individuals in which higher-level series of experiences have arisen out of the macromolecules. (According to a theory now widely accepted, the organelles are "captured" prokaryotic cells.) Even macromolecules, ordinary molecules, and atoms might be supposed to be compound individuals. As I mentioned earlier, once the ontological category of compound individuals has been accepted, then exactly *which* enduring things should actually be considered compound individuals, rather than mere aggregational societies, is an empirical question, to be settled in terms of whether their behavior seems to require a central agent with an element of spontaneity or self-determination. The basic point, however, is that our world involves hierarchies of compound individuals, in which more and more levels of compound individuals are involved. There are societies of societies, then societies of societies of societies, then societies of societies of societies of societies, and so on. Each higher level of experience and freedom is possible only because of the level below it. Human beings seem to be the most complex of the compound individuals on this planet, therefore the ones with the greatest degree of freedom.

We have, accordingly, two reasons for rejecting Principle 2, which says that the human being consists entirely of atoms and their subatomic constituents. On the one hand, there is a hierarchy of compound individuals. For example, organelles and cells need not be thought to be simply aggregations of atoms. Each can be thought to have its own level of actuality and therefore its own level of experience and agency. On the other hand, at the apex of this hierarchy of compound individuals there is a still higher temporally ordered society of occasions, the psyche or mind.

The idea that human behavior *must,* against all appearances, be as determined as that of a billiard ball has arisen because of the assumption that their respective organizations are analogous. The implication of this view is that all the purposive activities of human beings are, in Whitehead's words, "merely analogous to the rolling of the shingle on the beach" (*FOR,* 14). The actions of human beings, whether in giving a speech or building a ship, are said to be "purely governed by the physical laws which lead a stone to roll down a slope and water to boil." Whitehead adds: "The very idea is ridiculous" (*FOR,* 14). It *is* ridiculous, in that it contradicts our hardcore commonsense presuppositions. But it is widespread because the generally accepted ontology has implied that the behavior of human beings, no matter how much more complex and therefore unpredictable in fact, "must" in principle be explainable in terms of the same kinds of laws that apply to billiard balls and pebbles on a beach. This assumption, as we saw, is at the center of Searle's denial of freedom.

Given a panexperientialist ontology, however, in which more complex experiences can be emergent out of myriad less complex ones, we can develop a position consistent with those principles we presuppose in practice. The key idea is that "diverse modes of organization" can produce "diverse modes of functioning" (*MT,* 157). On the one hand, in inorganic aggregational societies, mutual influence "is predominantly of a formal character expressible in formal sciences, such as mathematics. The inorganic is dominated by the average. It lacks individual expression in its parts. Their flashes of selection (if any) are sporadic and ineffective. Its parts merely transmit average expressions" (*MT,* 27). In this kind of organization, in other words, the total functioning reflects the average result of partly spontaneous but uncoordinated activities. Although there are some spontaneous functionings in the individual actual occasions making up all things, "for lifeless matter these functionings thwart each other, and average out so as to produce a negligible total effect" (*AI*, 207). The scientific study of the behavior of such things, accordingly, can ignore the spontaneities of the individual members. Due to the law of large numbers, a science of average effects is adequate.

On the other hand, in compound individuals, especially humans and other higher animals, such a science is not adequate, not even in principle. The reason is that in these societies the spontaneities, far from being canceled out, give birth to a superior who can then coordinate these spontaneities into a coordinated effort. The rise of the dominant member depends on the bodily organization:

> Each animal body is an organ of sensation. It is a living society which may include in itself a dominant 'personal' [i.e., purely temporal] society of occasions. This 'personal' society is composed of occasions enjoying the individual experiences of the animals. It is the soul of man. The whole body is organized, so that a general coordination of mentality is finally poured into the successive occasions of this personal society. (*AI*, 211)

While being dependent on the bodily organization for its emergence, however, this higher-level society of experiences can then—again, thanks to the body's special organization—influence the body in return. "Owing to the delicate organization of the body, there is a returned influence, an inheritance of character derived from the presiding occasion and modifying the subsequent occasions through the rest of the body" (*PR*, 109). By virtue of this returned influence, this "downward causation," the mind can exercise unifying control—partial but real (*PR*, 108f.)—over the body, coordinating it to carry out its individual purposes. It is because of the dominating influence of these individual purposes that no science of the average can account for human behavior.

> An angry man . . . does not usually shake his fist at the universe in general. He makes a selection and knocks his neighbour down. Whereas a piece of rock impartially attracts the universe according to the law of gravitation. The impartiality of physical science is the reason for its failure as the sole interpreter of animal behavior. . . . The fist of the man is directed by emotion seeking a novel feature in the universe, namely, the collapse of his opponent. In the case of the rock, the formalities predominate. In the case of the man, explanation must seek the individual satisfactions. These enjoyments are constrained by formalities, but in proportion to their intensities they pass beyond them, and introduce individual expression. (*MT*, 28f.)

Given this difference in principle between humans and rocks, the hope to achieve a unified science by including human and other animal behavior within Galilean-Newtonian-Einsteinian science is based on a category mistake. There is no analogy. There is, to be sure, no ontological dualism. But there is an *organizational duality*, and the diverse organizations produce radically diverse modes of functioning, requiring radically diverse types of explanations. In compound individuals, the final causes, or purposes, of the dominant individual must be given a central role.

The inability of the materialistic vision to recognize this disanalogy depends, in large part, on having taken inorganic aggregational societies— Popper's "solid material bodies"—as the analogical basis, or paradigm, for understanding the ultimate actual entities of which these are composed. Searle's world composed of "mindless, meaningless physical particles" (*MBS*, 13) is the result. But, from the perspective of the distinction between such aggregational societies and compound individuals, this is a mistake. In Whitehead's words:

> In surveying nature, we must remember that there are not only basic organisms. . . . There are also organisms of organisms. Suppose for the moment and for the sake of simplicity, we assume without any evidence, that electrons and hydrogen nuclei are such basic organisms [this was written, we should recall, in 1925]. Then the atoms, and the molecules, are organisms of a higher type, which also represent a compact definite organic unity. But when we come to the larger aggregations of matter, the organic unity fades into the background. . . . It is a mere aggregation of effects. . . . Accordingly, the characteristic laws of inorganic matter are mainly the statistical averages resulting from confused aggregates. So far are they from throwing light on the ultimate nature of things, that they blur and obliterate the individual characters of the individual organisms. If we wish to throw light upon the facts relating to organisms, we must study either the individual molecules and electrons, or the individual living beings. In between we find comparative confusion. (*SMW*, 110)

Rocks do not provide the basis for understanding the nature and behavior of the more or less simple individuals of which they are composed. Compound individuals provide the better analogue. This is the basis for Whitehead's generalization from human experience to the ultimate units of nature and vice versa.

The double misapprehension on which materialism's determinism is based has been mutually reinforcing. The assumption that the ultimate units of nature are enduring, vacuous actualities has led to the inability to recognize the distinction in principle between aggregational societies and compound individuals, because *vacuous actualities would not be able to give birth to compound individuals.* (As Whitehead observed, "the aboriginal stuff, or material, from which a materialistic philosophy starts is incapable of evolution" [*SMW*, 107].) The nonrecognition of this distinction supports in turn the assumption that the ultimate units of nature must be analogous to aggregational societies of them. The panexperientialist perspective performs one of its greatest services in helping us see through this double and mutually reinforcing misapprehension, which has led many intelligent people, against all hard-core common sense, to assume that the behavior of human beings must be as determined as that of sticks and stones. One version of this assumption, widespread in the scientific and philosophical communities, is the belief that the laws of physics must fully describe and predict the behavior not only of inorganic things but also of living animals, including human beings. This assumption will be more fully explored in chapter 10.

In any case, the materialistic view of the actualities of which our bodies are composed has led to the view that even if there were a partially self-determining mind distinct from the brain, it would not be able to deflect the movements of the bodily members. Any freedom enjoyed by the mind, accordingly, would be epiphenomenal, impotent with regard to bodily behavior. The idea has been that the cells and their constituents would necessarily "blindly run," in the sense of being determined by the laws of physics and chemistry, regardless of whether there were a mind in the body or not.

The foregoing discussion in this chapter and the preceding one has laid the groundwork for rejecting this assumption. Besides portraying why we should think of the mind as distinct from the body and as having a degree of self-determining freedom, I have explored the reasons for thinking the ultimate units of the body to be momentary occasions of experience, each of which begins by prehending into itself aspects of the things in its environment. Unlike vacuous substances or windowless monads, accordingly, an enduring individual would be somewhat different in a different environment. Whitehead explicitly affirmed this idea while being fully aware of its controversial nature:

> Each individual occasion within a special form of society includes features which do not occur in analogous occasions in the external environment. The first stage of systematic investigation must always be the identification of analogies between occasions within the society and occasions without it. The second stage is constituted by the more subtle procedure of noting the differences between behaviour within and without the society, differences of behaviour exhibited by occasions which also have close analogies to each other. The history of science is marked by the vehement, dogmatic denial of such differences, until they are found out. (*PR*, 99f.)

The idea that the behavior of atoms and their constituents differs in living and nonliving bodies is, incidentally, not without support in recent science.[3] In any case, a third notion we have explored is that the body consists not simply of "atoms in the void," as Searle supposes, but of a hierarchy of compound individuals, so that there are several levels of actualities between the mind and the body's most elementary constituents.

With this set of alternative assumptions before us, we can give this response to Tennyson's dilemma: Yes, the particles in the body, like particles in a rock, blindly run, in the sense that their internal functioning never rises to the level of conscious experience. But they blindly run *in accord with the plan of the whole body,* which is often significantly affected by purposive influences originating from the body's mind. In Whitehead's words:

> The concrete enduring entities are organisms, so that the plan of the *whole* influences the very characters of the various subordinate organisms which enter into it. In the case of an animal, the mental states enter into the plan of the total organism and modify the plans of the successive subordinate organisms until the ultimate smallest organisms, such as electrons, are reached. Thus an electron within a living body is different from an electron outside it, by reason of the plan of the body.* The electron blindly runs either within or without the body; but it runs within the body in accordance with its character within the body; that is to say, in accordance with the general plan of the body, and this plan includes the mental state. (*SMW,* 79)

Does this idea imply that the laws of physics and chemistry are violated? Not at all: "No reactions between the material components of any animal body . . . in any way infringe the physical and chemical laws applying to the behavior of inorganic material" (*FOR,* 12). Sometimes, however, that proposition is confusedly equated with a quite different and entirely dubious proposition, which is that "in the transformations of matter and energy which constitute the activities of an animal body no principles can be discerned other than those which govern the activities of inorganic matter" (*FOR,* 12). This second proposition is affirmed whenever it is said that the behavior of a human being (or any animal) must be fully determined by the "laws of nature," meaning, usually, principles descriptive of the behavior of molecules in the laboratory. The second proposition, some materialists notwithstanding, is not at all identical with the first one and is not implied by it.**

---

*Whitehead is fully aware of the dogma that all electrons are identical. It is that dogma that he is directly challenging, saying that it is based on the fallacy of misplaced concreteness. He agrees, in other words, that all electrons, regardless of their locations, are identical with respect to various abstract features. But he does not agree that those abstract features are to be equated with the actual electrons in their full concreteness.

**This distinction is at the heart of the program of physicist-turned-theoretical-biologist Walter Elsasser for a "non-mechanistic biological scheme which does not contradict physics" (*AO,* 76). With regard to the choice presented by the mechanism-vitalism controversy, according to which "the observed biological regularities are either logico-mathematically derivable from the laws of atomic and molecular physics or else require specific modification of these laws," Elsasser says: "Our present theory does not agree with either of these ideas" (*AO,* 108). There are, he says, biological "regularities not deductively derivable from physics" (*AO,* 46). This fact involves no violation of the laws of quantum physics, however, because "the laws of quantum mechanics provide in general only necessary conditions for the phenomena and not sufficient ones, that is, they do not uniquely determine the happenings on the microscopic level" (*AO,*

The belief that the two propositions are equatable is based in part on the mythical view that laws are prescriptive, imposing behavior on the entities to which they apply. Once that idea, a hangover from the notion of laws as supernaturally imposed, is given up and we see laws of nature instead as habits, then the idea that laws fully dictate the behavior of molecules will be seen to be as groundless as the idea that human habits fully determine human behavior. I have the habit of stopping at stop signs. But in extraordinary situations, as when I am rushing someone to the hospital or when there is a gunman in the car telling me not to stop, I break that habit. In doing so, however, I have not violated some ultimate law of the universe. I have simply, because of extraordinary influences from my environment, acted differently than I and most of my fellow citizens normally act. That normal action provides the basis for the sociological laws of my community. But those laws do not dictate how I must act in all situations. Once we see that the laws of subatomic particles are not different in kind, only different in degree, being the "communal customs" of a lower level of nature (*AI*, 41), then we can shake free from the myth that behavior is regulated by laws applying indifferently in all situations.

The belief that the two propositions are equatable, so that the principles of physics would be violated if the behavior of particles within a body reflect principles that are not present in inorganic aggregational societies, is based on the assumption that inorganic aggregational societies such as rocks provide the privileged locus for studying the laws of physics. That assumption rests in turn on the assumption that inorganic aggregational societies such as rocks are more "natural" than living animals. Dualism dies hard. If we are truly nondualists, however, our doctrines about the "laws" of particle behavior will be based on observations of particles within living animal bodies as fully as on observations of them in inorganic aggregational societies. We will use each kind of observation to correct the conclusions derived from the other alone. One of the resulting laws would surely be, if the pan-experientialist view is correct, that the behavior of electrons, protons, and other subatomic particles is partly dependent on the immediate environment in which they find themselves. Our experience of, say, deliberately moving our hands gives strong prima facie evidence that this is true.

The idea that the feelings and purposes radiating from our minds into our bodies affect the activities of our bodies' ultimate constituents, there-

89). If Elsasser's view is accepted, accordingly, it is fully consistent with the empirical facts and quantum theory to believe that in living organisms, in the words of Whitehead (*FOR*, 12), "principles can be discerned other than those which govern the activities of inorganic matter." (Elsasser himself, guarding himself against any possible charge of vitalism [*AO*, 43, 46, 113, 128], does not make this claim, suggesting instead that the partial autonomy of organisms is "correlative to the intrinsic restriction of knowledge" rather than due to any organizing principle, which he seems to assume would entail vitalism [*AO*, 113].)

fore, violates no laws of physics, only a materialist dogma about such laws. An interactionist form of panexperientialism, accordingly, is able, while being consistent with our best scientific knowledge, to do justice to what we all presuppose about human mentality, which is that it is "partly the outcome of the human body, partly the single directive agency of the body, partly a system of cogitations which have a certain irrelevance to the physical relationships of the body" (*PR*, 108).

The last of these three features—cogitations with a certain irrelevance to the bodily activities—points to the most distinctive feature of the human mind. It is the supreme example of the mind's existence as an end in itself and for itself, in distinction from its instrumental function of helping the body survive. This brings us to the second question of this section: Why do animal minds, especially human minds, have more freedom to determine their own ends than do lower enduring individuals?

The answer was implicit in the notion of a hierarchy of compound individuals. The capacities of an occasion of experience are largely determined by the data that it can appropriate for its base. Very low-grade occasions, such as those in the life history of an electron, can appropriate only very little data. If molecules are compound individuals, so that there are molecular occasions, which can derive data from their subatomic constituents, they can appropriate a little more. Greater increases in richness of experience and in self-determining capacity would occur in macromolecules, then viruses, then bacteria and organelles (if all of these should be considered compound individuals). Another increase would occur in (eukaryotic) cells. At this level, Whitehead suggests, there is a significant increase in the capacity for conceptual appetition and thereby for novelty of response (*PR*, 102–4). The basis for this increased capacity for richness of experience and self-determination is all the data that pour into the living occasion from the many organelles, which had in turn integrated into an experiential unity data derived from billions of macromolecules, and so on. Billions and billions of living cells, organized in a central nervous system, can then pour data from their greater experiences into the dominant occasions that constitute the animal soul.

The emergence of the most complex kind of compound individual known to us, the human kind, involves the rise of a very high-level enduring individual, which, while not ontologically different from its lower-level forebears, involves a new kind of causal relation or, more precisely, an extreme exemplification of a kind of causal relation that had become increasingly important in the evolution of the higher animals. The observed difference in question needing theoretical explanation (without resort to vitalism or some other form of ontological dualism) is the fact that the abstract features of low-grade enduring individuals, such as protons, appear to remain virtually the same for millions or even billions of years, whereas human minds obviously change their characters over time, incorporating novel elements into their relatively enduring characters. While in one sense claiming self-identity with the little three-year-old freckle-faced boy some of whose experiences I remember, I also now embody all sorts of habits, character traits, sustained purposes, and attitudes that were in no way present in him and that were not even inevitable developments out of his identity between ages three and four. One aspect of this capacity of present experiences to incorporate and pass on a novelty arising in previous occasions of experience is the ability to carry through with purposes. The difference between a proton and a psyche in this respect is so striking that dualists can be partly forgiven their ontological indiscretion. The tendency of materialists to ignore the problem is also understandable. The panexperientialist perspective provides a way to deal with the problem without violating monistic pluralism.

The difference can be understood in terms of the novelty that may arise in the conceptual prehensions in the mental poles of occasions of experience within an enduring individual. There are two issues involved: (1) How significant is this novelty? (2) How do subsequent occasions of experience in the enduring individual respond to that novelty? With regard to the first issue, the higher-level occasions of experience differ from lower-level ones first of all in this respect: As we ascend from the occasions of experience in the life histories of electrons to the regnant occasions in organelles, cells, simple animals, simple mammals, nonhuman primates, and finally human beings, there are experiences in which the mental pole is of increasingly greater significance, which means that increasingly greater degrees of novelty can be originated by individual occasions of experience in responding to their worlds. The second issue, which is what role this novelty in individual occasions plays in the more or less enduring character of the enduring individual, requires for its explanation the introduction of further technical terms.

I have said that a prehension or feeling is *physical* if its object is a previous actuality (or set of actualities). However, physical feelings, thus defined, can be distinguished into "pure" and "hybrid" physical feelings. In a *pure physical feeling*, the previous actual occasion is felt *in terms of its own physical pole*, which means that what is passed on to the present occasion is what the past occasion had in turn received from previous occasions. Accordingly, even if some novelty cropped up in the mental pole of that previous occasion, it is bypassed by a pure physical prehension. What we usually think of as the "physical world" in the strictest sense—roughly, the world of subatomic entities, atoms, and ordinary molecules—is characterized (by hypothesis) almost entirely by pure physical feelings. The virtually indestructible proton is the paradigmatic instance, as it retains its character over many billions of years.

The fact that in such entities there is virtually no origination of novelty, along with the fact that whatever slight bit of novelty might be created by a wayward occasion is ignored by its ultraconservative successors, explains why there is almost complete uniformity at this level of nature. "There is a reign of acquiescence" (*AI,* 194). The so-called laws of nature are merely habits, to be sure, but the enduring individuals at that level are *so* habit-bound (at least when in inorganic surroundings) that the laws can appear to be imposed. All the causal relations at this level can appear to be "purely physical" because they *are:* All the efficient causation between events involves pure physical prehensions.

In a *hybrid* physical feeling, by contrast, the previous occasion of experience is prehended in terms of its mental pole, with its conceptual feelings. This is still a type of *physical* feeling, because the object felt is an actuality, not a mere possibility. But it is a *hybrid* physical feeling because that prior actuality is felt in terms of *its* prehension of *possibilities.* Among these possibilities may be some *novel* forms, meaning ones not simply received from the past world. If this occurs, then a future occasion of experience, by means of a hybrid physical feeling, can incorporate that novel form into its own physical pole. From then on this once-novel form can be passed on to subsequent occasions in the enduring individual by means of *pure* physical feelings. In this way, the origination of novelty is, to use Bergson's term, "canalized" (*PR,* 107).

The rise of life is associated with the rise of significant novelty of appetition along with causal processes significantly involving hybrid physical feelings. The sense that living things are not *purely* physical is thus supported by this explanation, because the mentalities of the living occasions of experience do play a significant role in the causal processes, thanks to the hybrid nature of the physical feelings. At the same time, the principle of continuity is not violated, because the change involves only a difference in emphasis, not the rise of some totally new principle. Whitehead's account has been given even further support since he wrote, as the discovery of new levels of organisms between simple molecules and living cells has made it even more difficult to specify exactly where "life" begins. We can understand the various levels—macromolecules (if they should be regarded as compound individuals), viruses, prokaryotic cells, eukaryotic cells—as characterized by increasingly significant hybrid physical prehensions.

This account prepares the way for an explanation of the distinctiveness of the human mind. At the level of eukaryotic cells, there has been a great increase in the capacity for novelty, and there is even some evidence of continuity of purpose over time, suggestive of the canalization of novelty through hybrid physical feelings (*PR,* 107; *AI,* 207). Nevertheless, the novelty possible is strictly limited. Even more limited seems to be the capacity for originating and sustaining purposes over time. At the level of the animal psyche, there is a great increase in both of these capacities. Whitehead uses the term "living person" for animal psyches to indicate this quantum leap. The term "living" points to the novelty of response characteristic of the mental poles of the occasions of experience in the animal mind. The term "person" points to the fact that this mind is a personally ordered society, in which each occasion of experience, besides incorporating feelings from the body, is significantly constituted by its prehension of its own past experiences, thereby sustaining its character as an enduring individual over time. Putting the two terms together into "living person" indicates that this type of enduring individual, unlike inorganic ones, sustains itself not simply in terms of a fixed essence but also by constantly incorporating new elements into itself, so that the enduring individual is significantly individualized by particular purposes that arose contingently at some moment in the past and are sustained for considerable periods of time, perhaps the remainder of the individual's life.

The human mind is the extreme example of a living person in this technical sense.

> When we come to mankind, nature seems to have burst through another of its boundaries. The central activity of enjoyment and expression has assumed a reversal in the importance of its diverse functionings. The conceptual entertainment of unrealized possibility becomes a major factor in human mentality. In this way outrageous novelty is introduced, sometimes beatified, sometimes damned, and sometimes literally patented or protected by copyright. The definition of mankind is that in this genus of animals the central activity has been developed on the side of its relationship to novelty. (*MT*, 26)

The minds of other animals seem to be occupied primarily with the survival and welfare of their bodies. The capacity of the human mind is such that it can engage in, to use the phrase of mathematical physicist-turned-metaphysician Whitehead quoted earlier, "a system of cogitations which have a certain irrelevance to the physical relationships of the body" (*PR*, 108).

We seem to ourselves to be so much more "mental" than other things because we *are:* Our mental prehensions are much greater in extent and intensity, and our relation to former occasions of our experience is based heavily on hybrid physical feelings, so that the distinctively mental aspects of our previous experiences are greatly constitutive of the base of our present experience. The resulting difference is so great—"The Rubicon has been crossed" (*MT*, 27)—that many, including the father of uniformitarianism, Charles Lyell,* have supposed a supernatural explanation to be nec-

---

*Lyell was famous for his uniformitarianism, according to which we are to assume that no types of causes operated in previous times that are not operating today. But he abandoned this uniformitarianism with regard to the human mind, saying that to explain its origin we must "assume a primeval creative power which does not act with uniformity" (*The Life and*

essary. But Whitehead has provided a way of explaining the difference so that it is only one of degree and can hence be understood naturalistically.

Although in developing the notion of the mind as a "living person" I have focused on the novelty received by an occasion of human experience from its own past, this is not the only source: "There is [also] the novelty received from the aggregate diversities of bodily expressions" (*MT,* 26). This point brings us back to the mind-body relation as that of the dominant occasion of a compound individual to those lower-level compound individuals (neurons) constituting the brain. The human mind, with its high level of mental functioning, is dependent on receiving data from the mental functionings of the brain cells. "The whole body is organized, so that a general coordination of mentality is finally poured into the successive occasions of [the dominant] personal society" (*AI,* 211). That is, the human mind depends on the fact that the billions of living occasions in the brain cells contribute not only the data that they have received from beyond but also their own enhancements and transmutations of these data: "The human body is to be conceived as a complex 'amplifier'. . . . The various actual entities, which compose the body, are so coordinated that the experiences of any part of the body are transmitted to one or more central occasions to be inherited with enhancements accruing upon the way" (*PR,* 119). For example, the transmutation of color from an emotion as felt in external nature to that color as we experience it involves an intermediate stage of transmutation effected by the bodily cells involved. In other words, a human mind, or anything analogous to it, would seem to presuppose for its emergence a living body:

> Apart from life a high grade of mentality in individual occasions seems to be impossible. A personal society, itself living and dominantly influencing a living society wider than itself, is the only type of organization which provides occasions of high-grade mentality. Thus in a man, the living body is permeated by living societies of low-grade occasions so far as mentality is concerned. But the whole is coordinated so as to support a personal living society of high-grade occasions. (*AI,* 208)

What does this perspective suggest about the possibility of computers with consciousness and freedom? Could, for example, consciousness arise from complexly organized silicon chips? From a panexperientialist perspective, on the one hand, this possibility could not be ruled out on the grounds that silicon atoms, being devoid of experience, could not give rise to con-

Letters of Charles Darwin, ed. Francis Darwin [London: John Murray, 1887], 2:210–11). Lyell spoke of a "creational law" that added "the moral and intellectual faculties of the human race, to a system of nature which had gone on for millions of years without the intervention of any analogous cause" (*On the Geological Evidences of the Antiquity of Man,* 3d ed. [London: John Murray, 1863], 469).

scious experience. Such atoms, by hypothesis, do have a lowly type of experience (at least if they are compound individuals; even if not, they would contain the experiences of their subatomic constituents). On the other hand, a direct jump from silicon (or any other simple) atoms to humanlike experience, with its consciousness and freedom, would be impossible. There is presumably a reason that it took some four billion years for that kind of transformation to occur in the evolutionary process. The reason suggested here is that the intervening levels of experience were necessary: Humanlike consciousness could only develop out of a central nervous system composed of units with the experiential complexity of eukaryotic cells; eukaryotic cell-like experiences could only emerge out of things with as much experiential richness as organelles; and so on down. So, for a computer to enjoy consciousness and freedom, it would have to have something like a brain composed of units something like the cells of our brains. This does not necessarily mean that carbon-based cells are necessary; we do not know but what life has been formed on planets in other galaxies out of different elementary materials. What does seem necessary is that the brain be composed of billions of compound individuals with a complexity and corresponding experiential richness like unto that of our own brain cells. Because fabricated things with these characteristics would be so different from any computers actual or even remotely possible today as to require another name, we can say that, from this perspective, computers cannot have freedom, consciousness, or any level of unified experience.

III. McGINN'S ATTEMPTED REFUTATION OF PANEXPERIENTIALISM

Before continuing the exposition of freedom, I will examine in some detail McGinn's attempted refutation of panpsychism, which was briefly mentioned in chapter 7. McGinn, as we saw, accuses panpsychism of being "outrageous" and "absurd." These accusations, however, follow partly from the fact that he examines only one version of panpsychism (the two-aspect version described by Nagel), assuming falsely that it is identical with all versions of panpsychism with respect to the criticized points, partly from the fact that McGinn evaluates panpsychism in terms of doctrines that he takes to be unquestionable even though the Whiteheadian position explicitly denies them, and partly because he holds panexperientialism to standards that materialism itself, by his own account, cannot meet.

That by "panpsychism" McGinn is thinking of something crucially different from the panexperientialism I have articulated is shown by his statement that "panpsychism claims . . . that all matter has mental attributes" (*CM*, 31). By thereby ignoring the Leibnizian distinction between true individuals (which are said to have experience) and mere aggregational societies (which are not), and by then imposing his own view that to have experience of any sort (which he intends his term "mental attributes" to cover) means having *conscious* thoughts, he concludes that panpsychism (of all varieties) entails that "bits of rock . . . enjoy an inner conscious life" and that "rocks actually have thoughts" (*CM*, 32). This is McGinn's main point in demonstrating to his readers that "panpsychism is metaphysically and scientifically outrageous" (*CM*, 32).

McGinn, however, also believes that absurdity follows even if one focuses on elementary particles. One part of his attempted *reductio ad absurdum* assumes that panpsychists hold that "elementary particles enjoy an inner conscious life" (*CM*, 32). But here he is imposing his assumption that to speak of experience is ipso facto to speak of *conscious* experience.

A second part of McGinn's argument about elementary particles is that if their mental states are causally efficacious, then "the mental properties of electrons bear upon how they will behave," so that "predictions about them will not be derivable from their physical properties alone: but we know this not to be the case" (*CM*, 32). In the light of all the discussions of quantum indeterminacy and the fact that the laws of quantum physics can only describe and predict the average behavior of large numbers of elementary particles, not the behavior of any given individual, this is an amazing "refutation." Most physicists and philosophers of physics would say (whether or not they themselves would adopt this interpretation) that the behavior of electrons is perfectly compatible with the supposition that they have an iota of mentality, in the sense of a power of self-determination.

For example, with regard to the question of whether the elemental units of nature "ever act in a way that is inexplicable from a purely physical standpoint," Seager says,

> Of course they do—the Quantum theory insists upon this. As a physical theory, QM [quantum mechanics] asserts that there is no explanation of certain processes since these involve an entirely random 'choice' amongst alternative possibilities. The world's behavior does leave room for an additional fundamental feature with its own distinctive role. (CIP, 283)

Having made this negative argument against McGinn's "completeness argument" (which says that a purely physical account of the world is complete, leaving no room for mental causation), Seager then gives a positive argument for affirming an iota of mentality at the quantum level, based on evidence from the two-slit experiment and the quantum eraser, which suggests that the world's elementary units respond to *information*. Discussing the significance of this fact, he says,

> Responsiveness to information is hardly foreign to the realm of mentality although here it applies in an admittedly very circumscribed and impoverished sense, but this is to be expected of a fundamental feature manifesting

itself at an elemental level. [Furthermore] the kind of information at issue is not just the bit capacity of classical information theory but something more like semantically significant information and this is a notion of information more akin to mentality. (CIP, 283)

Seager's argument from quantum physics is based on the orthodox interpretation thereof. The same conclusion follows, however, from Bohm and Hiley's ontological interpretation. For them, the idea that all elementary particles are influenced by *active information* is fundamental. From this point they draw the conclusion that "even an electron has at least a rudimentary mental pole, as well as a physical pole" (*UU*, 387). So, whether one prefers the orthodox or the ontological interpretation, there is evidently no reason to deny, and even reason to affirm, that nature's most elementary units have mentality that exerts causal efficacy. Accordingly, McGinn's first refutation of panpsychism, by portraying it as obviously absurd, fails in all its forms.*

McGinn's second attempted refutation hinges on his own assumption that all versions of panpsychism would necessarily hold his own position on the relation of the physical and the mental, which is that the mental is "supervenient" on the physical in the sense that "the mental is [wholly] determined by the physical" (*CM*, 29). Given McGinn's acceptance of the standard dualistic terminology, this means that experience, and thereby the mind, is fully determined by the purely physical properties of the brain. McGinn then argues that panpsychism, in attributing experience to all particles of matter, "only pushes the problem back a stage." That is, panpsychists must explain how "the mental properties of particles of matter are supervenient on their physical properties" (*CM*, 32). And if supervenience at that level requires no explanation, he says, it is puzzling why supervenience at the brain-mind level requires it (*CM*, 32).

This is another case, however, in which McGinn's target is quite different from the kind of panexperientialism articulated here. In this kind, there is no material substance with purely nonexperiential properties that either logically or causally precede its experiences (which McGinn calls its "mental properties"). Rather, an actual entity at any level is an "occasion of experi-

---

*McGinn's belief that any philosophy implying quantum physics to be incomplete can be rejected a priori perhaps reflects the idea that the physicist John von Neumann proved that, in Elsasser's words, "the validity of quantum mechanics is not compatible with the existence of any other type of regularity in nature which would not be derivable from quantum theory itself" (*AO*, 75). Elsasser, however, has argued that this proof depends on the assumption of an infinite universe of discourse populated entirely by homogeneous classes (in which all members are indistinguishable). The proof becomes invalid, Elsasser says, if one goes to "a finite universe of discourse in which radically inhomogeneous classes [the type we have in biology] exist" (*AO*, 75).

ence."* Such an entity exists first in its subjective phase, during which it is an experiential subject through and through; only afterward does it exist in its objective phase, exerting causal efficacy on other things, resulting in what McGinn means by "physical properties." So, if anything, the "physical" (in McGinn's sense, not Whitehead's) is supervenient on the experiential (which McGinn calls the "mental"). Accordingly, McGinn's whole line of criticism, which assumes that the relation between the mind and the brain must for all panpsychists be simply the macrolevel of the relation between two aspects of an actual entity at the microlevel, does not apply. (The relation between supervenience and panexperientialism will be discussed in chapter 10.) The fact that there is no emergence of the experiential out of the purely physical to explain at the microlevel, moreover, does *not* mean that the emergence of experience with conscious thoughts out of the brain need not be explained. At the microlevel, the existence of experience requires no causal explanation because, according to the metaphysics, it is the very nature of an actuality to be an occasion of experience. But the very *high level* of experience enjoyed by animals, and especially humans, does require a contingent, causal explanation.

McGinn's third refutation involves a dilemma: Either the elementary particles, according to panpsychism, have full-fledged consciousness, complete with sensations and propositional attitudes, or they do not, having instead merely a protoconsciousness. The former, McGinn says, would be "ridiculously extravagant," and I agree. But the latter, he argues, "in admitting that the proto-psychical falls short of the properly psychical, sacrifices its claim to derive the mind from phenomena of the same kind as mental phenomena" (*CM,* 33). McGinn's claim, in effect, is that any alleged psychical or experiential qualities that fall short of full-fledged *conscious* sensations and thoughts would be *different in kind* from them, so that panpsychists would have the same problem as materialists and dualists, having to explain the emergence of consciousness out of ontologically different kinds of entities.**

---

*Strawson, while evidently sharing the widespread intuition that the experiential must asymmetrically depend on the nonexperiential, does say that "it seems that we have no good reason to reject the idea that experience itself can be a substance—a substance process somehow incorporating both experiences and a subject of experience" (*MR,* 111f.), which is not a bad description of a Whiteheadian "occasion of experience."

**It is hard to take this point seriously. McGinn knows as well as anyone that what makes the mind-body problem insoluble for both dualists and materialists is that they affirm that things with an inner side (minds for dualists, brains for materialists) emerged out of things (insentient neurons) wholly devoid of an inside. For example, in describing the materialist's version of this emergence, he says: "Somehow or other sentience sprang from pulpy matter, giving matter an inner aspect, but we have no idea how this leap was propelled" (*PC,* 45). In attributing experience to all actualities, panexperientialism is, of course, attributing an inner aspect to all of them, so that no such leap need be posited. McGinn's attempt to claim that the

This claim, however, depends on McGinn's imposition of his own view, according to which the psychical or experiential necessarily involves conscious sensations and beliefs, so that the idea of nonconscious experience is nonsense—exactly the view that Whitehead spends much of his time arguing against. McGinn's view, furthermore, has absurd consequences: In saying that our conscious sensations and propositional attitudes cannot be explained by any properties of neurons if these properties "are not already sensations and propositional attitudes" (*CM*, 33), he is implying that an adult with conscious sensations and thoughts could not develop out of a baby unless the baby already enjoyed conscious beliefs as well as fully conscious sensations. These fully conscious sensations and thoughts, furthermore, would have to be ascribed to the fetus and even all the way back to the embryo, or at least to that point at which McGinn assumes the "sudden" emergence of consciousness to occur (*CM*, 14). One can perhaps be forgiven for wondering why panpsychism's alleged absurdity, even if it could be sustained, should be held by McGinn to count against it.

This last point brings me to the final problem with McGinn's treatment of panpsychism, which is that he holds it to a much higher standard of intelligibility than he does materialism. For example, he indicts panpsychism for "obscurity" on the grounds that it cannot clearly say "what *sort* of mental properties inanimate matter has" (*CM*, 33). Even if we look aside from the fact that McGinn had not examined Whitehead's attempt to do

---

emergence of conscious experience out of nonconscious experience would involve a leap over an ontological chasm like unto that of dualists and materialists seems to be more a debating point than a serious objection. In any case, in his later book McGinn himself, as we have seen, says that if neurons had protoconscious states, it would be "easy enough to see how neurons could generate consciousness" (*PC*, 28n).

It is on this issue, incidentally, that I find problematic Seager's otherwise excellent discussion of the criticisms of panpsychism. With reference to this criticism by McGinn, Seager says that if panpsychism must speak of "the generation of conscious experience from the combination of nonconscious entities, even if they are in some sense mental entities," then "panpsychism faces a problem which is strictly analogous to the generation problem facing physicalists" (*CIP*, 281). Seager, to be sure, believes that the acceptance of this point creates no problem for panpsychists, because they can say that the elementary units are "in some sense conscious" (*CIP*, 283n14). But what if some critic then claims that the real problem is the rise of *self*-consciousness (in the sense of reflexive consciousness)? Are we then to avoid this problem by saying that the elementary units are already self-conscious? Surely we need to be able to speak of evolution of more complex modes of experience out of less complex modes, and surely this evolution should include the emergence of experience in which some objects are clearly discriminated out of experiences in which objects are felt without being clearly discriminated. As I said earlier, however, the issue may be merely terminological: McGinn and Seager may be assuming that "nonconscious" means altogether void of experience. In that case, their point would stand—except that the position at issue would not be panpsychism or panexperientialism, which is precisely the denial that there are any "vacuous actualities."

just this, there would be a problem with his indictment. All panexperientialists, even those of us who find Whitehead's attempt suggestive, will agree that one cannot say *very much* about what it must be like to be an electron or even a cell. But as Berkeley pointed out (in arguing that the only intelligible meanings we have for "to be" are "to perceive" and "to be perceived"), McGinn and other materialists cannot say *anything at all* about what it means to assert the existence of what Whitehead calls "vacuous actualities," meaning things that are *actual* (so that their existence does not consist merely in *being perceived*) and yet are *vacuous* (so that they are not in any sense *perceivers*). Materialism, accordingly, is even more "obscure" than panpsychism; but McGinn does not lift this up as a reason to reject it. Likewise, McGinn had already stated in his 1982 book that he could give no explanation whatsoever as to how consciousness could arise out of matter that is completely devoid of an "inner" aspect (*CM,* 36), and by the time of *The Problem of Consciousness* he had decided the problem to be insoluble in principle. And yet he has concluded not that materialism must therefore be false but only that there must be something about our way of thinking that makes a solution impossible—a charitable interpretation indeed. In other words, although every possible version of panpsychism can be rejected as absurd on the basis of three objections stated in a brief treatment of one possible version of panpsychism (which differs significantly from the version of those philosophers who are recognized as the most distinguished advocates of panpsychism in the twentieth century), materialism is evidently regarded as irrefutable in principle. McGinn's so-called refutation of panpsychism seems, accordingly, little more than a reassertion of his starting point, that somehow we know that some version of materialism is true and that every version of panpsychism is false. In any case, having shown that McGinn's attempted refutation of panexperientialism fails, I return to the discussion of how Whiteheadian panexperientialism can explain the freedom we presuppose ourselves to have.

IV. COSMIC MIND AND THE HIGHER FREEDOMS OF THE HUMAN MIND

A question that could arise out of Section II is whether human beings (and perhaps similar or even more complex organisms on other planets) are the highest forms of compound individuals, or whether there is still a higher-level form. Another question that has not yet been addressed involves some of the apparently nonsensory forms of perception mentioned in chapter 5, such as our apparent capacity to apprehend logical, mathematical, ethical, and aesthetic forms, to have religious experiences, and to have telepathic and clairvoyant perceptions. This second question is: Is acceptance of these nonsensory perceptions compatible with the principle that all our experiences of things beyond ourselves originate in *physical* prehensions? This section is devoted to the relation between these two questions.

Whitehead did, in a sense, come to think of the universe as a compound individual (although this term, as well as its application to the universe, is Hartshorne's). He even, after having been a somewhat militant agnostic or even atheist most of his professional life, came temporarily to use the term "God" for the mind of the cosmos. He reportedly came to regret this usage, evidently having underestimated the extent to which this word inevitably suggests supernaturalism. In any case, he later spoke instead of the "Eros of the Universe" and the "Universe as One" (*AI*, 11, 295).

In one sense there is no analogy between the universe and ordinary compound individuals, because in the latter the regnant member's very existence arises out of its parts, whereas the mind of the universe is primordial. In another sense there is an analogy, in that the mind of the universe presupposes the existence of a universe—not necessarily our present one, but some universe or other. This is part of the naturalism of the view: A universe of finite actualities could not have been created ex nihilo but exists just as necessarily, just as primordially, just as naturally, as does the mind of the universe. Each presupposes the other (*PR*, 225). This notion precludes any supernatural intervention. Because the basic causal relations between actual occasions are metaphysical, part of the very nature of things (*AI*, 168), they cannot be overridden.

One of the questions answered by the notion of a cosmic mind—and, in fact, one that was fundamental in Whitehead's own acceptance of this notion—is that of the mode of existence of abstract entities, or possibilities. One formulation of the "ontological principle" is causal: To look for an effective cause is to look for an actuality. But another meaning involves our present question: "Everything must be somewhere; and here 'somewhere' means 'some actual entity' " (*PR*, 46). Whitehead agrees, in other words, with the widespread intuition that abstract entities, as mere possibilities, cannot exist simply on their own, free-floating in the void. This intuition has led most modern thought, having rejected any cosmic actuality in which they could subsist, to reject their existence altogether. This rejection implies that not only all moral and aesthetic norms but also all logical norms and mathematical relations must be thought to be created or invented, not discovered. The senior author of *Principia Mathematica*, not being able to accept this and having thought through the implications of the ontological principle, overcame his long-standing aversion to all theistic talk. Saying that "the general potentiality of the universe must be somewhere," he named this somewhere "the primordial mind of God" (*PR*, 46).

This affirmation allowed him to hold consistently to the notion that all conceptual experience is derived from physical experience. In my discussion of this topic, I said that the possibilities prehended in conceptual prehensions "are either possibilities that were already ingredient in the prehended actualities *or closely related possibilities.*" There I was presupposing what Whitehead calls "conceptual reversion." The problem with this category, Whitehead came to see, is that in referring to our capacity to lay hold of novel possibilities—meaning ones that had not been realized in the world we have physically prehended—it implied that some of the data of our mental experiences were not derivative from physical prehensions. However, by saying that all potentiality is in the mind of the universe and that our (nonsensory) physical prehension, in grasping everything in our immediate environment, prehends this universal mind as well, he attained what he considered "a more complete rational explanation": "The Category of Reversion is then abolished; and Hume's principle of the derivation of conceptual experience from physical experience remains without any exception" (*PR,* 250).

The larger implication is that all experience of ideals or normative values—logical, aesthetic, ethical—that cannot be explained in terms of derivation from experiences in one's past world can still be explained in terms of physical prehensions. Recalling that physical prehension is simply the reverse side of efficient causation, this perspective allows us to provide a naturalistic causal explanation of how abstract entities such as logical and ethical norms can influence us. McGinn has expressed the difficulty involved here: "Alleged causal relations between . . . abstract entities and human minds . . . [would be] funny kinds of causation" (*PC,* 53). Whitehead agrees, because such relations would violate the ontological principle, according to which only *actual* entities can exert efficient causation. In explaining such apparent causal relations in terms of the causal efficacy of the mind of the universe on our minds, we can understand it by analogy with the causal efficacy of our own minds on our brain cells. To put the issue back in perceptual terms, we can say that, just as our brain cells derive guidance from the mind by prehending its appetitions, so we can derive ideals from our prehension of the mind of the universe: "There are experiences of ideals—of ideals entertained, or ideals aimed at, of ideals achieved, of ideals defaced. This is the experience of the deity of the universe" (*MT,* 103).

Although the terms "deity" and "God" make most naturalists nervous, suspicious that supernaturalism is thereby implied, these terms do not contradict the claimed naturalism of Whitehead's position: Not only does the mind of the universe influence us in terms of ideals—or values, or possibilities, or "eternal objects," including both the objective and the subjective species—this is the *only* way in which it can influence us or anything else (except for religious experience, mentioned in the next paragraph, in which one might become aware of the cosmic mind's experience of the world, which Whitehead called its "consequent nature"). This influence of the mind of the universe is (by hypothesis) a fully natural part of the normal causal processes of nature. It does not involve any interruption of those processes or even a possibility of interrupting them. This is a *broader* naturalism than that of materialism, to be sure, but it *is* a naturalism. As a broader naturalism, it can be more empirical, because it can accommodate various types of data that from a materialist standpoint would require either supernaturalism or a priori denial.

This broader naturalism, besides accommodating mathematical, logical, ethical, and aesthetic experience, can do the same for distinctively religious experience. Genuine religious experience can be understood as the rising to consciousness of one's direct prehension of the mind of the universe. Whereas our awareness of truth, beauty, and goodness as normative values involves our awareness of the *content* of our prehensions of one dimension of the cosmic mind, religious experience would involve more the awareness of the actual *source* of those values, or at least the subjective form of that prehension, which can be called the subjective form of "the holy." Of course, we are, by hypothesis, prehending this cosmic mind all the time. The only thing special about those rare moments in which we have "an experience of the holy" is that this nonsensory prehension rises to the level of conscious awareness.

What, then, about those nonsensory perceptions included in chapter 5 that are usually called "extrasensory"—telepathy and clairvoyance? Can they be understood naturalistically? The usual assumption behind the a priori rejection of parapsychology (or psychical research), which studies ostensible extrasensory perception, is that it involves the study of relations that, if authentic, would be supernatural. This is a great misunderstanding. Naturalists should welcome parapsychology as the branch of science that, along with evolutionary biology, is most important for obviating the apparent need for supernatural explanations. That is, the two types of phenomena traditionally seen as most requiring such explanation were the existence of the world with its diverse species, including human beings, and those phenomena often called "miracles." Evolutionary biology (now expanded into evolutionary cosmology) overcomes the first of these; parapsychology suggests the fully natural character of the second. Of course, materialistic naturalists have generally dealt with these phenomena to their own satisfaction by the eliminative approach. But there is good evidence that these phenomena do occur (see the references cited in note 5 of chapter 5). A naturalistic view of the mind that cannot deal with such phenomena cannot be considered fully adequate. Whitehead's panexperientialism explains how extrasensory perceptions can occur. Unlike the explanations for aesthetic, ethical, religious, and even logical and mathematical experi-ence, this explanation requires no special reference to the mind of the universe.

Extrasensory perception can be understood as the occasional rising to conscious awareness of perceptions of other actual things—minds in the case of telepathy, the external features of aggregational societies in the case of clairvoyance—at a distance without the use of one's bodily sensory ap-paratus. The main reason for assuming this kind of perception to be im-possible has been the assumption that sensory perception is our basic, and in fact our only, mode of perception. Whitehead's demonstration that it is derivative from a more basic mode of perception, which is nonsensory, overcomes this reason for thinking that telepathy and clairvoyance could not be natural. A second reason for rejecting such perception as natural has been the view that any influence at a distance is impossible. This view was supported in the early modern period, as we saw in chapter 2, by the notion of matter as vacuous, as having no inner or "occult" (which simply meant *hidden*) capacities that might exert influence at a distance, so that all efficient causation had to be by contact. This view always had difficulty with gravitational attraction, and recent physics involving nonlocality may raise more problems. In any case, given an ontology in which the ultimate units are experiences, not solid bits of matter, it is not intuitively self-evident that influence at a distance is impossible.

With regard to the inner aspect of an actual entity, the distinction be-tween pure and hybrid physical prehension is relevant. Whitehead's sugges-tion was that whereas *pure* physical prehensions were quite likely limited to (spatially and temporally) contiguous events, *hybrid* physical prehen-sions might well include noncontiguous events, and he referred explicitly to telepathy as a fact requiring some such explanation (*PR,* 308). More generally, he says,

> We must allow for the possibility that we can detect in ourselves direct aspects of the mentalities of higher organisms. The claim that the cognition of alien mentalities must necessarily be by means of indirect inferences from aspects of shape and of sense-objects is wholly unwarranted by this philosophy of organism. The fundamental principle is that whatever merges into actuality, implants its aspects in every individual event. (*SMW,* 150)

My suggestion is that this nonsensory prehension of other noncontiguous experiences is occurring all the time and that what is unusual about an experience of "extrasensory perception" is nothing unnatural about its causal history but simply that it has risen to conscious awareness.

Although not discussed by Whitehead himself, psychokinetic causation can be given a similar explanation. If causation and physical prehension (perception in the mode of causal efficacy) are simply two sides of the same relation, then if there can be prehension at a distance, there can be causation at a distance. Accordingly, the same kind of psychic energy that causes extraordinary psychosomatic effects, such as ulcers, the placebo effect, and stigmata, might occasionally bring about effects directly on the world beyond the body. Once we have rejected both epiphenomenalism and the prejudice against influence at a distance, the effects could be accepted as fully natural. Whether or not such effects actually occur becomes an empirical question to be settled scientifically, not dogmatically.[4]

In sum, a naturalistic worldview can fully accept perceptions of abstract entities in logical, mathematical, ethical, and aesthetic experience, perceptions of and therefore causal influence on noncontiguous actual entities, and perceptions of an actuality felt to be holy. Such perceptions need be neither denied a priori nor considered supernatural.

Although the type of nonsensory perceptions generally labeled extrasensory are in a category different from that of the others discussed here, requiring no reference to cosmic mind for their explanation, they are important to them precisely because they are susceptible to verification scientifically, in terms of controlled experimentation. With regard to the other forms of ostensible nonsensory perception, no such testing is possible, so that alternative, reductionistic interpretations can always seem plausible to those sufficiently committed to the equation of perception with sensory perception. Insofar as tests of telepathy and clairvoyance provide scientific verification of the notion of nonsensory perception, however, then the resulting aura of credibility spreads to the interpretation of logical, mathematical, ethical, aesthetic, and religious experience in terms of genuine nonsensory perceptions.

Such an explanation of the capacity of the human mind to be aware of nonactual entities is an essential part of any account of the freedom of the human mind. For it is precisely the experience of the *alternative to the actual* that gives us our conceptual freedom over the actual. The ability to contrast *what is* with *what is not* is the basis alike for conscious criticism of our more primal appetitions and for the distinctively human enterprises of morality, religion, art, logic, mathematics, science, and philosophy. Having defined humanity in terms of our orientation toward novelty, Whitehead says,

> The introduction of novelty of feeling by the entertainment of unexpressed possibilities . . . is the enlargement of the conceptual experience of mankind. The characterization of this conceptual feeling is the sense of what might be and of what might have been. It is the entertainment of the alternative. In its highest development, this becomes the entertainment of the ideal. It emphasizes the sense of importance . . . [which] exhibits itself in various species, such as, the sense of morality, the mystic sense of religion, the sense of that delicacy of adjustment which is beauty, the sense of necessity for mutual con-

nections which is the understanding, and the sense of discrimination of each factor which is consciousness. (*MT,* 26)

All of these higher freedoms of the human mind, accordingly, result from our capacity to prehend novel possibilities entertained by the cosmic mind with appetition for them to be realized in the world. Materialism has been unable to account for human freedom in part because it rules out the possibility of a cosmic mind in which alternative possibilities could have residence and through which they could be made effective.

One of the reasons for the late modern denial of any kind of cosmic mind, of course, was that all such notions became suspect by association with the supernaturalistic conception of such a mind, which, among many other problems, supported the status quo against desires for greater freedom. The notion of the Eros of the Universe, however, has the opposite connotation. This cosmic mind, far from being opposed to freedom, is the ground of all freedom to transcend the past: "The novel hybrid feelings derived from God, with the derivative sympathetic conceptual valuations, are the foundations of progress" (*PR,* 247). Because of this constant lure to novel possibilities, "the pure conservative is fighting against the essence of the universe" (*AI,* 274). To affirm this kind of cosmic mind, accordingly, is not to threaten social and intellectual freedom but to undergird it.

V. DOES MORAL RESPONSIBILITY REALLY IMPLY METAPHYSICAL FREEDOM?

The previous section completed my exposition of the way in which the pan-experientialist worldview, with its concept of compound individuals, can account for our hard-core commonsense presupposition of freedom. My argument has been based on the claim that various types of responses shared by all human beings, including and especially those that assume that we and other people are morally responsible, reveal that we all in practice inevitably presuppose the reality of freedom, in the sense of the capacity for a significant degree of self-determination in the moment. Moral responsibility, in other words, implies metaphysical freedom. This claim, however, is not unchallenged. In this section I will examine two challenges to this claim, one by Peter Strawson, another by William Lycan.

My argument has been that to be adequate to the facts of our experience a philosophy must provide for human freedom in the metaphysical sense, which involves the denial that antecedent causal forces totally determine our actions. Some of the "facts of our experience" to which I have appealed are what Peter Strawson, in his essay "Freedom and Resentment" (in a book of the same title), calls "participant reactive attitudes," such as gratitude, resentment, shame, and feelings of obligation, guilt, and remorse (*FAR*, 5, 11, 15). I claim not only that such feelings presuppose that we and other people are morally responsible beings but also that this responsibility implies that we are significantly free in the sense that when we do something that leads to one of these attitudes or feelings, it is true that we could have acted otherwise. If we ourselves could never have acted other than we actually did, feelings of guilt, shame, remorse, and obligation would never be appropriate; if other people never could have acted other than they did, then our feelings of either gratitude or resentment toward them would never be appropriate. The fact that all people in all times and places have evidently had these and other feelings that presuppose freedom, along with that fact that it is evidently impossible to live without having some such feelings, is good evidence, I have argued, that we really have freedom in this sense. Strawson, however, does not agree. He, in fact, accuses those who infer the falsity of determinism from moral responsibility of having a "panicky metaphysics"—panicky because it fears that without the belief in freedom our moral attitudes would decay (*FAR*, 11, 25). Strawson's own account of our "participant reactive attitudes," however, fails to undermine the argument that they point to the falsity of determinism.

Strawson's view is that the correct explanation for them is sociological, not metaphysical, but that their sociological rootage runs so deep that they require no metaphysical rootage and that they, in fact, could even survive the metaphysical denial of freedom. Although it is not self-contradictory, he says, to suppose that the acceptance of metaphysical determinism would lead to "the decay or repudiation of participant reactive attitudes," he believes that the "human commitment to participation in ordinary interpersonal relationships is . . . too thoroughgoing and deeply rooted for us to take seriously the thought that a general theoretical conviction" would have this effect (*FAR*, 11). The question of how moral praise and condemnation are justified, Strawson argues, is to be answered solely in terms of "the general structure or web of human attitudes and feelings," which means in terms of human society: "The existence of the general framework of attitudes itself is something we are given with the fact of human society. As a whole, it neither calls for, nor permits, an external 'rational' justification" (*FAR*, 23). It is because of our human commitment to society, Strawson believes, that we can ignore the argument that if determinism is accepted, then continuing to react in ways that presuppose moral responsibility is irrational. Everything, Strawson, says, rests on "the nature of the human commitment that is here involved: it is useless to ask whether it would not be rational for us to do what it is not in our nature to (be able to) do" (*FAR*, 18).

Strawson's argument is problematic in several respects. Let us examine first the idea that "participant reactive attitudes," such as praising, blaming, and feeling guilty, rest on a "commitment" (rather than on a perception of how things really are, which would lead to a metaphysical assertion about freedom). Although Strawson's argument requires this idea, it is problematic—so deeply problematic, in fact, that he has trouble affirming it consistently. In the first place, the language of "commitment" suggests some sort of voluntary covenant. And yet Strawson seems to agree that people in all times and all places have shared such attitudes and feelings. Would it not be a marvelous coincidence if human beings in all times and all places, including the early, widely separated human communities, had made essentially the same voluntary covenant to react to themselves and each other as if they were morally responsible? Is this thought not more incredible than the thought that we really are partially free and that the universality of moral demands on ourselves and others is based in part on the universal recognition of this fact?

The notion that our moral attitudes are based on a voluntary covenant also implies that we could renounce them: Attitudes that have been freely adopted can be freely given up. This implication, however, would run counter to Strawson's claim that there is no need to resort to metaphysics to preserve the moral fabric of society because there is no real possibility that human beings would ever renounce the moral stance. To forestall this implication, Strawson rejects the voluntaristic implications of the notion of commitment. As we saw above, he says that it is "not in our nature to (be able to)" give up our moral reactions. This statement, along with repeated reference to us "as we are" (*FAR*, 11, 12), sounds more like a metaphysical assertion about human nature than a merely sociological statement about a widespread commitment. Furthermore, Strawson says that our commitment to participatory attitudes is similar to the "human commitment to inductive belief-formation," which, he says, is "original, natural, nonrational" and "in no way something we choose or could give up" (*FAR*, 23n). Aside from the question of whether we are stuck with this Humean, nonrational view of induction (see chapter 8, above), the problem raised by this statement is how we can speak meaningfully of a "commitment" if it is "in no way something we choose." I agree with Strawson that having moral attitudes toward ourselves and others is not something entirely chosen, so that it is not something that we could completely overcome, even by affirming the belief in total determinism. I hold, however, that this fact points to the *falsity* of the belief in total determinism. We cannot completely cease reacting to our own actions and those of others in terms of moral categories because belief in (partial) freedom is a hard-core commonsense notion that we inevitably presuppose in practice, even if we deny it in theory; and this fact provides the strongest possible evidence that total determinism is a false theoretical belief. Strawson's recognition that we cannot overcome our beliefs in moral responsibility, because we did not choose them, implies that these beliefs rest not on a mere "commitment" but on a "recognition" or a "perception."

A more general problem underlying Strawson's argument is that he seems to assume that the central concern behind what he calls the "metaphysics of libertarianism" is the belief that if a deterministic metaphysics becomes widely accepted, moral attitudes will decay. This would explain why he refers to the metaphysics of libertarianism as "panicky"—which suggests that he sees it as a product of wishful-and-fearful thinking. This kind of thinking surely does play a role, in some cases perhaps a central one. But the argument from our hard-core common sense is a different type of argument. It is based neither on the desire for freedom nor on the conviction that a general belief in freedom would be a good thing, but on the claim that universal and inevitable presuppositions of our practice show that *we know that we have freedom*. As a datum, not a mere desire, then, freedom, to the degree that it is inevitably presupposed in human practice, is something that our philosophy, to be adequate to the facts of our experience, must account for.

Some philosophers argue, however, that although moral responsibility entails moral freedom, moral freedom does not imply metaphysical freedom. A representative example of this argument is provided by William Lycan's chapter "Freedom of the Will and the Spontaneity of Consciousness" in his book *Consciousness*. Having affirmed materialism in general and functionalism in particular, both of which "suggest a causal determinism regarding human thought and action," Lycan sets out to show that the worry that his position is in conflict with the kind of freedom presupposed by moral responsibility is groundless (*C*, 113). He sets up the problem thus:

1. Every event has a determining cause. (That is, for any event *e*, there exists a set of antecedent causal conditions that are jointly sufficient for *e*'s occurrence; given those conditions, *e* could not but have occurred.) (The thesis of Determinism)
2. A human action is at least an event (i.e., a happening or occurrence). (Trivial)
3. If an action has a determining cause, then it is not a *free* action in the sense germane to moral responsibility.

Yet 4. (Many) human actions are free in the moral sense. (*C*, 113)

Lycan, pointing out that this is an inconsistent set, argues that it is Thesis 3 that must be rejected, which means that compatibilism (soft determinism) must be true. Of course, this position conflicts with my position, which is that freedom in the moral sense implies freedom in the metaphysical sense. Lycan recognizes that there are difficulties with compatibilism, but he believes that they must be defeasible because none of the other theses can be rejected: Thesis 2 is trivially true; Thesis 4 is supported by common sense; and Thesis 1 is supported by both common sense and science. I agree with regard to Theses 2 and 4. But I do not agree that Thesis 1 is supported by either science or common sense, let alone both of them.

Let us look first at Lycan's claim that "Thesis 1, one version of Determinism, is firmly endorsed by common sense" (*C*, 113). This is the case, he says, because "when any interesting event occurs we automatically assume there to be a sufficient cause." That, indeed, is the case. What is problematic about Lycan's claim, however, is an assumption that he has built into his notion of a "sufficient cause." This assumption, which is expressed in the parenthetical explanation of Thesis 1 quoted in the extract above, is that the "causal conditions that are jointly sufficient" for the occurrence of any event are always *antecedent* to that event. Now, it may be that modern soft-core common sense assumes this. But it is *not* assumed for all events by our hard-core common sense: The notion that every event must have causation sufficient to bring it about allows for the possibility that, for at least some events, part of that causation would be exercised by the event itself, so that it would be a partially *self*-determining event. Indeed, our hard-core common sense, far from disallowing this possibility, positively implies it with regard to some events, especially those human actions to which moral responsibility is ascribed.

Lycan prejudices the case in his favor by using for examples events—a toaster exploding, a human being developing a skin rash—in which the sufficient causes would indeed all be antecedent to the event. But even in his examples there are events in which this would not so obviously be the case. For example, after your toaster explodes, Lycan supposes, "you take it to an appliance repairperson" (*C*, 113). Involved in this event, however, is the event of *deciding* to take it to the repairperson (rather than, say, buying another toaster or simply doing nothing about it, thereby going without toast for a while). It is far from self-evident that the sufficient cause for the event of deciding to take it to the repairperson had to be totally antecedent to the event itself; certainly the explosion by itself did not dictate which subsequent course of action would be followed. Lycan, of course, probably believes that the explosion plus other antecedent causal conditions, such as genetic inheritance, parental influence, economic motivations, and love of toast, would jointly determine the "decision" to take the toaster to the repairperson, but he cannot claim that this belief is supported by the commonsense belief that every event has a sufficient cause. His claim that universal determinism is supported by common sense, accordingly, does not stand up.

Let us consider, then, his argument that universal determinism is supported by science. His argument is: "For a physical event to occur uncaused would (it seems) be for matter-energy to come into the system out of nowhere, which is disallowed by the conservation laws" (*C*, 114). Looking aside from the fact, which I have previously mentioned, that we have more reason to be confident of our belief in freedom than we do of the absolute and universal truth of the conservation laws, this argument about uncaused events is irrelevant. Those who affirm freedom usually think of free actions not as "*un*caused" but as (partially) *self*-caused. Although this has been pointed out *ad nauseam*, determinists continue to support their position by attacking the straw position of complete indeterminism, in the sense of events that would be wholly uncaused. Determinists, to be sure, may think that the notion of self-causation, or self-determination, is unintelligible, thereby philosophically indefensible. But, if so, they should make *that* argument (and against the best actual formulations of the notion, not made-up caricatures), rather than continue to pretend that the only alternative to complete determinism of all events by antecedent causes is the affirmation that all or at least some events are wholly devoid of causes. It would, indeed, be interesting to learn which philosophers have ever affirmed such an idea. In any case, Lycan has not shown that science supports universal determinism.

Lycan himself recognizes that his claim requires qualifications. One needed qualification arises from the fact that quantum physics suggests that determinism probably does not hold at the microlevel. Lycan argues, however, that these nondeterministic quantum phenomena "cancel each other out," so that "at the macrolevel determinism still holds as near as matters." He emends Thesis 1, accordingly, to read: "Every *physical macro*-event has a determining cause" (*C*, 114). Lycan's point here is that the qualification makes no difference to the question of human freedom, because human actions, no less than toaster explosions, are events at the macrolevel. His position thereby illustrates the assumption, to which materialism leads, that there is no organizational distinction between toasters (as aggregational societies) and human beings (as compound individuals), so that the "law of large numbers" applies as much to the latter as to the former.

Lycan's second qualification, however, does refer to the possibility of such a distinction. He says: "Suppose Cartesian Dualism is correct. Then there may be nonphysical mental events that are not determined; the mental has a way of seeming spontaneous. Let us therefore restrict the argument to physical events, since it is the physical aspects of human action that concern us primarily in moral evaluation" (*C*, 114). He then qualifies Thesis 2, emending it to read: "A human action (of the sort that concerns us) is a physical macro-event" (*C*, 114). By means of this qualification, he allows for the possibility that the *decision* to take the toaster to the repairperson might be partially free while still maintaining that the actual *taking* of it can be understood in fully deterministic terms.

One problem here is exactly how Lycan would develop the implications of the idea that the decision itself might not be fully determined by antecedent causal conditions. One possibility is that this free decision would then be one of the determining causes constituting the total sufficient causation for the body's subsequent movements. The determinism of the outer, bodily action would result significantly from the self-determination of the mind in making its decision. This would seem to be the implication of his supposition, which is that Cartesian dualism might be correct, because Cartesian dualism affirms *interaction* between body and mind. If this were what Lycan meant by "compatibilism," then few libertarians would have problems with it, because that is what they affirm: Human bodily action is significantly caused by the partially self-determining activity of the mind.

But Lycan most likely would *not* allow for this possible implication. He would be much more likely to say that even if there were "mental events" with a degree of genuine spontaneity, they could not sway the action of the body. His supposition, accordingly, is probably that a strong version of the epiphenomenalist form of dualism, a version that allows an element of self-determination by the mind, might be true. The point of stressing that *bodily* human actions are physical macroevents would be to insist on a complete reign of determinism in the physical world, including all bodily activities of human beings.

Even this more modest possibility, however, is surely one that Lycan does not take seriously: He had earlier explained (*C,* 2f.) why Cartesian dualism is extremely problematic, giving virtually the same reasons that I have summarized in chapter 6, and most of these reasons apply to an epiphenomenalist as well as an interactionist form of ontological dualism. For Lycan, however, the rejection of ontological dualism means the rejection of any sort of numerical distinction between the mind and the brain, because he, like most philosophers, simply assumes that any such distinction would necessarily entail an ontological dualism. Not considering the possibility of a nondualistic interactionism, he concludes from the rejection of dualism that some form of materialistic monism must be true. And this means that there is no distinction in principle, with regard to the issue of freedom and determinism, between a human action and the explosion of a toaster. Not only the taking of the toaster to the repairperson but even the decision to do so must be thought to be explainable in principle in terms of antecedent causes that fully determine the event. It is on this basis that Lycan concludes that in whatever sense we are morally free, it has to be a sense that is compatible with all of our actions' being physically (and metaphysically) determined.

Lycan's position, accordingly, can be seen to rest on the assumption that there is no difference in principle between the activity of a toaster and that of a human being. Both of them involve the activities of billions of events at the microlevel. These microlevel events may not be fully determined by antecedent causal conditions. But in the events at the macrolevel, human events no less than toaster events, whatever spontaneities there may be at the microlevel cancel out each other, leaving the macrolevel events understandable in principle in (at least virtually) deterministic terms. The distinction between aggregational societies and compound individuals, then, overcomes Lycan's primary argument for metaphysical determinism.

I will conclude this analysis of Lycan's position by examining his reason for rejecting Thesis 3 (that if an action is fully determined by antecedent causes, it is not a morally free action) instead of Thesis 1 (that all events are fully determined by antecedent causes). Lycan argues that Thesis 3 can be rejected but Thesis 1 cannot, because Thesis 1 is supported by both science and common sense whereas Thesis 3 is supported by neither, being a purely philosophical thesis, and he believes that "it is impossible in principle for a purely philosophical view or 'intuition' to defeat an alliance between common sense and science" (C, 115f., 147n4). It should be clear that I, too, endorse the idea that empirical evidence in general and hard-core commonsense notions in particular should be given priority over purely a priori philosophical argumentation. But I disagree completely with regard to the theses in question. Besides not agreeing that universal determinism is supported either by science or by (hard-core) common sense, I also believe that Thesis 3 *is* supported by (hard-core) common sense. The commonsense principle at issue is the law of noncontradiction: To reject Thesis 3 would be to imply that an action could be both free and unfree in the same respect.

The reason this is so is explained in an analysis provided by C. A. Campbell, which Lycan summarizes (C, 118). Campbell argues, against A. J. Ayer, that an act that was free in the sense that is germane to moral responsibility involves the freedom to have done otherwise *unconditionally* (not merely hypothetically—that is, *if* the person had had different desires at the time). Freedom in the sense that is presupposed in ascribing moral responsibility to ourselves and others, in other words, involves the freedom to have acted differently in a given situation in which all the antecedent causal conditions, including the person's desires, were just as they were. It would be self-contradictory, accordingly, to say that an act was physically determined and yet morally free.

Lycan repudiates Campbell's analysis, saying that it is "just a bare *assertion* that Ayer's analysis and others like it are incorrect, not an argument to *show* that (and why) hypothetical analyses are incorrect" (C, 118). What is involved here, however, is the very *meaning* of moral freedom, the kind of freedom that is presupposed in ascribing moral responsibility, and definitions are not matters of proof. All one can do is to provide an analysis of what one believes is generally presupposed about freedom when moral responsibility is ascribed. Such an analysis can be nothing other than a "bare assertion" containing the implicit question to the reader: "Don't you agree?" Ayer gave his bare assertion, and Campbell replied that he did not agree, implicitly asking the readers whether they did not find *his* analysis more in keeping with what they presuppose. So, Lycan cannot refute Campbell's analysis by pointing out that it is a bare assertion. The relevant question is whether it is a *correct* analysis of what people in general do presuppose about moral freedom.

Lycan claims that he does not agree with this incompatibilist analysis. But his claim is not convincing. On the one hand, he admits that it is arbitrary in a troubling way to say that being determined by *inner* antecedent causes is compatible with moral responsibility while being determined by *outer* causes is not (*C*, 117f.). On the other hand, it seems evident that he favors the compatibilist analysis not because of its intrinsic merits but because he believes that it *must* somehow be true because determinism is true. To show, by means of the concept of compound individuals based on panexperientialism, how metaphysical freedom is conceivable, accordingly, is to remove Lycan's main reason for supposing that moral responsibility does not imply metaphysical freedom.

Neither Peter Strawson nor William Lycan, in sum, has provided any good reason to doubt the claim that freedom, in the metaphysical sense of partial self-determination in the moment (so that one could have acted otherwise even had all the antecedent conditions been just as they were), is inevitably presupposed in practice, especially in our moral reactions. Although their compatibilist view, according to which the freedom we presuppose in our moral reactions is compatible with metaphysical determinism, has been the dominant view, its popularity has rested less on its intrinsic plausibility than on the deduction that it *must* be true, in spite of its apparent self-contradiction, because neither moral freedom nor metaphysical determinism could apparently be denied. Panexperientialism, however, by portraying all individuals as partially self-determining and showing humans (and other animals) to be compound individuals, not mere aggregational societies, removes the primary reasons for believing in metaphysical determinism and thereby the primary reason for supposing that compatibilism "must" be true, in spite of its apparent self-contradictoriness.

Insofar as we see that compatibilism *is* self-contradictory (as enunciated by Kim's principle of "causal-explanatory exclusion," to be discussed in the next chapter), we are left with our own self-determining freedom as a hardcore commonsense notion, to which any acceptable solution to the mindbody problem must do justice. One of the chief virtues of Whiteheadian panexperientialism, I claim, is that it can do justice to the kind and degree of freedom that we all inevitably presuppose in all our practices, including the practices of doing science and philosophy.

TEN

Supervenience and Panexperientialist Physicalism

Since the 1970s, the relation of the mind to the body has increasingly been discussed in the philosophical community in terms of "supervenience" (rather than "emergence"). Although I dealt with this notion in previous chapters in relation to some authors who have employed it, I did not focus on it as such. The other term in the title of this chapter, "panexperientialist physicalism," may seem oxymoronic. And, indeed, in previous chapters I discussed panexperientialism as an *alternative* to physicalism (as well as to dualism). However, in light of the fact that the panexperientialism advocated here says that every actual entity has a physical aspect, it could be regarded as a type of physicalism, to be contrasted with *materialist* physicalism. In this chapter I will so regard it, comparing it with materialist physicalism in terms of the way in which the mind can be said to be supervenient on the body.

I will carry out this comparison in terms of a discussion of the position of Jaegwon Kim, a highly respected philosopher who has been widely considered to be at least one of the leading analysts of the notion of supervenience, especially since the publication in 1993 of a collection of his essays as *Supervenience and Mind*. Although I have previously referred to this book here and there, I have thus far not subjected Kim's position to any sustained examination. My strategy will be to show that it is the acceptance of a materialist version of physicalism that has led Kim to a self-confessed "dead end" in his attempt to reconcile physicalism with the reality of mental causation, and that the panexperientialist version of physicalism would overcome the problems that led to this dead end. The purpose of this analysis is, of course, not to criticize Kim's honest effort to explore the extent to which materialist physicalism can do justice to our experience. The purpose is to make clearer, by means of this comparison, the nature of the panexperientialist position articulated in the previous chapters and the ways it can do more justice to the various dimensions of our experience than can the materialistic version of pluralistic monism.

I. KIM'S FAILURE TO RECONCILE MENTAL CAUSATION WITH PHYSICALISM

Kim's writings on the mind as supervenient on the body have revolved primarily around the effort to reconcile mental causation—"arguably . . . the central issue in the metaphysics of mind" (*SM*, xv)—with physicalism. His primary preoccupation, as he puts it, has been "the problem of delineating the place of mind in a physical world" (*SM*, xv). This is such a problem, he says, because of two basic assumptions: physicalism, "the claim that the world is fundamentally a physical world governed by physical law," and mental realism, "the view that mentality is a real feature of our world," which "requires that mentality have genuine causal powers, powers to affect other events and processes of this world, whether these are mental or physical" (*SM*, xv). The problem of reconciling mental realism with physicalism is felt more keenly by Kim than it is by some of his fellow physicalists because of a third basic assumption, which he calls "the principle of explanatory exclusion." This principle, which I endorsed in chapter 4, says: "No event can be given more than one *complete* and *independent* explanation" (*SM*, xii, 239). Although Kim tried, in essays written over the course of more than a decade, to reconcile these three assumptions, he confessed at the end of this period that he seemed "to be up against a dead end," with the problem of the mind appearing "intractable" (*SM*, 367). To see what led to this conclusion, we need to unpack his three basic assumptions, to see what each entails. I will begin with physicalism.

One dimension of physicalism, as Kim defines it, was mentioned above: the belief that the world is governed by physical law. Kim more characteristically speaks of physicalism as "the view that what is physical determines all the facts of the world" (*SM*, xv). This implies another principle, "the causal closure of the physical domain," which is "the assumption that if we trace the causal ancestry of a physical event, we need never go outside the physical domain" (*SM*, 280). This principle is a denial of "the Cartesian idea that some physical events need nonphysical causes." That Cartesian idea would contradict yet another way of formulating physicalism: the belief that "there can in principle be [a] complete and self-sufficient physical theory of the physical domain" (*SM*, 280).

These latter formulations, in insisting that every physical event has a physical cause, might seem compatible with the idea of an at least partly autonomous mental realm, according to which some mental events are not fully determined by physical causes. However, Kim's physicalism, in holding that "what is physical determines all the facts of the world," rules out this possibility. A "thoroughgoing physicalism," he says, cannot tolerate "the existence of irreducible psychological features or properties." The reason for this intolerance is that physicalism entails that physical theory can in principle provide "a complete and comprehensive theory of the world" as a whole (*SM*, 96)—not simply of the "physical domain" understood as a limited part of the world.

In speaking of "physical theory" as that which can in principle explain everything, Kim means, essentially, physics. "Not for nothing," he says, "do we think of physics as our basic science" (*SM*, xv). This point leads to yet another, and in some respects the crucial, implication of Kim's physicalism: ontological reductionism. All the observable behavior and properties of things are to be understood in principle "in terms of the properties and relationships characterizing their microconstituents" (*SM*, 96). Part and parcel of this reductionism is the claim that "macrocausal relations should be viewed as in general reducible to microcausal relations" (*SM*, 99), meaning those that are studied by physics.

Kim suggests that we describe this reducibility by saying that macrocausation is *supervenient* on the microcausation, which means that the former is entirely a function of the latter. In other words, "macrocausation is to be viewed as epiphenomenal causation" (*SM*, 99). The reducibility of the characteristics of wholes to those of their microparts is, more specifically, called "mereological supervenience." This doctrine "requires that each macrocharacteristic [including each causal relation] be grounded in some specific microcharacteristics" (*SM*, 101). It is, in other words, a doctrine of "upward determination" (*SM*, 353), according to which all observable properties of wholes are fully determined by their most elementary parts.

The fact that all macrocausation is to be regarded as supervenient and thereby as epiphenomenal, Kim has insisted, does not mean that it is illusory or unreal. Offering a *reductio ad absurdum* of that view, he says: "To take microreducibility as impugning the reality of what is being reduced would make all of our observable world unreal" (*SM*, 102). Kim will later have second thoughts about this claim, at least with regard to causation. But before looking at these later reflections, we need to examine his second basic assumption, which involves the reality of mentality and thereby of mental causation.

Kim takes it as virtually self-evident that eliminative materialism, with its denial of the reality of mentality, is an inadequate solution to the mind-body problem. And, on the basis of what he calls "[Samuel] Alexander's dictum"—namely, *"To be real is to have causal powers"* (*SM*, 348)—he says that the reality of the mental entails the reality of mental causation: *"What possible good could causeless and effectless entities do for us?"* (*SM*, 287). Mental causation involves not only the power of one mental event to cause another mental event, as when a pain leads to the decision to call a doctor, but also *psychophysical* causation, as when that decision causes one to walk to the telephone and dial it (*SM*, 286). One's theory should have a place for this "commonsense conviction in the reality of psychophysical causation" (*SM*, 105). The reason we need to make room for this conviction is that it is basic to "the whole framework of intentional psychology," in terms of which we ordinarily explain human behavior: "We standardly explain actions by . . . providing 'reasons for which' we did what we did; and . . . it is difficult to evade the conclusion that the explanatory efficacy of reasons derives crucially from their causal efficacy" (*SM*, 287). To renounce this idea, Kim says, "would render our moral and cognitive life wholly unintelligible to us, plunging us into a state of self-alienation in which we could no longer understand, or care, why we do what we do, or how our norms and beliefs regulate our deliberations and decisions" (*SM*, xv).

The efficacy of norms, just mentioned, is central to Kim's position; he believes that we must maintain both normative ethics and normative epistemology (*SM*, 236). The intentional psychological scheme, "within which we deliberate about ends and means, and assess the rationality of actions and decisions," is necessary because only within this framework are our normative activities possible.

> No purely descriptive framework such as those of neurophysiology and physics . . . can replace it. As long as we think of ourselves as reflective agents capable of deliberation and evaluation—that is, as long as we regard ourselves as agents capable of acting in accordance with a norm—we shall not be able to dispense with the intentional framework of belief, wants, and volitions. (*SM*, 215)

Kim concludes this reflection on our need for the intentional framework with the Kantian assertion that "our need for it arises out of the demands of practical reason, not those of theoretical reason" (*SM*, 215). Be that as it may, it is clear that this need imposes a constraint on theoretical reason: Our theoretical reason must not affirm epiphenomenalism. (Kim seems here to be implicitly appealing to the criterion of hard-core commonsense—that we must not deny in theory what we inevitably presuppose in practice.) Citing what William Kneale has called "the great paradox of epiphenomenalism," which arises from "the suggestion that we are necessarily mistaken in all our ordinary thought about human action" (*SM*, 105), Kim states that we must avoid this paradox (*SM*, 106). Kim himself formulates this paradox as a *reductio ad absurdum* (quoted above in chapter 5): "If our reasons and desires have no causal efficacy at all in influencing our bodily actions, then perhaps no one has ever performed a single intentional action!" (*SM*, 104).

The issue of epiphenomenalism arises, of course, because of Kim's first basic assumption, physicalism, which, in contrast with mental realism, is presented as a demand of our theoretical reason. (He supports the contention that physicalism seems unavoidable with the assertion that "if we take our science seriously—that is, if we are concerned to base our beliefs and judgments on our best knowledge of the world—it is difficult to resist the view that what is physical determines all the facts of the world" [*SM*, xv].) Kim has, accordingly, a seemingly impossible task: to reconcile opposing implications of practical and theoretical reason. In his own words: "The delicate task is to find an account that will give the mental a substantial enough causal rôle to let us avoid 'the great paradox of epiphenomenalism' without infringing upon the closedness of physical causal systems" (*SM*, 106). How can this be done?

One thing we know is that Kim will not solve this Kantian problem with a Kantian solution: The idea that theoretical reason deals with a merely apparent world, largely created by mind itself, is ruled out by Kim's physicalist assumption that "the world is fundamentally a physical world governed by physical law" (*SM*, xv). The question, accordingly, is: "How can the mind exert its causal powers in a world constituted by physical stuff and governed by physical law?" (*SM*, xv). Kantian compatibilism, accordingly, is not an option. But what about compatibilism without the Kantian rationale for it? Why not just say, with many philosophers (such as Lycan, treated above in chapter 9), that mental causation is compatible with the idea that all events are fully determined by physical causes? A purely physiological, mechanistic account of human behavior, on this account, would not rule out intentional psychology, with its rationalizing explanation of human behavior in terms of beliefs, desires, and volitions, which allows norms to play a role in shaping human attitudes and actions. This resolution, however, is ruled out by Kim's third basic assumption—his "principle of explanatory exclusion."

Although Kim believes that this principle obtains more generally, his application involves *causal* explanations; and, in fact, he sometimes refers to it as the principle of "causal-explanatory exclusion" (*SM*, 291). As such, it essentially rules out the idea that there can be two *sufficient* causes for any event. More precisely, it says that if one cause provides a sufficient explanation for any event, any other causal explanation is ruled out, unless that second explanation is simply an aspect of the first or reducible to it. For example, in the case of a man climbing a ladder to retrieve his hat from the roof, there would be no incompatibility between a purposive explanation and a physiological explanation if neither is considered *complete* in itself. That is, if the physiological explanation were regarded as merely a partial cause of the act, needing supplementation by reference to the man's beliefs and purposes, there would be no problem. But if, as physicalism claims, the physiological explanation is by itself a complete and thereby sufficient explanation, then there is no room for an explanation in terms of intentional psychology.* Or, rather, that is the case if the two explanations are also considered *independent,* so that neither is reducible to the other. With this latter proviso, Kim provides a possible opening for a form of compatibilism: Rationalizing explanations may be compatible with physical explanations, but only if they can be regarded as reducible to them.

Kim allows, however, for no *easy compatibilism,* in which one simply leaves the relation between the two types of explanation a mystery. Instead, he adds to the metaphysical exclusion principle, already stated, an epistemological corollary: "*No one may accept both explanations unless one has an appropriate account of how they are related to each other*" (*SM,* 257). With this corollary, Kim has stated the task of much of his writing over the past two decades: to try to provide such an account.

The approach to take, he has suggested, is to regard the mind-body relation as a type of mereological (part-whole) supervenience (*SM,* 168) and thereby to treat mental causation as a species of supervenient causation (*SM,* 103). That this must be the basis for a solution, Kim believes, follows from the fact that no other alternative seems conceivable. For an example, he employs "a typical case in which we would say a mental event causes a physical event: a sharp pain in my thumb causes a jerky withdrawal of my hand" (*SM,* 103). We surely could not say that the pain, or a decision resulting from it, acted telekinetically on the muscles of the arm, causing them to contract (*SM,* 103); rather, we must say that the pain somehow makes use of the physiological causal path from the brain. But it is also impossible, from Kim's viewpoint, to say that the mental event somehow initiated the causal path that led to the physical motion, and this for two reasons: The first is the usual problem of understanding how a nonphysical event could influence physical processes. The second reason is that such an influence, even if conceivable, would violate the closed character of physical theory. "It would force us to accept a conception of the physical in which to give a causal account of, say, the motion of a physical particle, it is sometimes necessary to go outside the physical system and appeal to some non-physical agency" (*SM,* 104). Having thereby ruled out mentality as an independent causal agent, Kim concludes that its causality must be dependent on, in the sense of supervenient on, physical causation.

---

*The idea that mental causation is a *partial* cause of the man's climbing the ladder, says Kim, "violates the causal closure principle in that it regards the mental event as a necessary constituent of a full cause of a physical event" (*SM,* 280). The idea that the mental and physical causes are each an independent *sufficient* cause of the effect would also violate the physical causal closure principle, as this idea would imply "that if the physical cause had not occurred, the mental cause would have occurred and caused the physical effect" (*SM,* 281).

Kim's resulting analysis is that "when a mental event M causes a physical event P, this is so because M is supervenient upon a physical event, P*, and P* causes P" (*SM*, 106). In terms of the above example, to say that a pain caused you to withdraw your hand means that the pain was determined by (supervenient on) a particular physical state and that this physical state then caused the withdrawal of your hand.

As made clear earlier, Kim's physicalism entails not only that no mental event can cause a physical event (except in the supervenient sense just explained) but also that every mental event must be fully explainable in terms of purely physical causation. That is, one mental event cannot directly cause another mental event, except in a supervenient sense. Accordingly, "when mental event M causes another mental event M*, this is so because M supervenes on a physical state P, and similarly M* on P*, and P causes P*" (*SM*, 106). In terms of the above example, let us say that we thought that the pain did not *directly* bring about the withdrawal of the hand but only by first causing another mental event, namely, the decision to withdraw the hand. According to Kim's explanation in terms of supervenience, to say that the pain caused the decision means that the pain was supervenient on a physical state and that this physical state then caused a second physical state, on which was supervenient the decision to move the hand. (And then, of course, by the above analysis, this second physical state caused, as a third physical state, the actual withdrawal.)

Does this explanation provide what Kim needs—an account that avoids epiphenomenalism while also maintaining physicalism's dictum that the physical realm must be causally closed and that, in fact, purely physical theory must be deemed adequate in principle to explain everything that occurs? Kim's explanation certainly remains true to physicalism. But does it avoid epiphenomenalism? At one time Kim evidently believed that it did. This belief is puzzling, given the fact that he was portraying mental causation as a species of supervenient causation, which he portrayed as epiphenomenal. He, in fact, explicitly described mental causation as "epiphenomenal causation" (*SM*, 107). Although it should have been clear thereby that physicalism, as he conceives it, makes it impossible to avoid "the great paradox of epiphenomenalism," he did not then think so, saying instead that his account seemed "sufficient to redeem the causal powers we ordinarily attribute to mental events" (*SM*, 107).

More recently, however, he has questioned the tenability of this position, asking whether it really is different from epiphenomenalism. There is, to be sure, a *technical* difference, as he had pointed out: The epiphenomenalist says that every mental state is *caused* by a corresponding physical state, whereas in Kim's account the mental state is *supervenient on* the physical state, the difference being that in the latter relationship the two levels are understood to be simultaneous, whereas the epiphenomenalist's causal relation allows for a time lapse between the physical state and its mental effect (*SM*, 359). But Kim now, besides seeing that he had given no reason as to why this should make a difference, adds that the epiphenomenalist might be happy to think of the mental as supervenient on the physical and even to attribute supervenient causation to the mental. This acceptance raises the question: "If 'supervenient causation' is something that even the epiphenomenalist can live with, might it not be 'causation' in name only?" (*SM*, 359). Kim now sees that there may be only "a very fine line" between epiphenomenalism and his own view that "mental causal relations are not among the fundamental causal processes of the world but are only supervenient or dependent on them" and that "any 'physicalistically correct' account of mental causation must . . . expos[e] itself to the charge of epiphenomenalism" (*SM*, 360).

The problem is that, given the two assumptions of causal exclusion and the closedness of the physical domain, "it is difficult to see how mental properties can have any role in the causation of physical events . . . : If a physical event has a sufficient physical cause, what causal work is left for an event consisting in the instantiation of some *nonphysical* mental property?" (*SM*, 360f.). In other words, in the account of supervenient causation, M_1 is said to be supervenient on P_1, which is said to be a sufficient cause of P_2.

> But if P_1 is a sufficient cause of P_2, what causal work is there for M_1 to contribute in the causation of P_2? . . . Given the assumption implicit in this model that fundamental causal processes occur at the physical level, the causal role imputed to M_1 in relation to an event at the physical level should strike us as something mysterious, and we should wonder what purpose could be served by this shadowy 'supervenient cause' that accompanies the physical cause. (*SM*, 361)

With this analysis, Kim has in effect rejected his own earlier claim that the analysis of mental causation as supervenient "does not treat mental phenomena as causally inert epiphenomena" so as to "reduce mental causation to the status of a mere chimera" (*SM*, 107).

Kim's (virtual) admission that his account has not attributed any real causal power to the mental is momentous, especially given his acceptance of Alexander's dictum that to be real is to have causal powers. It means that he has not, after all, provided a basis for saving the reality of the mental from elimination. "Why should we bother to save belief and desire, or qualia, if their presence or absence makes no difference to anything else and we can't use them to explain anything? Being real and having causal powers go hand in hand" (*SM*, 367). It is at this point that Kim says that he appears to be "up against a dead end."

And a serious dead end this is, given Kim's recognition of the necessity of affirming mental causation. Without this affirmation, as he pointed out, all of our ordinary, commonsense explanations of human action, in terms of beliefs, desires, and decisions, are undermined. There is no room for normative explanations and evaluations. And Kim's own *reductio*—"if our reasons and desires have no causal efficacy at all in influencing our bodily actions, then perhaps no one has ever performed a single intentional action!" (*SM*, 104)—reduces his own position to absurdity. Something must be amiss.

One way to state the mistake at the root of Kim's dead end is in terms of the conflict, as he portrayed it, between practical and theoretical reason. As he sees, we in practice cannot help but presuppose the efficacy of our conscious decisions. We walk to the refrigerator, for example, because we decide to get something to eat. In chapter 4, this efficacy of conscious decisions was included among our hard-core commonsense beliefs. In Kim's view, however, our theoretical reason, which tries to determine how the world really is, is constrained by a set of beliefs—those constituting "physicalism"—that are incompatible with our presupposition as to the efficacy of conscious decisions. This conflict forces a decision as to which of his two basic assumptions to modify. His choice is to take physicalism, as he has defined it, as virtually beyond question and thereby to try to redefine "mental causation" so as to make it compatible with this physicalism. In effect, accordingly, he takes his version of physicalism as more certain than our assumption as to the reality and thereby efficacy of conscious experience. I have argued, by contrast, that our hard-core commonsense beliefs should be regarded as the nonnegotiable elements in our belief systems. We would, accordingly, have an "intractable" problem only if two such beliefs seemed to be at loggerheads. That complex of beliefs constituting Kim's version of physicalism, however, does not belong to our hard-core common sense. It does, to be sure, constitute the dominant opinion within contemporary scientific and philosophical communities and, thereby, perhaps within the intellectual world in the West in our time. But this fact gives physicalism the status at best of *soft-core* common sense, and as such it should not be allowed to veto any hard-core commonsense beliefs. The way to avoid the dead end, accordingly, is to reconsider physicalism.

One way to reconsider physicalism would be to ask whether it should, after all, be given up for some other position. Dualists take this approach, and I took another version of this approach in the previous chapters of this book in advocating panexperientialism. Another approach, however, would be to ask whether physicalism itself can be reconceived so as to overcome the problematic features of the hitherto dominant version of it. This is the approach I am taking in this chapter.

From this perspective, Kim's problems arise from the fact that he has held a *materialist* version of physicalism. Of course, to speak of "materialist physicalism" is redundant, given the normal practice, followed by Kim (*SM*,

266n) and even by me throughout the earlier parts of this book, of using "materialism" and "physicalism" interchangeably. In this chapter, however, I suggest that we could distinguish the two terms, enlarging the meaning of "physicalism" so that it would have two versions, a panexperientialist as well as a materialist version.

In the next section, I will show that panexperientialism can plausibly be regarded as a form of physicalism. In the third section, I will show why it is the materialist version of physicalism, not physicalism as such, that created the problems that led Kim to a dead end, and why the panexperientialist version of physicalism would avoid these problems.

II. PANEXPERIENTIALISM AS A FORM OF PHYSICALISM

Given the widespread equation of materialism and physicalism, or at least the idea that to be a physicalist is to be a materialist, the idea of a nonmaterialist physicalism will seem strange, at least initially. There is, however, no consensus as to *exactly* what physicalism means, partly because, as Kim points out, there "appears to be no generally accepted account of exactly what it means to say that something is 'physical' " (*SM*, 340). I will here show that panexperientialism (as articulated in this book) concurs with physicalism as portrayed by Kim on most of its basic points, although the two positions give somewhat different formulations of the various underlying intuitions. Of course, it does not agree with the other form on *all* the points; if it did, there would be no reason to present it as an alternative. My twofold argument will be that (1) while panexperientialism shares most of the basic intuitions of materialist physicalism, (2) it differs with regard to precisely those aspects that led materialist physicalism to a dead end on the mind-body problem. The second part of this argument will be reserved for the next section. In the present section, I will show the similarity of the two positions, while also pointing to some of their basic differences, in terms of eleven more or less distinct points.

1. Perhaps the basic claim of physicalism is that every actuality is physical, in the sense that it has a physical aspect. In this regard, Kim quotes Donald Davidson's statement that "all events are physical; that is, every event has some physical property" (*SM*, 279). This definition permits at least some actualities also to have a mental aspect. What is ruled out is the notion of things, such as Cartesian souls, that are purely mental (*SM*, 126, 340). Whitehead's panexperientialism agrees: Every actual entity has a physical pole. There can be no purely mental actual entities.

2. In a closely related formulation, Kim speaks of "ontological physicalism" as "the claim that all that exists in spacetime is physical" (*SM*, 266). Panexperientialism agrees, in that space-time is constituted by actual entities, all of which have a physical pole. Panexperientialism does also speak

of "eternal objects," or "pure possibilities," which are not physical. But such objects, such as the number 2 or the color red, exist outside space-time. Although they, of course, become ingredient in some spatiotemporal loci, they are essentially outside the space-time continuum, being no more bound to one spatiotemporal locus than another. These wholly nonphysical entities, accordingly, do not contradict the point that *spatiotemporal* entities have a physical aspect.

3. Materialist physicalism also claims that, in actualities having a mental as well as a physical aspect, the physical is prior to the mental. Kim speaks, for example, of the "thesis of *primacy, or basicness, for physical properties in relation to mental properties*" (*SM*, 340). Panexperientialism agrees: The mental pole is always derivative from the physical.

4. In relation to his statement that "there appears to be no generally accepted account of exactly what it means to say that something is 'physical'," Kim suggests that one necessary feature of a definition would be that "a physical entity must have a determinate location in space and time" (*SM*, 340). Panexperientialism agrees. In Whitehead's system every actual occasion has a determinate spatiotemporal location relative to all others (*PR*, 25, 195).* This point is applicable to the "dominant occasions" belonging to a human mind as much as to any other actual occasions.

5. One of the conditions often given for being a "physical entity" is that of being an embodiment of energy. That Kim presupposes this condition is suggested by his proposal that "physical" be defined by reference to current theoretical physics, perhaps in conjunction with chemistry and biology (*SM*, 340). Panexperientialism, by virtue of its hierarchy of actual entities, could not, of course, accept such a reductionistic approach. It does agree, however, that all actual entities are capable of affecting, and being affected by, the entities studied by these sciences. This universal interactionism is possible because all actual entities are embodiments of "creativity," which, as explained in chapter 8, is an enlargement of the notion of energy as embodied in current physics. So, although some "physical entities" do not embody any of the forms of energy currently recognized by contemporary

---

*This aspect of Whitehead's philosophy, according to which every actual entity and therefore every occasion in the life history of every elementary particle is fully determinate, which involves its having a definite position relative to other particles (*PR*, 25), has been used as an argument against it. Abner Shimony has said that this element of Whitehead's philosophy is contradicted by quantum theory, according to which elementary particles have no definite position apart from being observed ("Quantum Physics and the Philosophy of Whitehead," chapter 19 of Shimony's *Search for a Naturalistic World View* [New York: Cambridge University Press, 1993], 2:291–309, esp. 298–99, 304. That indeed has been the dominant interpretation of quantum theory. Now, however, we have the ontological interpretation provided by Bohm and Hiley, which is equivalent mathematically and superior philosophically, in which a well-defined position is an intrinsic property of every particle (*UU*, 2, 110, 113).

physics, they all do embody creative power *that can be converted from or into* the creative power embodied in the entities studied by physicists. In this sense the physical *is* defined by reference to the entities of theoretical physics.

6. While claiming that there are no purely mental actualities, materialist physicalism says that some spatiotemporal things have *no* mentality. Kim says, for example, that "there can be, and presumably are, objects and events that have only physical properties" (*SM,* 340). Again, panexperientialism agrees—with one (all-important) proviso, that such things are not individual actualities but aggregates or aggregational societies of individuals. In such things (such as a rock) or events (such as a rock concert), there is no overall experience, therefore no mentality.

7. Because many materialists in speaking of "mentality" mean *conscious* mentality, the prior point could be taken simply to mean that some spatiotemporal things have no *conscious* mentality. Panexperientialism agrees with this point even with regard to individual entities, as the experience of the vast majority of them is said not to be conscious.

8. I cited earlier Kim's formulation of physicalism as the view that "what is physical determines all the facts of the world" (*SM,* xv). Given panexperientialism's view that all actual entities have a physical pole, it agrees. Indeed, at the center of Whitehead's philosophy is his "ontological principle," according to which only actual entities can act. All explanations must finally be in terms of actual entities: "to search for a *reason* is to search for one or more actual entities" (*PR,* 24).

This point holds true even with regard to aggregational societies of actual entities, as Whitehead says that they are efficient only by means of the causal efficacy of their component actual entities (*PR,* 91). The panexperientialist version of physicalism would, to be sure, resist what Kim, as a "robust materialist," assumes to be an alternative formulation of the same point, namely, "that what is material determines all that there is in the world" (*SM,* 63). That is, given the distinction that I am making between physicalism and materialism, the latter would mean that "vacuous actualities," devoid of experience, exert all the causal efficacy in the world (which is one of the basic points that led Kim into insuperable difficulties in affirming the reality of the mental). But the two kinds of physicalism do agree that all causal efficacy is exerted by "physical entities," as characterized in points 1 through 5 above.

9. One of the central tenets of Kim's physicalism, as we have seen, is the thesis of the closed character of the physical domain. This tenet is, in fact, virtually equivalent to the previous point, because this tenet insists that the actual world consists of a nexus of cause-effect relations among physical things that is not open to influence from alleged nonphysical agents. This point is affirmed not only by Whiteheadian panexperientialism's insistence

on the "ontological principle" but also by its rejection of both dualism and supernaturalism. Of course, in the panexperientialist version of physicalism, *all* individual actual entities are *physical-mental* actualities, and it would resist Kim's assumption that to say that every event has a physical cause must mean "that this physical cause, *in virtue of its physical property,* causes the physical event" (*SM,* 280; emphasis added). Panexperientialism holds that the physical-mental cause can exert causal efficacy on subsequent events in virtue of its mental as well as its physical aspect. But both views agree that there can be no occasional interruptions of the universal causal nexus among physical things.

10. Closely related is Kim's assertion of universal causal determinism, according to which "every event has a cause" or, more precisely put, "every occurrence has a temporally earlier determinative condition" (*SM,* 22, 76). Panexperientialism resists the completely deterministic interpretation of this idea, according to which the temporally prior condition *fully* determines every present event: When the event in question is an individual occasion of experience, it has a mental pole, which is partly self-determining. Given that (very important) qualification, however, panexperientialism agrees that every event is (more or less) determined by antecedent conditions. In fact, in line with the Einsteinian definition of the "past" for any event as everything that causally affects it, Whitehead says: "The whole [past] world conspires to produce a new creation" (*RIM,* 109). To be sure, he also recognizes, in line with the common distinction between "conditions" and "causes," that some past events are far more important in determining the character of a present event than others. In any case, panexperientialism accepts the assumption, which lies behind the scientific search for explanations in terms of efficient causes, that *all* events are causally conditioned by antecedent events. It even agrees that *some* events (namely, those devoid of experiential unity) are *fully* determined by antecedent events. There are no events that have no causes; there are no events that have purely nonphysical causes; and there are no events that are fully self-caused. In all this, there is agreement.

11. Besides holding that only physical things can exert causal influence, Kim's physicalism also maintains that all physical things *do* exert causal efficacy. This principle is contained in his endorsement of Alexander's dictum, "To be real is to have causal powers" (*SM,* 348). This point is central to the panexperientialism of Whitehead, who, although he was also influenced by Alexander, traces the point back to Plato, citing his statement that "the definition of being is simply power" (*AI,* 129). Accordingly, besides the fact that every occasion begins by being an effect of the past universe, every occasion also ends by being a cause (an "object" or "superject"), exerting causal power on future events. Each actual occasion is physical, accordingly, in the twofold sense that it begins with a physical pole, which means as an

effect of prior events, and concludes by becoming a causal ingredient in the physical poles of subsequent events.

Given all of these points of agreement or at least similarity, accordingly, thinking of panexperientialism as a version of physicalism would not seem to involve an implausible extension of the meaning of "physicalism" as established by prior usage. Of course, nothing of substance hangs on this point. Construing panexperientialism as a type of physicalism, however, may be helpful by showing how much more materialism and panexperientialism have in common than might otherwise be readily apparent. In any case, having made this point, I will, in the next section, show how Kim's problems, being rooted in the materialist version of physicalism, would be avoided in the panexperientialist version.

III. FROM MATERIALIST
TO PANEXPERIENTIALIST PHYSICALISM

In my analysis of materialism in previous chapters, I pointed out that although it rejects the Cartesian dualism of two kinds of actual entities, it does accept the Cartesian view of "matter" or "the physical" on which that dualism was based. The difference between Cartesian dualism and post-Cartesian materialism, accordingly, can be formulated in terms of the "material cause" of things in the Aristotelian sense—that is, the "stuff" that is instantiated by actual things. In Descartes's ontology, there are two fundamental kinds of stuff: Consciousness is the stuff that is instantiated by minds,* while bodies, or physical things, instantiate spatially extended stuff, thereby being wholly devoid of experience and spontaneity (in the sense of final causation, self-determination in terms of ends). Post-Cartesian materialism, which I am here calling materialist physicalism, holds in effect that this latter kind of stuff, this pure matter (now sometimes called matter-energy), is that which is instantiated in all actual things. Indeed, Kim characterizes his physicalism as the idea that the world is "constituted by physical stuff" (*SM*, xv). It is this idea that makes his physicalism incompatible with our hard-core commonsense presuppositions about our own experience.

This idea, for one thing, leads to Kim's complete causal determinism. His "physical stuff" is, in its individual instantiations, capable of exercising only efficient causation, not also final causation in the sense of self-determination. All the causality exercised on a present event, therefore, must come from prior events; no present event, including a moment of human experience, can exert causation on itself so as to be (partially) self-determining. Given this view, Kim must assume that "the existence and proper-

*McGinn, as quoted above in chapter 7, explicitly refers to consciousness as "a kind of stuff."

ties of an event are determined by its temporally antecedent conditions" (*SM*, 102).

This claim, insofar as it is generalized to *all* events, conflicts with our hard-core commonsense assumption that we, at least sometimes, exercise a degree of freedom, because this commonsense assumption, on analysis, can be seen to presuppose that an event in which we exercise this freedom is partly self-determining. The *sufficient cause* of the event would, accordingly, include not only its "temporally antecedent conditions" but also *the event itself*. Like everyone else, Kim himself presupposes a degree of freedom, as when he speaks of making choices (*SM*, 366) and of our ability "to intervene in the course of events and alter it to suit our wishes" (*SM*, 53). But his starting point leads to a position that implies the denial that this freedom is genuine.

To be sure, Kim seems to consider the complete causal determinism implied by his position a strength rather than a liability, in that it supports and is supported by theoretical (in the sense of scientific) reason. On the one hand, the thesis of causal determinism supports the scientific strategy of explaining events "in terms of their causal antecedents" (*SM*, 77). On the other hand, this thesis is said to be supported by the success of this strategy. Kim's statements reflect his awareness, however, that the success of this strategy is far from complete: He follows the statement about the success with the qualification, "limited though it may be"; and he says that the metaphysical thesis of causal determinism provides "an explanation of why this strategy *works as well as it does*" (*SM*, 76f.; emphasis added). It would be preferable to have a metaphysical position that, besides doing justice to the human freedom that we cannot help presupposing, correctly predicts the *degree* of success that the method of explaining events in terms of antecedents would have in various domains. Panexperientialism provides such a basis.

With regard to the universal stuff embodied in all actual things, the panexperientialist version of physicalism refuses not only the Cartesian dualism of stuffs but also the choice between the Cartesian material and mental stuffs (the choice that has led to the split, among would-be nondualists, between materialists and idealists). Regarding each of them as an abstraction from an abstraction, panexperientialism in effect combines them into a more inclusive stuff,* Whitehead's "creativity." By virtue of embodying

---

*Whitehead at one place seems to reject the term "stuff" as descriptive of the ultimate reality embodied in all actual entities, saying (with reference to the "neutral stuff" of certain realistic philosophers): "An actual entity is a process, and is not describable in terms of the morphology of a 'stuff' " (*PR*, 41). However, he is here rejecting less the idea that his "creativity" can be called a "stuff" than the idea that it can be described morphologically rather than as a dynamic

this creativity, individual actual entities have the capacity to exert at least an iota of self-determination before passing on the creative energy they have received from antecedent events to subsequent events. This modification of materialist physicalism provides one of the elements necessary to allow for freedom in human beings (and, to a lesser extent, other animals).

Another necessary element is the distinction between mere *aggregational societies,* such as rocks, on the one hand, and *compound individuals,* such as animals, on the other. In the latter, as explained in chapter 9, a higher level of actuality has emerged, thereby giving the society as a whole a unity of experience and activity. Kim's position, however, does not allow for such a distinction: "Atoms and their mereological aggregates exhaust all of concrete existence. . . . There is no room in this picture for any concrete existent not fully decomposable into atoms and other basic physical particles" (*SM,* 345).

This conclusion, like that of causal determinism, can be seen to follow from his assumption as to the nature of the universal stuff embodied in all actual entities or events. That is, besides being capable of exerting only efficient causation, this stuff is also, to use Whitehead's word, "vacuous," meaning wholly devoid of experience, so that events embodying it have no "inside." Such events exist wholly as objects for other things, not also as subjects for themselves. As such, they are incapable of *internal relatedness,* in the sense of being partly constituted by their appropriation of influences from other things. Given this idea, it is inconceivable that evolution could lead to the emergence of *higher-level actualities,* to which causal power could be attributed. In Whitehead's words:

> The aboriginal stuff, or material, from which a materialistic philosophy begins is incapable of evolution. . . . Evolution, on the materialistic theory, is reduced to the role of being another word for the description of the changes of the external relations between portions of matter. There is nothing to evolve, because one set of external relations is as good as any other set of external relations. (*SMW,* 107)

Given this view, all things big enough to be directly observed would be of the same type: We could not regard living cells or multicelled animals as being, or containing, higher-level actualities to which causal efficacy could be attributed. We would have to think of them, with Kim, as ontologically "decomposable into atoms and other basic physical particles," to which all causal efficacy would be assigned. There would, in other words,

---

process. For example, he elsewhere says: " 'Creativity' is another rendering of the Aristotelian 'matter,' and of the modern 'neutral stuff.' But it is divested of the notion of passive receptivity" (*PR,* 31).

be no difference in principle (but only in complexity) between living cells and living animals, on the one hand, and rocks and billiard balls, on the other. Accordingly, the former, which are more easily studied, can be taken as paradigms for understanding the causal principles involved in the latter. In Kim's words, "the paradigmatic examples of macroobjects and properties are medium-sized material bodies around us and their observable properties" (*SM*, 95). The implication is that all causation exerted within and by human beings must finally be reducible (ontologically if not epistemically) to the causal efficacy of the elementary particles constituting the human body. It is from this basis that Kim concludes that all mental causation must be epiphenomenal.

The argument for this conclusion runs as follows: (1) In material things such as rocks and bodies of water, the observable properties of the whole are mereologically supervenient on (totally determined by) the powers of the microconstituents (*SM*, 77, 96, 101). (2) In such things, therefore, "all causal relations involving observable phenomena—all causal relations familiar from daily experience—are cases of epiphenomenal causation" (*SM*, 95). (3) All observable things are of the same organizational type, so that human beings are analogous to material things such as rocks and bodies of water. (4) We should, accordingly, regard the mind—meaning that property of persons that we call mentality, which is observable in ourselves—"as an instance of mereological supervenience," meaning that its existence and properties are wholly determined by the microconstituents of the body (*SM*, 168). (5) Mental or psychological causation, therefore, "is to be construed as supervenient epiphenomenal causation" (*SM*, 95).

As this summary brings out, Kim's argument involves treating two very different kinds of "observability" as if the difference between them were irrelevant. That is, in the "medium-sized material bodies" such as rocks and bodies of water, which he takes as paradigmatic for "macroobjects" in general, the "observable properties" are observable *through our sensory perception,* especially vision and touch. With regard to the mind or mentality, however, the "observable properties," such as conscious thoughts, images, and decisions, are *not* outwardly observable through our physical senses. We know of the nature and reality of the mind only by introspection. Given these radically different ways in which they are "observed," it is not self-evident, to say the least, that "mental phenomena" should be regarded as analogous to observable physical phenomena such as the wetness of water and the hardness of ice. The conclusion that they must be analogous follows not from any evident similarity but as a deduction from the metaphysics of materialist physicalism, with its "Democritean doctrine of mereological supervenience, or microdeterminism" (*SM*, 96), according to which *all* the features of *all* wholes are ontologically reducible to the most elementary constituents of nature. This metaphysics, according to which these elementary constituents are devoid of experience and thereby of internal relations, does not allow for the evolutionary emergence of higher-level actualities with genuine causal powers of their own.

In panexperientialist physicalism, by contrast, the universal stuff embodied in all individuals is not vacuous energy but experiential creativity. A moment of human experience can, accordingly, be regarded as a full-fledged actuality with the power to receive and exert causal influence, not only because the brain cells are themselves regarded as centers of experience (so that there is no problem of *dualistic* interactionism) but also because it is the nature of actuality to be largely constituted by its appropriation of data from its immediate vicinity. The extremely rich (experiential) data provided by the human brain, accordingly, can be thought to allow the emergence of a higher-level actuality, which we call the mind. This emergence of human (and other animal) minds out of brains is not, furthermore, a unique type of emergence. Living cells themselves provide a lower-level example, in that the cell's living occasions of experience have emerged out of its more elementary constituents. Panexperientialist physicalism, accordingly, agrees with materialist physicalism in regarding the mind-body relation as a species of a more general type of relation. It differs, however, in distinguishing between mereological emergence in aggregational wholes, in which the emergent properties and causal powers are fully a function of the properties and powers of the parts, and the emergence of regnant occasions of experience in compound individuals, in which the higher-level emergent exerts causality—both final and efficient—of its own. Mental causation, accordingly, is not regarded as epiphenomenal. Besides the upward causation from the body to the mind, there is self-determination by the mind and, on the basis of this, downward causation from the mind to the body.

Could we, in the framework of panexperientialist physicalism, say that the mind is supervenient on the body, especially the brain? On the one hand, this might be confusing, insofar as "supervenience" has become identified with the idea of microdetermination, according to which all determination that is not horizontal is upward. On the other hand, however, the term "supervenience" was first used, according to Kim (*SM*, 134), as a variant of "emergence," and panexperientialism clearly says that the mind emerges from the brain. Also, as Kim says, "supervenient dependence does not represent a single, homogeneous type of dependence" (*SM*, 166). In fact, saying "Let one hundred supervenience concepts bloom!" Kim adds: "Each may have its own sphere of application" (*SM*, 155). What I am suggesting is that the part-whole relationship involved in compound individuals is different in principle from that involved in aggregational societies, so that a radically different concept of supervenience is required. Building on Kim's distinction between general and specific supervenience (*SM*, 157ff.), we can, with regard to the supervenience of the mind's experiences on the brain's activities, make a twofold point: The general fact that this relationship occurs is (at least usually) fully determined by the brain—by whether it is providing adequate support. But, although some of the specific experiences, such as pains, may be (at least virtually) determined by the brain (at least in what we usually consider "normal," as distinct from "altered," states of consciousness), others, such as thoughts and decisions, are not, but are based on the mind's self-determination. Panexperientialist physicalism, accordingly, rejects the view of materialist physicalism, enunciated by Kim, according to which all the mind's experiences are fully determined by the brain (SM, 76, 86, 278). The self-determination by the mind, furthermore, brings about effects in the brain.

This dual idea of self-determination and downward causation raises the question as to whether panexperientialism can affirm what Kim calls the core maxim of supervenience: "No difference of one kind without a difference of another kind" (SM, 155). Panexperientialists certainly cannot affirm this maxim in the sense in which it is intended by materialists, namely, that any difference in the mind's experience would depend on a difference in the brain but not vice versa. In other words, panexperientialism rejects the materialist doctrine that the dependence relation between brain and mind is asymmetrical, always running upward (SM, 76, 86, 278, 353f.). The maxim, however, can be affirmed in an interactionist sense: Not only does any change in the brain bring about a change in the mind; but any change in the mind brings about a change in the brain. This interactionism means, furthermore, that supervenience is not distinguished, as it is by Kim, from causation as another kind of determination. Rather, to say that the mind emerges out of the brain in each new moment means that it is causally dependent on the brain activities that occurred a fraction of a second earlier. This causal dependence is not, however, complete determination, because, as emphasized earlier, causal relations do not involve complete determination, at least when the "effect" is an individual actuality. And the human mind is evidently the individual actuality (at least on this planet) having the greatest power of self-determination. In any case, the mind's supervenience on the body is such that it can exert downward causation back on the body.

With this point, we come to the different meaning given by panexperientialist physicalism to the principle of the "closedness of the physical domain." Given the impossibility of conceiving of the emergence of higher-level physical individuals, the materialist version of physicalism interprets this principle to mean that all causal efficacy must be exerted by the level of physical entities studied by physics. Affirming downward causation by the mind on the body, accordingly, would violate this principle (SM, 356). It is this rejection of downward causation, of course, that has led Kim to the recognition that his position cannot do justice to our (hard-core) commonsense belief that, for example, we sometimes walk to the water fountain *because* we want a drink. The panexperientialist version of physicalism can affirm this belief because its "physical entities" are *physical-mental* entities, and because there are various levels of such entities, one level of which is that of the dominant occasions of experience constituting the human mind. To affirm the existence of minds or souls is not necessarily, as Kim assumes (*SM*, 126), to affirm the existence of things with mental but no physical characteristics. The closure of the system of physical causes to influence from nonphysical causes does not, accordingly, exclude human minds from the universal causal nexus. It does not even exclude downward causation on the body from the specifically mental aspect of the dominant occasions constituting the mind. This version of physicalism can, therefore, provide what Kim recognizes to be necessary: "an account of psychological causation in which the mental *qua mental* has [a] real causal role to play" (*SM*, 106). It can do this because it rejects Kim's contrary principle, according to which when causation is exerted by a "physical cause" with both physical and mental aspects, the causation always occurs solely by virtue of its physical aspect (*SM*, 280). According to panexperientialism, the causal efficacy can also occur by virtue of the mental aspect of an occasion of experience, meaning that aspect in which self-determination may occur.

This doctrine of panexperientialist physicalism entails yet another divergence from the materialist version. The latter takes the closedness of the physical domain to mean that *physical theory*, essentially equated with theoretical physics (*SM*, xv, 356), can in principle give a complete account of the world. For example, having said that "the causal closure of the physical domain" means that "if we trace the causal ancestry of a physical event, we need never go outside the physical domain," Kim adds:

> To deny this assumption is to accept the Cartesian idea that some physical events need nonphysical causes, and if this is true there can in principle be no complete and self-sufficient physical theory of the physical domain. If the causal closure failed, our physics would need to refer in an essential way to nonphysical causal agents, perhaps Cartesian souls and their psychic properties, if it is to give a complete account of the physical world. I think most physicalists would find that picture unacceptable. (*SM*, 280)

Indeed, both materialist and panexperientialist physicalists find dualistic interactionism unacceptable. The question, however, is the acceptability of the picture presented by materialist physicalism, according to which physics is supposed to be able, in principle, to give a complete causal account of every physical occurrence, even when such occurrences occur in human bodies. For example, Kim says, in a parallel passage, that rejecting the closure of physical theory would force us to accept a conception of the physical in which to give a causal account of, say, the motion of a physical particle, it is sometimes necessary to go outside the physical system and appeal to some nonphysical agency and invoke some irreducible psychophysical law. Many will find this just not credible. (*SM*, 104)

But how credible is Kim's scenario, according to which physics can in principle give a complete account of all the motions of the electrons in, say, the hands, throat, and mouth of an American president giving a speech? We all in practice assume that when speakers raise their hands, thereby (among other things) changing the spatial location of the electrons in them, they do so because they decided to do so; or, if we take the speaker's hand gestures to be involuntary, we at least assume that they occurred because of points the speaker had decided to make. And we assume that had the person decided to give a different speech, or no speech at all, the person's mouth and throat, and thereby all the physical particles therein, would have been in somewhat different states. According to the materialist version of physicalism, however, all the states of all the particles in a person's body would be *explainable in terms of physics, which takes no account of the person's mind—that is, the person's beliefs, desires, purposes, and decisions.*

The idea that physics by itself could predict, or even causally explain, all the movements of living human bodies is a pure pipe dream. Contemporary physical theory is not even remotely close to such a capacity. The idea that physics ever will have such a capacity, or even the more modest (and completely unverifiable) idea that physics in *principle* has such a capacity, is radically underdetermined by the evidence. In fact, most if not all of the relevant evidence, as the previous example illustrated, counts *against* the idea that physics can in principle provide a complete account of the physical world, especially given the existence of human and other animals in it. This idea is almost entirely a product of faith, inspired far less by evidence than by the metaphysics of materialist physicalism.* It can, indeed, be considered the form of superstition distinctive to the reductionistic worldview engendered by materialism.

This materialist physicalism rules out the influence of the mind's (partially) self-determining decisions on the physical processes in our bodies for two reasons. First, from its point of view, given its acceptance of the

---

*One of Kim's many virtues is that he recognizes the extent to which his positions are based more on metaphysical than on empirical considerations. For example, with regard to belief in psychophysical supervenience, according to which all psychological states are determined by brain processes, he says that the belief "seems to be based on broad metaphysical and methodological considerations . . . , buttressed by what empirical evidence there is for specific psychophysical correlations" (*SM*, 193).

Cartesian construal of the physical as devoid of experience and spontaneity, belief in "the mind" as an actuality distinct from the brain that could influence it is excluded, because this would imply dualistic influence of the experiential on the purely physical. Second, materialist physicalism's acceptance of causal determinism, along with the correlative acceptance of the idea that "science" provides precise predictive laws,* excludes the idea that a partially self-determining mind could affect the physical course of nature. It is these two metaphysically based exclusions that, as we have seen, prevent materialist physicalism from doing justice to our hard-core commonsense presuppositions about the reality and efficacy of our mental life.

Panexperientialist physicalism, with its alternative metaphysics, implies a different understanding of both causality and science, one that does not conflict with our inevitable presuppositions about ourselves. To begin with, having (like materialism) rejected the early dualists' supernatural deity who imposed absolute laws on nature, it also rejects the notion of absolute because imposed laws.** The so-called laws of nature are really its *habits*. This means that the laws of a particular domain are not prescriptive, specifying how its entities must behave, but descriptive, describing how they in fact do behave. It also means that the laws for different domains may be more or less exact if the habits they describe are more or less exactly followed in different domains.

That this is indeed to be expected follows from two other features of this metaphysical position: the distinction between lower and higher levels of individual actualities and the distinction between genuine individuals and aggregational societies of such. The latter distinction implies that there would be two kinds of laws. First, the laws applying to aggregational societies, which by definition have no overall experience and thereby no power of self-determination, would be absolute (or virtually so), so that predictability and repeatability would be (virtually) complete. This prediction indeed fits the results of the Galilean-Newtonian science of aggregational societies, such as billiard balls and stellar masses. Second, laws applying to genuine individuals, whether simple or compound, would be statistical, because all individuals have at least an iota of mentality and thereby spontaneity. This prediction is fulfilled, for example, by the laws of quantum physics, which predictively describe the behavior of groups of particles, not that of any individual particle.

---

*For Kim, science is nomothetic, so that, for example, if psychology cannot provide laws, it is not a science. Contained in this requirement is that the laws be *precise* laws, not mere generalizations (*SM*, 194, 199). Kim also seems to accept "the received view" that "events standing in a causal relation must instantiate a causal law" (*SM*, 288).

**That Kim still presupposes the idea of imposed laws is suggested by his statement that the world is "governed by physical law" (*SM*, xv).

The former distinction mentioned above—that between lower and higher levels of individuals—suggests that the habits of the higher-level ones will be less binding, so that as scientists move to increasingly higher levels the laws will become increasingly imprecise, gradually becoming what some would prefer to call mere "generalizations." This prediction also seems to fit the facts. For example, the laws applying to living cells are less predictive than the laws of physics and chemistry. The laws discoverable about multicelled life are even more distant from the (deterministic) ideal of complete predictability. Students of animal behavior are not even remotely close to having a predictive science. And, especially since the demise of behaviorism, the idea of having such a science of human behavior seems so impossible that the very idea of "social sciences" is widely disparaged, and many—still presupposing the notion that science must provide rather precise, predictive laws—say that we should take a hermeneutical, rather than a scientific, approach to human beings.

Although Kim is ambivalent about it (*SM*, xiii), he seems to accept a version of this disciplinary dualism, seeing no way around Donald Davidson's view that psychology is "a hermeneutic inquiry rather than a predictive science" because the laws of the mind "are *normative* rather than *predictive* laws" (*SM*, 211). Kim regards this as a Kantian rather than a Cartesian dualism, because it rejects interactionist dualism (*SM*, 214). It is, nevertheless, Cartesian in dividing the world into a purely physical realm, which is ruled by efficient causation, and a purely mental realm, in which there is only final causation, so that the mind is constrained only by "the norms and rules that guide actions and decisions, and form the basis of rational evaluations of our motives, cognitions, and emotions" (*SM*, 211).*

Surely, however, our psychological life is constrained by efficient causation—much of it from our bodies, in the form of hungers, thirsts, desires, pains, pleasures, and bodily limitations—as well as by ideal norms. Many of our decisions, in fact, notoriously involve a tension between these two

---

*This disciplinary dualism is reflected in Kim's recommendation that the right way to save vernacular psychology "is to stop thinking of it as playing the same game that 'cognitive science' is supposed to play—that is, stop thinking of it as a 'theory' whose primary raison d'être is to generate law-based causal explanations and predictions. We will do better to focus on its normative role in the evaluation of actions and the formation of intentions and decisions. If vernacular psychology competes against cognitive science in the prediction game, it cannot win" (*SM*, 264n46). Besides gratuitously granting to future "cognitive science" powers that its achievements thus far in no way support, this recommendation, in seeming to deny vernacular psychology any significant explanatory-predictive powers whatsoever, seems in strong tension with Kim's recognition, cited earlier, that we ordinarily "explain, and predict at least in a limited way, the behavior of our fellow human beings and ourselves" within the framework of vernacular or intentional psychology, with its motives, desires, beliefs, hopes, and decisions (*SM*, 261). Clearly what is needed is a viewpoint that allows us to combine physiological and normative factors—efficient and final causation—within a single explanation.

constraints, as in the conflict between desire and duty. The panexperientialist version of physicalism does justice to this fact by portraying the mind in each moment (that is, each dominant occasion of experience) as having both a physical pole, which is constituted by the causal influences from the physical environment, and a mental pole, which entertains ideal possibilities, including logical, ethical, and aesthetic norms. This way of regarding the human mind does not create a disciplinary dualism, furthermore, because both physical and mental poles are attributed to all animal minds and, in fact, to all individuals. Human psychology differs greatly, to be sure, not only because we have much less access to the psyches of other animals but also because their mentality is evidently so much less developed, so that they—at least most of them—seem incapable of entertaining norms as such. The difference is, nevertheless, one of degree, not of kind. This difference of degree, in fact, extends all the way down, to the simplest individuals. Insofar as a disciplinary dualism is entailed by panexperientialism, it involves not an ontological dualism between two kinds of individuals but only an organizational duality between compound individuals, such as animals, and aggregational societies, such as rocks. In any case, from this point of view, psychology is not to be excluded from the "sciences" because it cannot provide laws as predictive as those of physics, chemistry, and cell biology. Rather, the test is whether it provides true, testable knowledge about its domain, the human psyche. Part and parcel of such knowledge would be knowledge of the degree to which the mind can transcend efficient causation on the basis of normative ideals.

To those who have been informed by a materialistic, deterministic, reductionistic metaphysics, the suggestion that human psychology can in principle not discover laws as predictive as those of physics and chemistry, because there are no such laws to be discovered, will seem like defeatism. However, given our hard-core common sense, the results of scientific studies thus far, and the perspective of panexperientialist physicalism, it is simple realism. In fact, the primary virtue of panexperientialism is that, in spite of its initial implausibility (at least to those taught to see through dualist or materialist lenses), it enables us to coordinate our hard-core common-sense presuppositions with what we have learned about the world from the special sciences. It does this, with regard to the mind-body problem, by reconciling the element of truth in Cartesian dualism—that mind and brain are distinct and interact—with the truth in materialist physicalism—that all actual things are physical, so that there is no *dualistic* interaction.

Kim has been led to a dead end because, correctly seeing that a nonreductive materialism is impossible,* he believes that there are only three other options, all of which are extremely problematic: reductive material-

*See especially chapter 14 of *Supervenience and Mind,* "The Myth of Nonreductive Materialism."

ism, which reduces the psychological to the physical (as conventionally understood); eliminative materialism, which, realizing that reduction is impossible, excludes the psychological from its ontology; and ontological dualism, which rejects physicalism altogether. I have proposed a fourth option: a nonreductive, panexperientialist physicalism. The purpose of this final chapter has been both to make clearer the nature of this proposal and to illustrate how it overcomes the problems of the materialistic version of physicalism.

NOTES

CHAPTER 2: PARADIGMATIC AND WISHFUL-AND-FEARFUL THINKING

1. Susan Haack, "Double-Aspect Foundherentism: A New Theory of Empirical Justification," *Philosophy and Phenomenological Research* 53, no. 1 (March 1993): 116n8.

2. Brian Easlea, *Witch Hunting, Magic and the New Philosophy: An Introduction to Debates of the Scientific Revolution, 1450–1750* (Atlantic Highlands, N.J.: Humanities Press, 1980), 100–07, 113, 125, 130, 135, 137, 233–35; James R. Jacob, *Robert Boyle and the English Revolution* (New York: Franklin, Burt, 1978), 172.

3. Easlea, *Witch Hunting*, 112, 138; Eugene Klaaren, *Religious Origins of Modern Science: Belief in Creation in Seventeenth-Century Thought* (Grand Rapids, Mich.: Eerdmans, 1977), 93–99, 149, 173–77.

4. Klaaren, *Religious Origins of Modern Science*, 173–77; Alexandre Koyré, *From the Closed World to the Infinite Universe* (Baltimore: Johns Hopkins University Press, 1968), 178–84, 210–13.

5. Easlea, *Witch Hunting*, 108–15, 138, 158, 210; Robert Lenoble, *Mersenne ou la naissance de méchanisme* (Paris: Librairie Philosophique J. Vrin, 1943), 133, 157–58, 210, 375, 381.

CHAPTER 3: CONFUSION ABOUT COMMON SENSE

1. See Thomas Reid, *IHM*, and Paul Helm, "Thomas Reid, Common Sense and Calvinism," *Rationality in the Calvinian Tradition*, ed. Hendrik Hart, Johan van der Hoeven, and Nicholas Wolterstorff (Lanham, Md.: University Press of America, 1983), 71–89.

2. Reid, *IHM*, 268–69.

3. See David Ray Griffin et al., *Founders of Constructive Postmodern Philosophy: Peirce, James, Bergson, Whitehead, and Hartshorne* (Albany: State University of New York Press, 1993), 27–28, 60.

4. Of "the simple and original principles of [our] constitution," Reid said, "no account can be given but the will of our Maker" (*IHM*, 8). This position is exemplified today by Alvin Plantinga, "The Reformed Objection to Natural Theology," in Hart, van der Hoeven, and Wolterstorff, *Rationality*, 365.

5. Peter Ochs, "Charles Sanders Pierce," in Griffin et al., *Founders*, 60.

CHAPTER 5: DATA

1. George Santayana, *Scepticism and Animal Faith* (1923; New York: Dover, 1955), 15–20.

2. See Oliver Sacks, *The Man Who Mistook His Wife for a Hat* (New York: Harper & Row, 1987), and Blakemore and Greenfield, *MW*.

3. See Roger Lewin, "Is Your Brain Really Necessary?" *Science* 210 (December 12, 1980): 1232–34.

4. See John Bowker, *The Sense of God: Sociological, Anthropological, and Psychological Approaches to the Origin of the Sense of God* (Oxford: Clarendon, 1973).

5. The best and most readable recent overview of the field of parapsychology, especially from an experimentalist perspective, is Richard S. Broughton, *Parapsychology: The Controversial Science* (New York: Ballantine Books, 1991). On extrasensory perception in particular, see Stanley Krippner, "Telepathy" (112–32), and Rex Stanford, "Clairvoyance" (133–52), in *Psychic Exploration: A Challenge for Science*, ed. John White and Edgar D. Mitchell (New York: G. P. Putnam's Sons, 1974); Hoyt L. Edge, Robert L. Morris, John Palmer, and Joseph H. Rush, *Foundations of Parapsychology* (Boston and London: Routledge & Kegan Paul, 1986), 111–222; John Palmer, "Extrasensory Perception: Research Findings," in Stanley Krippner, ed., *Extrasensory Perception*, vol. 2 of *Advances in Parapsychological Research* (New York: Plenum Press, 1978), 59–244; and Stephen E. Braude, *ESP and Psychokinesis: A Philosophical Examination* (Philadelphia: Temple University Press, 1979). I have provided an evaluative summary of this evidence in chapter 2 of my *Parapsychology, Philosophy, and Spirituality: A Postmodern Approach* (Albany: State University of New York Press, 1997), which, although published first, was written after the manuscript for the present book.

6. William Barrett, "Some Reminiscences of Fifty Years of Psychical Research," *Proceedings of the Society for Psychical Research* 34 (1924): 275–95; Henri Bergson, "Presidential Address," *Proceedings of the Society for Psychical Research* 27 (1914–15): 157–75; David Bohm, "A New Theory of the Relationship of Mind and Matter," *Journal of the American Society for Psychical Research* 80, no. 2 (April 1986): 113–35; C. D. Broad, "The Relevance of Psychical Research to Philosophy," *Philosophy* 24 (1949): 291–309, reprinted in *Philosophy and Parapsychology* (Buffalo: Prometheus Books, 1978), ed. Jan Ludwig, 43–63; *Lectures on Psychical Research* (London: Routledge & Kegan Paul, 1962); and *Religion, Philosophy, and Psychical Research* (New York: Harcourt, Brace, 1953); Alexis Carrel, *Man the Unknown* (London: Harper & Bros., 1935); Sir William Crookes, "Address by the President," *Proceedings of the Society for Psychical Research* 12 (1897): 338–55; Hans Driesch, *Psychical Research: The Science of the Supernormal* (London: G. Bell & Sons, 1933); C. J. Ducasse, "Broad on the Relevance of Psychical Research to Philosophy," in *The Philosophy of C. D. Broad*,

ed. P. A. Schilpp (New York: Tudor, 1959), 375–410; and "The Philosophical Importance of 'Psychic Phenomena,' " *Journal of Philosophy* 51 (1954): 810–23, reprinted in Ludwig, *Philosophy and Parapsychology*, 128–41; Camille Flammarion, *Death and Its Mystery* (New York: Century, 1921); Sigmund Freud, "Psychoanalysis and Telepathy," in *Psychology and Extrasensory Perception*, ed. Raymond Van Over (New York: Mentor, 1972), 109–26; William James, *Essays in Psychical Research* (Cambridge, Mass.: Harvard University Press, 1986); Pierre Janet, "Deuxième note sur la sommeil provoqué à distance et la suggestion mentale pendant l'état somnambulique," *Revue Philosophique de la France et del l'Étranger* (August 21, 1886): 212–22; Gabriel Marcel, *The Influence of Psychic Phenomena on My Philosophy* (London: Society for Psychical Research, 1961); Gardner Murphy, "Are There Any Solid Facts in Psychical Research?" *Journal of the American Society for Psychical Research* 64 (1970): 3–7, reprinted in *Philosophical Dimensions of Parapsychology*, ed. James M. O. Wheatley and Hoyt L. Edge (Springfield, Ill.: Charles C. Thomas, 1976), 388–404; Gardner Murphy (with Laura A. Dale), *The Challenge of Psychical Research* (New York: Harper & Row, 1961); H. H. Price, "Psychical Research and Human Personality," *Hibbert Journal* 47 (1948–49): 105–13, reprinted in *Science and ESP*, ed. J. R. Smythies (London: Routledge & Kegan Paul, 1967), 33–45; and "Parapsychology and Human Nature," *Journal of Parapsychology* 23 (1950): 178–95, reprinted in Ludwig, *Philosophy and Parapsychology*, 371–86; Lord Rayleigh (John William Strutt), "Presidential Address," *Proceedings of the Society for Psychical Research* 30 (1919): 275–90; Charles Richet, *Thirty Years of Psychical Research* (New York: Macmillan, 1923; reprint New York: Arno Press, 1975); Henry Sidgwick, "Presidential Address," *Proceedings of the Society for Psychical Research* 1 (1882–83): 7–12, 65–69, 245–50.

7. See Charles Tart, *Altered States of Consciousness* (Garden City, N.Y.: Doubleday, 1972).

8. See Alan Gauld, *A History of Hypnotism* (Cambridge: Cambridge University Press, 1992).

9. See Herbert Benson, *Beyond the Relaxation Response* (New York: Berkeley, 1984); Bernie S. Siegel, *Love, Medicine and Miracles* (New York: Harper & Row, 1986); and Larry Dossey, *Meaning and Medicine* (New York: Bantam Books, 1991), and *Healing Words* (San Francisco: HarperSanFrancisco, 1993).

10. See Herbert Thurston, *The Physical Phenomena of Mysticism* (London: Burns and Oates, 1955), 32–129, and Michael Murphy, *The Future of the Body: Explorations into the Further Evolution of Human Nature* (Los Angeles: Tarcher, 1991), 484–502.

11. Michael Murphy, *Future of the Body*, 350–68, 535–39, 603–11.

12. See Stephen Braude, *First Person Plural: Multiple Personality and the Philosophy of Mind* (London and New York: Routledge, 1991).

13. Besides Broughton's *Parapsychology* (note 5, above), see also Joseph H. Rush, "Problems and Methods in Psychokinesis Research" (15–78), and Gertrude R. Schmeidler, "Research Findings in Psychokinesis" (79–132), in Stanley Krippner, ed., *Psychokinesis*, vol. 1 of *Advances in Parapsychological Research* (New York: Plenum, 1977); Helmut Schmidt, "Psychokinesis," in White and Mitchell, *Psychic Exploration*, 179–94; Joseph H. Rush, "Findings from Experimental PK Research," in Edge et al., *Foundations of Parapsychology*, 237–75; Stephen Braude, *The Limits of Influence: Psychokinesis and the Philosophy of Science* (New York and London: Routledge & Kegan Paul, 1986); Rex G. Stanford, "Experimental Psychokinesis: A Review from Diverse

Perspectives" (324–81); and Jule Eisenbud, "Paranormal Photography" (414–32), in *Handbook of Parapsychology*, ed. Benjamin Wolman (New York: Von Nostrand Reinhold, 1977).

14. See W. G. Roll, *The Poltergeist* (New York: Doubleday, 1972), or "Poltergeists," in Wolman, *Handbook of Parapsychology*, 382–413; A. R. G. Owen, *Can We Explain the Poltergeist?* (New York: Garrett, 1964); or Alan Gauld and A. D. Cornell, *Poltergeists* (London and Boston: Routledge & Kegan Paul, 1979).

CHAPTER 6: PROBLEMS OF DUALISM AND MATERIALISM AND THEIR COMMON ROOT

1. See *Descartes' Conversation with Burman*, trans. John Cottingham (Oxford: Oxford University Press, 1976), 28; Desmond Clarke, *Descartes' Philosophy of Science* (University Park: Pennsylvania State University Press, 1982), 27; or "Correspondence Between Princess Elisabeth and Descartes," trans. Donald Wayne Viney, in *Questions of Value: Readings for Basic Philosophy*, ed. Donald Wayne Viney (Needham Heights, Mass.: Ginn Press, 1989), 103–11.

2. Thomas Reid said that God, being omnipotent, can make ontologically heterogeneous things interact; see his *Essays on the Intellectual Powers of Man* (Cambridge, Mass.: MIT Press, 1969), 96–97, 99, 110, 118, 123, 220, 240, 318. On the "occasionalism" of Arnold Geulincx and Nicolas Malebranche, see F. C. Copleston, *A History of Philosophy*, vol. 4: *Descartes to Leibniz* (London: Burns Oates, 1960), 117–19, 188–90.

3. Paul M. Churchland, "The Ontological Status of Intentional States: Nailing Folk Psychology to Its Perch," *Behavioral and Brain Sciences* 11, no. 3 (1988): 507–8.

4. See note 5, chap. 5.

5. D. M. Armstrong, *A Materialist Theory of Mind* (London: Routledge & Kegan Paul, 1968), 364; Herbert Feigl, "Mind-Body, *Not* a Pseudoproblem," in *Dimensions of Mind*, ed. Sydney Hook (New York: New York University Press, 1960), 28–29; Keith Campbell, *BM*, 38, 48.

6. See John Beloff, *The Existence of Mind* (London: MacGibbon and Kee, 1962), 257–58; Paul Badham, "God, the Soul, and the Future Life," in *Death and Afterlife*, ed. Stephen T. Davis (London: Macmillan, 1989), 48–49; and H. H. Price, "Psychical Research and Human Personality," 38.

7. See note 13, chap. 5.

8. Julius Adler and Wing-Wai Tse, "Decision-making in Bacteria," *Science* 184 (June 21, 1974): 1292–94; A. Goldbeter and D. E. Koshland, Jr., "Simple Molecular Model for Sensing and Adaptation Based on Receptor Modification with Application to Bacterial Chemotaxis," *Journal of Molecular Biology* 161, no. 3 (1982): 395–416.

9. See Adolf Grünbaum, *Philosophical Problems of Space and Time* (New York: Knopf, 1963); "The Anisotropy of Time," in *The Nature of Time*, ed. Thomas Gold (Ithaca, N.Y.: Cornell University Press, 1967), 149–86; or *Modern Science and Zeno's Paradoxes* (Middletown, Conn.: Wesleyan University Press, 1967).

10. See Milič Čapek, *The Concepts of Space and Time* (Dordrecht: Reidel, 1976), xxxiv–xxxv, or "The Unreality and Indeterminacy of the Future in the Light of Contemporary Physics," in *Physics and the Ultimate Significance of Time: Bohm,*

Prigogine, and Process Philosophy, ed. David Ray Griffin (Albany: State University of New York Press, 1986), 301.

11. See my *God, Power, and Evil: A Process Theodicy* (Philadelphia: Westminster Press, 1976; reprinted with a new preface, Lanham, Md.: University Press of America, 1991) and *Evil Revisited: Responses and Reconsiderations* (Albany: State University of New York Press, 1991). The connection between naturalistic theism and this theodicy is explicitly made in my *God and Religion in the Postmodern World* (Albany: State University of New York Press, 1989), 5, 77–78.

12. See note 1, above.

CHAPTER 7: FULLY NATURALIZING THE MIND: THE NEGLECTED ALTERNATIVE

1. Immanuel Kant, *Critique of Pure Reason,* trans. Norman Kemp Smith (New York: St. Martin's, 1965), 381 (B 428).

2. See my "Pantemporalism and Panexperientialism" in Paul A. Harris, ed., *The Textures of Time* (Ann Arbor: University of Michigan Press, 1998).

3. David Bohm and B. J. Hiley say that their view implies that "in some sense a rudimentary mind-like quality is present even at the level of particle physics" (*UU,* 386). For C. H. Waddington's endorsement of Whitehead's view that all things are composed of "occasions of experience," see *The Evolution of an Evolutionist* (Edinburgh: Edinburgh University Press, 1975), 4–5. For Sewall Wright's endorsement of panpsychism, see PS or "Biology and the Philosophy of Science," in *Process and Divinity: The Hartshorne Festschrift,* ed. William L. Reese and Eugene Freeman (LaSalle, Ill.: Open Court, 1964), 113–20.

4. See Bernard Rensch, "Arguments for Panpsychistic Identism," *MN,* 70–78.

5. The book in question is *The Reenchantment of Science: Postmodern Proposals* (Albany: State University of New York Press, 1988). The review, by Ted Peters, appeared in *Zygon* 26, no. 3 (September 1991): 429–31. My response is in *Zygon* 27, no. 3 (September 1992): 343–44.

6. Paul Edwards, "Panpsychism," in *The Encyclopedia of Philosophy,* ed.-in-chief Paul Edwards (New York: Macmillan, 1972), 6:23–31. (In the forthcoming *Routledge Encyclopedia of Philosophy,* by contrast, the editor [Edward Craig] assigned the article on panpsychism to Timothy Sprigge, an advocate of the position, who does make the distinction between genuine individuals and mere aggregational clusters thereof.)

7. Ibid., 31.

8. John Eccles's objection to panpsychism for this reason, based on his equation of panpsychism as such with the parallelistic version of it, is brought out especially clearly by the fact that he considers it a form of materialism, the key point of which is that in the mind-brain relation "the brain is given complete mastery," with the brain events being entirely closed to influence from mentality (*HS,* 4, 8).

9. See Donald R. Griffin, *The Question of Animal Experience: Evolutionary Continuity of Mental Experience* (New York: Rockefeller University Press, 1976), *Animal Thinking* (Cambridge, Mass.: Harvard University Press, 1984), and *Animal Minds* (Chicago: University of Chicago Press, 1992).

10. I have developed this point in my introduction, "Time and the Fallacy of Misplaced Concreteness," in *Physics and the Ultimate Significance of Time*, 1–48, and in "Pantemporalism and Panexperientialism" (see n. 2, above).

11. See Milič Čapek, *The New Aspects of Time: Its Continuity and Novelties* (Dordrecht and Boston: Kluwer Academic, 1991), 135, 205, 211.

12. See Milič Čapek, "Time-Space Rather than Space-Time," in *The New Aspects of Time.*

CHAPTER 8: MATTER, CONSCIOUSNESS, AND THE FALLACY OF MISPLACED CONCRETENESS

1. For a biologist's nontechnical, readable account of the Whiteheadian-Hartshornean worldview oriented around the notion of feelings, see Charles Birch, *Feelings* (Sydney: University of New South Wales Press, 1995).

2. Alfred North Whitehead, *The Principle of Relativity.* For a recent report on the viability of Whitehead's theory, see Robert John Russell, "Whitehead, Einstein and the Newtonian Legacy," in *Newton and the New Direction in Science*, ed. G. V. Coyne, M. Holler, and J. Zycinski (Vatican City: Specola Vaticana, 1988), 175–92.

3. Charles Hartshorne, "Some Causes of My Intellectual Growth," *PCH*, 13.

4. Ibid., 23, 24.

5. Peter Ochs, "Charles Sanders Peirce," 67–68.

CHAPTER 9: COMPOUND INDIVIDUALS AND FREEDOM

1. I have analyzed Whitehead's somewhat confusing discussion of subjectivism in "The Subjectivist Principle and Its Reformed and Unreformed Versions," *Process Studies* 7, no. 1 (1977): 27–36.

2. See Charles Hartshorne, CI. For the way in which Hartshorne's conception involves an advance on Whitehead's, see John B. Cobb, Jr., "Overcoming Reductionism," in *Existence and Actuality: Conversations with Charles Hartshorne*, ed. John B. Cobb, Jr., and Franklin I. Gamwell (Chicago: University of Chicago Press, 1984), 149–63.

3. See the evidence cited in Mae-Won Ho, *The Rainbow and the Worm: The Physics of Organisms* (Singapore: World Science, 1993).

4. I have explained more fully how Whitehead's philosophy allows for various types of paranormal phenomena (but not retrocausation and therefore true precognition) in "Parapsychology and Philosophy: A Whiteheadian Postmodern Perspective," *Journal of the American Society for Psychical Research* 87, no. 3 (1993): 217–88.

BIBLIOGRAPHY

Adler, Julius, and Wing-Wai Tse. "Decision-making in Bacteria." *Science* 184 (June 21, 1974): 1292–94.

Armstrong, D. M. *A Materialist Theory of Mind.* London: Routledge & Kegan Paul, 1968.

Badham, Paul. "God, the Soul, and the Future Life." In *Death and Afterlife,* ed. Stephen T. Davis, 36–52. London: Macmillan, 1989.

Baker, Lynne Rudder. *Saving Belief: A Critique of Physicalism.* Princeton: Princeton University Press, 1987. Cited as *SB.*

Barrett, William. "Some Reminiscences of Fifty Years of Psychical Research." *Proceedings of the Society for Psychical Research* 34 (1924): 275–95.

Beloff, John. *The Existence of Mind.* London: MacGibbon and Kee, 1962.

Benson, Herbert. *Beyond the Relaxation Response.* New York: Berkeley, 1984.

Bergson, Henri. "Presidential Address." *Proceedings of the Society for Psychical Research* 27 (1914–15): 157–75.

Birch, Charles. *Feelings.* Sydney: University of New South Wales Press, 1995.

Blakemore, Colin, and Susan Greenfield, eds. *Mindwaves: Thoughts on Intelligence, Identity, and Consciousness.* Oxford: Basil Blackwell, 1987. Cited as *MW.*

Bohm, David. "A New Theory of the Relationship of Mind and Matter." *Journal of the American Society for Psychical Research* 80, no. 2 (April 1986): 113–35.

Bohm, David, and B. J. Hiley. *The Undivided Universe: An Ontological Interpretation of Quantum Theory.* London and New York: Routledge, 1993. Cited as *UU.*

Bowker, John. *The Sense of God: Sociological, Anthropological, and Psychological Approaches to the Origin of the Sense of God.* Oxford: Clarendon, 1973.

Braude, Stephen E. *ESP and Psychokinesis: A Philosophical Examination.* Philadelphia: Temple University Press, 1979.

———. *First Person Plural: Multiple Personality and the Philosophy of Mind.* London and New York: Routledge, 1991.

———. *The Limits of Influence: Psychokinesis and the Philosophy of Science.* New York and London: Routledge & Kegan Paul, 1986.

Broad, C. D. *Lectures on Psychical Research.* London: Harcourt, Brace, 1953.

———. "The Relevance of Psychical Research to Philosophy." *Philosophy* 24 (1949):

291–309. Reprinted in *Philosophy and Parapsychology*, ed. Jan Ludwig, 43–63. Buffalo: Prometheus Books, 1978.

———. *Religion, Philosophy, and Psychical Research*. New York: Harcourt, Brace, 1953.

Broughton, Richard S. *Parapsychology: The Controversial Science*. New York: Ballantine Books, 1991.

Campbell, Keith. *Body and Mind*. 2d ed. Notre Dame: University of Notre Dame Press, 1984. Cited as *BM*.

Čapek, Milič. *The Concepts of Space and Time*. Dordrecht: Reidel, 1976.

———. *The New Aspects of Time: Its Continuity and Novelties*. Dordrecht and Boston: Kluwer Academic, 1991.

———. "Time-Space Rather than Space-Time." In *The New Aspects of Time: Its Continuity and Novelties*. Dordrecht and Boston: Kluwer Academic, 1991.

———. "The Unreality and Indeterminacy of the Future in the Light of Contemporary Physics." In *Physics and the Ultimate Significance of Time: Bohm, Prigogine, and Process Philosophy*, ed. David Ray Griffin, 297–308. Albany: State University of New York Press, 1986.

Carrel, Alexis. *Man the Unknown*. London: Harper & Bros., 1935.

Chalmers, David. "Facing Up to the Problem of Consciousness." *Journal of Consciousness Studies* 2, no. 3 (1995): 200–19. Cited as FU.

Churchland, Paul M. *Matter and Consciousness: A Contemporary Introduction to the Philosophy of Mind*. Rev ed. Cambridge, Mass.: MIT Press, 1988. Cited as *MAC*.

———. "The Ontological Status of Intentional States: Nailing Folk Psychology to Its Perch." *Behavioral and Brain Sciences* 11, no. 3 (1988): 507–8.

Clarke, Desmond. *Descartes' Philosophy of Science*. University Park: Pennsylvania State University Press, 1982.

Cobb, John B., Jr. "Overcoming Reductionism." In *Existence and Actuality: Conversations with Charles Hartshorne*, ed. John B. Cobb, Jr., and Franklin I. Gamwell, 149–63. Chicago: University of Chicago Press, 1984.

Cobb, John B., Jr., and David Ray Griffin, eds. *Mind in Nature: Essays on the Interface of Science and Philosophy*. Washington, D.C.: University Press of America, 1977. Cited as *MN*.

Copleston, F. C. *A History of Philosophy*. Vol. 4: *Descartes to Leibniz*. London: Burns and Oates, 1960.

Cottingham, John, trans. *Descartes' Conversation with Burman*. Oxford: Oxford University Press, 1976.

Crookes, Sir William. "Address by the President." *Proceedings of the Society for Psychical Research* 12 (1897): 338–55.

Dancy, Jonathan. *Perceptual Knowledge*. Oxford: Oxford University Press, 1988.

Darwin, Francis, ed. *The Life and Letters of Charles Darwin*. 3 vols. London: John Murray, 1887.

Dennett, Daniel E. *Consciousness Explained*. Boston: Little, Brown, 1991. Cited as *CE*.

———. *Elbow Room: The Varieties of Free Will Worth Wanting*. Cambridge, Mass.: MIT Press, 1984.

Dossey, Larry. *Healing Words*. San Francisco: HarperSanFrancisco, 1993.

———. *Meaning and Medicine*. New York: Bantam Books, 1991.

Driesch, Hans. *Psychical Research: The Science of the Supernormal*. London: G. Bell & Sons, 1933.

Ducasse, Curt J. "Broad on the Relevance of Psychical Research to Philosophy." In *The Philosophy of C. D. Broad*, ed. P. A. Schilpp, 375–410. New York: Tudor, 1959.

———. "Minds, Matter and Bodies." In *Brain and Mind: Modern Concepts of the Nature of Mind*, ed. J. R. Smythies, 81–97. London: Routledge & Kegan Paul, 1965. Cited as MMB.

———. "The Philosophical Importance of 'Psychic Phenomena.' " *Journal of Philosophy* 51 (1954): 810–23. Reprinted in *Philosophy and Parapsychology*, ed. Jan Ludwig, 128–41. Buffalo: Prometheus Books, 1978.

Easlea, Brian. *Witch Hunting, Magic and the New Philosophy: An Introduction to Debates of the Scientific Revolution, 1450–1750*. Atlantic Highlands, N.J.: Humanities Press, 1980.

Eccles, John C. *Facing Reality*. Heidelberg: Springer-Verlag, 1970. Cited as *FR*.

———. *How the Self Controls Its Brain*. Berlin, Heidelberg, and New York: Springer-Verlag, 1994. Cited as *HS*.

Edelman, Gerald M. *Bright Air, Brilliant Fire: On the Matter of the Mind*. New York: Basic Books, 1992. Cited as *BABF*.

Edge, Hoyt L., Robert L. Morris, John Palmer, and Joseph H. Rush. *Foundations of Parapsychology*. Boston and London: Routledge & Kegan Paul, 1986.

Edwards, Paul. "Panpsychism." In *Encyclopedia of Philosophy*, editor-in-chief Paul Edwards, 6:23–31. New York: Macmillan, 1972.

Eisenbud, Jule. "Paranormal Photography." In *Handbook of Parapsychology*, ed. Benjamin Wolman, 414–32. New York: Von Nostrand Reinhold, 1977.

Elsasser, Walter F. *Atom and Organism: A New Approach to Theoretical Biology*. Princeton: Princeton University Press, 1966. Cited as *AO*.

Erickson, Millard J. *Christian Theology*. Grand Rapids, Mich.: Baker, 1985.

Feigl, Herbert. "Mind-Body, *Not* a Pseudoproblem." In *Dimensions of Mind*, ed. Sydney Hook, 24–36. New York: New York University Press, 1960.

Flammarion, Camille. *Death and Its Mystery*. Trans. E. S. Brooks. New York: Century, 1921.

Flanagan, Owen. *Consciousness Reconsidered*. Cambridge, Mass.: MIT Press, 1992. Cited as *CR*.

Ford, Marcus P. *William James's Philosophy: A New Perspective*. Amherst: University of Massachusetts Press, 1982. Cited as *WJP*.

Fraser, J. T. *The Genesis and Evolution of Time*. Amherst: University of Massachusetts Press, 1982. Cited as *GET*.

Freud, Sigmund. "Psychoanalysis and Telepathy." In *Psychology and Extrasensory Perception*, ed. Raymond Van Over, 109–26. New York: Mentor, 1972.

Gardner, Howard. *The Mind's New Science: A History of the Cognitive Revolution*. New York: Basic Books, 1985.

Gauld, Alan. *A History of Hypnotism*. Cambridge: Cambridge University Press, 1992.

Gauld, Alan, and A. D. Cornell. *Poltergeists*. London and Boston: Routledge & Kegan Paul, 1979.

Gier, Nicholas F. "Intentionality and Prehension." *Process Studies* 6, no. 3 (Fall 1976): 197–213.

Goldbetter, A., and D. E. Koshland, Jr. "Simple Molecular Model for Sensing and Adaptation Based on Receptor Modification with Application to Bacterial Chemotaxis." *Journal of Molecular Biology* 161, no. 3 (1982): 395–416.

Griffin, David Ray. *Evil Revisited: Responses and Reconsiderations.* Albany: State University of New York Press, 1991.

————. *God and Religion in the Postmodern World.* Albany: State University of New York Press, 1989.

————. *God, Power, and Evil: A Process Theodicy.* Philadelphia: Westminster Press, 1976. Reprint with new preface Lanham, Md.: University Press of America, 1991.

————. "Griffin Response to Peters." *Zygon* 27, no. 3 (September 1992): 343–44.

————. "Parapsychology and Philosophy: A Whiteheadian Postmodern Approach." *Journal of the American Society for Psychical Research* 87, no. 3 (1993): 217–88.

————. *Parapsychology, Philosophy, and Spirituality: A Postmodern Exploration.* Albany: State University of New York Press, 1997.

————, ed. *Physics and the Ultimate Significance of Time: Bohm, Prigogine, and Process Philosophy.* Albany: State University of New York Press, 1986.

————, ed. *The Reenchantment of Science: Postmodern Proposals.* Albany: State University of New York Press, 1988.

————. "The Subjectivist Principle and Its Reformed and Unreformed Versions." *Process Studies* 7, no. 1 (1977): 27–36.

Griffin, David Ray, John B. Cobb, Jr., Marcus P. Ford, Pete A. Y. Gunter, and Peter Ochs. *Founders of Constructive Postmodern Philosophy: Peirce, James, Bergson, Whitehead, and Hartshorne.* Albany: State University of New York Press, 1993.

Griffin, Donald R. *Animal Minds.* Chicago: University of Chicago Press, 1992.

————. *Animal Thinking.* Cambridge, Mass.: Harvard University Press, 1984.

————. *The Question of Animal Experience: Evolutionary Continuity of Mental Experience.* New York: Rockefeller University Press, 1976.

Grünbaum, Adolf. "The Anisotropy of Time." In *The Nature of Time,* ed. Thomas Gold, 149–86. Ithaca, N.Y.: Cornell University Press, 1967.

————. *Modern Science and Zeno's Paradoxes.* Middletown, Conn.: Wesleyan University Press, 1967.

————. *Philosophical Problems of Space and Time.* New York: Knopf, 1963.

Haack, Susan. "Double-Aspect Foundherentism: A New Theory of Empirical Justification." *Philosophy and Phenomenological Research* 53, no. 1 (March 1993): 113–28.

Hahn, Lewis Edwin, ed. *The Philosophy of Charles Hartshorne: Library of Living Philosophers XX.* La Salle, Ill.: Open Court, 1991.

Hannay, Alastair. *Human Consciousness.* London and New York: Routledge, 1990.

Hart, W. D. *The Engines of the Soul.* Cambridge: Cambridge University Press, 1988. Cited as *EOS.*

Hartshorne, Charles. *Beyond Humanism: Essays in the Philosophy of Nature.* Lincoln: University of Nebraska Press, [1937] 1968. Cited as *BH.*

————. "The Compound Individual." In Hartshorne, *Whitehead's Philosophy: Selected Essays, 1935–1970,* 41–61. Lincoln: University of Nebraska Press, 1972. Cited as CI.

————. *Creative Synthesis and Philosophic Method.* London: SCM Press, 1970. Reprint Lanham, Md.: University Press of America, 1983. Cited as *CSPM.*

————. *The Darkness and the Light: A Philosopher Reflects upon His Fortunate Life and Those Who Made It Possible.* Albany: State University of New York Press, 1990. Cited as *DL.*

————. "General Remarks." In Hartshorne, *Process Philosophy and Theology,* ed. Robert

Kane and Stephen H. Phillips, 181–96. Albany: State University of New York Press, 1989.

———. "Physics and Psychics: The Place of Mind in Nature." In *Mind in Nature: Essays on the Interface of Science and Philosophy*, ed. John B. Cobb, Jr., and David Ray Griffin, 89–96. Washington, D.C.: University Press of America, 1977. Cited as PP.

———. "Some Causes of My Intellectual Growth." In *The Philosophy of Charles Hartshorne: Library of Living Philosophers XX*, ed. Lewis Edwin Hahn, 3–45. La Salle, Ill.: Open Court, 1991.

Helm, Paul. "Thomas Reid, Common Sense and Calvinism." In *Rationality in the Calvinian Tradition*, ed. Hendrik Hart, Johan van der Hoeven, and Nicholas Wolterstorff, 71–89. Lanham, Md.: University Press of America, 1983.

Ho, Mae-Won. *The Rainbow and the Worm: The Physics of Organisms*. Singapore: World Science, 1993.

Honderich, Ted. "Mind, Brain, and Self-Conscious Mind." In *Mindwaves: Thoughts on Intelligence, Identity, and Consciousness*, ed. Colin Blakemore and Susan Greenfield, 445–58. Oxford: Basil Blackwell, 1987. Cited as MBSC.

Hoffman, Banesh (with Helen Dukas). *Albert Einstein: Creator and Rebel*. New York: Viking Press, 1972.

Humphrey, Nicholas. *Consciousness Regained*. Oxford and New York: Oxford University Press, 1983.

———. *A History of the Mind*. London: Chatto and Windus, 1992. Cited as *HM*.

———. *Soul Searching: Human Nature and Supernatural Belief*. London: Chatto & Windus, 1995.

Jacob, James R. *Robert Boyle and the English Revolution*. New York: Franklin, Burt, 1978.

James, William. *Essays in Psychical Research*. Cambridge, Mass.: Harvard University Press, 1986.

———. *A Pluralistic Universe* (published with *Essays in Radical Empiricism*). Ed. Ralph Barton Perry. New York: E. P. Dutton, 1971. Cited as *PU*.

———. *Principles of Psychology*. Vol. 1. New York: Henry Holt, 1890. Reprinted New York: Dover Books, 1950. Cited as *POP*.

———. *Varieties of Religious Experience*. New York: Longmans, Green, 1902. Cited as *VRE*.

Janet, Pierre. "Deuxième note sur la sommeil provoque à distance et la suggestion mentale pendant l'état somnambulique." *Revue Philosophique de la France et de l'Etranger* (21 August 1886): 212–22.

Kant, Immanuel. *Critique of Pure Reason*. Trans. Norman Kemp Smith. New York: St. Martin's, 1965.

Kim, Jaegwon. *Supervenience and Mind: Selected Philosophical Essays*. Cambridge: Cambridge University Press, 1993. Cited as *SM*.

Klaaren, Eugene. *Religious Origins of Modern Science: Belief in Creation in Seventeenth-Century Thought*. Grand Rapids, Mich.: Eerdmans, 1977.

Koyré, Alexandre. *From the Closed World to the Infinite Universe*. Baltimore: Johns Hopkins University Press, 1968.

Krippner, Stanley. "Telepathy." In *Psychic Exploration: A Challenge for Science*, ed. John White and Edgar D. Mitchell, 112–32. New York: G. P. Putnam's Sons, 1974.

Lenoble, Robert. *Mersenne ou la naissance de méchanisme*. Paris: Librairie Philosophique J. Vrin, 1943.

Lepore, Ernest, and Robert van Gulick, eds. *John Searle and His Critics*. Cambridge, Mass.: Blackwell, 1991. Cited as *JS*.

Levin, Michael E. *Metaphysics and the Mind-Body Problem*. Oxford: Clarendon, 1979. Cited as *MMBP*.

Lewin, Roger. "Is Your Brain Really Necessary?" *Science* 210 (12 December 1980): 1232–34.

Lewis, H. D. *The Elusive Mind*. London: George Allen & Unwin, 1969. Cited as *EM*.

———. *The Elusive Self*. London: Macmillan, 1982. Cited as *ES*.

Lovejoy, Arthur. "On Some Conditions of Progress in Philosophical Inquiry." *Philosophical Review* 26 (1917): 127–63.

Lycan, William G. *Consciousness*. Cambridge, Mass.: MIT Press, 1987. Cited as *C*.

Lyell, Charles. *On the Geological Evidences of the Antiquity of Man*. 3d ed. London: John Murray, 1863.

Madell, Geoffrey. *Mind and Materialism*. Edinburgh: Edinburgh University Press, 1988. Cited as *MM*.

Marcel, Gabriel. *The Influence of Psychic Phenomena on My Philosophy*. London: Society for Psychical Research, 1961.

McGinn, Colin. *The Character of Mind*. Oxford: Oxford University Press, 1982. Cited as *CM*.

———. "Consciousness and Space." *Journal of Consciousness Studies* 2, no. 3 (1995): 220–30. Cited as CS.

———. *The Problem of Consciousness: Essays Towards a Resolution*. Oxford: Basil Blackwell, 1991. Cited as *PC*.

Monod, Jacques. *Chance and Necessity: An Essay on the Natural Philosophy of Modern Biology*. New York: Random House, 1971. Cited as *CN*.

Murphy, Gardner. "Are There Any Solid Facts in Psychical Research?" *Journal of the American Society for Psychical Research* 64 (1970): 3–7. Reprinted in *Philosophical Dimensions of Parapsychology*, ed. James M. O. Wheatley and Hoyt L. Edge, 388–404. Springfield, Ill.: Charles C. Thomas, 1976.

Murphy, Gardner (with Laura A. Dale). *The Challenge of Psychical Research*. New York: Harper & Row, 1961.

Murphy, Michael. *The Future of the Body: Explorations into the Further Evolution of Human Nature*. Los Angeles: Tarcher, 1991.

Nagel, Thomas. "The Mind Wins!" (review of John Searle's *The Rediscovery of the Mind*). *New York Review of Books* (4 March 1993): 37–41. Cited as *NYR*.

———. *Mortal Questions*. London: Cambridge University Press, 1979. Cited as *MQ*.

———. *The View from Nowhere*. New York: Oxford University Press, 1986. Cited as *VN*.

Ochs, Peter. "Charles Sanders Peirce." In David Ray Griffin et al., *Founders of Constructive Postmodern Philosophy: Peirce, James, Bergson, Whitehead, and Hartshorne*, 43–87. Albany: State University of New York Press, 1993.

Owen, A. R. G. *Can We Explain the Poltergeist?* New York: Garrett, 1964.

Palmer, John. "Extrasensory Perception: Research Findings." In *Extrasensory Perception*, vol. 2 of *Advances in Parapsychological Research*, ed. Stanley Krippner, 59–244. New York: Plenum Press, 1978.

Passmore, John. *Philosophical Reasoning*. London: Duckworth, 1970. Cited as *PRE*.

Penrose, Roger. *The Emperor's New Mind: Concerning Computers, Minds, and the Laws of Physics*. New York: Oxford University Press, 1989.

Peters, Ted. Review of *The Reenchantment of Science: Postmodern Proposals* and *Spirituality and Society: Postmodern Visions*, ed. David Ray Griffin. *Zygon* 26, no. 3 (September 1991): 429–31.

Plantinga, Alvin. "The Reformed Objection to Natural Theology." In *Rationality in the Calvinian Tradition*, ed. Hendrik Hart, Johan van der Hoeven, and Nicholas Wolterstorff, 363–83. Lanham, Md.: University Press of America, 1983.

Pollock, John L. *How to Build a Person: A Prolegomenon*. Cambridge, Mass.: MIT Press, 1989. Cited as *HBP*.

Popper, Karl R. *Of Clocks and Clouds*. St. Louis: Washington University Press, 1966. Cited as *OCC*.

Popper, Karl R., and John C. Eccles. *The Self and Its Brain: An Argument for Interactionism*. Heidelberg: Springer-Verlag, 1977. Cited as *SAB*.

Price, H. H. "Parapsychology and Human Nature." *Journal of Parapsychology* 23 (1950): 178–95. Reprinted in *Philosophy and Parapsychology*, ed. Jan Ludwig, 371–86. Buffalo: Prometheus Books, 1978.

———. "Psychical Research and Human Personality." *Hibbert Journal* 47 (1948–49): 105–13. Reprinted in *Science and ESP*, ed. J. R. Smythies, 33–45. London: Routledge & Kegan Paul, 1967.

Quine, Willard. *Ontological Relativity and Other Essays*. New York: Columbia University Press, 1969.

Rayleigh, Lord (John William Strutt). "Presidential Address." *Proceedings of the Society for Psychical Research* 30 (1919): 275–90.

Reid, Thomas. *Essays on the Intellectual Powers of Man*. Cambridge, Mass.: MIT Press, 1969.

———. *An Inquiry into the Human Mind*. Ed. Timothy Duggan. Chicago: University of Chicago Press, 1970. Cited as *IHM*.

Rensch, Bernard. "Arguments for Panpsychistic Identism." In *Mind in Nature: Essays on the Interface of Science and Philosophy*, ed. John B. Cobb, Jr., and David Ray Griffin, 70–78. Washington, D.C.: University Press of America, 1977.

Rescher, Nicholas. *The Riddle of Existence: An Essay in Idealistic Metaphysics*. Lanham, Md.: University Press of America, 1984.

Richet, Charles. *Thirty Years of Psychical Research*. New York: Macmillan, 1923. Reprint New York: Arno Press, 1975.

Robinson, William S. *Brains and People: An Essay on Mentality and Its Causal Conditions*. Philadelphia: Temple University Press, 1988. Cited as *BP*.

Roll, W. G. *The Poltergeist*. New York: Doubleday, 1972.

———. "Poltergeists." In *Handbook of Parapsychology*, ed. Benjamin Wolman, 382–413. New York: Von Nostrand Reinhold, 1977.

Rosenfield, Israel. *The Strange, Familiar, and Forgotten: An Anatomy of Consciousness*. New York: Knopf, 1992.

Rosenfield, Leonora Cohen. *From Beast-Machine to Man-Machine*. Oxford: Oxford University Press, 1940.

Rush, Joseph H. "Findings from Experimental PK Research." In Hoyt L. Edge et al., *Foundations of Parapsychology*, 237–75. Boston and London: Routledge & Kegan Paul, 1986.

———. "Problems and Methods in Psychokinesis Research." In *Psychokinesis*, vol. 1 of *Advances in Parapsychological Research*, ed. Stanley Krippner, 15–78. New York: Plenum, 1977.

Russell, Robert John. "Whitehead, Einstein and the Newtonian Legacy." In *Newton and the New Direction in Science*, ed. G. V. Coyne, M. Holler, and J. Zycinski, 175–92. Vatican City: Specola Vaticana, 1988.

Ryle, Gilbert. *Collected Papers*, vol. II: *Collected Essays 1929–1968*. London: Hutchison, 1971.

———. *The Concept of Mind*. New York: Barnes and Noble, 1949.

Sacks, Oliver. *The Man Who Mistook His Wife for a Hat*. New York: Harper & Row, 1987.

Santayana, George. *Scepticism and Animal Faith*. New York: Dover, 1955.

Schmeidler, Gertrude R. "Research Findings in Psychokinesis." In *Psychokinesis*, vol. 1 of *Advances in Parapsychological Research*, ed. Stanley Krippner, 79–132. New York: Plenum, 1977.

Schmidt, Helmut. "Psychokinesis." In *Psychic Exploration: A Challenge for Science*, ed. John White and Edgar D. Mitchell, 179–94. New York: G. P. Putnam's Sons, 1974.

Seager, William. "Consciousness, Information, and Panpsychism." *Journal of Consciousness Studies* 2, no. 3 (1995): 272–88. Cited as CIP.

———. *Metaphysics of Consciousness*. London and New York: Routledge, 1991. Cited as *MC*.

Searle, John R. "The Mind-Body Problem." In *John Searle and His Critics*, ed. Ernest Lepore and Robert van Gulick, 141–46. Cambridge, Mass.: Blackwell, 1991. Cited as MBP.

———. *Minds, Brains and Science: The 1984 Reith Lectures*. London: British Broadcasting Corporation, 1984. Cited as *MBS*.

———. "Minds and Brains without Programs." In *Mindwaves: Thoughts on Intelligence, Identity, and Consciousness*, ed. Colin Blakemore and Susan Greenfield, 209–33. Oxford: Basil Blackwell, 1987. Cited as MBWP.

———. *The Rediscovery of the Mind*. Cambridge, Mass.: MIT Press, 1992. Cited as *RM*.

Shimony, Abner. *Search for a Naturalistic World View*. New York: Cambridge University Press, 1993.

Sidgwick, Henry. "Presidential Address." *Proceedings of the Society for Psychical Research* 1 (1882–83): 7–12, 65–69, 245–50.

Siegel, Bernie S. *Love, Medicine, and Miracles*. New York: Harper & Row, 1986.

Smart, J. J. C. "Materialism." In *The Mind-Brain Identity Theory*, ed. C. V. Borst, 159–70. London: Macmillan, 1979. Cited as M.

Sperry, Roger. *Science and Moral Priority: Merging Mind, Brain, and Human Values*. New York: Columbia University Press, 1983. Cited as *SMP*.

Stanford, Rex G. "Clairvoyance." In *Psychic Exploration: A Challenge for Science*, ed. John White and Edgar D. Mitchell, 133–52. New York: G. P. Putnam's Sons, 1974.

———. "Experimental Psychokinesis: A Review from Diverse Perspectives." In *Handbook of Parapsychology*, ed. Benjamin Wolman, 324–81. New York: Von Nostrand Reinhold, 1977.

Strawson, Galen. *Mental Reality*. Cambridge, Mass.: MIT Press, 1994. Cited as *MR*.
Strawson, Peter F. *Freedom and Resentment and Other Essays*. London: Methuen, 1974. Cited as *FAR*.
Swinburne, Richard. *The Evolution of the Soul*. Oxford: Clarendon, 1986.
———. *The Existence of God*. Oxford: Clarendon, 1979.
Tart, Charles. *Altered States of Consciousness*. Garden City, N.Y.: Doubleday, 1972.
Thurston, Herbert. *The Physical Phenomena of Mysticism*. London: Burns and Oates, 1955.
Viney, Donald Wayne, ed. *Questions of Value: Readings for Basic Philosophy*. Needham Heights, Mass.: Ginn Press, 1989.
Waddington, C. H. *The Evolution of an Evolutionist*. Edinburgh: Edinburgh University Press, 1975.
Whitehead, Alfred North. *Adventures of Ideas*. New York: Free Press, [1933] 1967. Cited as *AI*.
———. *The Aims of Education*. New York: Macmillan, 1929.
———. *The Concept of Nature*. Cambridge: Cambridge University Press, 1920.
———. *An Enquiry Concerning the Principles of Natural Knowledge*. Cambridge: Cambridge University Press, 1919.
———. *Essays in Science and Philosophy*. New York: Philosophical Library, 1947.
———. *The Function of Reason*. Boston: Beacon Press, [1929] 1958. Cited as *FOR*.
———. *Modes of Thought*. New York: Free Press, [1938] 1968. Cited as *MT*.
———. *The Organisation of Thought*. London: Williams and Norgate, 1917.
———. *The Principle of Relativity*. Cambridge: Cambridge University Press, 1922.
———. *Process and Reality: An Essay in Cosmology* [1929]. Corr. ed. Ed. David Ray Griffin and Donald W. Sherburne. New York: Free Press, 1978. Cited as *PR*.
———. *Religion in the Making*. Cleveland: World Publishing Co. (Meridian Books), 1960. Cited as *RIM*.
1. *Science and the Modern World*. New York: Free Press, [1925] 1967. Cited as *SMW*.
———. *Symbolism: Its Meaning and Effect*. New York: Macmillan, 1927.
Wills, Christopher. *The Runaway Brain: The Evolution of Human Uniqueness*. New York: Basic Books, 1993.
Wright, Sewall. "Biology and the Philosophy of Science." In *Process and Divinity: The Hartshorne Festschrift*, ed. William L. Reese and Eugene Freeman, 101–25. La Salle, Ill.: Open Court, 1964.
———. "Panpsychism and Science." In *Mind in Nature: Essays on the Interface of Science and Philosophy*, ed. John B. Cobb, Jr., and David Ray Griffin, 79–88. Washington, D.C.: University Press of America, 1977. Cited as *PS*.

INDEX

Eternal objects, 183, 205, 228. *See also* Possibilities

Events, 49n., 157. *See also* Actual occasions

Experience: aesthetic, 42–43, 206; and consciousness, 9, 71n., 78, 79n., 80, 92n., 106–107, 112, 127n., 202; creative, 152, 154; and duration, 102, 112–114, 148 (*see also* Duration); efficacy of, 37, 44–45; emotional, 139–140; as feeling, 104n., 112; as fundamental feature of mind, 7, 78; given elements of, 137–138, 149; human, 118, 124–125; logical, 26, 40–41, 42, 205–206; mathematical, 42, 205; moral, 26, 41, 42–43, 205–206; obvious facts of, 19–20; physical, 128, 205; religious, 26, 43, 206; self-conscious, 9, 10; in single-celled organisms, 9–10; stream of, 158; as stuff of mind, 127, 154; topsy-turvy interpretation of, 135–136; unity of, 35–36, 52; what-it's-likeness of, 64, 68, 105. *See also* Consciousness; Occasions of experience; Panexperientialism

External world, 34, 58, 138

Extrasensory perception, 30, 59, 111, 206–207. *See also* Nonsensory perception; Telepathy and clairvoyance

Evolution, 3, 9, 10, 31, 41, 123, 189, 233; and time, 62–63, 92; neo-Darwinian theory of, 31

Fallacy of misplaced concreteness, 117, 119, 122, 191n.

Farleigh, Peter, xi

Fechner, Gustav, 93, 95

Feeling, 107n., 112, 118, 248; causal, 153; conceptual (mental), 128–129, 136, 153, 158, 174, 205; intellectual, 127, 130–131; physical, 128, 152; virtual synonym for prehension, 128. *See also* Prehension

Feigl, Herbert, 59, 62n., 246 n.5

Final causation, 49–50; and efficient causation, 31, 49–50, 157–159, 240n., 241; as reasons, 69–70; as self-determination, 31, 51, 153, 182. *See also* Causa sui; Self-determination

Flammarion, Camille, 245 n.6

Flanagan, Owen, 1, 31, 37, 61, 67–68, 73, 79

Folk: beliefs, 38; empiricism, 174; philosophy, 101; physics, 173; psychology, 42n., 104, 173

Ford, Marcus P., 178

Foundationalism, 21

Fraser, J. T., 62–63

Freedom, 37–40, 163–217; as central to mind-body problem, 1, 2; compatibilist

and incompatibilist views of, 38, 164, 212–213; and compound individuals, 40; as difficulty for materialism, 52–54; distinctively human, 193–198, 203–209; and dualism, 40; moral and metaphysical, 164, 209–217; Pickwickian, 164n; as presupposed in practice, 2, 37–40, 53, 97, 163, 164, 212, 216–217, 232; as self-determination, 37–38, 167, 181–185, 213–214, 217. *See also* Determinism; Final causation; Self-determination

Freud, Sigmund, 44, 107, 127n., 245 n.6

Galilei, Galileo, 13

Gamwell, Franklin I., 248 n.2

Gassendi, Pierre, 13

Gauld, Alan, 245 n.8, 246 n.14

Geulincx, Arnold, 47, 50, 246 n.2

Ghost in the machine, 50, 167

Gier, Nicholas, 152n.

God, 204, 205–206. *See also* Theism

Goldbeter, A., 246 n.8

Great Exception, 61–62

Greenfield, Susan, 2

Griffin, David Ray, 243 n.3, 244 n.5, 247 nn.5, 11, 248 nn.1, 4, 10

Griffin, Donald, xi, 247 n.9

Grünbaum, Adolf, 62, 63, 246 n.9

Haack, Susan, 11, 243 n.1

Hannay, Alastair, 1

Hard-core commonsense notions, 16–21, 25, 32, 34–41, 94–95, 145–146, 166, 213, 226; knowledge of, 17, 58–59, 133–134; and scientific worldview, 32, 39–40

Hart, W. D., 51, 155

Hartshorne, Charles, xi, 23n., 152, 248 nn.2, 3; on compound individuals, 82, 178, 185, 204; on Husserl and Wordsworth, 149–150; as panpsychist, 78n., 81, 93, 95–97; and Whitehead's philosophy, 116, 149–150

Hegel, G. W. F., 27, 101

Helm, Paul, 243 n.1

Henry, Granville, xi

Hiley, Basil, 114n., 153, 200, 228n., 247 n.3

Ho, Mae-Won, 248 n.3

Hobbes, Thomas, 82

Hoffman, Banesh, 113n.

Honderich, Ted, 37

Hook, Sydney, 62n.

Hume, David: on conceptual and physical experience, 129, 136, 205; on efficient causation, 34, 35, 50, 58, 121, 133, 146; empiricism of, 129, 136, 174; on external world, 34, 58, 133; on induction, 111, 211; on practice, 18

Designer:	U.C. Press Staff
Compositor:	J. Jarrett Engineering, Inc.
Text:	10/12 Sabon
Display:	Baskerville
Printer & Binder:	Thomson-Shore